The World of Jonathan Swift

Essays for the Tercentenary collected
and edited by BRIAN VICKERS

Contributors

HERBERT DAVIS

HUGH SYKES DAVIES

IRVIN EHRENPREIS

BASIL HALL

GEOFFREY HILL

JOHN HOLLOWAY

PAT ROGERS

ANGUS ROSS

ROGER SAVAGE

W. A. SPECK

BRIAN VICKERS

The World of
JONATHAN SWIFT

Essays for the Tercentenary

collected and edited

By BRIAN VICKERS

HARVARD UNIVERSITY PRESS
CAMBRIDGE, MASSACHUSETTS
1968

PRINTED IN GREAT BRITAIN
BY A. T. BROOME AND SON, 18 ST. CLEMENT'S, OXFORD
AND BOUND BY THE KEMP HALL BINDERY, OXFORD

Contents

IN MEMORY OF

HERBERT DAVIS

(1893–1967)

Preface

This collection of new essays on Swift was intended for publication in the tercentenary year, 1967. Apologies are perhaps due for it being slightly late, but only one who has attempted the task will realize how difficult it is to commission and then co-ordinate the work of a dozen contributors from different Universities. But though not punctual we hope that the interest in understanding Swift's work did not expire on the last day of 1967.

I have described it as a collection of new essays, and that is true, although two have seen the light of day elsewhere: the late Herbert Davis's essay was first given as a lecture at Cambridge in the winter of 1965 (when he kindly agreed for it to be included in this volume) and was heard again at the Clark Memorial Library in 1966, where it was issued as a pamphlet together with a lecture on Defoe's irony by M. E. Novak. Dr. W. A. Speck had written his essay on Swift's politics for the *Dublin University Review* Swift issue of April, 1967, and it is here reprinted (in a corrected and expanded form) by kind permission of the editor.

We are also grateful for permission to quote from the standard editions of Swift's works, some of which are referred to throughout in abbreviated form:

To Basil Blackwell for the *Prose Works* edited by Herbert Davis (14 vols., 1939–1968): references are to volume and page number in the form (IX, 144) etc.

To the Clarendon Press for the *Poems* edited by Sir Harold Williams (3 vols., revised edition, 1958): the volumes are paginated consecutively, and references are to the page number only: (*Poems*, 851) etc.

To the Clarendon Press for the *Correspondence* edited by Sir Harold Williams (5 vols., 1965): references are to volume and page number in the form (*Corr.*, V, 127) etc.

Last but by no means least I must thank Sir Basil Blackwell for his encouragement and patience.

B.W.V.

Introduction

BRIAN VICKERS

In 1820 William Cobbett wrote an autobiographical letter to *The Evening Post* which recorded his childhood discovery of Swift. At the age of eleven his interest in gardens had been so much excited by reports of the splendours of Kew that he resolved to go there and try to find work: the next morning,

> without saying a word to anyone, off I set, with no clothes except those upon my back, and with thirteen halfpence in my pocket. I found that I must go to Richmond, and I accordingly went on from place to place inquiring my way thither. A long day (it was in June) brought me to Richmond in the afternoon. Two pennyworth of bread and cheese and a pennyworth of small beer which I had on the road, and one halfpenny that I had lost somehow or other, left threepence in my pocket. With this for my whole fortune, I was trudging through Richmond in my blue smock-frock, and my red garters tied under my knees, when, staring about me, my eye fell upon a little book-seller's window, on the outside of which was written, 'The Tale of a Tub, price 3d'. The title was so odd that my curiosity was excited. I had the threepence; but then I could not have any supper. In I went and got the little book, which I was so impatient to read, that I got over into a field at the upper corner of Kew Gardens, where there stood a haystack. On the shady side of this I sat down to read. The book was so different from anything that I had ever read before, it was something so new to my mind, that, though I could not understand some parts of it, it delighted me beyond description, and produced what I have always considered a sort of birth of intellect.
>
> I read on until it was dark, without any thought of supper or bed. When I could see no longer, I put my little book in my pocket and tumbled down by the side of the stack, where I slept till the birds in the Kew Gardens awakened me in the morning, when off I started to Kew, reading my little book.

He was successful in his attempt to get work: the benevolent gardener took him on, treated him kindly, and later,

> seeing me fond of books, lent me some gardening books to read; but these I could not relish after my 'Tale of a Tub', which I carried about with me wherever I went, and when I—at about twenty years old—lost it in a box that fell overboard in the Bay of Fundy, in North America, the loss gave me greater pain than I have since felt at losing thousands of pounds.[1]

This vivid account preserves the extraordinary impact that Swift had on Cobbett, and although at eleven he could not have perceived the full force of Swift's satire (he is not the only one 'not [to] understand some parts of' *A Tale of a Tub*), the experience is essentially that of all Swift's readers. We may not be prepared to spend our last penny on a copy of his works, but the unique nature of Swift's work both delights and fascinates two centuries later, and if a man does not undergo 'a sort of birth of intellect' in reading the great satires then, one is tempted to say, there must be something wrong with him. In our own time George Orwell, who had only imperfect sympathies for Swift, nevertheless confessed that

> he is one of the writers I admire with least reserve, and *Gulliver's Travels*, in particular, is a book which it seems impossible for me to grow tired of. I read it first when I was eight—one day short of eight, to be exact, for I stole and furtively read the copy which was to be given me next day on my eighth birthday—and I have certainly read it not less than half a dozen times since. Its fascination seems inexhaustible. If I had to make a list of six books which were to be preserved when all others were destroyed, I would certainly put *Gulliver's Travels* among them.[2]

Cobbett reading in 1773, Orwell in 1921, and innumerable people before and since testify to the hold that Swift has on them.

The qualities which maintain this universal interest are partly of historical, and partly of general significance. No reading of the Seventeenth Century is complete which does not take serious notice of Swift's criticism of the absurdities of that period—the easy optimism of the New Science and its often uncritical belief in the validity of experiment and the objective nature of research; the comparable complacency of that movement connected with science which demolished the Ancients in order to exalt the Moderns, an inversion of idols which Swift simply re-inverted with interest: I desired that the Senate of *Rome* might appear before me in one large Chamber, and a modern Representative, in Counterview, in another. The first seemed to be an Assembly of Heroes and Demy-Gods; the other, a Knot of Pedlars, Pick-pockets, Highwaymen and Bullies' (XI, 196); cant and ostentation in language, triviality and un-originality in literature, and, perhaps the most destructive of all these anatomies, the psychological and physiological processes which—then as now—nurture fanaticism and inspiration in religion: the *Mechanical Operation of the Spirit* is central both to Swift's intellectual standpoint as to his satiric methods. Very few writers in any country and any time have equalled this sustained criticism of the vice and absurdity of the preceding age. If Swift sometimes overbalances and is unjust to particular individuals—Bacon perhaps, Newton, Bentley, Dryden—then this is an occupational hazard of the satirist which time has corrected (as Johnson said of the attack on Bentley, 'Wit can stand its ground against Truth only a little while.'). To attack him on grounds of factual accuracy here is as silly as to accuse him of not having praised the positive achievements of that age, for the satirist is not bound to show both sides of the medal. Of course Swift does not merely look backward: few writers have equalled him in the intensity with which he exposed the evil and the ludicrous in their own times, and none compare with him in the range of the exposure, from the social *minutiae* of *Directions to Servants* and the *Polite Conversation* to the economico-statistical terrors of *A Modest Proposal* and to the all-inclusive satire on the stupidity and viciousness of man in *Gulliver*. This range is great in subject-matter as well as in tone, for if Swift could descend below the level of most men's sense of humour with his puns, nonsense-rhymes, and the private jokes of *The Journal to Stella* ('diurnal trifles' as Johnson called them), he could equally elevate the principle of fun to the unpredictable height of the *Bickerstaff Papers*, and if this vein seems parochial we must remember that for an amazingly concentrated period Swift's political satire dominated England, and that at a crucial stage in Irish politics his *Drapier's Letters* were singly and totally decisive.

When we draw up the balance-sheet of Swift's activities, even in this brief fashion, we can see that his involvement with past and present was as sustained in time as it was intense in effect. Some of these issues are irremediably dead, and the literary student today finds the linguistic and political satire hard to understand without much extra-literary information, while *A Tale of a Tub* is so complex that even with all the annotation so far provided we are still never quite sure at what point satiric targets merge and alter. But it can still be read and enjoyed before and without total study, and indeed a surprisingly large proportion of Swift's satire is directly available to the common reader with a minimum of apparatus—works like *A Modest Proposal*, *An Argument* [*against*] *the Abolishing of Christianity*, and *Gulliver's Travels* hardly need annotation, so completely have the 'keys' to the satire been integrated into the words themselves. In his *Apology for Smectymnuus* Milton wrote that satire, 'as it was born out of a tragedy, so ought to resemble his parentage, to strike high, and adventure dangerously at the most eminent vices among the greatest persons.'[3] Swift did precisely this, and if we need contemporary comment and modern scholarship to identify who 'the greatest persons' are, the 'most eminent vices' stand out plainly for every reader, today as tomorrow.

B

This is not to deny the need for literary criticism and elucidation but to stress that the major issues of Swift's satires are of permanent interest. Who can ever forget Gulliver's naive exposure of the anti-human (or super-bestial) practices of war? Yet today human ingenuity is being increasingly devoted to 'improvements' in weapons, and the Gulliver *de nos jours* could enthuse about the unspeakable advantages of the napalm bomb. Time has not glossed over the inherent weaknesses exposed here in social organization, or law, or politics. Human judgment is still as prone to purely relative contextual assessment, moral and intellectual, but nothing has shown this up so clearly as those games with magnifying and minifying in Books One and Two which turn out to have such disastrous consequences, or the even more fundamental split in Book Four between the human form and the human reason. Few (if any) satires since 1726 have penetrated as sharply into man's irrationality, malice, greed, pride and self-centredness as *Gulliver's Travels*. It, and several other works, are and always will be necessary reading if we want to preserve our moral perspectives. They are also eternally amusing.

Readers and critics have long paid tribute to the wit and accuracy of Swift's diagnosis of the evil side of man. But the critical achievement of the last thirty years has been to define and evaluate the techniques with which he made the attack. General studies of satire by David Worcester, R. C. Elliott, Alvin Kernan, L. Feinberg and R. Paulson,[4] and more particular studies of Swift's satirical method by Ricardo Quintana, Herbert Davis, W. B. Ewald, Martin Price, J. M. Bullitt, E. W. Rosenheim and others,[5] have enormously refined our understanding of the types of procedure by which man is here shown at his worst. The cumulative effect of this criticism has been to demonstrate for the first time the artistry with which Swift worked, the never-ending experiment with form. But one disadvantage of this emphasison Swift as a manipulator of masks, mirrors, personae, and all kinds of 'satiric devices' has been that we have lost sight of Swift himself, and the ultimate direction of this type of formalist criticism is to see him as a man who could mock everything but believed in nothing. I do not suggest that any of these subtle and illuminating books has reached this extreme position, but they have collectively weakened our view of Swift's positive attitudes, those straightforward, often conventional guards and limits which support the whole destructive fabric of raillery, invective, parody—satire in all its forms. This is perhaps a sophisticated failing, and it might be said that time would be better spent in correcting other persistent 'vulgar errors', such as that Swift was a purely negative person, a cynical and indifferent clergyman, or that the years of 'exile' in Ireland were spent in misanthropy and madness. In fact all of these errors will be attacked in the essays that follow, for the purpose of this book is not only to establish fresh lines of enquiry but also to correct persistent misinterpretations, and although there has been no collusion between the contributors, and certainly no party-line from the editor, the amount of agreement among them is remarkable.

The opening essay by Pat Rogers takes on precisely that weakness in modern criticism which I have referred to, the way that it has developed delicate tools to evaluate Swift's satiric techniques but is curiously unable to discuss the plain and obvious features of his positive beliefs (like those animals whose very sensitive eyes can see in the dark but are blinded by daylight). Dr. Rogers usefully relates Swift's work to the general eighteenth-century tendency to express balanced, straightforward moral and literary attitudes in highly complicated, disordered, and unbalanced forms, and goes on to show that Swift approved of authority in all spheres often in an institutional form and with the simple connotations of obedience and almost passive acceptance: innovation and rejection of authority are the steps to ruin. As Nigel Dennis has recently said, Swift 'loved authority more dearly than anything else', and even regarded liberty not as absolute freedom but rather 'as an arrangement of severe disciplines binding upon all persons from the King down to the lowest subject.'[6] It is a position very similar to that of Hobbes, and although Swift shows no signs of approving in detail the complex abstract social structure of *Leviathan* his satire certainly supports some of its basic assumptions—it is as if he were dedicated to exposing all those deviations from the norm which Hobbes did not stop to consider when outlining his system. To Swift as chronicler of 'mere nature' the most persistent vice is that Man constantly challenges authority, his incorrigible pride always ascending beyond his station—as, on a smaller scale, Swift wrote of himself in the *Verses* on his death:

> True genuine Dulness mov'd his Pity,
> Unless it offer'd to be witty. (*Poems*, 572).

If it did so it would immediately be exposed, often in ludicrous discrepancies between desire and achievement such as that cited by Dr. Rogers between the introduction to *Polite Conversation* and its contents —or one might add, between what we know to be the potential of the human body in strength, agility and speed, and what actually happens to it in *Gulliver's Travels*, both by physically humiliating the unhappy person of Gulliver and by the comparison of his body to the more 'practical' bodies of animals.

In the second part of his essay Dr. Rogers moves from this accurate and convincing analysis to make some more radical deductions: first that Swift, unlike most satirists, did not offer any ideal or norm of human behaviour; secondly, that he preferred 'a worthy profession' of goodness, although possibly hypocritical, to any obvious demonstration of badness; and lastly that because he did not bother to reveal his own opinions unequivocally he often confuses the issue in order not to lose any potential avenue for satire. These deductions qualify or perhaps contradict the picture of Swift's simple desire for authority which Dr. Rogers presented earlier, but although one may disagree with some of his assumptions (I personally do not believe that the satirist must offer an ideal alternative at the same time that he is exposing vice—in being dragged through the tour of human evil and absurdity in *Gulliver's Travels* I am not left wondering what rational or moral or charitable human behaviour would be like, or whether I would recognize it if I saw it. Swift knows that we can fall back—are forced back—on our moral sense, however occluded it may be)—nevertheless the other contradictions remain and have to be faced. It is interesting, for example, that Swift pays less attention to the discrepancy between appearance and reality in moral behaviour than do traditional satirists such as Ben Jonson and Pope, although one does remember that in Lilliput when a particularly inhuman punishment was carried out great 'encomiums on his Majesty's mercy' were produced; and also that if weak on the moral side Swift more than compensates for it by revealing the reality beneath appearances on the physical side, from the magnified patches of human skin in Brobdingnag to his incomparable inventories of Ladies' Dressing-rooms. In a sense these are much more damaging to human dignity than the evasions on the moral plane, for although our conscience is easily appeased and we find other people's face in satire's glass and not our own, we cannot change our bodies. Disagreement with Dr. Rogers there may be, but anyone who wishes to refute his thesis will have to produce one equally tightly argued and wide-ranging.

His diagnosis of Swift's desire for obedience to authority is carried further by Basil Hall, who begins by removing any doubts as to Swift's sincerity and devotion as a clergyman. (The Victorian assumption, which still prevails in some places, was that it is impossible to be both a cleric and a satirist—as Professor Hall dryly observes, men 'can forgive a clergyman almost anything save intelligence and wit.') But it was a piety and faith that concealed itself totally, avoiding the ostentation of being good, and Johnson's comments on it are still apposite: 'instead of wishing to seem better, he delighted in seeming worse than he was'—indeed Swift himself once diagnosed a similar human contradiction in his *Various Thoughts*, that 'Some People take more care to hide their Wisdom than their Folly' (IV, 244). Professor Hall usefully reminds us of a letter first published in 1966 which shows a similar split between surface and reality, as Swift performs a good deed while seeming to bark, and this use of Cerberus to conceal St. Julian goes deep into Swift's personality, being seen in literary and indeed personal terms in his constant fascination with raillery and its use of a hostile appearance to conceal a real warmth and friendliness (as subsequent essays by Geoffrey Hill and John Holloway record). Although Professor Hall would challenge Dr. Rogers on the validity of Swift advocating 'an outward show' in religion, he agrees with him on the importance to Swift of obedience to the Church as being 'essential to the moral stability of society', and explains the fixity of this belief by reference first to Swift's moral-psychological insistence on the need for limitation: 'Man's irrepressible self-sufficiency riding on his ruthless egotism needs the strongest curb' (the consequences of unrestrained inflation are devastatingly shown in *A Tale of a Tub* and *The Mechanical Operation of the Spirit*) and secondly to the destructive religious and political controversies of the period. His seemingly intolerant authoritarian attitude to liberty of speech and conscience derives from recent history: liberty had in fact produced anarchy in politics, and

> It is the same case in religion, although not so avowed, where liberty of conscience, under the present acceptation, equally produces revolutions, or at least convulsions and disturbances in a state . . . (IX, 263).

Evidently this respect for even an outward show is connected with the need for stability: it is as if in a Hobbesian view of society as a perpetual war amongst men Swift (like responsible leaders in a war between nations) is urging solidarity at least to the charitable and Christian potential of man: in a time of constant emergency we must suppress any signs of disbelief in the ideals for which we fight. The satirist and clergyman can be relied on to to expose evil and to show us virtue: our job is to keep up appearances.

This desire for restraint and obedience may seem to smack of the police state or church dictatorship, but Professor Hall's account of the alternatives—speculation into the ultimate Christian mysteries and either lessening the mysteries or ridiculing the speculation; doubt about the authority of scripture; faith by inspiration or by adherence to one of the new sects—is strong support for the view that Swift's position was a sensible one, if not indeed the only possible one. But it does not tally with more emotional views of faith (in an age of rational unbelief we demand that faith should be irrational and 'intensely personal'), and one of the most salutary effects of this exposition of Swift's view of religion is that it reveals the desperate need for religious stability felt throughout seventeenth-century Europe—particularly interesting are the quotations from Descartes and Charron here; indeed the latter's account of the Christian's duties of honesty, simplicity, willingness to believe, to elevate God and to humiliate man, read almost like a summary of Swift's own position. Naturally simplicity, modesty and self-depreciation are not likely to produce 'exciting' Sermons, but from this essay (and in the final section Professor Hall goes on to show those connections between the Sermons and the other religious writings which are seldom recognised) and from the work of Louis Landa[7] we can now understand why Swift's preaching was so straightforward and without the brilliance of his satire. Perhaps more important, we can see the connections between Swift as clergyman and Swift as satirist. For although the end-products are so different the preoccupations are the same: in defence of order, reason, virtue, sanity, and against that chaos and barbarism which is always threatening and which is the real nature of human 'progress,' that raid from 'Ignorance's Universal North': 'men degenerate every day, merely by the folly, the perverseness, the avarice, the tyranny, the pride, the treachery, or inhumanity of their own kind' (IX, 264).

If Swift the clergyman has been misunderstood, so has Swift the politician, and equally damaging criticism has been made of him on equally superficial evidence: Swift's critics have always been quick to attack apparent faults or inconsistencies without attempting to see the connections between theory and practice. W. A. Speck first demolishes the charge that Swift was a place-seeker and then defines his political theories by analysing his attitude to three major issues of the period, the origin of government, the position of the Church in society, and England's role in Europe. Dr. Speck shows the clear division between Whigs and Tories on each of these issues, and makes the important point that Swift's divided allegiance—being, as he described himself, a Whig in politics and a High-churchman in religion—is not due to any tendency towards compromise but rather to his peculiar position as a clergyman of the Church of Ireland, bitterly resenting both Catholic and Protestant extremes for their exploitation and destruction of the Irish Church and people: 'Swift shared the prejudices of the Irish clergy, and English politics therefore presented him with a real dilemma. Neither party both hated James II, the Catholic tyrant, and venerated Charles I, the Anglican martyr.' Dr. Speck (here, as elsewhere, reaching conclusions very similar to Professor Hall's), demonstrates the basic consistency in Swift's political principles—especially in his attitude to Church and State—and shows how the increasing intolerance of the Whigs against the Anglican church alienated Swift from them so that when Harley gained power in 1710 Swift 'could collaborate with this new ministry without discarding a single principle.' Thus it might be said that Swift's principles remained constant, but the parties' policies—and thus their implicit theories—changed. Once with the Tories he committed himself totally to them by prosecuting with great vigour the theory that 'the Whigs loved the War, while the Tories longed for peace', and to literary students it is no surprise to read a historian's judgment that 'Swift pushed [this theory] about as far as it would go.'

From this expert analysis of Swift's theory and practice of politics several points emerge which complement other estimates made here. The affinity with Hobbes, which Dr. Rogers and Professor Hall pointed to, is established further: Dr. Speck's analysis confirms that Swift was impressed by *Leviathan*, agreed with Hobbes's doctrine of sovereignty, and in espousing the contract theory inclined more towards the Hobbesian assumptions on which a contract was necessary (that otherwise 'mere nature' was a destructive extension of self-love) than to the Lockean version (where in the state of nature 'men were governed by reason, and life had been tolerable'). But Swift of course departs from Hobbes's ethical relativism in urging the claims of religion and virtue: 'he considered metaphysical sanctions to be necessary to preserve morality in civil society', even though the methods by which these are to be enforced suggest, as I argued above, the practices of a totalitarian society. The state, Swift believes, should support morality with discipline, and its rulers especially, being so much in the public eye, should give good examples of virtue and religion—even their domestic servants should be obliged to perform religious observance and to give 'the Appearance at least, of Temperance and Chastity' (II, 47). This idea of the enforcement of morality does not appeal to me or, I suspect, to anyone today, but one must concede that if a writer believes that society is perpetually on the point of breaking down into anarchy and barbarism then even good appearances are essential. Here indeed Swift's ideas on Church and State come together, as a desire for 'order and purity', but not in any placatory middle-of-the-road mood. As Dr. Speck says, 'On the real issues Swift was an extremist', and although his basic assumptions are orthodox the violence with which he attacked violations of them is the sign of a totally unorthodox passion of belief—he *almost* 'puts orthodoxy to subversive ends'. Swift's moral and intellectual energy was an invigorating and life-giving force, but also a dangerous one.

Professor Hall rightly pointed to Swift's rejection of scientific method as being based on a distrust of mechanist explanations for human behaviour, and this distrust has been well documented both in biographical terms and as it results in satire. But it does not seem to have been suggested that Swift ever attacked the father of seventeeth-century Science, Bacon, and in my first essay I attempt to provide evidence that a very strong antipathy existed and was expressed. If one reconstructs the climate of ideas in the 1690s it becomes apparent that not only are the latest manifestations of science admired—the Royal Society, Boyle, Newton—but that its 'only begetter' is being idolized, inflated to what even sympathetic readers of Bacon must admit to be an excessive size. Although Swift does not hesitate to take over some ideas from Bacon when they agree with his own thoughts (as Basil Hall wrote independently, 'while Swift rejects much that was offered to him from the past, he also accepts some things and modifies them for his own purposes'), his basic reaction is to satirize both the ideas of the master and his style. The first reaction, mockery of ideas, can be demonstrated with some confidence—the fact that Swift never referred to Bacon by name although quoting directly from the works is typical of his wish to mystify but also seems a challenge to contemporary adulators of him, and as far as I know, nobody in 'this *Bacon-faced* generation' spotted the references. The second argument is the more difficult, and not everyone will agree with all the details, but Bacon's style seemed archaic at that time, and certain features of it were definitely abhorrent to Swift; in the complete context of Swift's dislike of Bacon and what he stood for the thesis may convince. Indeed, given the antipathy it would be surprising if it did not result in parody, for as Irvin Ehrenpreis writes below, 'it is a well-known mark of the workings of Swift's imagination that he loves to speak in a parody of people he detests.' Some of my classifications of Swift's types of parody may be generally useful—knocking out the intermediary steps in an argument and so juxtaposing beginning and end in a ludicrous way; taking a favourite two-part structure and after a serious opening inserting a banal second half; re-deploying a stylistic device, changing its context, suppressing one part of it, inverting its sequence, compounding its parts—all roads leading to ridicule.

The critical difficulty with parody is that its point is not taken unless one knows the general or specific object being mocked—a study of technique alone will have no validity. Irony is a satirical method which is much less dependent on outside information, and continuing the development of this book from the analysis of the discernable bases of Swift's thought to that of the techniques and forms with which he made literature out of them, we come to irony, first from a linguistic point of view. Hugh Sykes Davies brings to his account of Swift's theory and practice of English the training of a historian of the language, and if the result is, in the first part of his essay, damaging to Swift, whose prescriptions for English vocabulary are shown to be repressive (but although misguided, very typical of his concern for what Basil Hall calls 'limitation' and Geoffrey Hill, below, 'reaction': control, stability), as compensation the second part offers a stimulating account of the method by which Swift produced some of his greatest satire. Mr. Sykes Davies proposes a linguistic theory of irony which is illuminating and, after some recent more laboured analyses, refreshingly simple. Whereas normal communication is a message which is transmitted and understood as intended, he argues that irony is a message which has to be systematically decoded to reveal a meaning very different to that apparent on the surface. Unlike parody, which depends on some external referent, irony must include within itself the key to its code, and one of the most powerful resources of the writer using it 'is to produce temporary confusion between the two, so that the receiver thinks that he is dealing with signals in the normal, uncoded mode of communication, when in fact he is receiving coded signals', and is thus given a shock which forces him to see the real meaning with greater intensity. (This theory might well be used to clarify *A Tale of a Tub*, where the switches from code to norm are often bewildering). Mr. Sykes Davies demonstrates the practical application of his theory with a brilliant analysis of several of the tactics used in *A Modest Proposal*, and he then connects it to the findings of the first part of his essay (that Swift wanted to restrict vocabulary to simple words) to draw a revealing link in the use of irony between code as opposed to norm, and simplicity or flatness of language as opposed to outright railing on the one hand and enthusiastic panegyric on the other. Swift frequently plays off the difference between these opposed modes to undercut the reader's response and to draw him into a direct and creative contact with the satire, as in that grim Kafka-like fable at the end of *Gulliver's Travels* on the evils of colonization, which begins in indignant railing and is then capped by an insidious panegyric of the admirable example set by 'the British Nation', which therefore rings completely hollow and is interpreted by its readers in quite the opposite direction—indeed one could add that because we are made to do the work ourselves we decode violently, with a revulsion and to an extent greater than Swift could ever have achieved by direct means. Mr. Sykes Davies has admirably illuminated how irony works at the linguistic level, and his essay is, I think, one of the most far-reaching in this volume.

His work on theory is complemented by the late Professor Herbert Davis discussing Swift's practice of irony. Both writers overlap in their reference to that great passage in *A Short View of Ireland* where Swift paints a glowing account of Ireland as it is shown by official English reports and then stops short—'But my heart is too heavy to continue this Irony longer', matching it with the depressing reality. This passage (written in 1728) is evidence of Swift's growing awareness of the nature of his use of irony, and in 1731 in the *Verses* on his own death he made the mock (?) serious claim to have invented or transformed it:

> ARBUTHNOT is no more my friend,
> Who dares to Irony pretend;
> Which I was born to introduce,
> Refin'd it first, and shew'd its Use. (*Poems*, 555).

The statement is true, of course, and Professor Davis perceptively charts the development and the interaction between author and persona. Modern criticism delights in finding complexities, and after all the dazzling varieties of mirror-images that have been discovered it is valuable to be reminded that Swift 'always remains himself in complete charge; he never becomes the sport of his own characters. . . . The puppets he is using are always being manipulated by his fingers, and their voices, however disguised, are always his voice'. Professor Davis rejects with equal rightness that school of critics which believes that Swift intended the Houyhnhnms to represent the Deists, and he is not incapable of a fine irony or two of his own, such as the comment that in the tract against abolishing Christianity 'a good many' of the points 'are rather outdated, depending as they do on such forgotten practices as assembling in Churches and other forms of Sunday observance.' Professor Davis finds *A Modest Proposal* to be 'the most perfect piece of writing that ever came from Swift's pen', and he makes an interesting comparison between its *persona* and Gulliver in his Letter to Sympson, both despairing over man; and one could add a point which strengthens the argument, for as Gulliver ends by saying 'I have now done with all such visionary Schemes for ever', so the

author of *A Modest Proposal* has experienced an identical disillusionment
with reform:

> as to my self; having been wearied out for many Years with offering
> vain, idle, visionary Thoughts; and at length utterly despairing of
> success, I fortunately fell upon this Proposal.
>
> (XII, 117)

The 'fortunately' is nicely placed.

But this agreement between Swift's *personae* raises a further issue,
the writer's own position on the scale between hope of reform and
despair. Herbert Davis argues that the ironic passage in *A Tale of a
Tub* which explains its definition of happiness as 'a perpetual possession
of being well deceived' is 'arranged to leave us with nothing but utter
scepticism', and at the end of his essay he suggests that Swift's marginalia on the Creed might be a sign of his own despair, recoiling from the
corruption of the world to that primitive faith which the author of *An
Argument* [*against*] *the Abolishing of Christianity* had said would be 'a
wild Project' to restore, that '*real* Christianity; such as used in primitive
Times (if we may believe the Authors of those Ages) to have an Influence upon Mens Belief and Actions . . . .' (II, 27). Satire, like true
Christianity, should have an influence upon men's belief and actions,
and the mere existence of satire is proof that men have always thought
that it could do so. Hugh Sykes Davies takes the other view, that
Swift does not reach despair or a negative position: he cites appositely
the debate in Peacock's novel *Melincourt* about the utility of moral
censure, in which Mr. Sarcastic's defence of satire as opposed to simple
moral denunciation echoes the words of Gulliver and the Modest
proposer:

> I tried [denunciation] in my youth, when I was troubled with the
> *passion for reforming the world;* of which I have been long cured,
> by the conviction of the inefficacy of moral theory with respect to
> producing a practical change in the mass of mankind. . . . It is not by
> reason that practical change can be effected, but by making a puncture
> to the quick in the feelings of personal hope and personal fear.

Mr. Sykes Davies concludes that in his unremitting use of satire Swift
was 'about as much of an optimist as any man can possibly be, provided
he is not a fool and is fully capable of understanding the knavery of
those around him', for his dedication to satire is proof that he believed
in the existence within man of a 'central core of decency' which could
be reached by satire and provoked to do good.

However, the problem is whether or not satire has ever had such an
effect: there is no doubt that lampooning has made people or policies

look ridiculous (Walpole; Wood's halfpence) but we have little evidence that it has ever worked a *moral* reform on man. In his own pronouncements Swift certainly believed that it could, and one may easily assemble evidence of this from the *Letters* or *Poems*—*Gulliver's Travels*, he says, 'are admirable Things, and will wonderfully mend the World'; the best motive for writing satire 'is a *Publick Spirit*, prompting Men of *Genius* and Virtue, to mend the World as far as they are able'; 'I write for their amendment, and not their approbation'; his satire was 'with a moral View design'd / To cure the Vices of Mankind.' But at the same time, in *A Tale of a Tub*, at the conclusion to that exposure of delusion in the mind of man it is suggested that even 'the Art of exposing weak Sides and publishing Infirmities' is among these delusions, and Gulliver's despair with man takes this scepticism to the limit: the satire has not worked. For

> instead of seeing a full Stop put to all Abuses and Corruptions, at least in this little Island, as I had Reason to expect: Behold, after about six Months Warning, I cannot learn that my Book hath produced one single Effect according to mine Intentions. . . . And, it must be owned, that seven Months were a sufficient Time to correct every vice and Folly. . . .

This outburst calls in question the whole function of satire, and one of the qualities that makes Swift greater than any other satirist in English or all but two or three in any literatures is his absence of complacency either about his personal success (unlike Pope) or, more fundamentally, about the form itself (as he reminds us elsewhere with his images of the mirror and the tennis-racket, we always try to direct it away from ourselves). But he writes with absolute consistency in Gulliver's role as a reformer full of 'visionary schemes', for Gulliver's insistence on the shortness of time needed for a reform tallies exactly with that of the true visionary, down almost to the estimate of time. Thus Milton at the end of *Areopagitica* has a vision of London as 'the mansion house of liberty', defending 'beleagured Truth' and anticipating with joy 'the approaching Reformation':

> What wants there to such a towardly and pregnant soil, but wise and faithful labourers, to make a knowing people, a Nation of Prophets, of Sages, and of Worthies? We reckon more than five months yet to harvest; there need not be five weeks; had we but eyes to lift up, the fields are white already.[8]

Gulliver's seven months, Milton's five, or even five weeks, would be enough, if there were 'the least Disposition to Virtue or Wisdom' in man. Now I am aware that Gulliver's rage with the Yahoos is a complicating factor which we must allow for, while not laughing off what he says. But I suggest that in reading the letter to Sympson we nevertheless do 'decode' his denunciation and apply it to ourselves, and our own experience of life and society now or (to stay with Gulliver's fundamentalism) in any six months following the publication of a major satire, is such that we laugh at Gulliver's anger because his impatience about reform although *right* is 'unreasonable' or 'unpracticable': it will never happen: people aren't like that: Milton's vision is one which will only come true in another world. I am not suggesting that there is a one-to-one connection between Gulliver's despair and Swift's life, for clearly this abandoning of any hope of reform could be just as much a rhetorical bluff as the conclusion to *The Dunciad*, where Pope envisages what it *would be* like if the forces of darkness *were to* triumph (I do not regard it, as some modern critics do, as a pessimistic prognostication of the end of the Enlightenment). But Gulliver's despair does expose a dilemma, that is in its original sense, an argument concluding both ways: either one regards it with cynical agreement—'of course, it's impossible to reform man', and sees the desire as yet another sign of human pride, as Montaigne does,[9] or one rejects it with the affirmation that man can improve himself morally, that he is the only living creature with this ability, that there is evidence that he does so, however feebly or irregularly, and that satire is the literary form that exists in order to remind him of his potential. These are, I think, the alternative conclusions, and I see no resolution to them— Swift has stated the problem definitively, and my contributors are right to see both sides.

Just as this volume offers two essays on irony, it brings together two on Swift's poetry, also complementary. Geoffrey Hill writes a wide-ranging but detailed survey of the themes and attitudes revealed in the poems, illuminating from another perspective what might be called the co-existence of extremes in Swift, here the presence in his poetry and in the social circumstances that produced it of both acceptance and rejection. His survey ranges from the early Pindarics (which, he argues, with their celebrations of a defeated man look forward to Swift's mock-serious poems of defeat on himself, equally victorious in the end), to the comic verse and street ballads; and from the harshest of political satire (Mr. Hill enters a much-needed defence of *The Legion Club*) to the depths of Swift's scatological exposures of female cosmetic. Mr. Hill endorses the verdict of Irvin Ehrenpreis on the intensity of this latter type of poetry: 'The complainants' case would be best proved if Swift were *not* intense on such subjects', and while making a perceptive point about necessary background information: 'so far as accusations of simple "bad taste" are concerned, there is no great difficulty in showing that, in terms of Eighteenth Century conditions of life, it would be virtually impossible to exceed plain reality' he is divided as to his response. He rightly finds modern criticism of the absence of 'compassion' in these pictures of 'nymphs' to be cant, yet he sees in Swift 'an appalling obsession with filth and disease', and one has to agree with his condemnation of the crude latrine humour of *A Panegyrick on the Dean, in the Person of a Lady in the North*, even though its description of excrement in terms of modish pastoral is at the same literary level as Pope's scatological games in *The Dunciad*. 'Obsession' does not seem to be the right word in terms of quantity, for as Irvin Ehrenpreis showed (*Personality*, p. 43) out of over three hundred poems only ten or a dozen are 'obscene', and I would argue it is not the right word in terms of quality, or satiric function.

In defence of Swift here one has to remember that whereas satirists have traditionally been allowed to strip off the finery of clothes to reveal naked and diseased humanity, Swift allied himself energetically to the satiric tradition[10] which discovered a further dimension, a resource that by 1730, say, woman has developed with unscrupulous ingenuity until it almost exceeds clothes in disguising power: artificial hair, crystal eye, false eyebrows, false teeth and a whole galaxy of contrivances to pad out the cheeks, breasts, hips, legs or any other deficiency (today cosmetic plastic surgery makes all things possible, and one could easily imagine Swift's reaction to the operating theatre). Swift first strips his nymphs, then humiliates them further, and the type of disgust which he produces can be paralleled both in secular satire of all periods and in Christian teaching designed to mortify the body (and with it man's pride) by reminding us forcefully of its inalienable relationship with dust, dirt, excrement and decay—only Swift made the great mistake of being witty about it and not solemn. If I disagree with Mr. Hill on this point, I am grateful for his subtle discriminations within Swift's *oeuvre*, for his demonstration of the close connection between public and private issues in Swift's poetry, for his reconstruction of the social context of the poems—a society where many people wrote verse and it is necessary in discussing influence to consider not only Butler or Rochester but also friends such as Thomas Sheridan—and for his discussion of the place of raillery in this society. After having thought of irony as a code we find it significant that in *Cadenus and Vanessa* Swift described how raillery could achieve a 'bite' (the trapping of a victim into mistaking a surface of either wit or seriousness for one's real feelings) and insisted that such an irony include its own key:

> But those who aim at Ridicule
> Shou'd fix upon some certain Rule,
> Which fairly hints they are in jest,
> Else he must enter his Protest:
> For, let a Man be ne'er so wise,
> He may be caught with sober Lies. (*Poems*, 707).

Again one sees the consistency of tone and method in Swift through much of literature and life.

From general we move to particular with Roger Savage's account of one poem, *A Description of the Morning*. It is generally appreciated that in the companion piece *A Description of a City Shower* Swift used the Augustan methods of applying a classical model to a modern subject in order to mock the moderns but the same process has never been noticed here. Dr. Savage removes the old idea that this is 'a piece of uncomplicated realism', and establishes authoritatively that unless we are aware of 'Augustan stock-responses to Swift's title . . . we are not likely to achieve more than a partial reading of his poem', by uncovering a whole tradition of 'dawn-scenes' imitated from Homer and Virgil. Some are 'straight' imitations in the pastoral mode, such as that found in Bysshe's *British Parnassus*, while others by poets such as Butler or Garth precede Swift in burlesquing it. Swift's version is remarkable for the precision with which he parallels every item in the traditional inventories with some sordid modern equivalent, and also, it seems to me, for the care for detail which makes his own version consistent in itself, a quite homogeneous account of how 'this end of town' starts the day's business. But at the same time, Dr. Savage argues, he does not simply destroy either past or present, but manages 'to preserve ideal epic dignity' while mocking the moral and social decadence revealed in modern society by the accidents of the comparison: there is a process of superimposition or parallel presentation at work (his diagnosis interestingly connects with what Hugh Sykes Davies has described as the 'running comparison' which the ironist makes us carry out 'between what is being said and what is being meant.')

This investigation of the 'set of hereditary images' which surrounded Augustan descriptions of the morning considerably clarifies not only the poem and its companion piece but also Swift's whole relationship to the past: as Dr. Savage finely puts it, Swift faced 'the dilemma of being a modern among ancients and an ancient among moderns.' Indeed, Dr. Savage takes the argument out further, into the two Swiftian topics that still most vex mankind, the scatological poems and

Book Four of *Gulliver*, interestingly connecting them to the two *Descriptions* and to the process by which Swift builds up an apparently exaggerated disgust: the poetic heroes who have worshipped 'angels without bowels' and discover that they too use chamber-pots; Gulliver incensed with human irrationality *and* with the human form; the author of the *Descriptions* criticising an Augustan city for the unavoidable failing of not being like Virgilian landscape. These are seemingly unreasonable positions in which nevertheless many positive injunctions are put forward: 'nymphs' should try to be hygienic, men should attempt to live up to human rationality, London should clean up both streets and morals. I find Dr. Savage's argument convincing and capable of further elaboration—thus it could be said that Swift has in all three cases used extremely violent means to engage his readers and provoke them to a fresh examination of human conduct, but that readers have persistently mistaken the means for the end, objecting to the violence as a personal insult and allowing their indignation to cloud their vision of the whole satiric process. Although not trying to minimise the violence nor its 'absolute' truth, perhaps we should try to be more detached, and, paradoxically, read his satire more coolly.

All the contributions so far have referred more or less substantially to *Gulliver's Travels*, and it is a fair reflection of the fascination and complexity that this work increasingly possesses that three whole essays should be given up to it. Not quite three, to be accurate, for in the first part of his study of 'the comedy of evil' Irvin Ehrenpreis analyzes the use of this effect in Juvenal, Molière and Brecht, but the most important of his conclusions have to do with Gulliver. In a short but extremely compressed essay Professor Ehrenpreis clarifies the apparently contradictory relationship between comedy and evil as seen in the work of four great satirists: the dark villains, Domitian, Tartuffe, Arturo Ui, are presented in all their evil, but although key-incidents show them in a potentially ridiculous light, their crimes remain serious enough for us not to regard them as mere irrational fools. Thus Professor Ehrenpreis poses us the question: 'How, then, can a reader avoid a continuous, guilt-ridden sense of ignoring horrors?' I would suggest that we may laugh but we do not ignore the horrors, even though our laughter might seem evidence that we do: the satirist exploits our sense of humour at the same time that he traps our moral sense, and we produce what is not a sign of delight but rather one which reinforces our horror (laughter has many varieties). Part of the contradiction, as Professor Ehrenpreis shows, is that these three satirists exclude themselves 'from any responsibility for the triumph of vice', whereas Swift involves himself in it, 'establishing himself in the immediate foreground of the scene'. Thus Swift's constant use of a *persona* is given a new explanation: whereas it is usually thought of as a device to create greater complexities and to free Swift from any simple identification with the direction of the satire, it can now be seen as a means of involving the audience in the whole satiric process: 'The author himself looks like the villain, and we find our reflection in both'. And whereas with other satire we can remain detached, in Swift we are not only indignant with the vice portrayed but have to admit that we are implicated in it, partly as representatives of the genus man, and partly as being consumers making up the market for which the vices are cultivated (superstition, greed, indiscriminate literary taste).

I will not paraphrase the steps by which Professor Ehrenpreis builds up this ingenious and convincing argument, nor his application of it to the *Letter of Thanks to the Bishop of St. Asaph* and to *Gulliver*, but I will say that it seems to me an attractive explanation of the peculiar two-way traffic between author and reader which exists in Swift's satire, and also of his peculiar intensity. Swift, it is argued, 'by risking more' than most satirists, 'wins more', but at the same time his intensity may cause him to lose more: this analysis of the satire on Wharton addressed to Asaph includes the comment that it is 'typical of Swift that when he does attack a man's character, he blackens it to a depth where the villainy seems to have no mitigation.' Similarly, Mr. Rogers has commented that Swift 'is at so little pains to make his own position clear or unassailable or visibly innocent (as satirists generally do) that he often compromises himself in order to demolish his victim the more effectually'. The violence that I described earlier has exactly this absolutist tendency, the desire to paint the portrait absolutely black, whether it be Wharton, or Celia in her dressing room, or the bestial side of man in the Yahoo—Swift is always wanting to take things as far as they will go, and he sometimes took them too far, or at any rate beyond the understanding of many of his readers, and beyond the sanity of his *personae*. But even in excess he was realizing to the full the potentialities of the form, and Professor Ehrenphreis has cast a good deal of light on the methods by which he did so.

The other two essays on *Gulliver's Travels* are concerned with it as a portrait of society. My own reconsiders the surprisingly neglected connection with More's Utopian society, not in terms of the content of each but rather in the way that the description of foreign customs is brought into critical and indeed destructive relationship with our own. The findings do not merely argue that Swift used *Utopia* more than has so far been supposed, and refined on its irony, but also try to illuminate

C

the way both writers apply the naive and ignorant partner in a dialogue to create fundamental objections to the ethics of human society. Angus Ross is more concerned with the content of the Societies visited by Gulliver, that is to their social organizations, either as (unwittingly?) revealing Swift's own assumptions about society or as deliberate pieces of satire: the Yahoos represent several types of social behaviour which Swift detested, but good and bad are evenly distributed throughout all the voyages. At the level of the individual, Gulliver is placed in a fairly respectable social position and one of his first tasks in each new milieu is to report back to his readers the level at which he moves: in Lilliput, as Dr. Ross puts it, 'because of his size, *and therefore importance*, he deals directly with the administration in the person of the emperor', he prides himself on being treated as superior even among 'persons of quality', certainly above the Treasurer. (Although Gulliver's transparent snobbery here makes mild but effective satire on human desire for social positions, it is also a wry echo of Swift's own 'reports back' in the *Journal to Stella*). In Brobdingnag he is physically and therefore socially inferior but is ultimately elevated (and us with him) only to be cast down; in Laputa he automatically associates with 'Persons of Distinction' and 'of better Quality', and amongst the Luggnaggians he has 'many acquaintance among Persons of the best Fashion'. This immediate gravitation towards the genteel levels of society is designed, I think, partly to show Gulliver's own social status, and partly to ingratiate him with those readers then as now who like to be assured that their hero is moving in the best circles. Both sides are undermined in Book IV, where the same unthinking and therefore curiously arbitrary social assumptions are kept up but now applied by Gulliver (he does not notice the incongruity, but we do) to horses: one of the visitors is 'an old Steed, who seemed to be of Quality', and there are several 'Horses and Mares of Quality in the Neighbourhood' (what, one is left to wonder, are the social differentia of gentility among horses?). Dr. Ross brings out clearly the variety of social structures and the satiric deductions to be made from them, noting another interesting incongruity in the Houyhnhnm Council when it debates whether the present 'Regulation of Children' is satisfactory, on which he comments: 'It would be interesting to know, though, whether "Children" and "Child" are slips by Gulliver or Swift.' Perhaps the former, as Swift used the opposite incongruity to good effect in *A Modest Proposal*, where the economic projector has been talking about human beings in terms of animals and unthinkingly applies the word 'soul' to them (XII, 110).[11] The type of analysis used by Dr. Ross could well be applied further to Swift, but already it has shown from a fresh position the remarkable inventiveness and care for detail that gives *Gulliver's Travels* its depth and realism.

Finally John Holloway makes a sympathetic and imaginative reconstruction of the most misunderstood period in Swift's life. The 'view from the *Letters*' is not a cheery one, but despite the physical torture that old age and disease forced upon him, Swift retained to the end many of his best qualities—his enormous physical vigour (one is reminded of Johnson's record of Swift at Moor-park fifty years earlier —'He thought exercise of great necessity, and used to run half a mile up and down a hill every two hours'), his interest in a wide circle of friends, inspiring warmth and affection at many levels, and his inexhaustible energy with words, which not content with the great works of this period (*The Drapier's Letters*, *Gulliver*, *A Modest Proposal*, and many of the finest poems) bubbles over into the nonsense letters and puns which he exchanged with Thomas Sheridan. The only directly literary element in the *Letters* of this period is the use of raillery to disguise true affection, and from the examples given here we see how flexible the 'decoding' process can be, and must endorse the judgment that the the form is 'a great and subtle compliment to the hearer, a major act of trust both in his intelligence, and in his nearness of feeling to you'. Swift himself thought that 'Raillery is the finest Part of Conversation' (IV, 91). Dr. Holloway provides us with a topography as well as a biography of the last years, and his technique of assembling small details to give a picture of every-day life is perhaps the best way of dealing with the *Letters*, for Swift was not the introspective or philosophical type of letter-writer, and like Dickens rather than Keats revealed his character and energy in close response to the immediate events in his working life. But even the assembling of fragments would not be worthwhile were it not for the 'rich immediacy and detail' of Swift's writing, and it does not seem excessive to rank the picture of Irish rural life that emerges with the first-hand grasp of experience shown in *Henry IV*, say, or *Bartholomew Fair*. At this stage of Swift's career the work is strangely separate from the life (with the exception of Wood's halfpence) and there is a still more surprising paradox in that these friendly trivialities, these rural discomforts, these sober pleasures, and the whole world bounded by remote Irish villages —should be the surroundings for 'perhaps the finest mind in the British Isles'.

This has been perhaps sufficient introduction to whet the reader's appetite for the essays which follow, and (more important) to show the connections between them. Whatever the criticisms to be made of this book, its authors will not, I am sure, be accused of disseminating vagueness or empty generalities. They have all been encouraged (if they needed encouragement) to become fully engaged with their subject—the thought and work of a great and complex writer—and to consider it in all the necessary detail without fear of losing impatient readers. The contributors represent severally many different approaches within literary criticism and some derive from other disciplines (philosophy, history, religion, linguistics, history of ideas), but their essays have been designed to interlock and to cover as wide as possible a spectrum of this enormously wide-ranging artist. Specialization and care for detail (though not hair-splitting or pedantry) are surely the only paths which will increase our understanding of Swift, and they are no bad qualities to display in a tercentenary year. Too often the anniversaries of great writers are greeted with hasty and indifferent work, the rehashing of old insights with well-meaning sentimentality and congratulations on the timeliness of it all. This is not that sort of book. But it is also not a book written for the higher ranges of the academic profession: the original stipulation was that the essays should consist of new work or detailed reassessment, but that each should contain within itself the information necessary to its own understanding. Editors tend to be biased, but I believe that this has been done, and that this book will be valuable to anyone interested in Swift and willing to come to grips with the diversity of problems that he poses.

But while dissociating ourselves from the merely commemorative market, we would not want to forget the immediate cause that has inspired our work, and to celebrate the happy event a modest but fitting epitaph can be taken from amongst the several that Swift wrote for himself, the conclusion of *The Life and Character of Dean Swift*, where the fair-minded speaker is given the last word:

> *Sir*, our *Accounts* are diff'rent quite,
> And your *Conjectures* are not right;
> 'Tis plain, his Writings were design'd
> To *please*, and to *reform* Mankind;
> And, if he often miss'd his Aim,
> The *World*, must own it, to their *Shame*;
> The *Praise* is *His*, and *Theirs* the *Blame*.
> Then, since you *dread* no further *Lashes*,
> You freely may *forgive his Ashes*. (*Poems*, 550).

NOTES

[1] William Cobbett, *Autobiography* ed. William Reitzel (London, 1947), pp. 13–14. The earlier edition (1933) of this compilation was entitled *The Progress of a Ploughboy to a Seat in Parliament, As Exemplified in the History of the Life of William Cobbett.*

² George Orwell, 'Politics vs. Literature: an examination of *Gulliver's Travels*', in *Shooting an Elephant and other essays* (London, 1950), p. 78.

³ Milton, *Apology for Smectymnuus*, in *Complete Prose Works*, ed. D. M. Wolfe et al. (New Haven, 1953–) I, 916.

⁴ David Worcester, *The Art of Satire* (New York, 1940; 1960). R. C. Elliott, *The Power of Satire* (Princeton, 1960). Alvin Kernan, *The Plot of Satire* (New Haven, 1965). Leonard Feinberg, *The Satirist* (Iowa, 1963) and *Introduction to Satire* (Iowa, 1967). Ronald Paulson, *The Fictions of Satire* (Johns Hopkins U.P., Baltimore, 1967).

⁵ Ricardo Quintana, *The Mind and Art of Jonathan Swift* (London, 1936; revised, 1953) and *Swift: An Introduction* (London 1955). Herbert Davis, *The Satire of Jonathan Swift* (New York, 1947), reprinted in *Jonathan Swift: Essays on his Satire and Other Studies* (London, 1964). W. B. Ewald, *The Masks of Jonathan Swift* (Oxford, 1954). Martin Price, *Swift's Rhetorical Art: A Study in Structure and Meaning* (New Haven, 1953) and *To The Palace of Wisdom* (New York, 1964). J. M. Bullitt, *Jonathan Swift and the Anatomy of Satire* (Cambridge, Mass., 1953). E. W. Rosenheim, Jr., *Swift and the Satirist's Art* (Chicago, 1963). Sheldon Sacks, *Fiction and the Shape of Belief: A Study of Henry Fielding with Glances at Swift, Johnson and Richardson* (University of California, 1964). Paul Fussell, *The Rhetorical World of Augustan Humanism: Ethics and Imagery from Swift to Burke* (Oxford, 1965).

⁶ *Jonathan Swift: A Short Character* (London, 1965), pp. 30 and 152.

⁷ Louis Landa, *Swift and the Church of Ireland* (Oxford, 1954).

⁸ *Areopagitica*, ed. cit., II, 554. Cf. John iv, 35.

⁹ Montaigne, *Essays*, II, 3 (tr. E. J. Trechmann (London, 1927), I, 340–1): 'it is contrary to Nature that we should despise and carelessly set ourselves at naught . . . It is on a par with our vanity to desire to be other than we are. We reap no fruit from such a desire, seeing that it contradicts, and hinders itself. He that, being a man, desires to be made an angel, does nothing for himself; he would never be the better for it.' But for Paul Fussell satire is unique in offering us 'a surface of contempt, disparagement, and ridicule masking something quite different, namely an implicit faith in man's capacity for redemption through the operation of choice. Satire works by taxing its targets with brutishness in order to turn them angelward.' (*op. cit.*, p. 112).

¹⁰ See Irvin Ehrenpreis, *The Personality of Jonathan Swift* (London, 1958), chapter 2, 'Obscenity', pp. 29–49, especially on contemporary poems satirizing artificial hair, teeth, eyes, etc., pp. 37–8, 43ff.—the 'anatomy' from *Quevedo's Visions* is especially close to Swift. As for the general issue of the satirist's right to use nauseating language to describe nauseating human behaviour, it is one which can hardly be denied as an essential and successful feature of satire from Horace, Juvenal, Persius and Catullus to Langland, Nashe, and Ben Jonson. That Swift's use of this device is both functional and authorized by the example of classical satire was ably argued by the author of *A Modest Defence of 'The Lady's Dressing-Room'* (V, 337–340), a pamphlet first published by Faulkner in 1732 and included by him in Swift's *Works* of 1746. (V, 358). The writer rhetorically despairs of the understanding of those readers who have been offended by it, and then states the moral function of this exposure of female uncleanliness:

I cannot but lament the prevailing ill Taste among us which is not able
to discover that useful Satyr running through every Line, and the
Matter as decently wrapp'd up, as it is possible the Subject could bear.
   Cleanliness hath in all polite Ages and Nations, been esteemed the
chief corporeal perfection in *Women*, as it is well known to those who
are conversant with the antient *Poets*. And so it is still among the young
People of Judgment and Sobriety, when they are disposed to marry.
And I do not doubt, but that there is a great Number of young Ladies
in this Town and Kingdom, who in reading that Poem, find great
Complacency in their own Minds, from a Consciousness that the
Satyrical Part in the *Lady's Dressing Room*, does not in the least affect
them.

                                                                  (V, 338)

He goes on to quote a passage from Horace (*Art of Poetry*, 179–188) which
is then given a completely bogus translation to make it appear obscene and
scatological. This amusing trick may raise doubts as to the seriousness of the
earlier argument, but it seems to me rather a separate *jeu d'esprit*, and one
must concede that the moral function of Swift's satire on women's uncleanliness can be consistently sustained, especially when there are so many and
so distinguished precedents. For the long tradition of satirizing feminine
decay beneath appearances, see David Worcester's category of 'grotesque
satire' with two dozen examples from Skelton to Thomas Mann (*The Art of
Satire*, pp. 61–3)—one could add a better example from Thomas Mann, the
appalling virtuosity with which he describes internal physical decay behind
a woman's apparently vivacious 'late-flowering lust' in a short story, *The
Black Swan*. That this is a satiric tradition which Swift used with all of his
verbal brilliance rather than a personal obsession can be seen from the width
of reference easily assembled by Mr. Worcester, or from Muriel Bradbrook's
note that 'Marston, Jonson and Webster have an almost identical vocabulary
to describe the painting of diseased woman which perhaps derives from
Roman satire (compare Maquerelle in *The Malcontent*, the empress in *Sejanus*
and the old lady in *The Duchess of Malfi*).' *The Growth and Structure of Elizabethan Comedy* (London, 1955), p. 236. Other examples in sixteenth and
seventeenth-century poetry and drama spring readily to mind. Herbert
Davis demonstrated how Swift deliberately parodied seventeenth-century
lyrics which carried on the banal praise of female beauty, even when diseased:
see his brilliant juxtaposition of three Corinna poems with Swift's '*Corinna
Pride of Drury-Lane*' in *The Beautiful Young Nymph Going to Bed* (*Jonathan
Swift: Essays on his Satire*, pp. 48–9). From many other eighteenth-century
exposures of female sluttishness one thinks first of Fielding's devastating
account of Jonathan Wild's visit to Miss Tishy Snap, or of Richardson's even
more disgusting description in *Clarissa* of Mrs.Sinclair's death-bed, where the
foul, worn-out mother is surrounded by her daughters and other whores, a
gallery of equally slimy, worm-eaten women: these are visions inspired by
Swift, perhaps, but the use of the *topos* of 'woman diseased and decayed
beneath external protection' is an equally valid extension of a satiric tradition.
   [11] This slip has also been noticed by John Holloway in his stimulating
essay 'An Analysis of Swift's Satire' in *The Charted Mirror* (London, 1960),
pp. 75–93, p. 88.

Swift and the Idea of Authority

PAT ROGERS

The great concentration of critical interest in Swift over the last
two decades has not been an unmixed blessing. It was, of course, all
to the good that we should have moved beyond the more inert kind of
biographical speculation. Endless disquisitions on Dean Swift's
marriage or Stella's parentage grow rather tiresome: and they are so
because (pace Mr. Denis Johnston) it is usually hard to see how settling
such issues—if they can be settled—would enhance our understanding
of Swift's work.[1] At the same time, there is some danger that we shall
substitute for the distortions of Thackeray, say, an equally cramping
orthodoxy of our own. In recent years Swift has been submerged in a
welter of intellectual traditions. He has been swamped in Anglican
rationalism, deeply embedded in the age of compromise, lost almost
without trace in the miasma of Gnostic self-sufficiency. He has dis-
appeared from view behind personae, he has been occluded by satiric
spectra, and he has been borne off into the night on allegorical vehicles.
There are indeed so many varieties of Swiftianism available that a note
on their discrimination might not come amiss.

I do not want to take up all the implications of this situation. It
might well be argued that there is a need to set Swift once more in a
landscape with figures. The informed reader of Leslie Stephen's era,
whatever his lack of sophistication regarding the history of ideas and
the theory of satire, tended to possess enviable awareness of the literary
relationships which moulded Swift's development as a writer. I wish,
however, to consider a different point. This is the fact that modern
criticism, predominantly 'rhetorical' in character, has had the effect of
reinforcing the view of Swift as a *negative* author.[2] For their own good
reasons, critics have emphasised the formal complexities which abound
in his writing. This has meant isolating the devious, the elaborate, the
disingenuous. We have been told about Swift's fondness for strategies
of indirection and misdirection. All this can easily obscure the simple
truth that Swift is a peculiarly affirmative writer, though of a special
sort. The stress on technique, necessary as it was, has concealed the
other elements in Swift which Victorian commentators brought out
more sharply—his straightforward, thoroughgoing, unequivocal side.
It is noteworthy that the plain take-it-or-leave-it manner of *The
Sentiments of a Church-of-England Man*, like the uncluttered whole-hog

proposal for correcting the English tongue, defeats more of our present
critical approaches than do the ingenious counter-bluffs of the *Vindica-
tion of Lord Carteret*.

I mention the stress on technique advisedly. We are prisoners more
than we like to admit of the doctrine of significant form. This is a
view of literary composition to which the Augustans, by their theory
of genre, gave notional assent. Nevertheless it is one which in practice
their great writers wisely chose to ignore.[3] Pope, wishing to endorse
sanity, proportion, good humour, civility, is forced by his own
rhetorical ends in *The Dunciad* to be often shrill, ill-humoured, unbalanced. Likewise Swift, in *A Tale of a Tub*, undertakes a defence—
one might even say a comic celebration—of rationality, humility and
freedom from pedantry. To do this he produces a work that in its
outward contours manifests exactly opposite qualities. It is true that
this is direct parody, and it might be argued that parody honours the
concept of significant form in the breach. But, even on this showing,
the *Tale* can hardly be 'a logically arranged encyclopedia of Gnostic
sufficiency', as Ronald Paulson has argued.[4] Either the *Tale* is confused
(a formal analogue of the moderns' undisciplined thinking), or else
it is logically ordered, in which case the joke disappears. The fact that
the illogicality is lucidly *displayed* to the reader is beside the point. I
shall return to the question of parody; but consider for a moment other
eighteenth-century writers. Fielding is driven towards the innovative,
the picaresque, the eclectic, the digressive, the episodic: his greatest
success is achieved in a book which is, by the traditional doctrine of
kinds, a hybrid: even a bastard form. The joke we miss today is that
the 'comic epic in prose' represents a deliberate contradiction in terms.
It is literally nonsense, something resembling the 'semantic shock'
technique practised by poets such as Dryden, Young and Churchill.[5]
Again, Johnson's most forthright utterance of Augustan principles
comes in that odd, betwixt and between composition *Rasselas*. The
main repository of his weightiest ideas is the occasional, journalistic
and therefore cramped formality afforded him by the *Rambler*. That
his ideas should emerge in this setting puts one in mind of the dog on
its hindlegs, a dog in a hobble skirt, what's more.

It seems clear that eighteenth-century parody grew up as something
more than the mere negative equivalent of a positive entity. Augustan
parodic constructions are things in their own right. *Peri Bathous* is a
carefully wrought anti-model, which functions as a rhetorical treatise
absolutely satisfactorily on its own terms.[6] It is a hornbook of pedantry
which sets out 'to collect the scatter'd Rules of our Art into regular
Institutes'. The task is carried out with as much pertinacity as ever

Bysshe employed to eke out *his* manual. The inverted system or anti-manual is a particularly common device. Both Arbuthnot and Swift compiled short discourses on 'The Art of Political Lying'. One thinks, too, of the pseudo-logic and mock consequentiality of the *Tritical Essay*. Such coherent rhetorical structures are, on one level, illusory: but on another they exist happily enough as the basis for a new, self-contained literary kind. (Much as 'Instructions to a Painter' lost their purely ironic colouring, and became an autonomous exercise: Swift's own *Directions for Making a Birthday Song* foreshadow his solemnly drawn-up *Directions to Servants*.) The point is that writers of the age belie significant form by using apparently 'negative' means to attain positive ends, and vice versa. This helps to clarify a major paradox which surrounds Swift himself. He enlists commonplace in the service of contrariety, but also contrariety in the service of commonplace. He puts orthodoxy to subversive ends.[7]

Swift cherished authority. But he did not do so on metaphysical grounds: his belief was as literal-minded as Mr. T. D. Weldon could wish. He was in general an adherent of established and particularly institutionally established authority; in church and state, in questions of style and linguistic usage, within the commonwealth of writers, in the sphere of personal ethics, in the regulation of domestic management, in learning and intellectual enquiry. He throws scorn on moderns, like the narrator of the *Tale*, who think to eclipse the authority of the ancients. Swift lays ubiquitous emphasis on the need —in religious matters above all—for a sanction more durable, more comprehensive and more widely testable than either the dictates of private conscience or the concept of grace can provide. Again and again through his works we come on the insistence that stability of doctrine has one necessary and efficient cause; and that is acceptance of the Church's supremacy, as it embodies true faith. He will admit some curtailment of the idea of passive obedience to the secular authority. *Examiner*, nos. 33 and 39, go surprisingly far in some ways in rejecting arbitrary power (though Swift's tactical purposes partly explain this). But in the matter of divine sanction, there is no such softening. The clearest statement occurs perhaps in the sermon *On the Excellency of Christianity*, but examples abound. Much of Swift's work reads like a gloss on Christ's speech in Book IV of *Paradise Regain'd*:

> . . . He who receives
> Light from above, from the Fountain of Light,
> No other doctrine needs, though granted true.

Swift accepts the orthodox tenet that submission to God's will is the truest freedom. Without considering the obvious Biblical texts, we may recall the great sermon by Ralph Cudworth, preached before the Commons in 1647:

> We think it is a gallant thing to be fluttering up to Heaven with our wings of Knowledge and Speculation: whereas the highest mystery of a Divine Life here, and of perfect happiness hereafter, consisteth in nothing but mere obedience to the Divine Will.[8]

('Mere', of course, has here the old force of 'absolute'.) But if it had all been said before, in many ways Swift said it better. Or at least he made the perils of withholding obedience more graphically clear than his immediate predecessors. With Pascal it is the gamble on faith we most naturally remember: the desperate bid for salvation in an absurd dilemma of meaningless but dimly seducing alternatives. With Swift the implications and effects of these wrong choices are conveyed much more explicitly. The results of opting against necessary authority are displayed and anatomised. He shows just what marauding forces are ready to slip into supply the gap left by the default of those things that should validate or sanctify one's religion.

Unlike most moralists, Swift describes mistaken choice *as* a choice, not as a non-choice. Abnegation of duty involves a parallel sin of commission. Consider this passage from the *Contests and Dissentions*:

> I think it is an universal Truth, that the People are much more dextrous at pulling down and setting up, than at preserving what is fix'd: And they are not fonder of seizing more than their own, than they are of delivering it up again to the *worst Bidder*, with their own into the Bargain. For although in their corrupt Notions of Divine Worship, they are apt to multiply their Gods; yet their earthly Devotion is seldom paid to above one Idol at a Time, of their own Creations; whose *Oar* they pull with less Murmuring and much more skill, than when they *share the Lading*, or even *hold the Helm*.
>
> (I, 219–220)

These 'corrupt Notions' do constitute a basis for moral decisions, perverted though the basis may be. Unlike the tender-minded school of Shaftesbury, Swift is never tempted to regard vicious behaviour as a denial of our humanity. It is simply an act of surrender to the unregenerate side of fallen man.

Rejection of authority, then, subsumes the innovating spirit. Swift describes how this makes for disorder; it promotes a set-up which is claustral, individualist, fissile by turns, where revolution breeds counter-revolution in perpetual anarchy. 'Whatever be the Designs of innovating Men,' he writes in *Examiner* no. 39, 'they usually end in a Tyranny.' (III, 146). In much the same way, 'new and affected modes of speech' are 'the first perishing Parts in any Language' (*Tatler*, no. 230; II, 177). Senseless change does more than corrupt (religion, or manners, or style): it takes away any cementing factor. Once this first step of rejection is taken, there is no longer any effective restraint. Speaking of the Puritans in the sermon on King Charles's martyrdom, Swift remarks, 'They did not think it sufficient to leave all the errors of Popery, but threw off many laudable and edifying institutions of the Primitive Church.' (IX, 221). Take but degree away. . . . Again, to ignore authority is to encourage a captious habit of mind, and to foster concern with the letter rather than the spirit. Hence Swift's dislike of refining, supersubtle argumentation. In Section XI of the *Tale* there is an illuminating passage. *Loquitur* the Hack (as I suppose we must now call him, by established usage—though it's rather as if we should be called on to refer to the narrator of the *Canterbury Tales* as 'the Poetaster', on account of his shifty proceedings, as well as his indifferent performance as raconteur.) At this juncture, reference is made to those 'whose peculiar Talent lies in fixing Tropes and Allegories to the Letter, and refining what is literal into Figure and Mystery.' (I, 121). One hesitates to think what Swift would have made of numerological experts on Spenser. Similarly in the sermon on the Trinity: 'Raising Difficulties concerning the Mysteries of Religion, cannot make Men more wise, learned or virtous.' In the same place, we hear of 'Rules of Philosophy, which have multiplied Controversies to such a Degree, as to beget Scruples that have perplexed the Minds of many sober Christians, who otherwise could never have entertained them.'[9]

A neat summation of the view against which Swift strove so resolutely can be found in Robert Boyle's *The Christian Virtuoso* (1690), a book not sufficiently regarded by Swift scholars hitherto. Boyle is concerned to argue that a scientist, far from being inhibited in his religious faith by his studies, is so much the more capable of true faith. He contends that the virtuoso, as he is 'both Willing and Fit to search out and discover Deep and *Unobvious Truths*', is peculiarly fitted to sound the deepest mysteries of revealed religion. His argument reaches a climax in a passage of unconscious self-immolation:

In short, whereas a Superficial Wit, such as is frequently found in Libertins, and often helps to make them such, may be compar'd to an *ordinary Swimmer*, who can reach but such things as float upon the Water; an Experimental Philosopher may be compar'd to a *skilful Diver*, that cannot only fetch those things that lye upon the Surface of the Sea, but make his way to the very Bottom of it; and thence fetch up Pearls, Corals, and other precious things, that in those Depths lye conceal'd from other men's Sight and Reach.[10]

Here is Boyle actually volunteering for the mud-diving games in *The Dunciad*, and filing at the same time his application for inclusion in Chapter VI of *Peri Bathous*, where the Didappers, the Porpoises, the Frogs and the Eels likewise flounder at the bottom of that stagnant pool which is the natural habitat of the species *Dunce*. Boyle hits on the exact figures by which Pope and Swift image scientific enquiry, and puts his virtuoso in the very posture which the Scriblerans saw as the true representation of the bathetic. His self-deflating phraseology is worthy of the narrator of Swift's *Tale*.

Irreligion, then, is promoted by excessive scruple. The duty of the Christian is to make early, total, unquestioning subscription to the faith, and then to allow himself to be regulated by that. He is not to seek about for moral imperatives, or proofs of divine pleasure and displeasure. He is not to look for arguments from nature for God's design in creating the world. Swift's Christian is a self-confessed duffer at what men of the time called 'the ethical calculus'. His business is not to exacerbate 'the quarrels we raise with nature' (as Gulliver puts it, in Brobdingnag), but to damp down such futile soul-searching. Thus Swift curiously approaches what might seem the antipodal ethic—that of the existentialist.

The latter asserts, equally, that it is pointless to keep a minute-by-minute journal of one's spiritual state, and to consult this before taking a given course of action. This characteristic slant of Swift's thinking has been fixed on by Martin Price:

> Swift's religious emphasis isolates the specifically moral and obligatory in Christianity, by insisting upon the immediate intuition of the right. . . . His central theme is the problem of moral cognition: to see one's duty is a simple act; yet all of man's powers are devoted to creating an escape.[11]

There are several ways in which we can trace Swift's insistence on the absolute primal necessity, the factor of *obligation*, in morality. For one thing, Swift places very little stress on what Paul Fussell refers to as the 'dynamics' of motivation.[12] Unlike Johnson, he is comparatively little interested in the genesis of a feeling such as envy. He carries out no elaborate survey of the etiology of sin, as Johnson does. The final result is that Swift's account of morality seems oddly behaviourist. No reading sermons off stones: simply, act well and trust to your commitment to God. Swift is as reluctant to take the High Priori road as Burke; yet his submission to unstated tenets assumes many first principles which he will not or cannot examine. Authority, on one level, is a means of evading all the problems historically associated with induction. It is a way of making epistemology, as well as metaphysics, redundant.

Now it is true that on occasions Swift can appeal ironically to authority. He sometimes sets up a bastard authority, as though to demonstrate that his creed is not mere quietism. Nothing is more fatal than total commitment to a spurious authority. Almost blasphemous weight attaches, consequently, to the craven show of deference to 'that great and profound Majority' who happen to think that the abolition of Christianity would be a good thing. (II, 27). More lightheartedly Swift demands of Isaac Bickerstaff that he is to 'make use of his Authority as Censor' and draw up an annual index to condemn barbarous neologisms and the like. (II, 176). The whole Partridge joke, in fact, resides in this very false claim of astrologers to be believed and trusted. The vulnerability as well as the danger of Partridge is that he offers to be subject to no external test, by reason of his oracular, uncheckable forecasts. Swift takes this to the logical extreme and supplies him for once with explicit predictions which are then shown to be only too accurate. Partridge is made to attain the fatal infallibility of Cassandra. Drest in a little brief authority, he is forced to sign his own death-warrant.

Finally, man in rejecting higher authority becomes presumptuous and self-sufficient. A good deal of the recent work on Swift has concentrated on this particular implication, and I shall not go over the same ground. It is, however, worth stressing the conventionality of Swift's position. I do not mean simply that the entire inheritance of Renaissance humanism was such as to suggest to Swift the pride which belongs to one who walks without the guide of authority. So much is evidently true: we may recall that in the *Encomium Moriae*, lounging next to Folly herself, 'you observe with that proud cast of her eye . . . φιλαυτία, Self-love'—solipsism and vanity, merged in the portrait.[13] But so general a debt is almost trivial. I was referring instead to the weight of Augustan rhetoric which lies behind Swift's critique. The most central repository is clearly the *Essay on Man*:

> In Pride, in reasoning Pride, our Error lies
> Men would be angels, Angels would be Gods . . .

Or this:

> Make God Man's Image, Man the final Cause
> Find Virtue local, all Relation scorn,
> See all in self . . . .

But the line goes back to Rochester ('This supernatural gift, that makes
a mite / Thinks he's the Image of the Infinite . . .'), as well as to Dryden
('For what could fathom God . . . were more than He. . . .'). We could
also find many famous parallels, in the same sources, to Swift's insistence, touched on earlier, that the basic truths of moral life are obvious
and attainable without laborious speculative enquiry. Equally, the
belief that man 'should resolve not to quit the rank which nature
assigns him, and wish to maintain the dignity of a human being'
(Johnson) was to be given memorable rephrasal by Burke: 'We are
born only to be men. We shall do enough if we form ourselves to be
good ones.'[14] In this light, Swift's statements of man's limited nature
may strike us not so much as disillusioned as unillusioned. In 1725 he
writes to Sheridan, 'Expect no more from Man than such an Animal
is capable of.' (*Corr.*, III, 94). The point is made more explicit in the
short piece *Of Public Absurdities in England*: 'It is the mistake of wise
and good men that they expect more Reason and Virtue from human
nature than taking it in the bulk, it is in any sort capable of.' (V, 79).
The corollary of such a belief is an obsessive preoccupation with that
higher authority which, alone, can save irrational and vicious mankind.

Swift as humanist legatee, then, conforms to type. What is special
about his exploitation of this inheritance, *qua* creative writer, is the
humorous use to which it is regularly put. The typical result of self-
sufficient pride is not merely folly, but *grotesque* error with high comic
potential. We recall Simon Wagstaff's fussy, bumbling introduction to
Polite Conversation:

> [England has] outdone all the Nations of *Europe*, in advancing the
> whole Art of Conversation to the greatest Height it is capable of
> reaching. And therefore, being entirely convinced, that the Collec-
> tion I now offer to the Publick, is full and compleat; I may at the
> same Time boldly affirm, that the whole Genius, Humour, Polite-
> ness, and Eloquence of *England*, are summed up in it. . . .
>
> (IV, 101)

After which, it need scarcely be added, the puny harlequinade of a few
posturing fribbles is set before us. Something approaching this occurs
quite early on in *Gulliver's Travels*, where we are told that the Emperor's
Lilliputian dominions extend five thousand blustrugs, 'to the Extremi-
ties of the Globe'. As an afterthought, 'about twelve Miles in Circum-
ference', says Swift in a parenthesis of Gibbonian destructive power.
(XI, 27). Lastly, there is clear indication of the comic applicability of
Swift's vision of man in the passage from Boyle already quoted. For
the Tory humanists, whatever their gloom, there was something
outrageously funny (in fitful bursts, at least) about human physicality.

In their pages besmirched, muddling, undignified dunces go fixedly about their vulgar concerns. Projectors, full of mean and low temporalities, mingle with half-crazed religious enthusiasts, their eyes rooted unswervingly on celestial regions as they blunder into every minor boobytrap of life. (This alternation of soaring *o altitudo* with grovelling futility is aptly caught in Pope's letter to Caryll of 14 August 1713.)[15] The proper image of ignoble man is in fact identical with the image of absurd man. The futile researches in the academy of Lagado present us with Swift's most telling identification of the sordid, the thriftless, the vainglorious and the laughable.

II

On the face of things, it would seem, Swift is a pillar of orthodoxy.[16] His ideas at large, no less than his literary manipulation of these ideas, point to a solid, middle-of-the-road mentality, resting securely on unquestioned assumptions. Yet finally there is something curiously contentless about his morality: an air less of genuine conviction than of assent for its own sake. In his early *Ode to the King*, there is the semi-ironic reflection, '. . . Else where's the Gain in being Great?' (*Poems*, 6). All through Swift's work we find a certain concealed scepticism about the sources and the sanctions of some forms of authority—notably political authority—at the same time as a heavy insistence is laid on the prescriptive rights of that authority. Swift was certainly interested in power as such: he would take over from Temple a marked emphasis on the importance of the *ruler* in any form of political organisation—an emphasis his friend Bolingbroke was also to underline. He discussed in more than one place, notably the start of the *Contests and Dissentions*, abstract questions of political power, its management and superintendence. Behind these discussions one can sense a personal tropism towards restraint and discipline as goods in their own right; something not far removed from Reynolds' version of 'authority'. A recent critic of Burke has remarked that, in the philosophy of the latter, 'God and providence appear to do the work of Hobbes's sovereign.'[17] Similarly it might be said that Swift is a Hobbesian despite himself. Anarchy is always round the corner. Power is valued not so much for what it fosters as for what it prohibits.

The explanation for this state of affairs was hinted at earlier. Swift attempts, through satiric means especially, to give orthodoxy the force we ordinarily associate with innovation. He seeks to attach a sense of shock to what is formally a reasonable and familiar attitude: for instance, the view that it would not be a good idea to relieve economic difficulties by eating up a large number of the babies alive within the community. (Swift presents matters so that we almost forget that nobody else had ever suggested this *would* be a good idea.) His overall strategies are geared to this leading purpose. It follows that any residual flavour of 'orthodoxy' which is not so transmuted in his work takes on a specially naked, unsatisfactory impression. His rhetoric has forced him into a position where any straight presentation of conventional thought appears jejune; where his inmost convictions fall flat on the page as figments of notional assent.

I think that this analysis in turn will explain a further paradox. In at least three respects Swift defeats the expectations we typically bring to satire. His stance seems almost that of the anti-satirist. Consider these issues.

(1) We usually expect the satirist to offer us an ideal alternative, if only implicit, to the follies he castigates. But Swift regularly destroys A by setting it against B, and then B by setting it off against A. We need only think of the notorious 'inside/outside' dilemma posed by the 'Digression on Madness'. He uses the butt end of his pistol when he has no more rounds left: and more than that, he confronts the victorious assailant with a magically restored victim. As Robert Elliott has said, 'Gulliver is at once target and purveyor of satire'.[18] Peter and Jack discredit one another in a prolonged *va-et-vient* of successive indignities. Again, Swift is sceptical regarding golden means, or at any rate about 'moderation' as currently practised—witness the sermon *On Brotherly Love*.

Some have claimed that Swift always does convey some implied norm. But (leaving aside the recognised thinness and insufficiency of Martin, who hasn't even the grace to disappear entirely, and makes periodic shifty entrances, like the untroubled absentee norm he is) I do not see how this view can be sustained. What, for instance, are we to make of Miriam Starkman's confident assertion that 'The *Apology* is scarcely satiric in either tone or intention. It is the norm of *A Tale of a Tub*'?[19] Or the repeated and quite desperate attempts to make Don Pedro the fixed point at the climax of *Gulliver*, if not indeed the semi-official hero—Don Pedro, a character whose existence seems to have gone totally unnoticed till about 1930?

Surely we needn't contort matters so. We should recall that in the *Mechanical Operation of the Spirit* the *summum bonum* is specifically aligned with Utopian commonwealths, philosophers' stones and the like as chimerical quests for the unattainable. Equally I believe that the Houyhnhnms represent an ideal of a sort, but one beyond the grasp of the limited human condition. I agree with Arthur Clayborough when he says that 'The Houyhnhnms are at once grotesque and ideal; Gulliver is at once crazed and ennobled by contact with them.'[20] There is, I think, no norm—only a demonstrable non-human perfection outside the compass of a part-Yahoo like Gulliver. Structurally, the ideal becomes for Swift little more than a noise off, almost wholly irrelevant to the exposure of Gulliver himself.

(2) We expect the satirist to scourge hypocrisy, to expose pretence by reference to reality, profession by reference to true (but unexpressed) motives. Swift, on the other hand, in that climactic passage of the 'Digression on Madness' reveals the innards as no more acceptable than the outer layer of things. Although he does, in the sermon *On the Excellency of Christianity*, pick out the fact that Christian wisdom is 'without hypocrisy' as one of its differentiae, elsewhere he seems strangely indulgent towards this fault. In general, a worthy profession is seen as better than nothing. The whole of the *Project for the Advancement of Religion* is based on the premise that it is better to have a show of morality in high places than do without altogether. To modern eyes, this looks suspiciously like an ethic of sweeping under the carpet.

Yet Swift's point is more serious than that. He writes with characteristic starkness in his *Thoughts on Religion*, 'The want of belief is a defect that ought to be concealed where it cannot be overcome.' (IX, 261). This in turn rests on the view that, 'having used his best efforts to subdue his doubts, the Christian should see that they have no influence on the conduct of his life'. This aspect of Swift's thought has been well put by Nigel Dennis—

> All Swift's satire is directed against the hundreds of ways human beings have discovered of avoiding being good; all his benevolence goes out to those who have resisted the ostentation of being bad—who would rather be a mere negation of evil than a distinguished example of it.[21]

'The ostentation of being bad'—there is the clue to much of Swift. His literary techniques are developed with the express aim of giving what is traditional and respectable some of the life, the panache and the glamour which properly belongs to what is bold and extreme. To this end he presents folly as madly systematic, not free: he presents vice as dull and repetitive. Sleepers in church are described as 'dozed and besetted with indecencies'; there is nothing enlivening about dissipation. The foolish participants in the comic opera which is *Polite Conversation* are given none of the best tunes. They are not, properly speaking, given any tunes at all—only meaningless recitative. Silliness is more boring than plain good sense.

D

(3) Another way in which Swift stands practically unique amongst satirists lies in his toleration of cant, providing it has good practical effects. Just as he gives low marks for blinkered sincerity, so he himself rejects the ostentatious probity which has been the satirist's favourite rhetorical pose. As Elliott says, he has it both ways by making Gulliver both *ingénu* observer and misanthropic participant;[22] equally, he is at so little pains to make his own position clear or unassailable or visibly innocent (as satirists generally do) that he often compromises himself in order to demolish his victim the more effectually. He will commend Carteret with ironic care for totally absurd reasons; he will argue against the extirpation of the Christian religion on palpably inane grounds. Never can any satirist have left so many handles for wilful miscontruction of the author's viewpoint as he did in the *Tale*. Leslie Stephen once remarked that the condition of having the scoffers on your side was to be on the side of the scoffers.[23] It is a necessity at which Swift did not balk. He cared more (unlike, one suspects, many of his critics) for morality than for satiric identity. He never confused the functions of moral allegory with those of the *pièce justificative*. This often makes life harder for commentators.[24]

I have tried to show that there is no radical inconsistency between Swift's expressed belief in publicly sanctioned authority (unconvincing as it sometimes appears, in his non-satiric pieces such as the *Project for the Advancement of Religion*) and his norm-less satiric works. In both cases Swift's position is one of rooted orthodoxy. It is a technical consideration whether or not his satire requires the structural presence of orthodox belief. If not, Swift was perfectly happy to suppress his fundamental positive beliefs (traditional as they were), instead of wrenching the work to display them. He would not, I think, have been much disturbed by the knowledge that critics of our own day would confuse means with ends, and label him 'negative'. Critics were not the species of authority he most revered.

NOTES

[1] Johnston, *In Search of Swift* (Dublin, 1959), p. 6.

[2] A representative example is the phrase 'negativistic satire', used by Gordon McKenzie, 'Swift: Reason and some of its Consequences', *University of California Publications in English* VIII (1940), pp. 101–129 (the phrase quoted appears on p. 127). Similarly Gilbert Highet speaks of a medley of emotions present in *Gulliver's Travels*, 'whose effect is generally negative and destructive' —*The Art of Satire* (Princeton, 1962), p. 150.

[3] Martin Price's recent book, *To the Palace of Wisdom* (New York, 1964), is actuated by a similar conviction regarding the nature of eighteenth-century literature. Price expressly states as an aim of the work his desire to stress 'the dialectical excess as much as the balance and moderation of the Augustans' (Preface, p. vii in the Doubleday Anchor paperback ed., N.Y., 1965).

[4] Paulson, *Theme and Structure in Swift's Tale of a Tub* (New Haven, 1960), p. 233. E. W. Rosenheim, too, writes of the 'Digression on Madness': 'The *persona's* argument . . . is neither sarcastic nor parodic in any simple meaning of these terms; it is rather a systematic exposition of wrongness,' *Swift and the Satirist's Art* (Chicago, 1963), p. 149. Elsewhere (p. 147), Rosenheim speaks of an 'internal logic of error'. I believe that sequentiality as comprehensive as this would *undercut* more of the satire than it would reinforce.

[5] The formula 'semantic shock' is borrowed from W. C. Brown, *The Triumph of Form* (Chapel Hill, 1948), p. 93. Dryden's 'deviates into sense' is a famous instance of the technique Brown describes. I have attempted to extend its application to Young in an article, 'Poetry as a Means of Disgrace', *Cambridge Review* LXXXVII (1965), pp. 133–145.

[6] On *Peri Bathous* as a 'duncely' rhetoric of satire, see Alvin Kernan, *The Plot of Satire* (New Haven, 1965), pp. 27–35: as well as Price, p. 216.

[7] McKenzie (p. 113) comes to a fairly similar conclusion regarding Swift's 'orthodoxy', from a very different standpoint. On the other hand John Traugott has written scathingly of the conservative, domesticated Swift who emerges from recent criticism: see 'The Refractory Swift', *MLQ* XXV (1964), pp. 205–211.

[8] Cudworth, *A Sermon Preached before the Honourable the House of Commons. At Westminster, March* 31, 1647 (Cambridge, 1647), p. 19.

[9] *Prose Works*, IX, 166–167, 160: and see *Thoughts on Religion*, IX, 262.

[10] *The Christian Virtuoso . . .The First Part. By T. H. R. B. Fellow of the Royal Society* (London, 1690), pp. 48–50.

[11] Price, *op. cit.*, p. 183.

[12] Fussell, *The Rhetorical World of Augustan Humanism* (Oxford, 1965), p. 75.

[13] *The Praise of Folly*, tr. John Wilson (Oxford, 1931), p. 16.

[14] Johnson, *Rambler* 183, in *Works*, ed. Murphy (London, 1824), V, p. 253; Burke, *Thoughts on the Cause of our present Discontents*, in *Works and Correspondence* (London, 1852), III. 172.

[15] Pope, *Correspondence*, ed. Sherburn (Oxford, 1956), I, 185.

[16] For a general discussion of the importance of the concept of 'authority', see G. R. Cragg, *Reason and Authority in the Eighteenth Century* (Cambridge, 1964), *passim*.

[17] Harvey C. Mansfield, Jr., *Statesmanship and Party Government* (Chicago, 1965), p. 234. I would like to thank my colleague, Dr. Derek Beales, for drawing this book to my attention as well as for the loan of his personal copy.

[18] Elliott, *The Power of Satire* (Princeton, 1960), pp. 184–222, amplifies this view of Gulliver's role in convincing detail.

[19] Starkman, *Swift's Satire on Learning in A Tale of a Tub* (Princeton, 1950), p. 112.

[20] Clayborough, *The Grotesque in English Literature* (Oxford, 1965), p. 153.

[21] Dennis, *Jonathan Swift* (London, 1965), p. 48.

[22] Elliott, *op. cit.*, p. 190.

[23] Stephen, *Swift* (London, 1882), p. 43.

[24] For the view that, in satire, 'ideals are present only to set off the evil, and tell us nothing of the satirist's values', see S. Sacks, *Fiction and the Shape of Belief*, pp. 8–9, and R. Paulson. *The Fictions of Satire*, p. 20 n.

"*An Inverted Hypocrite*": Swift the Churchman

BASIL HALL

After *Gulliver's Travels* was published, Swift wrote to Pope that: 'A Bishop here said, that Book was full of improbable lies, and for his part, he hardly believed a word of it'. (*Corr.*, III, 189). Remarks like this gave Swift, combined with his other talents, the character of a wit —most dangerous for a clergyman in search of a career, as he himself noted in his *Essay on the Fates of Clergymen*. ' . . . the *Clergy*; to whose Preferment nothing is so fatal as the Character of Wit, Politeness in Reading, or Manners, or that Kind of Behaviour, which we contract by having too much conversed with Persons of high Station and Eminency; these Qualifications being reckoned by the *Vulgar* of *all Ranks* to be Marks of *Levity*, which is the last crime the world will pardon in a *Clergy-Man*.' (XII, 40). There are several matters on which Swift has been misunderstood but especially in his views on religion, for he has repeatedly from his own time to the present been condemned for being a' divine who is hardly suspected of being a Christian'. It is forgotten that he wrote to Archbishop King of Dublin (who, three years after *A Tale of a Tub* had appeared, attempted to reconcile the existence of moral evil with the omnipotence and goodness of God in a book soon to become famous): 'I very much applaud your Grace's sanguine Temper, as you call it, and your Comparison of Religion to paternal Affection; but the World is divided into two Sects, those that hope the best, and those that fear the worst; your Grace is of the former, which is the wiser, the nobler, and the most pious Principle; and although I endeavour to avoid being of the other, yet upon this Article I have sometimes strange Weaknesses. I compare true Religion to Learning and Civility which have ever been in the World, but very often shifted their Scenes; sometimes leaving whole Countries where they have long flourished, and removing to others that were before barbarous; which hath been the Case of Christianity itself, particularly in many parts of *Africa*, and how far the wickedness of a Nation may provoke God Almighty to inflict so great a Judgement, is terrible to think.' (*Corr.*, I, 117).

Here is to be seen Swift's grim awareness of the basic sinfulness of humanity, a sinfulness which was a potential threat of barbarism, only held in check by the State maintaining religion seen in morality and obedience supported by learning. Swift also shows here his fear that if that religious grip were to slacken through men's pride and folly then God's Providence would judge the nation at fault by allowing it to revert to that barbarism which is man's natural condition unaided by Revelation. Failure to recognize these aspects of Swift's religious viewpoint can gravely distort our understanding of Swift's purposes as a satirist.

Nevertheless, the themes which Swift chooses in this analysis of his own religious views are not usually central in judgements of him as a man or as a writer. On the contrary, it is more usual to think that Swift was fundamentally irreligious; that he was using a career in the Church for personal ambition, since he lacked a political post; that he showed no respect for traditional Christian beliefs; that his religious writings are political tracts with pious titles; and that his handful of sermons are the chilled product of a rationalism without insight or conviction. In 1713 Robert Molesworth wrote to his wife: 'They have made Swift Dean of St. Patrick's. This vexes the godly party beyond expression'. (*Corr.*, I, 350n). But not even the ungodly were delighted: Dean Smedley who shared with Swift little save his ecclesiastical title and ended as a refugee debtor in the Indies, claimed to have fixed this poem to the door of St. Patrick's Cathedral on the day when Swift was instituted as Dean:

> Today the Temple gets a Dean
> Of parts and fame uncommon
> Used both to pray and to prophane
> To serve both God and Mammon.
>
> This place he got by wit and rhyme
> And many ways more odd
> And might a bishop be in time
> Did he believe in God.
>
> Look down St. Patrick look we pray
> On thy own church and steeple
> Convert the Dean on this great day
> Or else God help the people.
>
> And now when'er his deanship dies
> Upon his tomb be graven
> A man of God here buried lies
> Who never thought of heaven.[1]

Swift well knew that so many men including his fellow clerics then as now can forgive a clergyman almost anything save intelligence and wit, and he vainly tried to correct the bad impression left by his *Tale of a Tub* in an Apology prefaced to later editions. He was probably right in believing that Sharp, Archbishop of York, had told Queen Anne, no doubt with the approval of her companion the Duchess of Somerset, that the author of *A Tale of a Tub* was unsuitable for preferment in the Church.[2] Swift had the last word, caustic and contemptuous:

> By an old redhair'd, murd'ring Hag pursued,
> A crazy Prelate, and a royal Prude.
> By dull Divines, who look with envious Eyes,
> On ev'ry Genius that attempts to rise. . . . (*Poems*, 193).

thus demonstrating to those who might have promoted him to a bishopric, the pungent articulate force which frightened them from the solemn choice of doing so.

Leslie Stephen, though addressing a more discriminating audience than that at the lecture where Thackeray had said of Swift 'He puts his apostasy out to hire . . . and his sermons have scarce a Christian characteristic',[3] could still be no less obtuse: 'He felt the want of some religion and therefore scalped poor Collins' and ' . . . the dogmas of theologians were mere matter for the Homeric laughter of the *Tale of a Tub*'. Stephen, who resigned his Holy Orders and was more concerned with 'honest doubt' than with 'earnest religion', shows his obtuseness fully in his final judgement on Swift—'He had not the unselfish qualities or the indomitable belief in the potential excellence of human nature to become a reformer of manners, or the speculative power to endeavour to remould ancient creeds.'[4] This reflects as great a failure in understanding Swift as that of Thackeray (at a different level of intelligence), for Swift deliberately avoided and rejected from the first *Odes* to the final *Legion Club* those two purposes which Stephen assumes to be acceptable to his own contemporaries, that is, belief in the potential excellence of human nature and the speculative attempt to revise the Christian faith.

Nor does Swift escape misrepresentation in our own time, for the only book so far written comprehensively on the subject of Swift's religious thought, Canon Looten's *La Pensée religieuse de Swift et ses Antinomies* (Lille, 1935), asserts that he not only undermined Christian doctrinal traditions but also the possibility of a Natural Theology—he pretended to defend Christianity and then stabbed it in the back.[5] Dr. Leavis in his essay on Swift's irony has received a far wider audience than Canon Looten and his judgements are elsewhere often deservedly magisterial, but he can write thus: 'Of Jack we are told "nor could all the world persuade him, as the common phrase is, to eat his victuals like a Christian"; it is characteristic of Swift that he should put in these terms, showing a complete incapacity even to guess what religious feeling might be, a genuine conviction that Jack should be made to kneel when receiving the Sacrament', and: 'He showed the shallowest complacencies of Augustan good sense'.[6] However, the historian well-read in the sacramental controversy between Catholics and Protestants in the sixteenth and seventeenth centuries will realise that Swift's phrases can be matched from clerical controversialists before him; while it does not excuse his coarse phrase it does provide it with a recognisable context. Again, who more bitterly than Swift opposed 'the shallow complacencies' of Bolingbroke and Shaftesbury, those arbiters of 'Augustan good sense', precisely because he knew them to be shallow? Dr. Leavis writes further: 'An outward show is, explicitly, all he contends for in the quite unironical *Project for the Advancement of Religion*, and the difference between the reality of religion and the show is, for the author of the *Tale of a Tub*, hardly substantial'.[7] To state that Swift's concerns in that pamphlet are surface matters, 'an outward show' is imperceptive, as will be shown later in this essay. The criticism that Swift's religion was superficial, since it had no essential ground in his life, is in itself a failure to get beneath the surface.

For a great number of contemporary writers the close relation of the Church and society has ceased to be conceivable today. They generally assume, when considering the Christianity of past times, that its faith and practices should be interpreted by our current views of what constitutes personal piety and loving kindness to others, and these views alone are considered to be the standards of Christian sincerity. This is no place to describe what is latent here, the over-simplification and sentimentalism about the person and work of Christ expressed by many of the literate and articulate in our time, aligned with naivety about the nature of the Church, its organisation, beliefs and practices, and indeed about the Bible upon which these are grounded. One consequence of this is that unction of the 'secular' Tartuffe, which is the hypocrisy of the religiously superficial or un-committed. Swift, with passionate conviction, concealed the practice of his personal piety since it was nobody's business but his own; and with equally passionate conviction he rejected emotionalism in faith and practice as contemptible, erroneous and irreligious. We may think he overdid this; but at least we should examine impartially, and with patience, his reasons for doing so, which were complex and profound as well as rational and coherent, for they were one with other attempts to resolve the problem of the relation of a Church of convinced believers to a society of reluctant believers which has faced the Churches since the time of the Emperor Theodosius. That Swift inherited, and loyally struggled for, a traditional Anglican solution here can be seen demonstrably in his life. If Swift was a pretender to religion, and merely a professional writer who adopted Christian formulas and *mores* for the sake of earning a more secure income than Grub Street or politics provided, then this could be shown by investigation of the evidence. His enemies in his life-time provided abuse and innuendo but no evidence; too many of his detractors today substitute for investigation an intuition (relying on uninformed conceptions) of what is appropriate to 'religion' and on their cultivated aesthetic response to his sharper ironies.

Swift's religion as country parson and as Dean of a cathedral contains no inner contradictions in the framing of his religious ideas, nor any break between his inner convictions and his outward pastoral activity: he is consistent throughout. A man's religion is tested by his prayers; consider these words from a prayer for the dying Stella, which began with an appeal for her need, and contains these phrases: 'O All-powerful Being, the least Motion of whose Will can create or destroy a World. . . . Accept, O Lord, these Prayers poured from the very Bottom of our Hearts. . . . Forgive the Sorrow and Weakness of those among us, who sink under the Grief and Terror of losing so dear and useful a Friend.' (IX, 253–5). To the unaccustomed ear this may sound wholly formal, but even the *Sacra Privata*, a famous collection of private prayers and religious diary, by Swift's contemporary, Bishop Wilson (like Swift ordained by the Bishop of Kildare after graduating from Trinity College, Dublin), provides no more moving language. The all-powerful will that could create or destroy a world, and the grief and terror at the heart of life are themes central to Swift's religion. For him, when one contemplates the evil state of men and the latent chaos in the world, only an all-ruling Providence can save men from the vertigo of terror. He could find no lasting comfort in Archbishop King's attempt to resolve the problem of evil. Two statements by Swift in letters to friends, when facing the death of the innocent and the young, may be added. To the Reverend James Stopford he wrote after the death of Stella, 'For my part, as I value life very little, so the poor casual remains of it, after such a loss, would be a burden that I must heartily beg God Almighty to enable me to bear', and after referring to the 'folly' of having too close friendships because the pain of loss is so great, added: 'Dear Jim, pardon me, I know not what I am saying; but believe me that violent friendship is much more lasting, and as much more engaging, as violent love. Adieu'. (*Corr.*, III, 145). When Lord

Oxford's daughter died Swift wrote: 'To say the truth, my Lord, you began to be too happy for a mortal; much more happy than is usual with the dispensations of Providence long to continue', and then after the statement, harsh in our eyes, that God punished Oxford 'where he knew your heart was most exposed' and rewarded with a better life 'that excellent creature he has taken from you', added ' . . . I know not, my Lord, why I write this to you, nor hardly what I am writing. I am sure it is not from any compliance with form; it is not from thinking that I can give your Lordship any ease. I think it was an impulse upon me that I should say something: And whether I shall send you what I have written, I am yet in doubt'. (*Corr.*, I, 405–6). There are, possibly, those for whom these quotations show little beyond the fact that Swift like other men felt melancholy in the face of death: but if they catch no force of feeling and sincerity behind the religious expression in them then they will indeed find no meaning in Swift's writings on religion, nor could they detect the religious background in his other more familiar work. The advice to Oxford to bow to Providence was a commonplace of the time as *The Works of the Learned and Pious Author of the Whole Duty of Man* clearly shows, but Swift's framing of it and his addition is wholly from his own heart.

For this was the private heart of Swift, which he least of all men was willing to wear on his sleeve; but others could observe his pastoral activities. Swift wrote to Stella once about a sermon he was to give in London: 'I shall preach plain honest stuff'[8]—any of the fashionable world who came to listen to the greatest wit in England would be deservedly disappointed, and his surviving sermons are models of plain direct Christian teaching set within the theological pattern of his Church. No exception can be taken to his work as a parish priest at Kilroot and later at Laracor. He used his income for restoring the dilapidated Church at Laracor, built a parsonage, and introduced week-day services and regular preaching every Sunday. Bolingbroke called him 'an inverted hypocrite' in pretending to the onlooking world that he had little religion, preferring to conceal his faith and practice from the eyes of others. Dr. Johnson may be the judge here, not least because he was no admirer of Swift, a fact that puzzled Boswell, who was: 'The suspicion of his irreligion proceeded in a great measure from his dread of hypocrisy; instead of wishing to seem better, he delighted in seeming worse than he was. He went in London to early prayers, lest he should be seen at Church; he read prayers to his servants every morning with such dexterous secrecy that Dr. Delaney was six months in the house before he knew it. He was not only careful to hide the good which he did, but willingly incurred the suspicion of evil which he did not. He forgot what himself had formerly asserted, that hypoc-risy is less mischievous than open impiety.'[9]

Some biographers describe him as parsimonious and avaricious, but contemporaries witness to his charities (though many of these were so effectively concealed that they were unknown to outsiders)—'to ask him for a pound was often to receive five' was a generous comment in his lifetime. A recently discovered letter shows his characteristic brusqueness masking a generous purpose: 'Sir: there is a Rascally Cousin of mine called John Swift, his Father is my Cousen German, called Mead Swift, as great a Rascal as his Son. He was a son of my Uncle Godwin as arrant an old Rascal as either. I was desired to be a trustee of the Marriage Settlement, along with a Rogue of an Attorney one Kit Swift another son of old Godwin.'[10] It is a matter of verifiable fact, and not mere opinion, that in spite of the scornful severity of language Swift used here, his dealings with John Swift were more than benevolent, they were generous and fatherly. Swift always emphasized 'the works of love'; for example, in writing to Pope, 'Pray God reward you for your kind Prayers. You are a good Man & a good Christian, & I believe your Prayers will do me more good than those of all the Prelates in . . . Europe, except the Bishop of Marseilles'. (*Corr.*, IV, 335). Here he is writing to a Catholic, and behind his usual irony about bishops he makes exception for M. de Belsunce who remained to confess and comfort the sick and dying in the great plague at Marseilles in 1720. This was a practical demonstration of true religion that Swift, who usually had little good to say for 'Papists' but who approved them when they showed self-denying pity for others, was always ready to recognize.

Of his energy shown in supporting the rights of the Irish clergy in the matter of tithes and first-fruits, and in his administrative efficiency as Dean there can be no doubt, for the useful and able book by Pro-fessor Landa has demonstrated it.[11] He could fight tenaciously with city and Archbishop for the rights of his cathedral, and for his rights as Dean with his chapter. Swift was a loyal supporter of the religious principles of the Revolution, but perhaps he carried this a little far in erecting a monument for the grave of the Duke of Shomberg, a hero of the Battle of the Boyne, which included words that challenged the meanness of the Duke's relations in Germany in failing to provide enough money for the memorial. Most utterances of George II are of little worth, but his comment on this is memorable: 'God damn Mr. Swift, does he mean to make me quarrel with the King of Prussia?'[12]

All his life as a clergyman Swift struggled tenaciously for improve-ment in the status of the clergy, which meant improvement in their economic security. The purpose of this, as it had been for Archbishop Laud before him, was to ensure the authority of the Church throughout the country since this was in his eyes essential to the moral stability of society. He feared confusion, that 'Gothic barbarism' would return, and was certain that politicians alone, even the monarchy and Parliament alone, could not prevent collapse—the Church was the God-given instrument of order in society. Take away that support and confusion and terror would reign. He was far removed from the easy assumptions that used to be made about Augustan optimism.

II

Some literary critics tend to ignore a writer's declared intentions and seek to determine the structure and aims of his work by other routes. Even those who would shun this method nevertheless share with it all too often when they assume that Swift's assertion of his religious convictions and moral intention is camouflage for his real purpose. Modern literary criticism has produced many brilliant analyses of the surface of the satires, but is curiously silent about the assumptions behind them, and here a traditional literary-historical method, the analysis of the history of ideas, is more fruitful for real understanding of Swift's work. It should be clear from the start that he does not represent Augustan complacencies about man and society, for his view of the human situation, and his private world mirror the confusion of purpose in England prior to the Revolution of 1689. Voltaire once said of Swift: 'pour le bien entendre, il faut faire un petit voyage dans son pays'—but Swift's country was more than England or Ireland, it was a private landscape in which dark shadows were cast. Swift reflects in his writings, beneath the surface force and clarity, the anxieties and doubt of the seventeenth century mind, and not the forward-looking optimism of his contemporary Shaftesbury—his Gulliver was not travelling to the 'Heavenly City of the Eighteenth Century Philosophers'.

Through the long gestation of the hidden years under Sir William Temple at Moor Park Swift was struggling to clarify for himself the problems posed for his generation by theologians, politicians, scientists and philosophers including those who represented both the old and the new ways of thought. Some he rejected outright, some he came to terms with—it is a measure of the force of his intelligence that they were his own terms. That he should have chosen (after the rebellious years at Trinity College, Dublin, and the years of service, humiliating to his proud mind, as an ambiguous amanuensis to Temple) to express his inward struggle through Odes modelled on those of Cowley, may be surprising. But Cowley's *Odes* represent precisely the form current at the time to express general ideas, though these mostly lacked the content which Swift struggled to articulate—that he failed to be lucid for the only time in his career as a writer is largely a measure of the intellectual crisis he endured. These few Odes have been studied more than once in accounts of Swift's origins as a writer, but some further comment may still be allowed. They refer to fears which were to be recognisable in Swift's work throughout his life: 'The Tyranny of Years'. 'A Destroying Angel stands (By all but Heaven and me unseen)'; 'Ignorance's Universal North . . . with blind Rage break all this peaceful Government'; *'The Wits* . . . own th' Effects of Providence, And yet deny the Cause'; '. . . ev'n the Extravagance of Poetry Is at a loss for Figures to express Men's Folly'. (*Poems*, 6, 7, 25, 19, 21). To understand why the disciple of the polished Temple, who arranged the beauty of his formal gardens to celebrate calm and reasoned hopefulness, should look aghast at:

> Disjointing shapes as in the fairy land of dreams. . . .
> No wonder, then, we talk amiss
> Of truth, and what, or where it is: (*Poems*, 35)

requires a closer look at Swift's environment. It should never be forgotten that Swift was born and partly bred in Ireland, an Ireland weakened by the destructive force of Cromwell's policy of 'To Hell or Connaught', by the mutual distrust of the English and Scottish planters, by political corruption and religious divisions between Anglican and Presbyterian and the consequent neglect of Churches and piety. He had to flee with others from Dublin when the invasion came in the North, before the Battle of the Boyne made Ireland safe for Protestants again. Ireland for him became an image of a brutalized peasantry, half-dead religion, corrupt administration, and English misgovernment. Not only this but he had a mixed political and religious inheritance, shown in his comparative neglect of his sister who sympathised with his mother's Puritan and nonconformist ancestry, whereas he himself preferred to rejoice in that clerical grandfather Thomas Swift who was, he wrote once with bitter exaggeration, 'persecuted and plundered two and fifty Times by the Barbarity of Cromwell's Hellish Crew'. (*Corr.*, V, 150). He had barely come of age when the Revolution took place, which (though he was after a fashion of his own a Tory Highchurchman) he always supported as the satisfactory and abiding answer to the unresolved problems left by the Civil War and only masked by the Stuart Restoration. He never lost his horror of the blind destructive force of Cromwell's army, nor his disgust with the frenzied religious 'enthusiasm' he associated with the 'toleration' of the sects under the Commonwealth. It is fundamental for understanding Swift to realize that he saw the generation preceding his birth as containing a religion which meant fanaticism, and politics which meant tyranny; and he saw the irrationality and intolerance of that time as breeding 'atheism' and moral collapse in his own day.

Amid these confusions, and faced by 'atheism and immorality'—
' . . . men degenerate every day, merely by the folly, the perverseness, the avarice, the tyranny, the pride, the treachery, or inhumanity of their own kind'. (IX, 264). Swift found little help in earlier patterns of religion in that century. In view of the critical approach to Scripture shown in the London Polygot Bible edited by Bishop Walton (accused by the Independent minister, John Owen, of leading men to doubt the authority of the Hebrew and Greek originals by putting out so many versions and variant readings), and made explicit in the writings of the French Oratorian, Richard Simon[13]; and in view of the stalemate induced by the prolonged and exhausting controversy between Catholics and Protestants, each trying unsuccessfully to outflank the other by proving the finality of one system over the other, Swift could not propose *simpliciter* the authority of Scripture, or the authority of a Church based on a system of dogmas. His solution to this problem will be discussed later; it is sufficient to record here his recognition of the failure of Catholics, Puritans and Anglicans (both Laudian and merely Erastian), to give a final solution:

> For, sure, we want some guide from Heav'n to show
> The way which ev'ry wand'ring fool below
> Pretends so perfectly to know;
> And which for ought I see, and much I fear,
> The world has wholly miss'd;
> I mean, the way which leads to Christ:
> Mistaken Ideots! see how giddily they run . . .
> Each fond of erring with his guide . . .
> Others, ignorantly wise,
> Among proud Doctors and disputing Pharisees:
>
> (*Poems*, 39).

Nor did the young Swift see any peculiar hope lie in the post-Revolutionary parties and their shifting alliances. He knew in Temple a distinguished servant of the State, a diplomatist wise in Courts and politics, and in the *Ode to Sir William Temple*, he could write:

> The wily Shafts of State, those Juggler's Tricks
> Which we call deep Design and Politicks . . .
> Methinks, when you expose the Scene,

> Down the ill-organ'd Engines fall; . . .
> How plain I see thro' the Deceit. (*Poems*, 29)

As will be shown later his solution will not be to cry the shibboleth of a current political faction.

Why did not a mind as penetrating as Swift's concentrate on philosophy at a time when philosophical studies outstripped in quality and contemporary appeal the outmoded systems of theologians? His suspicion of the validity of speculative reasoning has already been mentioned, for it was early in life that he had seen the possibility of self-delusion in most of men's speculations, above all the delusion of making one's own thinking the standard for determining truth. His later appeal to reason was not to establish it as a self-justifying end, but to use it to explode illusions like burst balloons, and to support that balancing of religion and virtue under Providence which alone gave stability to men's purposes. Moreover, he had been taught and loathed at Trinity College, Dublin, the traditional systems of logic, still founded on Aristotle—Smeglesius, Keckermannus, and Burgersdicius—which he mocked to Temple:[13]

> 'Tis you must put us in the Way:
> Let us (for shame) no more be fed
> With antique Reliques of the Dead,
> The Gleanings of Philosophy,
> Philosophy! the Lumber of the Schools. . . .
> And we the bubbled Fools
> Spend all our present Stock in hopes of golden Rules.
>   (*Poems*, 27)

Since he came of age in the flowering of scientific method which had gone beyond Baconian induction to the precision of measurement established by the mathematics of Cartesianism, it might be assumed that so pragmatic, logical and lucid an intelligence as that of Swift would have turned to these studies for stability and hope. But his mockery at the pretensions and the methods of scientists is well-known and occurs not only in Gulliver's account of Laputa. There were two levels of hostility here. First, Swift had acquired from Temple an attitude to experimental science which appealed to his own temperament too, that enquiries into natural phenomena did not provide an adequate basis for establishing stability and values in human society private and political. Secondly, Swift suspected scientists of a total self-sufficiency which ignored the possibility that they also could be the victims of all too human folly, jealousy and egotism. Therefore, he both mocks and fears this new approach to the problems posed by the human situation, which demonstrated that natural phenomena are a better starting point than supernatural sanctions. While he could accept the attack by the Royal Society on the Aristotelian scholasticism of the universities, yet he could not accept the apologetic of Thomas Sprat (himself a clergyman) and others, that scientific method and the basic truths of Revelation were complementary—he foresaw the probability of unrestrained inquiry disturbing the delicate balance of stability in society. He believed, and showed it in his own fable of the bee and the spider in *The Battle of the Books* that 'sweetness and light' are the product of a balanced understanding of human nature, whereas the mechanical and mathematical arts produce imbalance and show neither sweetness nor light. The ironic contrasts of size in Lilliput and Brobdingnag are the product not so much of Rabelais as of pondering on the consequences of the improved techniques of microscopy.[14]

Swift could not believe that these inquiries listed among others by Sprat: 'Observations on the Bills of Mortality: on the leaves of Sage: on small living Flies in the Powder of Cantharides: of insects bred in Dew: . . . of the teeth of Lupus Marinus, that they are the same thing with the Toad-Stones set in Rings: . . . of Bernacles: . . . of stones taken out of the Heart of Man',[15] would improve human relationships. Sprat had noted uneasily that experiments 'are inconstant' and that ' . . . it is probable that the trials [experiments] of Future Ages will not agree with those of the present, but frequently thwart, and contradict them. . . .'[16] Swift was to use this argument forcefully in showing on Glubbdubdrib Aristotle confessing that he made many errors in natural philosophy; and on showing Gassendi and Descartes holding views of nature that are exploded because, ' . . . new Systems of Nature were but new Fashions, which would vary in every Age; and even those who pretend to demonstrate them from Mathematical Principles, would flourish but a short Period of Time, and be out of Vogue when that was determined'. (XI, 182). Swift's pessimism about human nature set in a natural world resistant to human control, and subject to decay and death, denied to him the possibility of belief in a progress and improvement in the world, or the acceptance of the Cartesian method applied to scientific discovery, which would move masterfully from the known to the further knowable.

This much attention has been given to Swift's rejection of scientific methods because his rejection is total, and without this finality we might misread his aims, but, having been shown, it can be left aside; whereas, of religious, political and philosophical themes, while he rejects much that was offered to him from the past, he also accepts

some things and modifies them for his own purposes. He rejected the
scientists because they identified their work with the 'mechanical'.
For Swift life could only be livable in terms not of mechanism but of
the understanding of human nature itself, which was capable of being
possessed by blind destructive forces only to be controlled by the
harmonizing of reason and Revelation, by 'virtue and religion', limited
by the unquestioning acceptance of the authority of the constitution of
the British State and of the canonical requirements of the established
Church of England. The idea of limitation here is essential in Swift's
thought. Man's irrepressible self-sufficiency riding on his ruthless
egotism needs the strongest curb. Swift felt the vertigo arising from
his horror of the destructive mindless energies of human folly, illusion
and vice: he felt the terror of the incursion of barbarism, of that wrath
of God which would allow 'religion and civility' to depart from a
nation as the penalty for its pride in itself and ignorance of Providence.
Also he felt the slow disintegrative force of time; the loss of purpose,
of innocence and of hope. In his account book, on the news of his
mother's death he wrote: 'I have now lost my barrier between me and
death'. (V, 196). Again he wrote on another occasion: 'I was 47
Years old when I began to think of death; and the reflections upon it
now begin when I wake in the Morning, and end when I am going to
Sleep.' (*Corr.*, III, 354). He came to the conclusion that death must be
intended by Providence as a blessing to men, and his Struldbruggs are
a fearful demonstration of it. A poem that has been misunderstood
as a cynicism more appropriate to Voltaire than to Swift the clergyman,
The Day of Judgement, shows him not dismissing the last judgement as a
childish superstition, but as challenging the last pride of man: that he
is worthy to stand before God for judgment. It is Swift's final condemnation of the vanity and complacent stupidity of men, he records
God speaking:

> "You who thro' Frailty step'd aside,
> And you who never fell—*thro' Pride*;
> You who in different Sects have shamm'd,
> And come to see each other damn'd . . .
> The World's mad Business now is o'er,
> And I resent these Pranks no more.
> I to such Blockheads set my Wit!
> I damn such Fools!—Go go, you're bit."

But the poem began:

> With a whirl of Thought oppress'd,
> I sink from Reverie to Rest.
> An horrid Vision seiz'd my Head. . . . (*Poems*, 578–9)

Unlike Chesterfield who wrote of the poem to Voltaire as one worldly mocker at religious myths to another, Swift indeed was appalled by the 'horrid Vision'. Further, he had written elsewhere, 'Miserable mortals! can we contribute to the *honour and Glory of God*? I could wish that expression were struck out of our Prayer-books'. (IX, 263).

The self-sufficient energies of men, if they are not to become destructive, need to be subjected to limitation. What this meant and how it was to be achieved can be seen in considering how Swift faced the philosophies of his time.

III

Swift addressed himself at Moor Park to the intellectual crisis of the late seventeenth century: *A Tale of a Tub*, long in his mind, when finally achieved is, for all its confidence and brilliance, still a summing up related to the stresses of the seventeenth-century situation and is not a prologue to the optimism of the works of Shaftesbury. Swift, seeking answers to that intellectual crisis, recognised the need to replace the traditional assumptions of pre-Cartesian philosophy and pre-Revolution churchmanship. He had seen how the Puritan theology of the covenants could destroy the stability of the State in the Civil War, and also had seen that the Laudian answer to the Puritans by insisting on *De iure divino* episcopacy, depending on absolutist monarchy, equally endangered stability. He was also aware of the route tried before him by well-informed laymen who found little assurance in clerical orthodoxies. Bacon could be cited as an influence of this type of thinking on the young Swift: but Bacon shared the religious-intellectual framework of later Calvinism, or Elizabethan Protestantism, as his own confession of religious belief shows.[17] This had little attraction for Swift. While Sir Thomas Browne could offer something to meet his needs, it was another more thoroughly critical layman, Thomas Hobbes, who opposed the religious extremisms of Puritanism and Laudianism and provided an alternative which attracted Swift's attention for a time. It is certain that he had studied Hobbes, for he had been Stella's Abelard and on the night of her funeral he wrote among reflections on her life: 'She understood the nature of government and could point out all the errors of Hobbes, both in that and religion'. (V, 231). But Swift owed something to Hobbes, perhaps more than he realized, for he could echo Hobbes's summing up on morals: 'he deduced the manners of men from human nature; virtues and vices from a natural law; and the goodness and wickedness of actions from the laws of states'. Further, Swift knew from his wide reading of books of travels that morals tend to be relative and vary with climate and religion, and

E

that one cannot accept *simpliciter* the traditional ethics of the Church. Hobbes in his chapter '*Of the Natural Condition of Mankind, as concerning their Felicity, and Misery*' ignores the traditional Christian doctrine of original sin, but is even more pessimistic than St. Augustine, for without external restraint there are ' . . . no arts; no letters; no society; and which is worst of all, continual fear, and danger of violent death; and the life of man, solitary, poor, nasty, brutish, and short.'[18] Swift accepted the doctrine of original sin, and a more Christian answer to it than Hobbes proposed for the natural man, but Hobbes's pessimistic view of human nature unrestrained Swift could surely share—the Yahoo is part of a similar vision. Hobbes had written that man has the exclusive privilege of forming 'general rules called *theorems*... But this privilege is allayed by another; and that is by the privilege of absurdity; to which no living creature is subject, but man only. And of men, those are of all most subject to it, that profess philosophy'.[19] The quotation calls to mind, first, Swift's early struggle to free himself from 'general theorems'; secondly, Gulliver's description of the Houyhnhnms who, puzzled by his shoes and stockings, neighed to each other and used 'various Gestures, not unlike those of a Philosopher, when he would attempt to solve some new and difficult Phaenomenon'. (XI, 210).

Yet Swift rejected Hobbes's system more than once as intolerable, however much he may have recognised the truth of some of his psychological insights, and there is more in common with Locke's ideas (though not with his philosophical system) in Swift's writings than with those of Hobbes. Locke wrote about metaphysical speculation in words which Swift would have approved, since it 'let loose our Thoughts into the vast Ocean of *Being*. Thus men extend their inquiries beyond their capacity. . . .'.[20] Locke also called Christian theology 'not a notional science, but a rule of righteousness'.[21] Both these general statements of Locke can be plainly found echoed in Swift's writings. How far Descartes disturbed or stimulated Swift would be difficult to determine, and the fact that Molyneux translated *Le Discours sur la Méthode* at Dublin when Swift was in his second year there at Trinity College may be one more fact without determinable consequences in the hidden life of a man of genius. But whether derived from him or not Swift reflects in his own work not Descartes' concern to demonstrate ultimate truth by mathematics but the view of Descartes that morality could be reduced to a few maxims: 'To obey the laws and customs of my country, constantly adhering to the religion in which God has given me the grace to be instructed from my childhood and governing myself in all other things by the wisest and least exaggerated opinions which were commonly received in practice by the most sensible of those with whom I had to live . . . to be as firm and resolute in my actions as I could be: . . . always to try to conquer myself rather than fortune.'[22] As Dean of St. Patrick's, for example, Swift was committed (as he once noted) to conquering himself rather than fortune.

A disciple of Montaigne who may have been one of the sources in which Swift found ideas common to Montaigne and his school, Pierre Charron, certainly wrote lines that Swift (whether he knew them directly, or mediated through Temple's conversation, or some other source) reflected in his own writings: 'Il faut estre simple, obéissant, et debonnaire pour estre propre a reçevoir religion, croire et se maintenir sous les loix, par réverence et obéissance, assujettir son jugement et se laisser mener et conduire à l'authorité publique. . . . La religion est en la connaissance de Dieu, et de soy-mesme; . . . son office est d'elever Dieu au plus haut de tout son effort, et baisser l'homme au plus bas, l'abatre comme perdu, et puis luy fournir des moyens de se relever, luy faire sentir la misère et son rien, afin qu'en Dieu seul, il mette son confiance et son tout. . . . La vraye science et le vray estude de l'homme, c'est l'homme'.[23]

For some the question may arise whether these citations are necessary or fruitful in understanding Swift: but if the principle of interpretation proposed earlier in this essay is accepted (that Swift must be understood against the background of the thought of his time, especially of its 'laicized religion', or else we tend at least to misrepresent him), then Charron and the rest are relevant. Camille Looten, Philip Harth and John Traugott have produced discussions of influences upon Swift's religious views and the mould of his thought.[24] However, together with the reason already given for the citations above, it is difficult to accept Traugott's attempt to make Swift largely a disciple of Anglo-Catholic Laudianism, or his statement that Swift participated 'in the same intellectual, political and religious cause to which Sir Thomas More became a martyr':[25] the one is an anachronism, the other an oversimplification. This kind of situation arises by giving more attention to the writings of Swift than to their historical context and to the development of Swift's mind. Harth gives a useful and valid study of the 'Anglican rationalists'—his own phrase—from Chillingworth through Glanvill and the Cambridge Platonists to Stillingfleet: but that the range of Swift's balanced thought can usefully be discerned in their writings is not to me self-evident, for he would have regarded half of them with boredom (how could Cudworth's discursive platonizing be reconciled with Swift's desire for reducing religious truths to the simplest principles?). Rather, Swift had to deal with the complications of Montaigne's 'Que sais-je?' and with Hobbes, Locke and Descartes, and by name and inference these recur more often in his writings than those other authors cited in Harth and elsewhere.

Certain truths for Swift are the basic realities of the Christian faith: that Christ is God; that the Trinity is a mystery of faith to be affirmed and not subtly disputed; that man is corrupt in nature, and needs the bridle of moral law interpreted by the Church, not with elaborate casuistry but by plainly determined principles of virtue; that episcopacy is the only lawful authority for the ordination of the Christian ministry; that the sacraments of baptism and holy communion are mysteries of fundamental importance—a position to be accepted without arguing it either by the interminable regress of historical analysis or by the interminable logomachy of the metaphysical analysis of the nature of regeneration or of the real presence. He shows his lifelong loyalty to the High Church principle that the teaching authority of the church is not subject to the State, not only in his frequent virulent attacks on Henry VIII as a lustful, godless tyrant who sought to be authority in the Church and despoiled her goods, but also in his early *Ode to Dr. William Sancroft*, the Non-juring martyr for the Church's independence, and in all his later writings.[26] 'The Church *of England* is no Creature of the Civil Power, either as to its Polity or Doctrines. The Fundamentals of both were deduced from Christ and his Apostles and the Instructions of the purest and earliest Ages'. (II, 79). Again, 'although the Supreme Power can hinder the Clergy or Church from making any new Canons, or executing the old; from consecrating Bishops, or refusing those that they do consecrate: or, in short, from performing any Ecclesiastical Office, as they may from eating, drinking and sleeping; yet they cannot themselves perform those Offices, which were assigned to the Clergy by our Saviour and his Apostles; or, if they do, it is not according to the Divine Institution, and consequently null and void.' (II, 77).

On the basis of this quotation some might consider Swift as a representative of the old Laudian high-church theology, and that therefore he would have supported the Non-Jurors who on the ground of the Divine Right of Kings refused to take the Oath of Allegiance to William and Mary out of loyalty to James II. Nevertheless, Swift, always a supporter of the Revolution of 1689 and always opposed to excessive zeal in religion, wrote of the Non-Juring Schism: 'it seemeth to be a Complication of as much Folly, Madness, Hypocrisy, and Mistake, as ever was offered to the World'. (*Corr.*, II, 222). For him they had made the mistake of destroying balance and proportion, of refusing to accept limitation, and thereby they had opened the door to religious fanaticism. Decency, proportion, restraint, he shared these attributes of Augustan classicism and required them of the young cleric seeking advice: 'I should be glad to see you the Instrument of introducing into our Style, that Simplicity which is the best and truest Ornament of most Things in human Life, which the politer Ages always aimed at in their Building and Dress, (*Simplex munditiis*) as well as their Productions of Wit.' (II, 177). This is not merely the elegant posture of a Chesterfield, nor even the more informal sympathetic and balanced 'politesse' of a Temple: these rules are the closely-held bridle upon fanaticism. The complaint of Socinians and Deists in his time was that the Christian's God was an arbitrary tyrant, or an unintelligible mathematical surd of a three in one, who should be thrust to a further distance from man and his rationalities; so they slackened or ceased to grip the reins upon man's sinful energies and rationalistic questionings. Swift, on the contrary, would find the views of a Bolingbroke and of the Deists about God's tyranny in omnipotence to be both psychologically and intellectually contemptible. For him man needs powerful restraints to master the weakness and passions in his flesh and in his reason. That there is no solid firm foundation of virtue but in a conscience firmly directed by the principles of religion is the theme not only of his sermon *On Conscience*. If a Bolingbroke, a Collins or a Tindal should reply, from one or other of their critical positions in regard to Revelation, 'how do you explain or justify the grounds or mysteries of the Revelation you affirm to be the controlling principle behind the teaching of a decent limitation', Swift replies: 'There seems to be a manifest Dilemma in the Case: If you explain them [the Mysteries], they are Mysteries no longer; if you fail, you have laboured to no Purpose.' (IX, 77). The authority of the Church enduring through seventeen centuries suffices. Go beyond that limitation and you may emphasize piety until it becomes fanaticism and can end in the disgusting *Mechanical Operation of the Spirit*; or you may emphasize the 'free rights of the reason' and end in atheism leading to that condition described in Hobbes's *Leviathan*; or you may emphasize enthusiastic preaching and end in bawling from a tub; or you may give over to the State your need for an ideology and an ethic and you end in an intolerable tyranny. Like Goya's terrible painting of the Colossal Man striding destructive and unseeing through trampled screaming refugees against a black apocalyptic sky (*El Coloso o el Pánico*) Swift's mind pictured the horror basic in man if he were to be set free from all limitations—his own attacks of vertigo were not psychosomatic, but perhaps they had a horrible inevitability when seen in relation to his private vision of what could happen in the world.

This powerful emotion was not forced into his writings on religion: he preserved there the appearance of calm through intense self-discipline. Nor should we overlook his deep sense of responsibility, not only in his calling as clergyman but as a writer, for the demonic power within him was continually subject to the mastery of his will; his feeling for form, his desire for serenity according to the 'simplicity of former ages' covers that inner depression and fear.

IV

From the first collected editions of his works onwards Swift's writings on religious subjects have not been brought together, instead many of them are placed with tracts on political or Irish affairs. This has tended to leave the impression on those who begin the study of Swift that he had very little to say on religious matters from committed Christian convictions. For example, *An Argument To prove, That the Abolishing of Christianity in England, May, as Things now Stand, be attended with some Inconveniences, and perhaps, not produce those many good Effects proposed thereby*, is an ironical presentation of Swift's fundamental convictions about that faith of which he said elsewhere, 'in the capacity of a clergyman' he had been 'appointed by providence for defending a post assigned me, and for gaining over as many enemies' as he could. (IX, 262). This well-known phrasing of his conception of his calling, by its suppression of personal feeling is frequently misunderstood as an example of his opportunism, and taken with the fierce intensity of *A Tale of a Tub* or the milder irony of *An Argument . . . [against] abolishing Christianity*, shows to superficial judges that his religious writings need not be taken seriously. Again, his self-depreciation as a preacher is taken at its face value by too many commentators. One would have to be well acquainted with Swift to understand his aside to a neighbouring parson: 'Those sermons You have thought fitt to transcribe . . . were what I was firmly resolved to burn and especially some of them the idlest trifling stuff that ever was writt'. (*Corr.*, I, 31), and the reluctant agreement that Dr. Sheridan could have some of them: 'they may be of use to you, they have never been of any to me.' (IX, 98). Landa has shown that Swift paid careful attention to sermon preparation and provided evidence that Swift at St. Patrick's Cathedral listened carefully to the sermons of visiting preachers and offered criticisms of them afterwards.[27]

In an age when the writing and publishing of sermons was a major and lucrative part of publishing, it is characteristic of Swift that he sought to keep his preaching for those whom it concerned. Those eleven sermons that survive emphasize Swift's own expression of themes he thought central to the needs of his people at that time. That more of Swift's sermons have not survived is probably in part due to his realistic clear judgement which recognised that possibly sermons in general, but certainly his own, should be kept out of the hands of Curll—or the Duchess of Somerset. While Swift deals with the great doctrinal and moral truths of the Christian faith as did other preachers before and after him, yet we can also, in certain of the sermons, see summarized his characteristic views, which have been discussed here: the balance between Church and State, against fanatical deviations to left or right; and the need for accepting without unnecessary argument the authority of the fundamental truths of Revelation. The sermons show beyond doubt that Swift fulfilled his own statement: 'I believe that thousands of men would be orthodox enough in certain points, if divines had not been too curious, or too narrow, in reducing orthodoxy within the compass of subtleties, niceties, and distinctions, with little warrant from Scripture, and less from reason or good policy.' (IX, 262).

His sermon on the commemoration of the Martyrdom of King Charles I sets forth in simple terms that careful balance which he regarded as the only barrier against the return to barbarism. His intense feeling here marks his concern with what were fundamentals for him. It is significant that unlike most High Churchmen Swift does not merely praise Charles as a religious martyr, a non-pareil, for he had too much realism to fail to see how far Charles and Laud had endangered the stability of the Church by *de iure divino* principles. He also points out that Charles introduced 'a practice, no way justifiable, of raising money; for which, however, he had the opinion of the judges on his side: For, wicked judges there were in those times as well as in ours'. (IX, 221). He then accuses the Long Parliament of having claimed all authority to itself and so destroying the balance of the constitution. The Irish rebellion and massacre of Protestants, the factious schisms and heresies in England, and the beginning and progress of Atheism, he blames on the Puritan parliament, and even the turning to Catholicism of James II is also derived from its intransigence. In simple terms there lies behind this sermon as in his other writings where these themes occur the view that Puritan fanaticism in religion led to the destruction of the necessary, the fundamental, relation of Prince, Lords, Commons and Church, with interrelated powers and responsibilities—here is the basic political religious answer of Swift to the needs of the English nation. Over against this he saw Dissenters demanding toleration, and indeed more than this, even comprehension within a Church establishment modified to suit them; for Swift this would be the return to the very position Charles I had faced before the Civil War broke out. Therefore, said Swift, it is an intolerable demand: Dissenters will not be persecuted, but the settlement of the Church of England made in 1662 must not be altered to suit them. They cannot expect the comprehension within the established Church which some of them sought, particularly the Presbyterians, since their views and practices would destroy the proper balance between Church and State in their weakening if not overturning the traditional worship, mysteries of the faith, and canonical practice of the Church of England, and in their constantly threatening to use the 'right of conscience' to oppose the State, or the Church settlement, after the manner of the Catholics. Dissenters must accept the limitations of their position, and be thankful for the measure of toleration they receive without demanding more. Behind his political philosophy and those varied writings which express it, lie the fundamental convictions of Swift about the right relation of Church and State (for him the State would disintegrate without the support of the Church and what, under God, it represented), and about the nature of man, foolish, proud and rebellious, which needs restraint, or limitation, by a moral order grounded not on speculative reason, always volatile, but on Revelation.

The vigorous, indeed harsh, rejection of what Puritanism and its heir, Dissent, stood for, which Swift urged succinctly in the *Sermon upon the Martyrdom of Charles I*, is expanded and applied in his straightforward tracts: *A letter from a Member of the House of Commons in Ireland concerning the Sacramental Test*; *The Sentiments of a Church-of-England Man*; *A Preface to Bishop Burnet's Introduction*; *The Presbyterians' Plea of Merit*; *The Advantages proposed by repealing the Sacramental Test*; and, by the method of ironical inversion, in the tract, *Reasons . . . for Repealing the Sacramental Test in Favour of the Catholicks*. In his discussion of the grounds for maintaining the Sacramental Test Swift shows that the Dissenters have liberty to own their property and to practise their religion undisturbed—what more can they want or deserve in view of their past rebellious disposition? Elsewhere Swift, for example, describes them as *Puritans*, and other Schismaticks, [who] without the least Pretence to any such Authority, by an open Rebellion, destroyed that legal Reformation . . . murdered their King and changed the Monarchy into a Republick.' (XII, 290). For him the Presbyterians, especially the Scottish planters of Ulster, need to be kept under the tightest rein, for the Scots of Ulster are 'an industrious People, extreamly devoted to their Religion, and full of an *undisturbed* Affection towards each other', who by 'Parsimony, wonderful *Dexterity in*

Dealing' and their solidarity advance their own power and reject anything to do with the Church of Ireland. (II, 116). They complain like other dissenters that it is unconscionable that Holy Communion should be made the test of political loyalty for those wishing to serve the State; no doubt, says Swift, but if they were offered instead an oath to be loyal to the constitution of Church and State they would claim it to be against conscience, and 'this is no sincerity in arguing', for the circle comes round again. The argument of these tracts is forceful, showing his inevitable stylistic vigour, and lighting up the facets of his fundamental position on the Church's function under God and in the State. He gives no place to Bishop Burnet's plea for leniency to Dissent, for such authors treat this subject *tamquam in republica Platonis, et non in faece Romuli*—here again his realism, without illusions, is as apparent as the force in the quotation. Since Burnet was a former Presbyterian, a Scot and the kind of Whig whose views Swift loathed, he described him as one who 'was absolute party-mad, and fancied he saw Popery under every bush'. (V, 184). For Swift 'toleration' is of little use, since when it once was tried (that is, under the Commonwealth) it corrupted the essentials of religion by the unlimited liberty of professing all opinions.

The mind that prepared the sermon *On the Martyrdom of Charles I* and the following sentences from the sermon *On Brotherly Love*: 'This Nation of ours hath for an Hundred Years past, been infested by two Enemies, the Papists and Fanaticks, who each, in their Turns, filled it with Blood and Slaughter, and for a Time destroyed both the Church and Government'; 'There are too many People indifferent enough to all Religion; there are many others who dislike the Clergy; and would have them live in Poverty and Dependence: Both these Sorts are much commended by the Fanaticks [that is, Dissenters] for moderate Men, ready to put an End to our Divisions, and to make a General Union among Protestants'. (IX, 172, 175)—this mind also prepared consistently these Tracts dealing with the problems posed by Dissent. We fail to do Swift justice if we do not recognize too that these writings are all of a piece with one of his major purposes in *A Tale of a Tub*: to attack the turbulence of Jack and his followers which is Dissent in action, and the fantasies of the Aeolists which represent the irrationality and emotional fanaticism of Dissent.

But Dissent was not the only focus of Swift's smaller writings on religious matters. Matthew Tindal, a leading Deist, had written *The Rights of the Christian Church* on which Swift wrote *Remarks* which were not finished and were published posthumously, but which should not be overlooked. For Tindal wanted to make the Church wholly subject to the State, a view which Swift is often accused of holding. But Swift in fact opposed this: establishment does not give being to the Church by act of Parliament, any more than the existence of God can be demonstrated by being conferred, as it is, by act of Parliament. 'But the Church of *England* is no Creature of the Civil Power, either as to its Polity or Doctrines. The Fundamentals of both were deduced from Christ and his Apostles, and the Instructions of the purest and earliest Ages, and were received as such by those Princes or States who embraced Christianity, whatever prudential Additions have been made to the former by human Laws, which alone can be justly altered or annulled by them.' (II, 79). Authority in the clergy comes from Christ, but the right to exercise it lies in civil governments: once again Swift is demonstrating man's tendency to confuse cause and appearances. We today may reject Swift's argument in the *Remarks* and oversimplify our criticism of him here, but if we do then we are overlooking the fact that Swift was reproducing a doctrine of classical Protestantism. His argument on this theme is neither improbable nor inconsistent, but is the central doctrine of Anglicanism from Richard Hooker onwards.

In his *Sentiments of a Church-of-England Man* he insisted without qualification that a member of that Church 'ought to believe a God, and his Providence, together with revealed Religion, and the Divinity of *Christ*' (II, 4), and that he must accept episcopacy as most agreeable to the primitive institution of the Church and most suited for preserving order and purity. Morality and religion may be miscalled the prejudices of education by freethinkers, but in doing so they demonstrate their wish to have liberty for their vices and self-sufficient opinions. Confusion between the executive and legislative power (a confusion which Swift says Hobbes himself made and was the foundation of the political mistakes in his books) is the basis for unintelligent attack on Church and State relations by those who wish to alter them. 'The Freedom of a Nation in fact consists in an absolute *unlimited legislative* Power, wherein the whole Body of the People are *fairly* represented; and in an *executive* duly *limited*.' (II, 23). Here is one ground for understanding how Swift could combine Whig and Tory principles in a period when a man must be one or the other undiluted—like the Whig Bishop Burnet or the Tory Bishop Atterbury, 'party-mad'. Swift did not apostatize in changing from the new style of Whigs to the Tories, he held to his integrity of judgement on what would best serve the State and the Church, Revelation and morality. He did not change his views: with the political developments of the early eighteenth century it was the party lines which changed. Swift was a Tory churchman of 1662, and a Whig of 1689—and in essentials remained so. His failure to achieve a bishopric lay partly in his holding to these convictions when such appointments largely went by party. In 1708 he wrote, at the end of *The Sentiments of a Church-of-England Man*, 'I should think that, in order to preserve the Constitution entire in Church and State; whoever hath a true Value for both, would be sure to avoid the Extreams of *Whig*, for the Sake of the former, and the Extreams of *Tory* on Account of the latter.' (II, 25).

Swift plainly thought of the Church not only as having its own divine origin, although since it was established in law it was subject in its canons and practices of government to the executive and legislative powers of the State, but also as being essential to society, intended by God's providence for this purpose, among others, to demonstrate, encourage, and give pastoral care to the moral well-being of the members of the community. We can find these beliefs recommended as capable of being advanced even at the lowest level of princely example and encouragement in *A Project for the Advancement of Religion, and the Reformation of Manners*; shown in *Gulliver's Travels* in the views of the King of Brobdingnag; and the sermons *On the Testimony of a good Conscience* and *The Duty of Mutal Subjection*. Johnson thought that *A Project for the Advancement of Religion*, while showing great purity of intention, was 'if not generally impracticable, yet evidently hopeless': but something like it was successfully advocated and realized under Victoria the Good, at least to the extent that it allowed the 'hypocrisy which is the tribute that vice pays to virtue'.

Near the end of *A Project* Swift quotes Machiavelli on the value of reducing things to their first principles: therefore, he urges, we should clarify where the roots of abuses in religion and morality lie, and attack them at those roots. This piece has been described by Dr. Leavis as a call for 'outward show in religion'; for Johnson, however, it urged more 'zeal, concord and perseverance' in religion than men are capable of. Swift himself agreed that on the method he advocated there might arise nineteen hypocrites for one good man: but that ratio would be worth it, from the quality of the good men. What he had condemned in *A Project*, he condemned more forthrightly in similar terms in his sermon *On the Testimony of Conscience*: 'So, that upon the Whole, there is hardly one Vice which a meer Moral man [that is, 'those Men who set up for Morality without regard to Religion'] may not upon some Occasions allow himself to practise. . . . And the Reason we find so many Frauds, Abuses, and Corruptions where any Trust is conferred, can be no other, than that there is so little Conscience and Religion left in the World, or at least that Men in their Choice of Instruments have private Ends in view, which are very different from the Service of the

Publick.' (IX, 153, 157). Without recourse to his stylistic brilliance on the one hand, nor to the exhortatory tone and appeal to emotion too common in the pulpit on the other, Swift states plainly in this Sermon his view of the human condition and some of the basic principles which lie behind all his writings.

Swift's pamphlet *A Letter to a Young Gentleman lately entered into Holy Orders* is used most frequently by those concerned with his analysis of a good prose style and how it should be formed, but his purpose here was focused on giving advice on the professional equipment of a clergyman—advice which achieves more good sense in short space than many similar efforts on the pastoral training of the clergy. Once again he is seen reducing the complex and contradictory to first principles and then advising that these should be directed with the greatest concentration of force to the appropriate targets. Among other sound points Swift, approving for once of a Dissenter, claims that he had been 'more informed by a Chapter in the *Pilgrim's Progress*, than by a long Discourse upon the *Will* and the *Intellect*, and *simple* or *complex Ideas*'. (IX, 77). In his own sermon *On Sleeping in Church* he provides an irony and an indignation lacking in *A Letter* which forcefully exemplify part of its intention—the two should be read together for to some degree they complement each other. In *A Letter* he writes: 'For a Divine hath nothing to say to the wisest Congregation of any Parish in this Kingdom, which he may not express in a Manner to be understood by the meanest among them': in *On Sleeping in Church* he writes more pungently that 'Refinements of Stile, and Flights of Wit, as they are not properly the Business of any Preacher, so they cannot possibly be the Talents of all. In most other Discourses, Men are satisfied with sober Sense and plain Reason; and, as Understandings go, even that is not over frequent'. (IX, 66 and 217).

Swift the ironist of *An Argument* [*against*] *Abolishing Christianity* shares something of the Erasmian tradition of the *Praise of Folly*, for the humanist element in Swift's early reading is not only to be found in Montaigne, but the method and the style of *An Argument* are peculiarly Swiftian and have made it a frequent choice for representative selections from his writings. He tells us of the sad fate of two young gentlemen who 'by meer Force of natural Abilities, without the least Tincture of Learning; having made a Discovery, that there was no God, and generously communicating their thoughts for the Good of the Publick; were some Time ago, by an unparalleled Severity, and upon I know not what *obsolete* Law, broke *only* for *Blasphemy*'. But how many of those to whom *An Argument* is familiar know the following, from a sermon, *On Sleeping in Church*, which shows Swift's method of turning the enemy's weapon against him, his contempt for the 'tritical', and his concern for plain but forceful discourse: 'these Men, whose Ears are so delicate as not to endure a plain Discourse of Religion, who expect a constant Supply of Wit and Eloquence on a Subject handled so many thousand Times; what will they say when we turn the Objection upon themselves, who with all the lewd and profane Liberty of Discourse they take, upon so many thousand Subjects, are so dull as to furnish nothing but tedious Repetitions, and little paultry, nauseous Commonplaces, so vulgar, so worn, or so obvious, as upon any other Occasion, but that of advancing Vice, would be hooted off the stage.' (IX, 214). The main theme of *An Argument* is seen where Swift ironically affirms that he has no intention of defending the real Christianity of the apostolic age, for to restore it is a wild project; he is only defending nominal Christianity on such grounds as that it would be useful to have one man who could read and write in a parish, and that the abolition of the Christian religion might bring in popery, though he admits that parsons could provide useful recruits for the army and the fleet since they are a tiresome set of men whose only duty it is to bawl one day in seven. The complementary form of *An Argument* can be found in the sermon *On the Excellency of Christianity* where we can compare the assertion in the former 'to offer at the Restoration of *real* Christianity would indeed be a wild Project', with this: 'Why doth not Christianity still produce the same effects? [as among the primitive Christians] it is easy to answer, First, That although the number of pretended Christians be great, yet that of true believers, in proportion to the other, was never so small; and it is a true lively faith alone, that by the assistance of God's grace, can influence our practice. Secondly, we may answer, That Christianity itself hath very much suffered by being blended up with Gentile philosophy'. (IX, 249). Behind all this, however, there is the constant theme with Swift, the need for maintaining an educated, well-ordered, well-provided for and respected body of clergy: he recurs again and again to the damage caused to the Church and, therefore, to society, through the poverty and disrespect accorded to the clergy. For example, in the unfinished piece *Concerning that universal Hatred which prevails against the Clergy*, the ground is never mere professional assertion, but is that moralism basic to Swift's world-view, that the clergy are the God-given agents for maintaining moral stability in society.

It has been shown how certain of his sermons interpret briefly and underline his other writings on religious themes, but the sermons can also be shown as reinforcing the purposes of the great satires and indeed the whole of his writings. Eleven sermons were published out of the many Swift preached as parish priest and later as Dean, and it is an open question whether even these came to be published through his intention that they should survive. They are usually neglected in considering his literary achievement because of failure to find in them his stylistic brilliance, the assumption that sermons are insignificant for literary criticism, and the frequent but erroneous belief that Swift must have found preaching a tiresome distraction from his real interests as a writer, and therefore that what he preached would hardly relate to his major works. Nevertheless, here in the sermons Swift states plainly without masks, inversions, or stylistic devices the point of view and the beliefs which lie behind the great satires and the political and religious essays. His judgement on human nature, so often described as pessimistic, negative or even cynical, is repeated in the sermons, where he shows that he inherits and believes profoundly in the moral realism of the traditional Christian doctrine of Original Sin. On man's desperately sinful condition Swift has no doubt: man left to himself is a creature of pride, vanity, lust, stupidity, and folly. It is significant that John Wesley could quote with approval *Gulliver's Travels* on man's depravity in his tract on *The Doctrine of Original Sin*. Swift's positive conclusion to his sermon *On the Testimony of Conscience* should be pondered by those who fail to see any connection between Swift the Dean and Swift the satirist: 'It plainly appears, that unless Men are guided by the Advice and Judgment of a Conscience founded on Religion, they can give no Security that they will be either good Subjects, faithful Servants of the Publick, or honest in their mutual Dealings; since there is no other Tie thro' which the Pride, or Lust, or Avarice, or Ambition of Mankind will not certainly break one Time or other.' (IX, 158). That a stable society cannot be created by man's own resources without reference to the Church the guardian of Revelation is not only the implication of the satires, and the affirmation of the religious essays, it is the blunt purpose, as has already been shown, of the sermon *On the Martyrdom of Charles I*, and is energetically expressed in the sermon *On Brotherly Love*: 'A Moderate Man, in the new Meaning of the Word, is one to whom all Religion is indifferent, who, although he denominateth himself of the Church, regardeth it no more than a Conventicle. He perpetually raileth at the Body of the Clergy, with Exceptions only to a very few, whom he hopeth and probably upon false Grounds, are as ready to betray their Rights and Properties, as himself. He thinks the Power of the People can never be too great, nor that of the Prince too little; and yet this very Notion he publisheth, as his best Argument, to prove him a most loyal Subject. Every Opinion in Government, that differeth in the least from his, tendeth directly to Popery, Slavery and Rebellion. . . . Lastly, his Devotion consisteth in drinking Gibbets, Confusion, and Damnation; in profanely idolizing the Memory of one Prince [William III] and ungratefully trampling upon the Ashes of another' [Queen Anne] (IX, 178). Here we have in fact the character of a new Whig, for Swift, the very ground of instability in the State. That Swift thought this kind of writing proper for a sermon shows his realism, and his contempt for the pious platitude that politics should not enter the pulpit.

A useful introduction to Swift's Irish tracts and to the *Drapier's Letters* is provided by the sermon *Causes of the Wretched Condition of Ireland*, for it contains a clear and forceful summary of the Irish problem in which the endemic troubles of, for example, absentee landlords, and numbers of starving beggars, are set down. Another sermon *Doing Good* is subtitled *On the Occasion of Wood's Project* where Swift strikes at 'the meanest instrument' who 'by the concurrence of accidents, may have it in his power to bring a whole kingdom to the very brink of destruction, and is at this present endeavouring to finish his work'. He adds:

Perhaps it may be thought by some, that this way of discoursing is not so proper from the pulpit. But surely, when an open attempt is made, and far carried on, to make a great kingdom one large poor-house, to deprive us of all means to exercise hospitality and charity, to turn our cities and churches into ruins, to make the country a desert for wild beasts and robbers, to destroy all arts and sciences, all trades and manufactures, and the very tillage of the ground, only to enrich one obscure, ill-designing projector, and his followers; it is time for the pastor to cry out, that the wolf is getting into his flock, to warn them to stand together, and all to consult the common safety.
(IX, 235–6)

Again, the sermon *On False Witness* is about much more than the evil of malicious gossip, for in faction-ridden Ireland Swift notes the scandal of another feature of Irish politics, the Informer, 'evil Instruments who . . . are always ready . . . to offer their Service to the prevailing Side and become Accusers of their Brethren. . . .' (IX, 180). He points his congregation to the way to defend themselves against false accusation and the activities of the *agent-provocateur*, showing that innocence is always the best protection for those who are to be as harmless as doves, but adds pointedly that they should be as wise as serpents in keeping to loyalty.

In his sermon *On the Excellency of Christianity* Swift challenges the contemporary assumptions made by the Deists, and by Bolingbroke and Shaftesbury, that the virtues of the Greeks and Romans were the

highest examples of the good life and accessible without the need of
the Christian Revelation. He argues that even the best philosophers of
Greece and Rome showed defects in morals which were 'purely the
flagging and fainting of the mind for want of a support by revelation
from God'. (IX, 247), and that Plato with all his refinements left 'the
wise and the good man wholly at the mercy of uncertain chance, and
to be miserable without resource'. (IX, 246). This is complemented
by his sermon *On the Trinity* where—with some theological astuteness—
he gives a positive answer to the Deists' criticism of Trinitarian
orthodoxy, and a statement of the essential themes of the orthodox
reply to the Anti-Trinitarians, and also the characteristic challenge of
man's rationality: '*Reason* itself is true and just, but the *Reason* of every
particular Man is weak and wavering, perpetually swayed and turned
by his Interests, his Passions, and his Vices.' (IX, 166).

A final group of three sermons shows Swift fully committed to
pastoral concern about the obligations of love and service which men
owe to each other. In two of them he emphasizes a theme unacceptable
to our unitary view of society but which was fundamental to the
political outlook of his time. In *The Duty of Mutual Subjection* by taking
literally the words 'Be subject one to another' (though he recognized
as do modern commentators that the intention here is to emphasize
humility) Swift affirms that, since society is hierarchical, each man has
his station and his obligations; and in *The Poor Man's Contentment* he
consoles the poor by pointing out that vices and miseries beset the
rich and powerful, that wealth is not a blessing, and that the poor man
is free from its insistent temptations. Swift is saved from smugness
here by the forthrightness of his demand that the poor man should be
helped and cared for by the richer, by reminding the poor that Christ
was born among them, and by sharply affirming that virtue does not
reside with rank and wealth. The sermon *On Conscience* demonstrates
clearly Swift's grim view of the sinful condition of men, not least of
those who appear to live with virtue before the world but who are in
reality hypocrites and self-seekers, and he allows no place to those who
substitute Honour for virtue, mocking 'The Catechism of Honour,
which contains but two Precepts, the punctual Payment of Debts
contracted at Play, and the right understanding the several Degrees of
an Affront, in order to revenge it in the Death of an Adversary'.
(IX, 153). Here Swift the preacher agrees with Swift the political
observer and the satirist, in saying 'There is no way of judging how
far we may depend upon the Actions of Men, otherwise than by
knowing the Motives, and Grounds, and Causes of them; and, if the
Motives of our Actions be not resolved and determined into the Law

of God, they will be precarious and uncertain, and liable to perpetual Changes . . . a Religious Conscience is the only true Foundation upon which Virtue can be built.' (IX, 154, 156).

In these eleven sermons can be found in little space the focal points of Swift's view of man, society, the Church and the State, Ireland, Christian faith and virtue, together with his repudiation of those who will not accept a decent limitation for the sake of order—the religious extremist, the self-confident rationalist, and the factious party-man, in all their ramifying activities disturbing that balance without which life would become intolerable. In his sermon *On the Excellence of Christianity* he said: '[The Christian religion] is *without hypocrisy*; it appears to be what it really is; it is all of a piece. By the doctrines of the gospel we are so far from being allowed to publish to the world those virtues we have not, that we are commanded to hide, even from ourselves, those we really have, and not to let our right hand know what our left hand doth'. (IX, 248). Here in his own words to his congregation at St. Patrick's is the key to Swift's 'inverted hypocrisy'. It points to what 'really is' and was 'all of a piece' with his religion. The Swift of the satires concealed from being obvious the religious motivation of his thought not through indifference nor merely as the stylistic necessity of avoiding 'tritical' moralizing, but through conviction: 'we are so far from being allowed to publish to the world those virtues we have not, that we are commanded to hide, even from ourselves, those we really have.'

NOTES

[1] *A Supplement to Dr. Swift's Works* (ed. J. Nichols), 1779, vol. III, p. 226
[2] For Swift's view that Archbishop Sharp told Queen Anne that the author of *A Tale of a Tub* was unfit for appointment as a bishop see *Poems*, 193, n. 2. Swift had referred to the Duchess of Somerset, formerly Baroness Percy, daughter of the last Earl of Northumberland in his poem *The Windsor Prophecy* (1711), as 'Carrots from Northumberland'.
[3] *The English Humourists of the Eighteenth Century: Swift*. W. M. Thackeray, *Works: The Biographical Edition* (1898), vol VII, p. 441.
[4] *History of English Thought in the Eighteenth Century* (3rd edn., 1927), vol. II, pp. 373–4.
[5] Looten, *op. cit.*, p. 9.
[6] *The Common Pursuit* (Peregrine Books edition, 1962), p. 85 and p. 87.
[7] Leavis, *op. cit.*, p. 85.
[8] *Swift's Journal to Stella*, ed. Harold Williams, 1948, vol. I, p. 126.
[9] Samuel Johnson, *Lives of the English Poets* (Everyman, 1958 edition), vol. II, pp. 268–269.
[10] *The Times Literary Supplement*, No. 3,347, p. 356, April 21, 1966.
[11] L. A. Landa, *Swift and the Church of Ireland* (Oxford, 1954).
[12] R. W. Jackson, *Jonathan Swift: Dean and Pastor*, p. 111.

F

[13] These logical text-books were first referred to by Emile Pons, *La Jeunesse de Swift* (Strasbourg, 1925), p. 128, but have now been convincingly put into the context of Swift's satire by R. S. Crane, 'The Houyhnhms, the Yahoos, and the History of Ideas', in *Reason and the Imagination*, ed. J. A. Mazzeo (London, 1962), pp. 213–253, and in R. S. Crane, *The Idea of the Humanities*, 2 vols. (Chicago, 1957), II, 261–282.

[14] See the classic essays by Marjorie Nicolson, reprinted in *Science and the Imagination* (Ithaca, New York, 1956).

[15] Thomas Sprat, *The History of the Royal Society of London for the improving of Natural Knowledge*, (London, 1667), p. 242.

[16] Sprat, op. cit., p. 243.

[17] A-M. Schmidt, *Calvin and the Calvinistic Tradition*, trans. R. Wallace, 1960, pp. 153–161.

[18] *Leviathan*, ed. M. Oakeshott (Blackwell, Oxford, 1946), p. 82.

[19] *Leviathan, ed. cit.*, p. 27.

[20] Locke's *Works* (3rd edition; London, 1727) I, 2.

[21] *Ibid.*

[22] Descartes, *Oeuvres*, Bibliothèque de la Pléiade (Paris, 1953), p. 141.

[23] Pierre Charron, *Petit Traite de la Sagesse* (Paris, 1646), p. 327 and p. 334. Swift owned a copy of 'Charron of Wisdom 2d. and 3d. Books. Lond. 1697'–1745 Sale Catalogue, item no. 648.

[24] Philip Harth, *Swift and Anglican Rationalism*: *The Religious Background to the Tale of a Tub*, Chicago, 1961. Looten, *op. cit.* John Traugott, 'A Voyage to Nowhere with Thomas More and Jonathan Swift,' reprinted in *Swift*: *A Collection of Critical Essays*, ed. E. Tuveson, New York, 1963.

[25] Traugott, *op. cit.*, p. 160.

[26] Swift attacks Henry VIII in several places, for example, *Concerning the Universal Hatred which Prevails against the Clergy*; *Remarks upon a Book The Rights of the Christian Church*; The *Ode to Sancroft*.

[27] Landa, Introduction to the Sermons (IX, 97–137) and *Swift and the Church of Ireland*, p. 193.

From Principles to Practice:
Swift and Party Politics

W. A. SPECK

Swift began Anne's reign as a Whig and ended it as a Tory. A glance at a list of his English correspondents gives some indication of the completeness of this change. (*Corr.*, I, xxi ff.) In the first half of the reign nearly all his private correspondence was with Whigs, including Lord Halifax and his fellow writers Joseph Addison and Richard Steele. After 1710 their names almost completely disappear, and new ones occur, most of them Tories such as Henry St. John and Francis Atterbury. From Halifax to Atterbury Swift's correspondents spanned the political spectrum from Junto Whig to Jacobite Tory. His relations with the Whig Lords who composed what was called the Junto are particularly remarkable. Late in 1710 he brought out the fifth edition of *A Tale of a Tub*. As usual it contained a dedication to Lord Somers. Before the year was out Swift published, in *A Short Character of Thomas, Earl of Wharton*, one of Somers' Junto colleagues, what must be one of the most savage attacks on a politician to appear in print.

This change is the key to Swift's politics. If we could explain it we would solve the knottiest problem of his political allegiance, for he never changed again. Yet, like the meaning of his major satires, his motives present riddles to which it is possible to give several explanations.

I

His political career might be explained in terms of pure self-interest. Swift could be credited with seeking nothing more than advancement in the Church, in order to obtain which he attached himself first to the Whigs, when they were in power, and then to the Tories when they came into favour. As we shall see, he considered that self-love was the spring of human action, and there seems to be no valid reason for believing that he exempted himself with a self-denying dispensation from this law of nature. His begging letters to the great differ from the masses which they received only in being well written. His disappointment when his reward turned out to be nothing better than the Deanery of St. Patrick's was no more philosophic than any other man's, being expressed in the most spiteful complaints against personalities who had blocked the path to preferment. The Queen herself, who opposed his promotion because of *A Tale of A Tub*, he called a 'royal prude', while of the Duchess of Somerset, whom he suspected of being the chief obstacle, he wrote: 'From her red locks her mouth with venom fills, And thence into the royal ear distils.' (*Poems*, 193–6.)

If we accept this view, the explanation of Swift's apparent volte-face becomes easy. He was neither Whig nor Tory but a place-seeker, one of those who gravitated towards the men in power whatever their party politics. Some contemporary observations square with this view. White Kennett's description of Swift in 1713 is of the complete hanger-on at court:

> Dr. Swift came into the coffee house, and had a bow from everybody but me. When I came to the antechamber to wait before prayers, Dr. Swift was the principal man of talk and business, and acted as a master of requests. He was soliciting the earl of Arran to speak to his brother the duke of Ormond, to get a chaplain's place established in the garrison of Hull for Mr. Fiddes, a clergyman in that neighbourhood, who had lately been in gaol, and published sermons to pay fees. He was promising Mr. Thorold to undertake with my lord treasurer, that, according to his petition, he should obtain a salary of 200 per annum, as minister of the English Church at Rotterdam. He stopped F[rancis] Gwynne, esq., going in with his red bag to the Queen, and told him aloud that he had something to say to him from my lord treasurer. He talked with the son of Dr. Davenant to be sent abroad, and took out his pocket book and wrote down several things, as *memoranda*, to do for him. He turned to the fire, and took out his gold watch, and, telling him the time of the day, complained it was very late. A gentleman said 'he was too fast'. 'How can I help it,' says the doctor, 'if the courtiers give me a watch that won't go right? . . .' (*Corr.*, V, 228–9.)

This is of course a malicious story, by an inveterate enemy of the Dean. But even his best friends were prepared to believe that he cut his coat entirely according to the court cloth. The Earl of Oxford, when he was steadily losing ground to Lord Bolingbroke in 1714, 'twitted him [Swift] with the comparison of the rat which leaves a falling house.'[1]

Yet Oxford was mistaken. Swift, as far as possible, stayed loyal both to him and Bolingbroke. When Oxford was finally dismissed he received a letter from the Dean, written before the event but fully anticipating it, in which Swift pledged his allegiance to him in unequivocal terms. (*Corr.*, II, 44–5). He made no effort to ingratiate himself with the Whigs on Anne's death, when it was still possible for supporters of her last ministry to make their peace with the incoming regime. James Brydges, one of those who did, was written off by Swift as 'a great complyer with every Court'. (V, 260.) It would be a great miscarriage of justice to apply the same verdict to Swift himself.

It is well known that he intervened in English politics primarily to obtain financial relief for the clergy of the Church of Ireland. In 1704 their English brethren were granted Queen Anne's Bounty, by which the Crown made over revenues received from the Church since the Reformation to the augmentation of inadequate stipends. In 1707 Swift visited England in order to solicit a similar arrangement for the Irish clergy. Despite strong backing from Ireland, and personal solicitation with leading politicians, the negotiations got nowhere. The Whigs who were then in power were not prepared to extend Queen Anne's Bounty to Ireland. Three years later, when the Tories came into power, Swift was still in the position of a supplicant on behalf of his colleagues, and therefore turned to the new government. This time he met with success, and his conversion could therefore be ascribed to the rejection of his mission by the Whigs, and the accomplishment of its objectives by the Tories.

However, the negotiations over Queen Anne's Bounty broke down in 1708, not on some arid technicality, but a point of principle. The government made the extension of the Bounty to Ireland conditional on the Irish clergy's consenting to the repeal of the Irish Test Act. This Act, passed in 1704, was intended, like its English counterpart, to keep dissenters out of public office, and to give Anglicans a monopoly of political power. Swift refused to countenance such a deal, to the extent of writing a pamphlet against any proposal to repeal the Act. (*Corr.*, I, 84–7, 94–6; *Works*, II, 109–125). This is the most convincing proof that he was not a mere place seeker, for had he been prepared to comply with the court he could reasonably have expected the reward of a good living. Instead he jeopardised his career in the Church when his principles came into conflict with those of his Whig friends. The answer to the riddles of Swift's politics must therefore be sought not in his actions but in his ideas.

II

A useful way of examining Swift's political views is to outline the main issues of the period, and then to see which attitudes he adopted to them. This is the method which I have used in this essay.

Society in the late seventeenth-century was divided by differences of opinion on three major issues: the origin of government; the position of the Church in society; and England's role in Europe.

Divergent views on these questions underlay the conflict between the Whig and Tory parties.[2]

The debate over government concerned not its nature but its origin. On the nature of government the majority of both parties seem to have been in agreement. England was admitted to be a mixed monarchy, wherein monarchical, aristocratic and popular elements offset each other, and none should be allowed to preponderate. On the origin of government, however, and particularly whether it was sacred or secular, there was considerable disagreement.

One view upheld the theory of the divine right of kings. The full-blown theory involved arguments from the Scriptures to back up indefeasible hereditary right from Adam to the Stuarts. Its corollary was the doctrine of passive obedience and non-resistance, since it was sinful to oppose the Lord's Anointed on any pretext whatsoever. After the Revolution of 1688, however, this view became increasingly unrealistic, and many modified it to the notion of the Divine Right of Providence, arguing that the downfall of James II and the success of the Prince of Orange was a judgment of God on the House of Stuart.[3] This was not a particularly satisfactory compromise for most adherents to the traditional view, since it was a doctrine to which Cromwell could have subscribed quite cheerfully.

Opposed to the divine right school was the view that men formed civil society to suit themselves. This concept found expression in various forms of the contract theory, the most well-known being that government was a contract between the ruler and the ruled. According to this school the Revolution of 1688 had come about because James II had broken the original contract, and the people had therefore exercised their right to depose him and elect a new ruler.

The Whigs subscribed to the contract theory, while most Tories continued to uphold the idea of divine and even of hereditary right, though the party lines were becoming less sharp on this issue as more and more Tories found divine right increasingly untenable despite the subtle modification made to it in an effort to square it with reality.

The question of the Church produced a sharper dichotomy. It turned on the position of the Church of England in English society, which had been profoundly affected by the Revolution. The Anglican monopoly of authorised worship was broken by the Toleration Act of 1689, which allowed Protestant dissenters who believed in the Trinity to worship in their own conventicles. In the state the monopoly of political power apparently vouchsafed to the Anglicans by the Corporation and Test Acts of Charles II's reign was being infringed by dissenters who practised what was known as occasional conformity in order to qualify for office. Under the terms of the Corporation Act members of borough corporations were obliged to take communion in the Church of England at least once in the year before their appointments. Since most of them were elected annually this meant an obligatory annual visit to an Anglican communion service. The Test Act required men appointed to office under the crown to take communion within three months after their appointment. Thereafter there was no necessity to enter an Anglican church again. Many dissenters broke the spirit of these laws by sticking strictly to the letter. These developments undermined the traditional place of the Church in society, but it faced a direct frontal attack from the press after 1695. In that year the Licensing Act expired, and the result was an avalanche of literature which would never have got past the old ecclesiastical censors. This literature was not merely dissenting, but aired every current heresy, and there were plenty about, from Atheism to Socinianism.

Faced with this situation many Anglicans raised the cry 'the church in danger'. They demanded that the State should step in to restore the former status of the Church with all the constitutional machinery available. Parliament should pass an Act to stamp out the practice of occasional conformity. Convocation should be summoned to defend Anglican orthodoxy and to suppress heretical literature. Such advocates of compulsion formed what was called the 'high church party'. Their opponents the 'low church party', were against the use of force to safeguard the church, and the invasion of the liberties upheld in the Revolution settlement. Compulsion should only go as far as putting the existing laws into execution.

These divergent views were reflected in the political parties. Though not all Tories shared the 'high church' outlook, the advocates of force were all to be found in the ranks of the Tory party, while the more moderate approach of the 'low church party' found favour with the Whigs.

While the religious issue was a constant theme in late seventeenth-century politics there were times when the question of England's role in Europe was more dominant. The Revolution transformed England's relations with the continent. From being a minor power which tended to support France she became a major power completely committed to stopping French expansion. This involved her in two costly and prolonged wars against Louis XIV. During the second of these conflicts, the War of the Spanish Succession, which lasted from 1702 to 1713, differences appeared between the two parties, initially over the strategy to be adopted, but later over what war aims to puruse. As the war went on, the objectives of the allies became more and more ambitious. At first committed to little more than obtaining Louis XIV's recognition of the Protestant succession in England, security for the Dutch in the Low Countries, and a fair share of the Spanish Empire for the Habsburg claimant to the throne of Spain, the allies eventually undertook to place the Habsburg candidate on the throne of Spain itself, a war aim summed up in the slogan 'No Peace Without Spain'. Insistence on this principle rendered more than one French overture for peace abortive. Later it became clear that the Bourbon claimant of the Spanish throne was so firmly entrenched that the war might have to be protracted indefinitely unless the allies dropped their demand that he should make way for his rival. This divided the English political parties. The Whigs continued to insist on 'No Peace Without Spain', while the Tories asserted that this was needlessly prolonging the war, and that in order to reach a peace settlement it must be dropped.

Such in brief were the major political issues of the period. Political propagandists distorted the nature of these differences, Whigs by asserting that the Tories were conniving with Popery, Jacobitism, and Louis XIV's aim of world domination, Tories by claiming that the Whigs were a gang of republican, presbyterian war-mongers. In his more ferocious sallies against the Whigs after 1710 Swift himself was quite capable of such wilful misrepresentation. Thus in his *Advice to the Members of the October Club* he warned those diehard Tories against the wicked Whigs: ' . . . a perpetual War encreases their Mony, [and] breaks and beggars their *Landed Enemies*. The Ruin of the Church would please the Dissenters, Deists, and Socinians, whereof the Body of their Party consists. A *Commonwealth*, or a *Protector*, would gratify the *Republican Principles* of some, and the Ambition of others among them.' (VI, 78).

Thinking men, seeing that the reality scarcely squared with these notions, and that the bulk of both parties consisted of Anglicans committed to the Hanoverian settlement, dismissed the propaganda as lies, and concluded that at bottom there was really no difference in principle between Whigs and Tories. Swift in his more moderate writings frequently took this line.[4] In an early contribution to the *Examiner* he explained his determination

> to let the remote and uninstructed Part of the Nation see, that they have been misled on both Sides, by mad, ridiculous Extreams, at a wide Distance on each Side from the Truth . . . .

> outrageous Party-Writers . . . inflame small Quarrels by a thousand Stories, and by keeping Friends at Distance, hinder them from coming to a good Understanding, as they certainly would, if they were suffered to meet and debate between themselves. For, let any

one examine a reasonable honest Man of either Side, upon those Opinions in Religion and Government, which both Parties daily buffet each other about; he shall hardly find one material Point in difference between them. (III, 14–15).

But behind the exaggerated rhetoric of the propagandist lay real enough disagreements over questions concerning government, religion and involvement in Europe. At bottom the conflict between the parties involved the clash of rival political theories. When Swift took them seriously he reached firm enough conclusions about them.[5]

Swift did not dispute the nature of government, being a leading champion of the balanced constitution.[6] But he did join in the controversy over the origin of the State.

As an Anglican clergyman Swift might have been expected to side with the advocates of the divine right of kings. And indeed we find him admonishing his flock in a sermon: 'All government is from God, who is the God of order, and therefore whoever attempts to breed confusion or disturbance among a people, doth his utmost to take the government of the world out of God's hands, and to put it into the hands of the Devil. . . .' (IX, 238.) This even smacks of passive obedience and non-resistance, and in *The Sentiments of a Church-of-England Man* he subscribed to that doctrine: 'The Question originally put, and as I remember to have heard it disputed in publick Schools, was this; Whether under any Pretence whatsoever, it may be lawful to resist the supreme Magistrate, which was held in the Negative; and this is certainly the right Opinion.'

Yet Swift's version of the doctrine of passive obedience as developed in the *Sentiments* gives the traditional view a peculiar twist.

But many of the Clergy, and other learned Men, deceived by a dubious Expression, mistook the *Object* to which *Passive Obedience* was due. By the *Supreme Magistrate* is properly understood the Legislative Power, which in all Government must be absolute and unlimited. But the word *Magistrate* seeming to denote a *single Person*, and to express the *Executive Power*; it came to pass, that the Obedience due to the *Legislature* was, for want of knowing or considering this easy Distinction, misapplied to the *Administration*. Neither is it any Wonder, that the Clergy, or other well-meaning People should often fall into this Error, which deceived *Hobbes* himself so far, as to be the Foundation of all the political Mistakes in his Book. . . .

(II, 16)

The reference to Hobbes is significant. As we shall see, Swift was very impressed by some of the ideas expounded in the *Leviathan*. For the moment it is sufficient to note that he agrees with the doctrine of sovereignty, which had been very forcibly expressed by Hobbes. The sovereign power in the state could not logically be lawfully resisted. But the sovereign power was king in parliament, not the king alone. This was Swift's version of the doctrine of passive obedience. It would not have appealed to its traditional advocates, though it anticipated the Tory defence of Dr. Sacheverell's advocacy of the doctrine in his notorious sermon.

Elsewhere in the *Sentiments of a Church-of-England Man* Swift had implied that he was no believer in divine hereditary right: 'He doth not think . . . any one regular Species of Government, more acceptable to God than another.' (II, 14). He did not even uphold the divine right of Providence. In his first political tract, *A Discourse of the contests and dissensions between the nobles and commons in Athens and Rome*, published in 1701, he wrote: 'all Forms of Government having been instituted by Men, must be mortal like their Authors . . . .' (I, 228). As to the contract theory, although in the *Discourse* Swift left the matter open, observing '. . . it seems to me, that a free people met together, whether by compact or family government. . . .' (I, 196), years later, in his marginal comments on Burnet's *History of His Own Time*, he came out unequivocally in favour of it. When Burnet discussed the work of the Convention parliament of 1689, he described a party 'who thought that there was an original contract between the king and the people of England; by which the kings were bound to defend their people, and to govern them according to law, in lieu of which the people were bound to obey and serve the king'. Alongside this passage Swift wrote: 'I am of this party . . . ' (V, 291).

Now the contract theories then in vogue argued that before a contract was agreed men lived in a state of nature, but there were two conflicting views about the condition men were in during the state of nature. Hobbes had reasoned that in that state men were governed by their passions, and each sought his own selfish advantage, so that life had been poor, solitary, nasty, brutish and short. Locke, on the other hand, had argued that in the state of nature men were governed by reason, and life had been tolerable. Men contracted out of the Hobbesian state of nature to avert destruction and out of Locke's to avoid inconvenience.

There are indications throughout Swift's works that he subscribed to Hobbes's view of human nature rather than to Locke's. Thus in *Thoughts on various subjects* he argued: 'The Motives of the best Actions will not bear too strict an Enquiry. It is allowed, that the Cause of most Actions, good or bad, may be resolved into the Love of our selves: But the Self-Love of some Men inclines them to please others;

and the Self-Love of others is wholly employed in pleasing themselves. This makes the great Distinction between Virtue and Vice. Religion is the best Motive of all Actions; yet Religion is allowed to be the highest Instance of Self-Love.' (IV, 243) His sermon *On doing Good* opens: 'Nature directs every one of us, and God permits us, to consult our own private Good before the private Good of any other person whatsoever.' (IX, 232) When developing this argument he used an expression which might have been penned by Hobbes himself: ' . . . the law of nature, which is the law of God, obligeth me to take care of myself first . . .' But the fullest indication that he shared Hobbes's view of human nature, and of the state of nature, is to be found in Gulliver's fourth voyage. This voyage to the Houyhnhnms still taxes the ingenuity of scholars, but it seems possible that here Swift is presenting a perfect case study of the rival views of the state of nature. The horses represent the Lockean state, which is governed by reason, and the Yahoos the Hobbesian state, which is governed by the passions. There can be no doubt from Swift's direct comparisons with civil society that he himself subscribed to what we might call the pessimistic school of human nature.

Hobbes had argued in the *Leviathan* that reason could control the passions, and that self-interest rationally considered would lead men to consent to being subjected to absolute power. Swift himself was inclined to the view that 'reason were intended by Providence to govern our passions . . .' (IX, 263), but on the evidence of Gulliver's fourth voyage he had little faith in its efficacy. Reason corrupted rather than controlled the passions. Thus after Gulliver had informed his Houyhnhnm host about the institutions and customs of Europe, the horse told him that 'he looked upon us as a Sort of Animals to whose Share, by what Accident he could not conjecture, some small Pittance of *Reason* had fallen, whereof we made no other Use than by its Assistance to aggravate our *natural* Corruptions, and to acquire new ones which Nature had not given us'. (XI, 259). Elsewhere Swift argued, in his sermon on *The Testimony of Conscience*:

Fear and Hope are the two greatest natural Motives of all Men's Actions: But, neither of these Passions will ever put us in the Way of Virtue, unless they be directed by Conscience. For, although virtuous Men do sometimes accidentally make their Way to Preferment, yet the World is so corrupted, that no Man can reasonably hope to be rewarded in it, merely upon account of his Virtue. And consequently, the Fear of Punishment in this Life will preserve Men from very few Vices, since some of the blackest and basest do often prove the surest Steps to Favour: such as Ingratitude, Hypocrisy,

Treachery, Malice, Subornation, Atheism, and many more which human laws do little concern themselves about. But when Conscience placeth before us the Hopes of everlasting Happiness, and the Fears of everlasting Misery, as the Reward and Punishment of our good or evil Actions, our Reason can find no way to avoid the Force of such an Argument, otherwise then by running into Infidelity. (IX, 155).

Metaphysical sanctions, therefore, Swift considered to be absolutely necessary to preserve morality in civil society. He was also persuaded that the State should back them up with the discipline of a State Church. This is the theme of his *Project for the Advancement of Religion and the Reformation of manners*:

. . . human Nature seems to lie under this Disadvantage, that the Example alone of a vicious Prince, will in Time corrupt an Age; but the Example of a good one will not be sufficient to reform it without further Endeavours. Princes must therefore supply this Defect by a vigorous Exercise of that Authority, which the Law hath left them, by making it every Man's Interest and Honour to cultivate Religion and Virtue; by rendering Vice a Disgrace, and the certain Ruin to Preferment or Pretensions: All which they should first attempt in their own Courts and Families. For Instance, might not the Queens' Domesticks of the middle and lower Sort, be obliged upon Penalty of Suspension, or Loss of their Employments, to a constant weekly Attendance on the Service of the Church; to a decent Behaviour in it; to receive the Sacrament four times a Year; to avoid Swearing and irreligious profane Discourses; and to the Appearance at least, of Temperance and Chastity? Might not the Care of all this be committed to the strict Inspection of proper Officers? Might not those of higher Rank and nearer Access to Her Majesty, receive her own Commands to the same Purpose, and be countenanced or disfavoured according as they obey? Might not the Queen lay her Injunctions on the Bishops and other great Men of undoubted Piety, to make diligent Enquiry, and give Her Notice, whether any Person about Her should happen to be of Libertine Principles or Morals? (II, 47–8).

This system of a moral police force to encourage virtue and discourage vice was to be extended throughout the country.

'Suppose for Instance, that itinerary Commissioners were appointed to inspect every where throughout the Kingdom into the Conduct (at least) of Men in Office, with respect to their Morals and Religion, as well as their Abilities; to receive the Complaints and Informations that should be offered against them; and make their Report here upon Oath, to the Court or the Ministry; who should reward or punish accordingly.' (II, 49).

Coming from Swift such a McCarthyite nightmare might be considered satirical of the ultra-authoritarian. But unlike another modest proposal which he made this seems to have been written in all seriousness. On the question of whether or not the Church should be safeguarded by the power of the State Swift came down emphatically on the side of the authoritarians.[7]

In the absence of the coercive machinery suggested in the *Project* he considered that the existing structure of the Church of England offered the next best thing. Thus one of the *Sentiments of a Church-of-England Man* was 'a true Veneration for the Scheme established among us of Ecclesiastical Government; and although he will not determine whether Episcopacy be of Divine Right, he is sure it is most agreeable to primitive Institution, fittest, of all others for preserving Order and Purity, and under its present Regulations, best calculated for our Civil State.' (II, 5).

At this point Swift's ideas on Church and State coincided. Between them the Anglican Church and contractual government were the best guarantees of 'order and purity'. Both were threatened by Papists, dissenters, and heretics. The law should therefore curb their capacity for mischief. This had been done completely in the case of Catholics, though dissenters were allowed a limited toleration. Swift's Church of England man expressed the following sentiments on this score:

... He is for tolerating such different Forms in religious Worship as are already admitted; but, by no Means, for leaving it in the Power of those who are tolerated, to advance their own Models upon the Ruin of what is already established. . . To prevent these Inconveniences, He thinks it highly just, that all Rewards of Trust, Profit, or Dignity, which the State leaves in the Disposal of the Administration, should be given only to those, whose Principles direct them to preserve the Constitution in all its parts. (II, 6).

As for heretical literature:

He thinks it a Scandal to Government, that such an unlimited Liberty should be allowed of publishing Books against those Doctrines in Religion wherein all Christians have agreed; much more to connive at such Tracts as reject all Revelation, and, by their Consequences, often deny the very Being of God. (II, 10).

III

Such were Swift's principles with regard to Church and State. He upheld them with reasonable consistency, though as he himself wrote: 'If a Man would register all his Opinions upon Love, Politics, Religion, Learning, and the like; beginning from his Youth, and so go on to old

Age: What a Bundle of Inconsistencies and Contradictions would appear at last'. (I, 244). He did change his mind, for instance, on the degree of toleration to be allowed to dissenters. In 1704 he 'wrote against the bill that was against occasional conformity'. (*Corr.*, I, 44). In 1714 he argued:

> . . . the Church of England should be preserved entire in all Her Rights, Powers and Priviledges; All Doctrines relating to Government discouraged which She condemns; All Schisms, Sects and Heresies discountenanced and kept under due Subjection, as far as consists with the Lenity of our Constitution. Her open Enemies (among whom I include at least Dissenters of all Denominations) not trusted with the smallest Degree of Civil or Military Power; and Her secret Adversaries under the Names of Whigs, Low-Church, Republicans, Moderation-Men, and the like, receive no Marks of Favour from the Crown, but what they should deserve by a sincere Reformation. (VIII, 88).

Yet although such inconsistency might be expected of a man who changed from Whig to Tory between 1704 and 1714, Swift's transference of his allegiance cannot be attributed to a change of principles. He continued to uphold a Whig view of the State even after 1710, and protested with some sincerity to his former friend Steele in 1713, 'I have in print professed myself in politics, to be what we formerly called a Whig.' (*Corr.*, I, 359). On the other hand there can be little doubt that his outlook had always been fundamentally Tory with regard to the Church.

The anomaly of a State Whig and a Church Tory, such as Swift was, has recently been ingeniously explained. Swift, it has been alleged, by nature compromised between two extremes, and was therefore naturally a moderate in his politics.[8] The view certainly squares with the *Sentiments of a Church-of-England Man*, wherein Swift commented:

> Now, because it is a Point of Difficulty to chuse an exact Middle between two ill Extreams; it may be worth enquiring in the present Case, which of these a wise and good Man would rather seem to avoid: Taking therefore their own own good and ill Characters with due Abatements and Allowances for Partiality and Passion; I should think that, in order to preserve the Constitution entire in Church and State; whoever hath a true Value for both, would be sure to avoid the Extreams of *Whig* for the Sake of the former, and the Extreams of *Tory* on Account of the latter. (II, 24–5).

But to describe Swift as a moderate because when he was a Whig he detested dissenters, and when he was a Tory he disliked Jacobites, is to mistake political slogans for the substance of politics. On the real issues Swift was an extremist. He had little time for divine right theories of government, whether hereditary or providential, and came out wholeheartedly in favour of the contract theory. On the other hand he regarded the Anglican Church as an essential bulwark of the constitution, and wanted its position to be safeguarded by the full rigour of the law.

Now though there was no earthly reason why men should not, in the American phrase, 'split tickets' on different issues, it was remarkably uncommon at this time in English politics. The likeliest explanation of Swift's anomalous role on the political stage of early eighteenth-century England is that he was a clergyman of the Church of Ireland. James II's policy of replacing Anglicans with Catholics in key position both in Church and State had gone much farther in Ireland than in England. However much he might have interfered with privileges of the Church of England he had ridden rough-shod over those of the Church of Ireland. Thereafter there was absolutely no love lost between the Irish clergy and the hereditary Stuart line. For them Divine Right was killed stone dead at the battle of the Boyne. Their experiences had also given them a deeper hatred of the Catholics than was usual among the English clergy. At the same time the history of Ireland earlier in the seventeenth-century did little to endear them to the dissenters. Swift's own hatred of both denominations on this score comes, ironically, in his sermon *On Brotherly Love*: 'This Nation of ours hath for an Hundred Years past, been infested by two Enemies, the Papists and Fanaticks, who each, in their Turns, filled it with Blood and Slaughter, and for a Time destroyed both the Church and Government.' (IX, 172). Hatred of what James II had done in Ireland turned the Irish clergy into Whigs. Swift himself claimed to have told William III 'that the highest Tories we had with us would make tolerable Whigs there'. (II, 283: note to II, 118). On the other hand hatred of what papists and dissenters had done in Ireland turned them towards the Tories. As Archbishop King informed Swift in February 1709, 'Mr. Stoughton preached a sermon here, on the 30th of January, King Charles's martyrdom, that gives great offence. . . . Assure yourself this had an ill effect on the minds of most here; for, though they espouse the Revolution, they heartily abhor forty-one.' (*Corr.*, I, 124)

Swift shared the prejudices of the Irish clergy, and English politics therefore presented him with a real dilemma. Neither party both hated James II, the Catholic tyrant, and venerated Charles I, the Anglican martyr.

Swift first came into contact with English politicians through his connection with Sir William Temple. Since most of those he met socially were Whigs this might have predisposed him towards that party. But he did not take politics seriously until 1701, when the impeachment by the Tories of four Whig Lords prompted him to publish *A Discourse on the contests and dissensions between the nobles and the commons in Athens and Rome*. Even this was more in the nature of an academic exercise than a polemical tract, and it was not until 1702, when he met Somers and Halifax, that he became closely involved in English politics.

Swift later wrote the following account of his attitude to the parties at that time:

> It was then I first began to trouble myself with the differences between the principles of Whig and Tory; having formerly employed myself in other, and, I think, much better speculations. I talked often upon this subject with Lord Sommers; told him, that, having been long conversant with the Greek and Roman authors, and therefore a lover of liberty, I found myself much inclined to be what they called a Whig in politics; and that, besides, thought it impossible, upon any other principle, to defend or submit to the Revolution: But, as to religion, I confessed myself to be an High-churchman, and that I did not conceive how any one, who wore the habit of a clergyman, could be otherwise: That I had observed very well with what insolence and haughtiness some Lords of the High-church party treated not only their own chaplains, but all other clergymen whatsoever, and thought this was sufficiently recompensed by their professions of zeal to the church: That I had likewise observed how the Whig Lords took a direct contrary measure, treated the persons of particular clergymen with great curtesy, but showed much ill-will and contempt for the order in general: That I knew it was necessary for their party, to make their bottom as wide as they could, by taking all denominations of Protestants to be members of their body: That I would not enter into the mutual reproaches made by the violent men on either side: but, that the connivance, or encouragement, given by the Whigs to those writers of pamphlets, who reflected upon the whole body of the clergy, without any exception, would unite the church, as one man, to oppose them. . . (VIII, 120).

When the Whigs came to power in 1708 they embarked on a series of measures which did cement the great majority of Anglican clergymen into an alliance against them. Swift himself drew the line when they proposed to repeal the Test Act in Ireland, and identified himself with the Tory opposition to the other measures:

> We opposed Repealing the *Test*, which would level the Church Established, with every snivelling Sect in the Nation. We opposed the Bill of General Naturalisation, by which we were in danger to be

over-run by Schismaticks and Beggars: The Scheme of breaking into the Statutes of Colleges, which obliged the Fellows to take holy Orders; the Impeachment of Dr. *Sacheverill*; the hopeful Project of limiting Clergymen what to preach; with several others of the same Stamp, were strenuously opposed, as manifestly tending to the Ruin of the Church. (VI, 130)

In 1710 Robert Harley engineered the overthrow of the Whigs and took over the direction of affairs at the head of a predominantly Tory ministry. Since Harley had been one of the chief architects of the Act of Settlement in 1701, which confirmed the Revolution Settlement by placing the succession in the House of Hanover, Swift's fears that an alliance with the Tories implied the repudiation of the Revolution were set at rest. He could collaborate with this new ministry without discarding a single principle.

Harley's role in Swift's conversion was crucial. Though they were very far from seeing eye to eye on all things, especially on Church matters, the new Prime Minister had a programme which he knew Swift's able pen could help him to get through—peace with France. Swift never sacrificed consistency with regard to Church and State, and so never fully appreciated the real division between the English parties on these abstract issues, but on the concrete question of peace or war he recognised a Whig or a Tory when he saw one. 'By this time,' he wrote in the *History of the Four Last Years of the Queen*, 'all Disputes about those principles, which used Originally to divide [Whig] and Tory, were wholly dropped, and those Fantastick Words ought in justice to have been so too; Provided we could have found out more convenient Names, whereby to distinguish Lovers of peace from Lovers of War.' (VII, 3). This was just the conviction which he needed to give him the enthusiasm of the real convert.[9]

The notion that the Whigs loved the war, while the Tories longed for peace was based on the supposition that the Whig party represented the moneyed men of the City, who profited from the loans raised by the government to finance the war, while the Tory party represented the men of landed estates who suffered from the heavy land taxes levied for the same purpose. This is not the place to determine whether or not this theory had any real basis in fact. What is to the immediate point is that Swift pushed it about as far as it would go. He embarked on one of the most controversial campaigns in the history of political journalism, and developed the theory into a thesis that the war had been a conspiracy between the Duke of Marlborough and military men in general, the Whigs, the City and the Allies, to enrich themselves at the expense of the Tory gentry. The opening shots in this campaign were

G

fired in his very first contribution to the *Examiner*, which came out on 2 November 1710:

> Let any Man observe the Equipages in this Town; he shall find the greater Number of those who make a Figure, to be a Species of Men quite different from any that were ever known before the Revolution; consisting either of Generals and Colonels, or of such whose whole Fortunes lie in Funds and Stocks: so that *Power*, which, according to the old Maxim, was used to follow *Land*, is now gone over to *Money*; and the Country Gentleman is in the Condition of a young Heir, out of whose Estate a Scrivener receives half the Rents for Interest, and hath a Mortgage on the Whole; and is therefore always ready to feed his Vices and Extravagancies while there is any Thing left. So that if the War continues some Years longer, a Landed Man will be little better than a Farmer at a rack Rent, to the Army, and to the publick Funds. (III, 5).

This campaign reached its height in November 1711 with the publication of his most effective pamphlet, *The Conduct of the Allies*. Its theme was that the allies had made Britain bear the main burden of the Grand Alliance while they reaped all its advantages. In the course of developing this argument Swift stated the conspiracy thesis at its baldest:

> But the common Question is, If we must now Surrender *Spain*, what have we been Fighting for all this while? The Answer is ready; We have been Fighting for the Ruin of the Publick Interest, and the Advancement of a Private. We have been fighting to raise the Wealth and Grandeur of a particular Family; to enrich Usurers and Stock-jobbers; and to cultivate the pernicious Designs of a Faction, by destroying the Landed-Interest. The Nation begins now to think these *Blessings* are not worth Fighting for any longer, and therefore desires a peace. (VI, 58–9).

This attack on the Whigs and allies did much to make the Tory peace popular.[10] Yet for Swift it was flying in the face of fortune. For a few years he revelled in the favour of the great Tory politicians, but when the Whigs came into their own in 1714 they did not forget the man who had libelled them so mercilessly. Nor did George I, who as Elector of Hanover had been one of the allies whose conduct Swift had castigated. Swift left London before Anne's death, despairing of saving the Tory cause when its leaders were like 'a Ship's Crew quarrelling in a Storm, or while their Enemies are within Gun Shott.' (VIII, 87). The death of the Queen merely hastened his departure from the country, and he landed in Ireland before George I arrived in England. Twelve years were to pass before he returned to London. He never re-entered the charmed circle of the court. If Swift's authorship of *A*

Tale of a Tub debarred him from high ecclesiastical preferment under Anne, his propaganda for the Tories sentenced him to exile from high political circles under the Hanoverians.

He was intellectually as well as physically remote from the political world of the Hanoverians. His views on the Church, if not on the State, became increasingly outmoded as Whig latitudinarian principles triumphed. The great Dean of St. Patrick's was not at home in the 'pudding time' of the Vicar of Bray, when 'moderate men looked big'. His politics were of an earlier epoch, firmly set in the last four years of Queen Anne. Something of Swift's nostalgia for that era can be detected in the dating of Gulliver's last voyage, wherein the traveller became the guest of the most civilised creatures he ever encountered, between September, 1710, the month in which Queen Anne dissolved parliament and made her final break with the Whigs, and February 1715, when the first General Election to be held under the Hanoverians finally broke the power of the Tories. In choosing those dates Swift surely had in mind the period when he, too, had lived in a world more sympathetic to his views.

NOTES

[1] British Museum Additional MSS 47027, pp. 259–60. Sir John Percival to Daniel Dering, 22 June, 1714.

[2] In *English Politics in the early Eighteenth Century* (Oxford, 1956), Robert Walcott denied the validity of a two-party political context, and offered instead a multi-party framework. His thesis, never generally accepted by historians, must be emphatically rejected following its demolition in two major contributions to the period: Geoffrey Holmes, *British Politics in the Age of Anne* (1967); and J. H. Plumb, *The Growth of Political Stability in England* 1675–1725 (1967). It was most unfortunate that both these works appeared too late to be taken into account by Irvin Ehrenpreis in the second volume of his *Swift: the man, his works and the age* (1967), which, unhappily, relies on Walcott's thesis (see especially, pp. 252–4).

[3] G. Straka, 'The Final Phase of Divine Right Theory in England', *English Historical Review* (1962), lxxvii, 638–658.

[4] It was a commonplace among political writers in Anne's reign to deplore the existence of parties. Usually this was no more than conventional, and hypocritical, political piety. Almost always the other side was blamed for the fall from grace—one's own party being 'the honest interest', while the other side was 'the faction'. Swift appears to have been more genuine in his exhortations to virtue; cf. *The Sentiments of a Church-of-England Man* (II, 1–2).

[5] The trouble is to know when Swift was taking them seriously. As with his major satires so in his political writings it can be difficult to decide if he is speaking himself, or if he is using a 'mask'. In reconstructing his political thought I have relied chiefly on his sermons, and on two pamphlets which seem to me to contain far more of Swift's own views, and far less propaganda, than most others which he wrote in Anne's reign: *The Sentiments of a Church-*

of-England Man, written in 1704, but not published until 1711; [see Irvin Ehrenpreis, 'The Date of Swift's Sentiments', Review of English Studies n.s. (1952), iii, 272–4]; and A Project for the Advancement of Religion and the Reformation of Manners.

⁶ The need to uphold the correct balance between Crown, Peers and people was the main theme of his first pamphlet, A Discourse of the Contests and Dissensions . . . in Athens and Rome', (1701), (I, 193–236).

⁷As late as 1728 Swift was still thinking seriously about a moral reform of public life. In the fragmentary Notes for a 'Proposal for Virtue' recently published for the first time (XIV, 14–15), one of the points made is that 'In private life Virtue may be difficult by passions infirmityes, temptations, want of power, strong opposition, etc., but not in publick administration; there it makes all things easy' (XIV, 14).

⁸ Kathleen Williams, Jonathan Swift and the Age of Compromise (University of Kansas Press, 1958), pp. 100–101.

⁹ Cf. A Discourse of the Contests . . . in Athens and Rome, where Swift wrote of 'an univeral Fear and Apprehension of the Greatness of the Power of France, whereof the People, in general, seem to be very much, and justly possessed. . . .'(I, 235).

¹⁰ For a detailed discussion of Swift's effectiveness as a propagandist for the Harley Ministry see Michael Foot, The Pen and the Sword (1957).

Swift and the Baconian Idol †

BRIAN VICKERS

The study of the intellectual sources (and so, the targets) of Swift's earliest and most allusive satires has so far been focused quite successfully on the second half of the seventeenth century. We are now in a good position to judge just how Swift has satirized or parodied Anglican Rationalists, Cabbalists, Alchemists, the Royal Society and its *Transactions*, Boyle, Dryden, and most recently, L'Estrange. But in concentrating on the work published nearest in time to Swift, we have lost sight of work produced earlier, but still very current in Swift's day, that of the father-figure behind much seventeenth-century thought, Francis Bacon. I want to suggest that Bacon stood for many things that Swift detested, and that Swift expressed his scorn, as so often, in parody, mocking Bacon's opinions, attitudes, and even his style.

There can be no doubt, first, that Swift knew Bacon, and that the men closest to Swift in his formative years not only knew but admired and were influenced by the 'father of experimental philosophy'. Swift himself owned several copies of Bacon, as we see from the catalogues of his library[1]: in the list which he drew up in 1715 among 'miscellaneous folios' we find: 'Bacon, Advancement of Learning—2s. 6d.' and among the smaller books, 'Bacon's Essays, 1691.' The first is not the original version written in English and published by Bacon in 1605 as *The Twoo Bookes of Francis Bacon Of the proficience and aduancement of Learning, diuine and humane* but the expansion of that into nine books published in Latin in 1623 as the *De Augmentis Scientiarum*, and translated back into English by Gilbert Wats (1640, second edition 1674). This was in fact the normal text of the *Advancement* to be used in this period, and equally typical is Swift's copy of the *Essays* in that it also contains Bacon's *Colours of Good and Evil* and *The Wisdom of the Ancients* in the translation of Sir Arthur Gorges.[2] And in the Catalogue of Swift's books to be sold after his death[3] item 627 is

* Baconi Fran. Opera Omnia. Lond. 1630.[4]

We do not know the whereabouts of any of these books, and the loss is

† I should like to record my thanks for helpful criticism of this essay to Mr. George Watson, Professor Denis Donoghue, and above all to the late Professor Herbert Davis, who corrected several errors and encouraged me to take the argument beyond the mere listing of parallels to the consideration both of Swift's general attitude to Bacon and of the ways in which he constructed his parodies.

especially tantalizing for the last one, as the asterisk shows, contained marginalia—I should guess in the vitriolic mode which he shares with another unsympathetic annotator of Bacon, Blake.

So there is evidence that Swift owned, read, and scribbled on Bacon. He was also exposed to the influence of his teachers at Trinity College, Dublin, and Irvin Ehrenpreis[5] and Edward Rosenheim[6] have shown that the new philosophy was flourishing there in the Dublin Philosophical Society. A prominent experimenter was Ashe, Swift's 'tutor and lifelong friend', and in the few excerpts that Ehrenpreis gives from Ashe there are (inevitably) several Baconian echoes. Swift may have respected Ashe, but he certainly detested another Dublin advocate for the new science, Bishop Narcissus Marsh, one of whose papers on acoustics is definitely parodied in *A Tale of a Tub*. When Swift moved from Ireland to England, the situation is repeated: again the senior person to whom he looks for intellectual guidance is one who reads and respects Bacon. In Sir William Temple's works there are many echoes of Bacon, and in *Ancient and Modern Learning* Temple, despite his preference for the Classics, had named Bacon as one of 'The great Wits among the Moderns', so it is doubtless in deference to his patron's respect that in *The Battle of the Books* the arrow shot at Bacon by Aristotle misses its mark. (I, 156). Swift may have deferred to Temple here, but what Herbert Davis has described as 'the difficulty of adapting himself to Temple's standards both in life and in letters' (I, xiii) results—could only result—in opposition to this Idol of the last age. Nor was Swift deterred by the last biographical detail I shall cite, the curious fact that he was actually related to Bacon[7]—although he was proud of his ancestry, it was not enough to alter some of his deepest antipathies.

To get a clearer picture of what Bacon represented for Swift we must look first at the status of the new science. Bacon's impact on seventeenth-century science has been magnificently analysed by Richard Foster Jones in his *Ancients and Moderns: A Study of the Rise of the Scientific Movement in 17th Century England* (1936; second edition, 1961). Professor Jones has documented in great deatil the stages by which Bacon's influence spread: there is no substitute for reading his account, I merely want to select some of the relevant points. First, characteristic of the age, the universal chorus of praise, extolling Bacon in the most extravagant terms: Bacon as 'the Masterbuilder' of the new system (Jones, p. 89), 'the Learned and incomparable Author' (p. 161), 'the Master . . . from whom I received my first light' (p. 161), 'that Patriarck of Experimental Philosophy' (p. 191), 'that Great Genius of Rational Nature' (p. 221), 'my heroic Master', 'honoured Lord and Master' (p. 292). Not only minor figures praised

him, but important ones too, especially those writers associated with
the Royal Society: Thomas Sprat writing the *History of the Royal Society*
gives Bacon the credit for inspiring its foundation: he 'had the true
Imagination of the whole extent of this Enterprize as it is now set on
foot' (Jones, p. 234). In the frontispiece to the *History* Bacon shares
pride of place with Charles II; in the *Ode to the Royal Society* by Cowley
Bacon is described as the Moses who first led us to that promised land;
Dryden, in his verses to Dr. Charleton confidently predicts that

> The World to Bacon does not only owe
> Its present knowledge, but its future too.

Joseph Glanvill finds Bacon 'illustrious', 'immortal', 'deep and
judicious', praising the 'mighty Design . . . *recommended* by the *Glorious
Author*, who began *nobly* and directed with an *incomparable conduct* of
Wit and *Judgment*'; he is 'that great Man', the 'noble Advancer of
Learning, whose name and parts might give credit to any undertaking'.
(Jones, pp. 239, 240, 305).

The praise continues from the mouths of distinguished scientists
too: the Frenchman Samuel Sorbière, who made a voyage to England
in 1663 and did not like much of what he saw, makes an exception for
Bacon, and in terms of a remarkable panegyric:

> But to speak the Truth, the Lord Chancellor *Bacon* has surpassed all
> the rest in the Vastness of his Designs, and that Learned and Judici-
> ous Tablature he has left us. . . . This undoubtedly is the greatest
> Man for the Interest of Natural Philosophy that ever was, and the
> Person that first put the World upon making Experiments that way.[8]

Still more impressive is the testimony of the greatest English scientist
of the age, Robert Boyle: Professor Jones records that

> Every mention of Sir Francis is instinct with praise, and he is
> mentioned again and again in Boyle's writings. He is most frequently
> 'excellent Verulam' or 'illustrious Verulam', but the unvarying
> tribute finds varied expression: 'a great and candid philosopher',
> 'that great ornament and guide of philosophical historians of nature',
> 'one of the most judicious Naturalists that our Age can boast',
> 'that great Restorer of Physics', 'our famous experimenter', 'the
> first and greatest experimental philosopher of our age', and 'the
> great architect of experimental history' (p. 170).

And this is only a fraction of Boyle's eulogies.

It is tiring to read such endless, boundless praise, even in this
relatively short list of allusions which modern scholarship has retrieved:
how possibly to gauge what the actual situation was in the 1690's?
No wonder that one of the few opponents of the Royal Society, Henry

Stubbe, should exclaim bitterly of the uniformity of 'this *Bacon-faced*
generation' (Jones, p. 258, 340). For Bacon had excelled in so many
different fields—scientist, philosopher, statesman, apologist for the
government in politics and religion, lawyer, essayist, and so on. As
Oldenburg wrote, dedicating Volume 5 of the *Philosophical Transactions*
to Boyle: in Bacon's time,

> It cannot be doubted, but that *England* had then better knowledge of
> the abstrusities, many troubles and burthens of our Municipal Laws,
> and Chancery, which lay long and much upon his shoulders; And
> that he bore the stress of State affairs in almost all King *James's* days,
> and in Queen *Elizabeth's* later days; That he adorned the solemn
> Addresses, and was the Extra-Ordinary Pen-man for most Apologies,
> Deliberations, and gravest Adviso's in Parliaments, and otherwise:
> Here they saw also, how he excelled in the best Theology of that Age,
> and in the Politest of Civil and Moral Essays: And therefore here
> they might justly wonder, how a person so publickly immersed in all
> Civil Interests should find leisure to do any thing at all in *Philosophy*;

—and particularly that without any specialised training or scientific
apparatus 'he should so much transcend the Philosophers, then living,
in judicious and clear instructions, in so many useful Observations and
Discoveries; I think I may say beyond the Records of many Ages'.[9]
Faced with an achievement as widespread as this, it is not surprising
that writers should strain after the highest possible terms of comparison
for this polymath who still dominated culture: 'our English *Plato*';
'our English *Trismegistus*'; 'our English *Aristotle*'; 'that great Dictator
of Learning' (Gibson, items 356, 632, 648, 391).

And if you read Section V of *A Tale of a Tub* in connection with
this reverence for Bacon's polymathic learning then the attack on 'a
certain Author called *Homer*' (I, 74–80) takes on a new interest. In the
famous letter to Burghley (first published in 1657 in Rawley's important
collection of miscellaneous works, the *Resuscitatio*)—Bacon had written
'I have taken all knowledge to be my Province'[10]: the Modern Author
complains of 'Homer' that 'whereas, we are assured, he design'd his
Work for a compleat Body of all Knowledge Human, Divine, Political,
and Mechanick; it is manifest, he hath wholly neglected some, and
been very imperfect in the rest'. Certainly Bacon can be said to have
'designed' his work as a complete system in a way which Homer did
not: as a contemporary of Swift's wrote, from Bacon's 'works may be
deduced the whole system of natural knowledge', and Bacon's own
division of knowledge into human and divine seems to be mocked
here. I would not claim that everything in this section refers to Bacon,
for the irony is complex and perhaps deliberately confused, but it is

odd that several of the detailed faults or omissions of 'Homer' refer to topics on which either Bacon has himself written or where writers have claimed him as patron. As R. F. Jones has shown (p. 123f.,), even the Alchemists professed to be inspired by Bacon (it is certainly true that he made much use of the Alchemists' assumptions and methods), and in works of Vaughan which Swift refers to Bacon is familiarly taken as approving Alchemists (Gibson 621, 622)—even Rapin, in his *Reflexions upon Ancient and Modern Philosophy* describes Bacon as a Cabbalist (Gibson, 555). The very titles of some works by Bacon seem to be echoed, too: Oldenburg had referred to his ability in law, theology, and politics, and among the works which had been printed by this time and were well known are his *Elements of the Common Laws of England* (which includes *Rules and Maxims of the Common Law* and the *Use of the Common Law*), and two tracts on the *Controversies of the Church of England*. Yet the writer of the *Tale* has 'a Fault far more notorious to tax this Author with; I mean, his gross Ignorance in the *Common Laws of this Realm*, and in the Doctrine as well as Discipline of the Church of *England*'.

This parallel could, of course, be just a coincidence—but as so often, I think that Swift's satire, although thought to be only vaguely allusive, is specific yet distorted: you see a direct reference, but at the same time there is something oblique about it too. Take some of the smaller references here: Bacon is very fond of citing the discoveries of the compass and gunpowder as evidence of modern inventors' excellence—but then, so is every other supporter of the moderns; the jibes about the spleen and 'Salivation without Mercury' certainly point to aspects of Bacon's medical and mineral knowledge known and respected at this time[11]; and as for the unsatisfactory nature of 'Homer's long Dissertation upon *Tea*', it is interesting to note that in 1663 there appeared a work called *The Vertues of Coffee* 'Set forth in the works of the Lord *Bacon* his *Natural Hist.[ory]*'. (Gibson, 623). Bacon seems to be everywhere—as indeed he was in the seventeenth century—but the difficulty is to know where to stop in suggesting allusions. The peculiar quality of Swift's satiric attacks on particular victims is that he advances fiercely on them yet withdraws very quickly, so leaving the reader who is trying to identify the victim in a state of hesitation, lacking the confidence to make a consistent identification. Of course Swift knows what he's doing—as he makes his annotator say, 'I believe one of the Author's Designs was to set curious Men a hunting thro' Indexes, and enquiring for Books out of the common Road'. Having been caught myself, I think that the real joke is that in Swift's day the works of Bacon were not 'out of the common road'—few less so, as the vast numbers of editions remind us: by 1702 no less than 230 editions of his works in English, Latin, French, German, Italian—a staggering figure.

To Swift, and his contemporaries, then, Bacon stands as a monument of human learning, particularly in the new science, towards which (and especially to the abuses of which) Swift had deep and long-persisting antipathies,[12] from the parody of scientific jargon in the *Tale* to the mock transactions of the Royal Society of Laputa, and that sublime dismissal of Newton: 'The Man it seems was knighted for making Sun-Dials better than others of his Trade, and was thought to be a Conjurer, because he knew how to draw Lines and Circles upon a Slate, which nobody could understand.'[13] The most important aspect of Bacon's scientific thought so far as Swift is concerned is, paradoxically, not the constructive programme of observation, experiment, and co-operation, (I say paradoxically, given Swift's hatred of systems and system-builders), but the preliminary destructive movement, the demolition of previous systems, in Bacon's imagery the clearing of the ground before building afresh. Bacon refers mockingly to Aristotle's attack on his predecessors: 'Aristotle, after the Ottoman fashion, thought that he could not reign safely unless he put all his brethren to death' (B, 4, 358), yet Bacon constantly attacks Aristotle, Plato and all other classical philosophers, though keeping some respect for the Atomists. You find Bacon reminding himself in his notebook of 1608 to go on attacking the Ancients—'Discoursing skornfully of the philosophy of the graecians' (B, 11, 64), and besides innumerable hostile references to Aristotle, he composes a whole work of destruction, the *Redargutio Philosophiarum* ('The Refutation of Philosophies'). A typical instance of this violence comes from a work called *The Masculine Birth of Time*,[14] where he harshly arraigns the philosophers of antiquity:

> Let Aristotle first appear; whom we charge (1) with abominable Sophistry; (2) useless Subtilty; and (3) a vile sporting with words. . . . Let Plato next appear; whom we charge with being (1) a well-bred Sophister; (2) a tumid Poet; and (3) a fanatical Divine. . . .

This violence would not have endeared him to Swift, who in his alignment on the Ancient's side is bound to see Bacon as the most offensive Modern.

Bacon's attack on the Ancients was echoed by all his followers—indeed, he can be said to have set the tone for several generations of abuse. This is another development which has been clearly analyzed by R. F. Jones, who describes 'reverence for antiquity' as 'the most significant obstacle to the advancement of science', and shows just how Bacon's influence became dominant, though interpreted with even more virulence (pp. 43, 46, 146). Another Baconian attitude which was influential and should be mentioned here as Swift links it to the preceding one, is the paradox which Bacon used to discredit stultifying reverence for the past, the paradox that the present age is in fact antiquity: as Bacon expresses it: 'And to speak truly, *Antiquitas saeculi juventus mundi.* These times are the ancient times, when the world is ancient, and not those which we account *ordine retrogrado*, by a computation backward from ourselves' (B, 3, 291). This idea was associated with Baconians throughout the century[15] (e.g. Jones, p. 78, 120, 138, 305), and was taken up by Swift three times in these early satires, in the *Mechanical Operation of the Spirit*, where it is linked with 'a sort of Modern Authors, who have too *literal* an Understanding; and, because Antiquity is to be traced *backwards*, do therefore, like *Jews*, begin their Books at the wrong End, as if Learning were a sort of *Conjuring*' (I, 186); he refers to it again in *The Battle of the Books*, with a marginal note adding 'According to the Modern Paradox' (*Ibid.*, 147). In the *Tale* Swift adds a footnote which links the process by which 'our Illustrious *Moderns* have eclipsed the weak glimmering Lights of the *Antients*' quite clearly with Bacon:

> The Learned Person here meant by our Author, hath been endeavouring to annihilate so many Antient Writers, that until he is pleas'd to stop his hand it will be dangerous to affirm, whether there have been ever any Antients in the World.
> (*Ibid*, 78; just before the attack on 'Homer'.)

Swift adds the wit by which the paradox is inverted yet again, and so deflated.

There is one last point common to the Baconian scientific movement which Swift seizes on, the image very frequent in Bacon of Truth being hid in a well, or in a mine, to be reached by digging—himself as a 'pioneer in the mine of truth'. (B, 3, 219; 3, 503; 4, 88–90, etc.). This image is repeated and elaborated by the Baconians: John Webster in his *Academiarum Examen* (1654) naturally enough attacks Aristotle's Philosophy for being full of 'speculative and fruitless conceits', not fit to 'lead man practically to dive into the internal centre of natures abstruse and occult operations: But is only conversant about the shell, and husk, handling the accidental, external, and recollacious qualities of things confusedly', unsatisfying to a 'discreet and wary understanding, that expects *Apodictical*, and experimental manuduction into the more interiour clossets of nature' (Jones, p. 137–8). Similarly Thomas Vaughan attacks the Aristotelians with the same image: 'for verily as long as they lick the shell in this fashion and *pierce* not *experimentally* into the *Center* of *things* . . .' (Jones, p. 125), and Oldenburg praises two of Boyle's tracts for containing 'most diving Researches into some of the deepest Recesses of Nature, that ever appear'd in Publick; . . . .'[16] This Baconian image of penetrating the surface into the heart of truth is, I suggest, mocked by Swift in the Hack's complaint about the 'superficial Vein among many Readers of the present Age, who will by no means be persuaded to inspect beyond the Surface and the Rind of Things; whereas, *Wisdom* is a *Fox*, who after long hunting, will at last cost you the Pains to dig out. . . .' (I, 40). The language is of course far removed from the jargon of the scientists, but it is in the direction of taking the basic image—the coat of the cheese, the shell of the nut—and applying it quite literally but adding a subversive, irreverent detail—a maggot, a worm. As ever, by the time Swift has finished with the parody, the object of it is quite devalued: we now see the absurdity inherent in this idea of diving down, penetrating some thing in order to discover truth; the zeal of the scientist is revealed to resemble the zeal of a worm or a maggot—as Swift observed elsewhere, 'Climbing is performed in the same posture as creeping'.

Not all of Bacon's influence was limited to the scientific movement, however, and Swift picks up various ideas and attitudes of Bacon for satiric comment, especially in *A Tale of A Tub*. Analysis of all the references to Bacon in this work show that Swift concentrates his attack not in the central allegory of the three brothers, but in the more literary sections, the digressions, particularly associating Bacon with the absurdities of the Modern Author, as if to suggest that the idol of the last age has been totally devalued. Several critics have commented on Swift's scorn for human pride in man as the measure of all things, as seen in the title of one of the works promised by the Modern Author: Kathleen Williams sees Book 4 of *Gulliver* as the culmination of Swift's 'lifelong attack on the pride of man, especially the pride which convinces him that he can live by the light of his unaided reason, the pride that Swift himself sums up, in the title of his imaginary discourses in *A Tale of a Tub* as *An Universal Rule of Reason, or Every Man his own Carver*.' (I, 80). Nigel Dennis relates the title to Swift's praise of England before chaos, the reign of Charles I: 'Belief in a single authority has been replaced by a detestable individualism that Swift describes in another admirable phrase: *Every Man his own Carver*'.[17]

But Swift did not invent the phrase: it is another jibe at Bacon, this time for his use of the post-Machiavellian concept of *virtù*, the Renaissance idea that a man's innate qualities can allow him to transcend social limitations. Bacon discussed the idea in the *Advancement of Learning*, and developed it at length in Book 8 of the *De Augmentis*, beginning with the two quotations he was very fond of:

> This wisdom for oneself the Romans, though excellent guardians of their country, took much knowledge of; 'For', says the comic poet, 'a wise man fashions his fortune for himself'. And it grew into an adage amongst them, 'Every man is the maker of his own fortune.' (B, 5, 57).

The Latin phrase is *'Faber quisque fortunae suae'*, and it recurs many times in Bacon,[18] and was definitely associated with him, for this section (together with other excerpts from the *De Augmentis* on related aspects of world advancement) was issued as a separate treatise, the *Faber Fortunae*. As such it was reprinted no less than seven times between 1641 and 1685, usually together with the Latin translation of the *Essays*.[19] It found its audience, naturally enough, in bourgeois hopes of advancement, and had certainly 'come home to the bosom of' Samuel Pepys, for as R. C. Cochrane has recently shown,[20] Pepys owned and loved this work. The phrase is usually translated as 'Architect of Fortune', or 'Carpenter', though Philemond Holland, translating Livy, rendered it as 'Every man should be his own carver'[21]: Swift chooses the version nearest to banality, and yet another Baconian bulwark is undermined.

Bacon's *Faber Fortunae* has long since dropped out of general awareness: so, too, has his *Wisdom of the Ancients*, a collection of fables (re-interpreted to show the needs and intentions of the new science) which was very popular in the seventeenth century, and often reprinted with the *Essays*, as indeed in the copy Swift owned. Fables and parables were attractive to Bacon as modes of communication which, like his favourite form, the aphorism, could contain pregnant thought in an unpretentious and flexible frame. He often alludes to their popularity in antiquity, and when he does so he tends to lump them all together in an unnecessarily long list of similar details, writing in the *Advancement* that 'Religion sought ever an accesse, and way to the *Mind*, by *Similitudes*; *Types*; *Parables*; *Visions*; *Dreams*' (B, 4, 406; Wats p. 218). Swift mocks both the idea and the list-form directly in describing the oratorical machines as 'a great Mystery; being a Type, a Sign, an Emblem, a Shadow, a Symbol'. (I, 37). Again in his Preface to *The Wisdom of the Ancients* Bacon argues that

> in the first Ages . . . all Things were full of Fables, Enigma's, Parables, and Similies of all sorts: By which they sought to teach, and lay open, not to hide and conceal knowledge . . . for as Hieroglyphicks preceded Letters, so Parables were more Ancient than Arguments. (B, 6, 698; *Essays*, 1706 ed. Sig. O₆ʳ).

The last reference to hieroglyphics (which occurs also in the *Advancement*, B, 3, 344) has been noted by editors in connection with similar reference in the *Tale* (I, 59; GS, 97), but it has not been seen that Bacon's earlier point is mocked there too:

> In consequence of these momentous Truths, the *Grubaean* Sages have always chosen to convey their Precepts and their Arts, shut up within the Vehicles of Types and Fables. (I, 40).

Swift does not merely mock the idea and its expression: he distorts it, for Bacon explicitly said that the function of this genre was 'to teach, and lay open, not to hide and conceal': Swift has their Precepts 'shut up within the Vehicles', so making it rather pointless and suggesting total liberty to the interpreters. Bacon is deflated not only by such distorted parody, but by association—he is now a 'Grubaean' (so much more portentous than merely 'Grub-street') sage. And not only is his theory of fables mocked, but possibly his practice, for Bacon often uses fables (e.g. B, 3, 470), though never in such a banal way as the Modern's apologist.

Swift also takes occasion to satirize Bacon's use of the normal Renaissance division of the intellectual faculties—the will, appetite, affections, reason, imagination. We are familiar with Swift's devaluation of the concepts themselves, often by imagery, as when he uses the Platonic image of man as a charioteer controlling the horses of reason and the passions and deflates it by taking it literally and then inverting the real positions: '. . . when a Man's Fancy gets *astride* on his Reason. . . .' (I, 108; Swift's italics). This of course, is another distortion, the Platonic charioteer being reduced to a (possibly bareback) rider. So on the same page of the *Advancement* where he had found Bacon listing 'Similitudes; Types; Parables' he now finds him using the traditional separation of the faculties, and making it easier to understand by expressing it in a metaphorical, concrete form: Gilbert Wats' translation even improves on it, by adding after 'Nuncius' or 'messenger' the explanatory 'or common Atturny':

> *Logique intreateth of the understanding and Reason*; *Ethique of the Will*; *Appetite*; *and Affections*; the one produceth *Decrees*; the other *Actions*. It is true that the *Imagination* in both Provinces, Iudiciall and Ministeriall, performes the Offices of an Agent or Nuncius, or common Atturney. For *Sense* sends over all sorts of Ideas unto the *Imagination*, upon which, *Reason* afterwards sits in Judgment: And *Reason* interchangeably sends over selected and approved Ideas to the *Imagination*, before the Decree can be acted. . . . Neither is the *Imagination* a meer and simple Messenger, but is invested with, or at leastwise

usurpeth no small Auctoritie besides the duty of the message. (Wats p. 218; B, 4, 405–6).

Once familiar with Swift's techniques of deflation through parody you can almost predict which element he will seize on: the rather ludicrous idea of these separate bodies buzzing about according to a well-observed code of discipline and employment. So he makes the Modern's Narrator say in his closing paragraph:

> In my Disposure of Employments of the Brain, I have thought fit to make *Invention* the *Master*, and to give *Method* and *Reason*, the Office of its *Lacquays*. (I, 134).

There is the deflation, made doubly cutting with another inversion: Reason is for the Narrator not master but servant, and at that a concretely menial one—and the mock gains greatly from the precision with which it is delivered. All's fair in Love, War and Satire.

So far I have been considering examples of Swift's derisive attitude to some aspects of Bacon's influence: I want to produce some more evidence of derision attached to Bacon himself, particularly his style, but first I should like to suggest that Swift was not above borrowing some ideas from Bacon seriously, that is to say that the debts may fit into a satiric context but they are not mocked in themselves. Some allusions of this kind have already been noted by A. C. Guthkelch and D. Nichol Smith in their edition of *A Tale of a Tub*.[22] As a transition from satirical to serious, on the same page of the *Tale* (I, 108: GS 172) where we have just found the parody of Bacon's personification of the intellectual faculties they note two borrowings from Bacon which add definite substance to Swift's argument yet receive relatively slight satiric treatment. As so often the borrowing occurs during a digression, that 'concerning Madness': Swift's theme is that Happiness is '*a perpetual Possession of being well Deceived*', and he begins with the power of the imagination: ' 'tis manifest, what mighty Advantages Fiction has over Truth; and the Reason is just at our Elbow; because Imagination can build nobler scenes, and produce more wonderful revolutions than Fortune or Nature will be at Expence to furnish' (there is a hint of something ridiculous in the last clause, as in the whole next sentence). The editors cite the well-known passage in the *Advancement* on poetry: 'The use of this Feigned History hath been to give some shadow of satisfaction to the mind of man in those points wherein the nature of things doth deny it. . . . Therefore, because the acts or events of true history have not that magnitude which satisfieth the mind of man, poesy feigneth acts and events greater and more heroical' (B, 3, 343). An immediate reaction on reading this passage in Bacon could be to speculate on the falseness and the delusion involved, by reference to 'true history', in the creation of this imaginary world. And this is just how Swift proceeds, reducing the idea to absurdity:

> How fade and insipid do all Objects accost us that are not convey'd in the vehicle of *Delusion*? How shrunk is every Thing, as it appears in the Glass of Nature? So, that if it were not for the Assistance of Artificial *Mediums*, false Lights, refracted Angles, Varnish, and Tinsel; there would be a mighty Level in the Felicity and Enjoyments of Mortal Men. (I, 109; GS 172).

Common sense alone tells us that this is an absurd overstatement of the relationship between truth and delusion: yet it is an absurdity which has been carefully controlled by Swift and at several points it recalls familiar passages in Bacon. Guthkelch and Smith note the main resemblance, to the Essay 'Of Truth', and to a dispassionate, slightly cynical, point of Bacon's:

> this same truth is a naked and open day-light that doth not shew the masks and mummeries and triumphs of the world, half so stately and daintily as candle-lights. . . . Doth any man doubt, that if there were taken out of men's minds vain opinions, flattering hopes, false valuations, imaginations as one would, and the like, but it would leave the minds of a number of men poor shrunken things . . . unpleasing to them selves? (B, 6, 377–8).

That account is of course properly qualified, Swift's simple and extreme (his parody of Bacon often consists of knocking out the intermediary steps and so ridiculously juxtaposing beginning and end). The images of 'the glass' and 'refracted Angles' look like further exaggeration in Swift—so they may be, but they call up another famous passage, Bacon's account of the Idols, the innate distortions within human judgment. The 'human understanding', he writes, 'is like a false mirror, which, receiving rays irregularly, distorts and discolours the nature of things by mingling its own nature with it'. And again, the 'Idols of the Cave are the Idols of the individual man. For every one (besides the errors common to human nature in general) has a cave or den of his own, which refracts and discolours the light of nature. . . .' (B, 4, 54).

Swift here seems to have compounded the two accounts, and though he uses the result to a satiric end, the initial borrowing seems to be a serious one—I think there are more such debts.[23] For the *Meditation on a Broomstick* Swift may have remembered in Bacon an example of the classical commonplace of man as an inverted tree which is much closer to Swift's use of it than any cited so far. In *The Battle of the Books* the image of the spider and the bee has long been attributed to Bacon,[24] but he is also a probable source, amongst other things, for one of the key ideas of the satire: in his devastating history of intellectual abuses in *The Advancement of Learning* Bacon describes how Luther, in his controversy with Rome and the decadent Church, found no assistance in contemporary culture and turned to the classics for help, thus starting a battle between the Ancients and the Moderns in the Sixteenth Century: Luther,

> being no ways aided by the opinions of his own time, was enforced to awake all antiquity, and to call former times to his succors to make a party against the present time; so that the ancient authors, both in divinity and in humanity, which had long time slept in libraries, began generally to be read and revolved. (B, 3, 282–3).

That is an exact parallel for the Battle that Swift was contemplating, together with a very suggestive detail—the ancients 'had long time slept in libraries.'

In *A Tale of a Tub* Bacon and his followers take quite a beating, but there are nonetheless some serious borrowings. From the same section in the *Advancement* (and it is a section which Swift knew well, rightly so, as it is one of the most brilliantly destructive passages in Bacon) we might pick out Bacon's final dismissal of the schoolmen, who instead of being sources of light were in fact 'fierce with dark keeping'—that is, with imprisonment for lunacy—like Malvolio (B, 3, 287). Again in the 'Digression concerning Madness' Swift neatly develops this idea to discredit *his* enemy philosophers (although Bacon's name does not appear amongst them, the context suggests that he is in fact included: see below, Appendix B, p. 125–6) of the 'Grand Innovators' in philosophy, 'several of the chief among them' were generally thought to have been

> Persons Crazed, or out of their wits. . . . Of this Kind were *Epicurus*, *Diogenes*, *Apollonius*, *Lucretius*, *Paracelsus*, *Des Cartes*, and others; who, if they were now in the World, tied fast, and separate from their Followers, would in this undistinguishing Age, incur manifest Dangers of *Phlebotomy*, and *Whips*, and *Chains*, and *dark Chambers*, and *Straw* (I, 105).

Swift's technique here is to take a destructive attitude and enlarge it until all its potential grotesqueness is revealed. On smaller points Bacon is a more likely source for the scientific allusions than Sir Thomas Browne, for his 'Natural History', the *Sylva Sylvarum*, was much better known than the *Pseudodoxia Epidemica* (by 1685, 20 editions as against 3) and another remarkably popular work of Bacon's, the *History of the Winds* (by 1696 a dozen Latin editions, two French and

H

two English translations) provides some suggestive ideas for the
Aeolists section. There are other places where Swift seems to be
taking over ideas from Bacon without mocking them, but this is
perhaps enough to establish the point, and not to make it too important
—mockery outweighs it.

II

Swift's attitude to Bacon's ideas may be ambivalent, but there is no
hesitation in his reaction to Bacon's style: mockery. As a prose-writer
Bacon belongs essentially to the Elizabethan and Jacobean modes, for
despite some modern theories of him being a Senecan, he is one of the
most fluently traditional and Ciceronian writers in English, with a
great imaginative grasp of metaphor. Swift does not satirise the Ciceronian techniques of syntactical parallelism used by Bacon (and by Swift
himself occasionally), but attacks two distinct features, the first being
an antipathy common to his age but with an added personal force for
Swift, disapproval of imagery in prose. The greatest influence on this
change of taste was the Royal Society, and their effect on prose has
been well documented.[25] But it is interesting to look at current reactions
to Bacon's style, especially his imagery. Readers were certainly aware
of its characteristics: Thomas Sprat has left us two accounts of Bacon's
style,[26] and in the first, (in his *History of the Royal Society*) he praises it
without reservations:

> He was a Man of strong, cleer, and powerful Imaginations: his
> Genius was searching, and inimitable: and of this I need give no
> other proof, then his Style it self; . . . The course of it vigorous, and
> majestical; the Wit Bold, and Familiar; the comparisons fetch'd out
> of the way, and yet the most easie. . . .

Sprat recognises the originality in Bacon's imagery, but is prepared to
tolerate it for the confidence with which it is done—'comparisons
fetch'd out of the way, and yet the most easie'.

Sprat provides a still clearer example of his awareness of post-
Restoration linguistic decorum when he attacks Sorbière for having
suggested that Hobbes was much influenced by Bacon through having
been his amanuensis, and that Hobbes has '*Studied his manner of turning
Things: That he just expresses himself in that Way of Allegory, wherein the
other excell'd.*' Sprat replies intelligently:

> I scarce know Two Men in the World that have more different
> Colours of Speech than these Two Great Wits: The Lord *Bacon*
> short, allusive, and abounding with Metaphors, Mr. *Hobbs* round,
> close, sparing of Similitudes, but ever extraordinary decent in them.
> The one's Way of Reasoning proceeds on Particulars, and pleasant

Images. . . . The other's bold, resolv'd, settled upon general
Conclusions. . . .

That is, incidentally, a very good description of Bacon's use of imagery
—'abounding with metaphors', his whole reasoning process proceeding
on 'Particulars, and pleasant Images'; but the main point there is that
Sprat does not condemn Bacon for using imagery in prose though he is
very well aware of the change of taste,[27] as seen by his later charge
that the French have not reformed themselves enough: '. . . there might
be a whole Volume composed in comparing the Chastity, the Newness,
the Vigour of many of our *English* Fancies, with the corrupt and the
swelling Metaphors wherewith some of our Neighbours, who most
admire themselves, do still adorn their Books' (*Ibid.*, p. 172).

Perhaps Sprat excuses Bacon on the grounds of his scientific
eminence. Certainly the only other criticism of Bacon's style that I
know of in the seventeenth century expresses itself with some hesi-
tance: in 1684 Gilbert Burnet, in the preface to his translation of More's
Utopia, notes the remarkable change in style since 'the last age', one so
marked that

> even the great Sir *Francis Bacon*, that was the first that writ our
> Language correctly—in some places has figures so strong, that they
> could not pass now before a severe Judg. (Gibson, 498).

Yet Burnet concludes that Bacon is 'still our best Author', and we have
seen how Oldenburg praised him for having written 'the politest of
Civil and Moral Essays'. Certainly the publishing history of the
Essays bears both men out, as this continued to be the most popular of
Bacon's works, with some thirty editions by 1700. But it is worth
noting that on the number of occasions when Swift refers to Bacon, or
quotes from him (he refers to the *Essays* several times)[28] he never
allows a word of praise to escape—he is the 'severe Judge' whose
reaction points the way to later Augustan disapproval of Bacon's
style, shown by Budgell, Goldsmith, and Hume. Swift's distrust of
metaphor is well-known, and is so strong that he would not be likely to
make exceptions—it leads him even to disapprove of the most revered
authorities:

> I have been often offended to find St. Paul's allegories, and other
> figures of Grecian eloquence, converted by divines into articles of
> faith. . . . . I may venture to insist further, that many Terms used in
> Holy Writ, particularly by St. *Paul*, might with more Discretion be
> changed into plainer Speech, except when they are introduced as
> part of a Quotation. (IX, 262; 66).

His suspicion of imagery is historically related to the taste of his
age with its distrust of metaphysical wit and Puritan enthusiasm for

their excesses, for imagery which expands beyond the bounds of rational control. Yet in these early satires, and especially *A Tale of A Tub*[29] the language is extremely rich in imagery and in literary allusion, and the two qualities are, I think, related, for they both reflect Swift's formative literary background at this time and the nature of his satire, which is directed as much against books, writers, and styles, as against political enemies, or the vagaries of human conduct. At any rate, we find him using similes and metaphors with greater freedom, and in greater abundance, than he was to do in later years. More than this, his way of using them seems to show a definite Baconian influence.

Bacon is very fond of analogies, more so, perhaps, than any other prose-writer in English. Very often these occur in the most explicit form possible—'It is (in/with) A as (in/with) B'. Here are half-a-dozen examples from works readily available to Swift:

> But it is in life as it is in ways; the shortest way is commonly the foulest, and surely the fairer way is not much about.[30]

This analogy can be compared directly with what seems to be Swift's *reductio ad absurdum* of it—'For in *Writing*, it is as in *Travelling*: If a Man is in haste to be at home... I advise him clearly to make the straitest and the commonest Road, be it ever so dirty ...' &c. (I, 120—see whole paragraph).

> For it is in knowledge as it is in plants. (AL; B, 3, 404).
>
> it is in praise as it is in gains (*Essay* 'Of Ceremonies', B, 6, 500).
>
> And certainly it is with the kingdoms on earth as it is in the kingdom of heaven (*Resuscitatio*; B, 14, 17)
>
> It is in expense of blood as it is in expense of money (*Ib.*; B,11, 404).
>
> For it is in Proofs as it is in Lights; there is a direct Light, and there is a reflexion of Light, or Back-Light. (*Baconiana*, p. 30; B, 12, 317).

Bacon is using the device formally, perhaps even stiffly, to propose a relationship between his two terms which will be mutually illuminating. The analogy is often ingenious, but always serious.

In Swift's hand it becomes another complex satirical instrument, directed at times against its user as well as against its victim, by adding a ludicrous second term to the quite conventional first term:

> It is with *Wits* as with *Razors*, which are never so apt to *cut* those they employ'd on, as when they have *lost their edge*. (*Tale*, I, 29).
>
> For it is with Men, whose imaginations are lifted up very high, after the same Rate, as with those whose Bodies are so. (I, 100).

The beginning of the analogy (as Swift uses it) is formal, and the reader thinks it is going to continue seriously—he begins to assent to the proposition—and then the trap springs:

> I conceive therefore, as to the Business of being *Profound*, that it is with *Writers*, as with *Wells*. . . . (I, 133).

> But, I believe, it is with Libraries, as with other Coemeteries. . . . (*Battle*, I, 44).

> For, I think, it is in *Life* as in *Tragedy* . . . (*Spirit*, I, 180).

In one of these parodies Swift manages a double hit at Bacon's expense, combining his fondness for analogy with that of citing a proverb to back up his argument: 'The old *Sclavonian* Proverb saith well, That *it is with* Men, *as with* Asses; *whosoever would keep them fast, must find a very good Hold at their Ears*' (p. 128). It can be seen, I think, that Swift mocks the formal, almost pompous manner of the explicit analogy, and makes it still more pompous by the apparent modesty of the introductory 'I believe'.

Mockery is present, though not so easily seen, in Swift's use of the analogy in its less open form, the simple 'like' or 'as', which he employs mainly for damaging comparisons, and in the same way as before, he uses Bacon semi-seriously. Fluency of simile is of course not unique to Bacon, (though used to an enormous degree by him) but of all the seventeenth century prose writers he is the one nearest in manner as in tone to the Swift of these satires. It was a quality in Bacon's prose style that Sprat had praised ('The *Comparisons* fetch'd out of the way, and yet the most easie') and which Budgell was to find 'tedious' (—'as fond of out-of-the-way similies as some of our old play-writers'). Some of those 'fetch'd out of the way' are parodied by Swift in the *Tritical Essay* and ingenuity is certainly one characteristic of Bacon's analogies. Another is their 'homeliness'[31]—the majority of them are drawn from areas of experience common to all men, and so their impact is universal. In the *Essays*, for example we find: 'Money is like muck, not good unless it be spread' ('Of Seditions', B, 6, 410) and 'Fortune is like a market, where many times, if you can stay a little, the price will fall' ('Of Delays', B, 6, 427).

Frequent, too, is the comparison with animals—'Suspicions amongst thoughts are like bats amongst birds, they ever fly by Twilight' ('Of Suspicion', B, 6, 454), or with insects, as in the famous account of the Schoolmen as spiders. These analogies are often destructive, as in the account of misanthropic men, who are 'not so good as the dogs that licked Lazarus' sores; but like flies that are still buzzing upon anything that is raw' ('Of Goodness and Goodness of Nature', B, 6, 404); or in this analogy for the schoolmen's 'degenerate learning': 'Surely, like as many substances in nature which are solid do putrefy & corrupt into worms, so it is the property of good & sound knowledge to putrefy & dissolve into a number of subtile, idle, unwholesome, and (as I may term them) vermiculate questions . . .'[32] (B, 3, 285); or in this pungent progression:

> Superstition without a veil, is a deformed thing; for as it addeth deformity to an ape to be so like a man, so the similitude of superstition to religion makes it the more deformed. And as wholesome meat corrupteth to little worms, so good forms and orders corrupt into a number of petty observances. (B, 6, 416).

Swift uses very similar analogies in the section of the *Tale* on Critics, as part of a self-conscious attempt by the Modern Author at finding analogies for criticism:

> *True Criticks* are known by their Talent of swarming about the noblest Writers, to which they are carried meerly by Instinct, as a Rat to the best Cheese, or a Wasp to the fairest Fruit (p. 63).

or

> A *True Critick* in the Perusal of a Book, is like a *Dog* at a Fest, whose Thoughts and Stomach are wholly set upon what the Guests *fling away*, and consequently, is apt to *Snarl* most, when there are the fewest *Bones*. (p. 64).

Not that Swift doesn't have considerable skill with analogies in his own right—here is one which is essentially Baconian, but moves to a subtle and witty conclusion as good as any of Bacon's:

> *Criticism*, contrary to all other Faculties of the Intellect, is ever held the truest and best, when it is the very *first* Result of the *Critick's* Mind; As Fowlers reckon the first aim for the surest, and seldom fail of missing the Mark, if they stay for a Second. (p. 63).[33]

For the root comparisons within the metaphor it is not possible to be confident about Swift's allusion to Bacon: though there are similarities,[34] they are not as convincing as the specifically Baconian scientific images, or the use of metaphor in dividing up the faculties of the mind, both already considered. One use of imagery, however, does seem to be parodied, and that is the assembling of a continuous series of metaphors in consecutive sentences or clauses. This typifies much of the exuberance of Elizabethan and Jacobean prose, and if Bacon was the most widely known prose-writer of that period[35] in Swift's time, then he is most likely to be the butt of Swift's satire—or at least the echoes of this archaism by hack-writers a generation after the Royal

Society's reforms. So the Modern Author is made to defend Grub-Street against its audience's inability to

> inspect beyond the Surface and the Rind of Things; whereas, *Wisdom* is a *Fox*, who after long hunting, will at last cost you the Pains to dig out: 'Tis a *Cheese* . . . 'Tis a *Sack-Posset* . . . *Wisdom* is a Hen . . . 'Tis a *Nut*. (p. 40).[36]

This passage (which comes immediately before the reference to the 'Grubaean Sages') is, of course, much more banal than anything in Bacon, who often constructs wonderfully fluid and imaginative sequences of metaphor, as in the attack on those who seek in knowledge, for motives of personal comfort or gain, 'a couch . . . a terrace . . . a tower of state . . . a fort or commanding ground . . . or a shop . . . and not a rich storehouse, for the glory of the Creator and the relief of man's estate' (B, 3, 294). One sequence, though, while it is not in this form of direct metaphorical statement, comes quite close to the Modern Author's example; in one of the *Essays* which Swift quotes from elsewhere (X, 120), Bacon writes that

> Wisdom for a man's self is, in many branches thereof, a depraved thing. It is the wisdom of rats, that will be sure to leave a house somewhat before it falls. It is the wisdom of the fox, that thrusts out the badger who digged and made room for him. It is the wisdom of crocodiles, that shed tears when they would devour. (B, 6, 432).

Another passage in the Essays, the opening of the unfinished 'Of Fame' (B, 6, 519 and *Resuscitatio*) should be compared with Swift's mock sequence of images for Fame in the *Tale*, (p. 118). With Swift's evident hostility to Bacon, and the incomparable literary sensitivity implied by his gifts for parody, we cannot neglect the possibility that here too the Baconian idol is being steadily undermined. If the last few paragraphs (on the nature of the images being parodied) are more speculative than the earlier ones (on the way the analogies are introduced) then we can at least agree that Bacon's way of using imagery lies behind that of many seventeenth-century writers, and that if the spear seems to be directed at the Puritans or L'Estrange, then it pinions Bacon too.

III

The second aspect of Bacon's style which Swift mocks is the use of supporting material—quotations, maxims, allusions—all abundantly employed by Bacon. The first edition of the *Essays* in 1597, for example, contains only three such references: the final version of 1625, the one known to the world, has over three hundred. *The Advancement of Learning* is equally heavily ornamented with quotations, *sententiae*, proverbs, fables, references of all kinds—indeed the argument often depends on them. In attacking this technique (and he makes many scornful references to the easy reliance on pre-formed maxims and *sententiae*, quite apart from attacking Bacon) Swift is sharing the general dislike of banality, for inevitably by 1700 many of the stock Classical and Renaissance tags were wearing rather thin,[37] and Swift seems to have been unduly sensitive to this—he read too closely, perhaps, or refused to give imaginative assent to an argument which depended too much on quotations or maxims. He writes bitterly in the Preface to the *Tritical Essay* about his recent reading: '*I have been of late offended with many Writers of Essays and moral Discourses, for running into stale Topicks and thread-bare Quotations, and not handling their Subject fully and closely.*' (I, 246). Arguments should be worked out fully and on their own terms, not bolstered up with scraps introduced from elsewhere and used as if they automatically carried authority or assent. The effects of Swift's dislike of banality on the way he himself uses quotations have been well brought out by Edward Rosenheim:

> For all his adherence to the Ancient cause, in both the *Tale* and *The Battle of the Books*, his employment of classical allusions and invocation of ancient authorities are usually marked by strong suggestions of irreverence. When classical sources, precedents, and conventions are employed in the mocking attack upon various contemporary victims, they too are likely to become plainly 'vulgarized' in the process. Similarly, for Swift, the classical tag or proper name, the judgments of antiquity, have little magic in their own right; when he introduces them it is likely to be in implicitly heavy quotation marks or with a destructive intention to which the reader had better remain alert. (Op. cit., p. 234).

The destructive intent here is all the more sharp, I suggest, in that Swift mocks not only the quotations and maxims used by Bacon, but also the maxims which Bacon formulated himself, and even his manner of introducing such tags.

The difficulty of establishing the first point is, obviously, that Bacon is not the only person to use these tags—one could not base the argument on the common use of '*ira furor brevis est*' or '*meum* and *tuum*', and there are a number of parallels where the parody includes Bacon but cannot be said to be directed at him alone.[38] However, there are some definite jibes: editors of *The Battle of the Books* have recognised that the opening of the first of Bacon's *Essays*, 'Of Truth'—(and the most famous opening words of any essay in English)—'*What is Truth?* said jesting Pilate; and would not stay for an answer.' (B, 6, 377),[39] is destructively adapted to the dullard of criticism: 'MOMUS having thus delivered himself, staid not for an answer' (I, 154). That crude deflation sets the tone here, as elsewhere in Swift's parodies, whereby a valid stylistic ploy is redeployed and made to look stupid. In *A Tale of A Tub* Bacon is from this angle, too, associated with the Modern Author, even to having a common method of collecting quotations: the Narrator's boast of having gathered 'flowers' from modern authors, 'digested with great Reading, into my Book of *Common-places*' (I, 134) though of course applicable to many Renaissance writers, does recall Bacon's frequent advice to prepare 'a good digest of common-places' (e.g. B, 3, 398). Certainly it is through the literary mechanism of the *Tale* that Swift attacks: on the first page, in the 'Author's Apology', there seems to be an allusion to Bacon, who had announced, rather confidently, in the Dedication to his *Essays* that 'I do conceive that the Latin volume of them (being in the universal language) may last as long as books last.' (B, 6, 373). Swift's comment looks like a parody of this, with a more modest corrective qualification: '*Therefore, since the Book seems calculated to live at least as long as our Language, and our Tast admit no great Alterations . . .*' (p. 1). There are several such random blows, as later in this section, the offhand remark '*But Religion they tell us ought not to be ridiculed*' (p. 3) certainly recalls Bacon's maxim (which, at the other end of the seventeenth century must have looked rather futile): 'As for jest, there be certain things which ought to be privileged from it; namely religion.' (Essay 'Of Discourse', B, 6, 455). And in the introduction Swift has his Narrator equate the new science and hack poetry as products of modernity by joining the resort of each, Gresham's College and Will's Coffee-House: 'they both are Seminaries, not only of our *Planting*, but our *Watering* too?' (I, 39): that innocuous-looking image points to Bacon, who had used it in the *Advancement* with just the same division: 'And because founders of Colleges do plant and founders of lectures do water' . . . (B, 3, 324; the same image comes in passages reprinted in the *Resuscitatio*, B, 6, 314; 14, 481).

When Swift wants to mock a particular quotation used by Bacon, he makes it ridiculous either by suppressing some part of it, or by putting it in a slightly different context. Bacon is fond of using a quotation from Plutarch to illustrate the point that men's abilities vary according to their occupation:

> that which was said by Themistocles, arrogantly and uncivilly being applied to himself out of his own mouth, but being applied to the general state of this question pertinently and justly; when being invited to touch a lute, he said *he could not fiddle, but he could make a small town a great state*. (*AL*, B, 3, 280; in Wats's translation it comes twice, p. 24, 425; also *Essays*, 6, 444).

Swift takes the saying, twists it into an 'either-or' frame, and adds his
own conclusion:

> For all Human Actions seem to be divided like *Themistocles* and his
> Company; One Man can *Fiddle*, and another can make *a small Town
> a great City*; and he that cannot do either one or the other, deserves
> to be kick'd out of the Creation. (I, 62).

That is a clear case of parody by distortion and addition: here is one by
conflation and reduction. Swift remembers two passages in the
Advancement, the first near the beginning, on the criticism of the dangers
of learning—people say 'that knowledge hath in it somewhat of the
serpent, and therefore where it entereth into a man it makes him swell
—*Scientia inflat* [Knowledge puffeth up]' (B, 3, 264); and the second
near the passage on the imagination mocked earlier, where Bacon
writes that '*Syllogisms* consist of Propositions, Propositions of words,
words are but the currant tokens or markes of the Notions of things'
(Wats, p. 224; B, 4, 411). Swift neatly runs both points together:

> Because, First, it is generally affirmed, or confess'd, [a damaging
> addition] that Learning *puffeth Men up*: And Secondly, they proved it
> by the following Syllogism; *Words are but wind*; *and Learning is
> nothing but Words*; Ergo, *Learning is nothing but Wind*" (I, 96–7).

That is of course an inspired conflation and association of the two
ideas, and the reductive possibility of the syllogism is given full weight.
It would be unsporting to complain of the distortion which Bacon's
points have suffered—indeed the beauty of Swift's tactics is to move
you into a position where you cannot complain, where you concede
the ridiculous inherent in the original, and concede it so clearly that
whenever you re-read the original you will remember the ridiculous
too.

The second sort of stylistic parody in the *Tale* which I find is that
of Bacon's habit of constructing maxims in his own person, giving
general rules about life, often about human nature. In the Essay which
Swift seems to know best, 'Of Truth', and in the section which he has
already used in the 'Digression concerning Madness', Bacon observes
shrewdly that it is not the difficulty of finding the truth 'that doth
bring lies in favour; but a natural though corrupt love of the lie itself',
for 'A mixture of a lie doth ever add pleasure' (B, 6, 378). This confident maxim summing up distortions in man is mocked twice by
Swift, first as the narrator speculates on the reasons for man's tendency
to perverse imaginative flights:

> Whether a Tincture of Malice in our Natures, makes us fond of
> furnishing every bright Idea with its Reverse . . . (I, 99).

Again, 'Reverse' makes the whole process seem pointless. The second parody is still more devastating, catching up as well that way of Bacon's in introducing analogies in the form 'it is with' X 'as with' Y, which Swift has already had sport with. The Narrator is now suggesting that quite trivial occasions produce much of modern literature— '*a rainy Day, a drunken Vigil, A Fit of the Spleen*', and seeks for support, naturally enough, in the Modern's Idol:

> To confirm this Opinion, hear the Words of the famous *Troglodyte* Philosopher: '*Tis certain* (said he) *some Grains of Folly are of course annexed, as Part of the Composition of Human Nature, only the Choice is left us, whether we please to wear them* Inlaid *or* Embossed; *And we need not go very far to seek how that is usually determined, when we remember, it is with Human Faculties as with Liquors, the lightest will be ever at the Top.* (I, 116)

A remarkably complex piece of satire, at the same time making its main point, that these effusions are irredeemably ephemeral, and achieving several hits at Bacon, enlivened by a bit of nonsense ('Inlaid *or* Embossed'). First Swift parodies the normative maxims of human nature ('some Grains of Folly are of course annexed', where the 'of course' supports the ' 'Tis certain' to suggest a pontificating tone), and mocking another Baconian maxim too, that 'There is in human nature generally more of the fool than the wise' (Essay 'Of Boldness', B, 6, 402). He also deflates both the way of introducing the analogy, and the analogy itself (as before, the first term seems serious, the second *is* ridiculous)—one can even find parallels in Bacon for this image of liquids floating but not mixing[40]: I do not suggest that Swift refers to them, but rather that his acute sense of style can intuitively construct a Bacon-like image. And the *coup de grâce* is the off-hand pseudo-scholastic reference to the 'Troglodyte' philosopher: this 'still awaits explanation' the editors say (GS, 183)—in this context of ironic deflation of Bacon I think we can well connect 'troglodyte' or 'cavedweller' with the philosopher famous for his concept of the 'Idols of the Cave'.

By such alternately crude and subtle means Swift carries out his undercover dislodgement. This last reference to Bacon was the most specific—usually a parody is introduced with an unflattering 'they say', 'I have heard', 'they tell me', where the vagueness suggests that the source is not even worth mentioning, so obscure it must be. The third element in his parody of Bacon's style is directed against the master's habit of introducing an observation or analogy with the word 'For', so setting up a causal relationship between the argument and its illustration. This is a particularly useful technique for the aphorist, as an explanatory or limiting device, and is remarkably prominent in Bacon, as can be seen from the examples given already here. A particularly concentrated specimen of this habit is the Essay 'Of Envy', in which, as R. Tarselius points out,[41] of seventy-six head clauses in all, no less than twenty-one begin with the explanatory 'for', so showing Bacon's 'obvious tendency to sum up his argumentation in conclusive observations starting with *for*'. Swift latches on to this habit too, catching its tone and movement, as in many examples already quoted, and in others: 'For, I have somewhere heard, it is a Maxim . . .' (I, 14); 'For, as to be a *true Beggar* . . .' (p. 62); 'For, to enter the Palace of Learning at the *great Gate*, requires an Expense of Time and Forms; therefore . . .' (p. 91)—and the next sentence begins 'For, the Arts are all in a *flying* March, and therefore . . .'(p. 91); and 'For, as it is the Nature of Rags, to bear a kind of mock Resemblance to Finery . . . so . . .' (p. 128). I suspect that the incidence of this construction declines in Swift's later works, though I have not made a search—at any rate here it is another blow against a great user of maxims.

The last blow against Bacon in this way comes in a work which I have wanted to discuss separately, the *Tritical Essay*, which assembles a great number of 'stale topics and threadbare quotations' and disposes of them *en bloc*. The very density of the assemblage of quotations and maxims makes reading difficult, as Herbert Davis has commented: 'It is too thorough a parody to be witty; and it is perhaps not often read. But it is a part of Swift's campaign against dullness, an early disciplinary measure against the banalities of composition' (I, xxxv). Like any parody (only more so) it is witty and very funny once the object of attack is identified, and rather pointless until then. I think that a large part of its target is the archaic persistence as a model for literary composition of Bacon's style, and particularly his way of supporting and illustrating a point with example, quotation, and analogy. Whereas these are perfectly acceptable in their original context of argument, where they come as the clinching 'homely' or imaginative appeal after an often quite abstract discussion, Swift isolates and compounds them, deftly seizing on that tendency towards truism which is basic to the maxim, and uses them to expound a (deliberately) stale series of topics. The effect is rather like taking away a painting and exhibiting the easel which had supported it: basically, Swift abandons the arguments, and runs together all the conventional props which had maintained it—no wonder they look ridiculous.

The difficulty with this sort of allusion, as I have already said, is that these tags are not the personal property of Bacon: nevertheless, almost half of the *Essay* consists of tags which Bacon had used, some of them in a quite distinctive way. And where Swift does not echo Bacon, he invents something himself in the true Baconian manner, only more stupid, as in such aphorisms as: 'All rivers go to the Sea, but none return from it' (p. 250) and 'there is nothing in this World constant, but Inconstancy'[42] (p. 251). Already we see Swift's wonderfully destructive ability to make the parodied object look silly: here our reaction to the aphorism on its own is to say 'Yes, we know that'—its whole value to Bacon in its intended context is that its immediate appeal for our assent can win acceptance for the argument to which it is attached.

At its simplest, Swift's mockery is direct and unadorned:

> *Bacon*: 'For the truth and falsehood, in such things, are like the iron and clay in the toes of Nebuchadnezzar's image; they may cleave, but they will not incorporate.' (*Essay* 'Of Unity in Religion'; B, 6, 383).
> *Swift*: 'For such Opinions cannot cohere; but, like the Iron and Clay in the Toes of *Nebuchadnezzar's* Image, must separate and break in Pieces.' (p. 247).

That is one of Bacon's most remarkable and quirky quotations from any source—it was enough merely to repeat it, though there is an added twist as the iron and clay in Swift's version not merely do not 'incorporate' but actually 'break in Pieces' (which is ridiculous). At other times Swift will deflate by just omitting certain transitions:

> *Bacon*: '*Democritus* and *Epicurus*, when they publisht and celebrated their Atomes; were thus farre by the more subtile witts listned unto with Patience: but when they would avouch that the Fabrique and Contexture of all things in Nature, knit and united it selfe without a *Mind*; from a fortuitous Concourse of those *Atomes*, they were entertain'd with Laughter by all.'[43] (Wats, p. 166–7; B, 4, 365).
> *Swift*: 'how can the *Epicureans* Opinion be true, that the Universe was formed by a fortuitous Concourse of Atoms?' (p. 247).

Again simply by changing the sequence of an anecdote Swift can deflate it: Bacon is very fond of this tale, in this order:

(a) *Socrates* was pronounced by the *Oracle* of *Delphos*, to be the *wisest man* of Greece;

(b) which he would put from himself, in *modesty*, saying, *There could be nothing in himself to verifie the Oracle except this; That he was not wise and knew it; And others were not wise, and knew it not.* (*Resuscitatio, Apophthegms* nos. 257 and 81; B, 7, 158; also B, 3, 388; 4, 412).

Here Swift has only to reverse the sequence 'Oracle; Socrates' disclaimer' to make both look ridiculous:

(b) *Socrates*, on the other Hand, who said he knew nothing,

(a) was pronounced by the Oracle to be the wisest Man in the World (p. 247).

Another familiar quotation in Bacon is destroyed by adding[44] a tiny detail:

> *Bacon*: 'Question was asked of *Demosthenes*, 'what was the chief part of an orator?' he answered 'action': what next? 'Action' what next again? 'action'.' (*Essay* 'Of Boldness'; B, 6, 401, also *Baconiana* (1679) p. 67, in different form).

> *Swift*: '*Demosthenes* being asked, what was the first Part of an Orator, replied *Action*: What was the Second, *Action*: What was the Third, *Action*: And so on *ad infinitum*' (p. 249).

By that small touch the rather simple device of repetition is made to seem pointless, mechanical, unending.

Swift also satirizes the way in which these maxims and quotations are introduced, and here the satire may move out against hack writers, for Bacon is never as banal as this, or it may be suggesting that the whole process is tired. The common anecdote of Alexander weeping because he had no more worlds to conquer (B, 7, 142) is introduced by Swift with the words 'I have read in a certain Author, that . . . ' (p. 247), so pretending—as some hacks did—that he had just discovered the quotation himself, and also being oddly secretive about its source. Again he mocks the coyness of such phrases as 'as we say' to introduce an unusual expression by applying it to the totally familiar 'Catch time by the forelock' (p. 250; B, 6, 427). Swift deflates the portentous introduction of a maxim by printing in capital letters 'HOWEVER', as a prelude to 'the first step to the Cure is to know the disease' (p. 247). This last is one of Bacon's favourite analogies (from the *Essays* alone: B, 6, 409–10, 412, 424), although one could not be sure that Bacon is the sole target, nor with Democritus' image that Truth 'lieth hid in certain deep mines and caves' (B, 3, 351; 8, 109, etc.), which Swift devalues by taking literally—'as the Philosopher observes, she lives in the Bottom of a Well' (p. 247). I feel more certain about this allusion:

> *Bacon*: 'For although sometimes a looker on may see more than a gamester' (*AL*, B, 3, 428); 'Lookers-on many times see more than gamesters' (*Essay* 'Of Followers and Friends'; B, 6, 495).

> *Swift*: 'since a Stander-by may sometimes, perhaps, see more of the Game than he that plays it.' (p. 247).

Here Swift's hesitancy, ('*may*; *sometimes*; *perhaps*') is subtly deflating, suggesting that he is unsure of the point and that it may be a silly one (cf. Herbert Davis's comment below, p. 159, on the cautious reservations in the title of the *Argument* [*against*] *the Abolishing of Christianity*), and in another parody of a quotation which seems unique to Bacon he devalues it by the insolently off-hand introduction:

> Bacon: 'One of the Seven was wont to say: *That Laws were like Cobwebs;* *where the small Flies were caught, and the great brake through.*' (*Resuscitatio,* *Apophthegms* no. 303; B, 7, 150).

> Swift: 'After which, Laws are like Cobwebs, which may catch small Flies, but let Wasps and Hornets break through' (p. 250).

Both the throw-away start and the new exactness about the insects involved make the maxim—or the Laws—look silly.

A number of the maxims which Swift mocks and which are used by Bacon cannot be definitely described as targets here, though the evidence of context may be more persuasive: the first two paragraphs are particularly dense with possible allusions, and there are hardly three consecutive sentences without some point used by Bacon. Sometimes Swift's wit works by an exaggeration of a Baconian position: Bacon quotes with approval Aristotle's dictum that 'the nature of every thing is best seen in his smallest portions' (Wats, p. 166; B, 3, 332) also the familiar tag that nature does nothing in vain (B, 3, 470); but he could not have contemplated Swift's development of these ideas:

> I think it as clear as any Demonstration in *Euclid*, that Nature does nothing in vain; if we were able to dive into her secret Recesses, we should find that the smallest Blade of Grass, or most contemptible Weed, has its particular Use; but she is chiefly admirable in her minutest compositions, the least and most contemptible Insect most discovers the Art of Nature. . . . (247–8)

The damaging effect here comes partly from the banal repetition, partly from the counterweight exaggerations ('most contemptible', 'most discovers') and partly from the over-enthusiastic language ('dive into her secret Recesses') which is very near the Baconian images of penetration quoted earlier. Although 'contemptible' is one of Swift's favourite words in deflating man, there is a curious parallel either in Bacon or in the work of an ardent Baconian, Henry Power, who in his *Experimental Philosophy* (1664) praises the microscope, and calls in Bacon's testimony with an exact quotation from the master:

> The Eye of the Understanding, saith he, is like the Eye of the Sence; for as you may see great Objects through small cranies or Levels; so you may see great Axioms of Nature, through small and contemptible Instances and Experiments. (Jones, p. 191; B, 2, 377).

Swift is perfectly capable of debasing the concept on his own initiative, and if it be not agreed that this passage is not another source, then it shows how little is needed for the master parodist to distort the serious into the ridiculous. By a series of subtle re-adjustments Swift makes this giant of the last age seem nothing more than a purveyor of the tritest maxims.

IV

Swift's subversive attacks on the idol of the seventeenth century are most concentrated in the early satires, at a time when his own purely literary surroundings were at their richest. It is extremely difficult to tease out his parodies, and those of Bacon are but one strand in the bewildering net of satiric allusion, at its most complex in *A Tale of a Tub*, written when (as he writes in the *Apology*) *'The Author was then young, his Invention at the Height, and his Reading fresh in his Head'* (p. 1). Because of the freshness of his reading Swift could achieve an easy, riotous confusion of targets and of satiric effects applied to each target, and it is here that Bacon receives his hardest knocks. But for *Gulliver's Travels* Swift had obviously been doing some careful reading in a variety of works, so that it may not be surprising to find there further allusions to Bacon, mostly satiric, and as before covering several aspects of Bacon's work.

Bacon the moralizer on human nature is echoed, in his dispassionate maxim on the changing function of a wife: 'Wives are young men's mistresses; companions for middle age; and old men's nurses' (*Essay* 'Of Marriage and Single Life'; B, 6, 382). Swift's revision puts it into a curiously fashionable social context:

> For, their Maxim is, that among People of Quality, a Wife should be always a reasonable and agreeable Companion, because she cannot always be young. (XI, 62).[45]

Swift's attitude to Bacon does not seem very hostile here, nor does it in deference to Bacon the moralist, whose uncompromisingly ethical point, that

> Goodness . . . of all virtues and dignities of the mind is the greatest . . . and without it man is a busy, mischievous, wretched thing; no better than a kind of vermin.[46]

is surely one inspiration for the King of Brobdingnag's equally moral conclusion (on the basis of the select evidence):

> I cannot but conclude the Bulk of your Natives, to be the most pernicious Race of little odious Vermin that Nature ever suffered to crawl upon the Surface of the Earth. (XI, 132).

These are examples of a process which we have seen elsewhere, Bacon's ideas (usually those which themselves attack mankind for some fault) being taken over non-ironically and then applied to a satiric purpose. But Bacon also comes in for deflation, too, most obviously in his role of founder and theorist of the new science. The Royal Society of Laputa is a jibe at all scientific academies, not just that proposed in the *New Atlantis*, but it does catch the specifically Baconian ideal of the humanitarian ends of science, 'for the relief of man's estate', mocked both in the 'universal artist' who has spent thirty years 'employing his thoughts for the improvement of human life', and in the language of the professor with his project whose 'usefulness' would soon be known to the world.[47] This section also contains an unmistakably specific reference to Bacon, who had rather naively stated that in his method any fool could assist: 'the course I propose for the discovery of sciences is such as leaves but little to the acuteness and strength of wits, but places all wits and understandings nearly on a level', or again, leaving 'but little to individual evidence; because it performs everything by surest rules and demonstrations' (B, 4, 62–3, 109). On Swift's scale of satiric exaggeration this idea is immediately transformed by that professor with his random word-forming frame:

> Every one knew how laborious the usual Method is of attaining to Arts and Sciences; whereas by his Contrivance, the most ignorant Person at a reasonable Charge, and with a little bodily Labour, may write Books in Philosophy, Poetry, Politicks, Law, Mathematicks and Theology, without the least Assistance from Genius or Study. (XI, 182–4).

What a dreadful prospect! And though he has distorted Bacon's point, we have to concede that the ridiculous was inherent in it.

Finally Bacon the political theorist is put down. One of the more pioneering sections of the *Advancement of Learning* was that Machiavellian account in Book 8 (the part excerpted as the *Faber Fortunae*) of how to study men, how to know their motives, intentions, and methods so that you could predict how they would behave. It was filled with observation from life, precepts, little tips such as that if we want to 'purchase and procure unto our selves good information touching particular Persons, with whom we negociate and have to deale' then we must get information about 'their natures, their desires, their ends, their customes, their Helps and Advantages, whereby they are chiefly supported and are powerfull; and againe, of their weaknesses and disadvantages, and where they lye most open and are obnoxious; of their Friends, Factions, Patrons and Dependancies; and again of their Opposites, Enviers, Competitors; as also their Moodes, Times, and Criticall seasons of easy Accesse.' Bacon also classifies the particular functions or activities of man which may be studied here:

I

The *knowledge of Men* six wayes may be disclosed and drawne out; by their *Faces* and *Countenances*, by *Words*, by *Deeds*, by their *Nature*, by their *Ends*, by the *Relations* of others.[48]

And he goes into great detail on each function—for the '*Visage* and *Countenance*' for example, there are

certaine subtile motions and labours of the *Eyes*, *Face*, *Lookes*, and *Gesture*, whereby as *Q. Cicero* elegantly saith, is unlockt and open'd— *Ianua quaedam animi—the gate of the mind*. (Wats, 401–3; B, 5, 59–61 *et seq.*)

Despite his comprehensiveness, Bacon has left out one important human function, and given some of the suggestive details here ('where they lye most open and are obnoxious', their 'Criticall seasons of easy Accesse', and the 'subtle motions and labours' which unlock 'the gate of the mind') it is not surprising—indeed given Swift's attitude to Bacon it is inevitable—that in his 'School of Political Projectors' Swift should have re-applied this sort of advice to an inescapably human function of whose existence he never tired of reminding us:

Another Professor shewed me a large Paper of Instructions for discovering Plots and Conspiracies against the Government. He advised great Statesmen to examine into the Dyet of all suspected Persons; their Times of eating; upon which Side they lay in Bed; with which Hand they wiped their Posteriors; to take a strict View of their Excrements, and from the Colour, the Odour, the Taste, the Consistence, the Crudeness, or Maturity of Digestion, form a Judgment of their Thoughts and Designs: Because men are never so serious, thoughtful, and intent, as when they are at Stool; which he found by frequent Experiment: For in such Conjunctures, when he used merely as a Trial to consider which was the best Way of murdering the King, his Ordure would have a Tincture of Green; but quite different when he thought only of raising an Insurrection, or burning the Metropolis. (XI, 190).

That superb mock of Bacon's attitudes to life and his objective style (which Swift sustains with such phrases as 'to take a strict View' and 'found by frequent Experiment', even rising to a Baconian maxim— 'Because Men are never so serious', etc.—all of course in Swift's well-practised trick of mounting an absolute split between style and meaning)—this great parody concludes with the exact type of Baconian utilitarian praise: 'The whole Discourse was written with great Acuteness, containing many Observations both curious and useful for Politicians. . . .'

This final *reductio ad cloacam* is a fitting place at which to end, for it sums up at their strongest Swift's derisive feelings about Bacon. The deflation of the idol of the last age is accomplished on a wide front with a remarkable range of satiric devices, the most brilliant being parody. Why Swift should have been so subtle and secretive about attacking Bacon (never referring to him by name in the satirical allusions) is hard to establish: perhaps he wanted to see if all those who praised Bacon knew him well enought to recognise specific satire, or perhaps he just wanted to mystify, as he did in all his publishing (the only work printed in his lifetime with his name on it was the *Proposal for Correcting . . . the English Tongue*—but he nevertheless usually expected to be recognised.) At any rate he covered his tracks so well here that the relationship does not seem to have been suspected, in itself an ironic detail which he would have enjoyed. If challenged he might have replied in indignation as Gulliver does in his *Letter to Sympson* that 'I see myself accused of reflecting upon great States-Folk; of degrading human Nature'—as unthinkable as to be charged with 'attacking the great Lord Chancellor Bacon, founder of the experimental philosophy, polymath of learning, and model for the politest style in Essays'. But I for one would not have believed him.

NOTES

[1] See the 1715 catalogue reprinted by T. P. Le Fanu, *Proceedings of the Royal Irish Academy* (Vol. 37, 1927; pp. 270, 273).

[2] See R. W. Gibson, *Francis Bacon. A Bibliography*, 1597–1750 (Oxford, 1950; Supplement, 1959) items 141–2 and 26. This bibliography (hereafter referred to as 'Gibson') also contains a list of allusions to Bacon up to 1750 (items 257 to 680).

[3] Reprinted by Harold Williams, *Dean Swift's Library* (Cambridge, 1932).

[4] The date is an error, possibly of one figure in the title-page date: there were two 'complete editions' published by this date in London, one in 1638, the other in 1730, though the second, the *Opera Omnia* edited Blackbourne (Gibson, 238) is nearer in title than the first, the *Operum moralium et civilium* edited Rawley (Gibson, 196–7). If the second one was in fact the edition owned by Swift, this would explain why it does not figure in the 1715 catalogue, and would also be evidence of Swift's continuing interest in Bacon.

[5] See his biography. *Swift: The Man, His Works, and the Age*, Vol. 1: *Mr. Swift and his Contemporaries* (London, 1962) chapter 8.

[6] See *Swift and the Satirist's Art* (Chicago and London, 1963), pp. 72–76.

[7] According to Sir Frederick Falkiner, (Swift, *Prose Works*, edited Temple Scott, London 1897–1908, Vol. 12, pp. 57–8) his ancestor Barnham Swift 'took his name Barnham from his mother Ursula, cousin german' of Bacon. In his *Autobiographical Fragment* Swift refers with approval to Barnham, 'a noted Person who passed under the name of Cavaliero Swift, a Man of Wit and humour' (V, 187).

⁸ Samuel Sorbière, *A Voyage to England* (London, 1709), p. 32.

⁹ *Philosophical Transactions*, Vol. 5, For *Anno* 1670, Sig. *3ᵛ–*4ʳ.

¹⁰ Bacon, *Works* ed. J. Spedding *et al*. (London, 1857–1874; hereafter referred to as 'B') Vol. 8, p. 109. Part 1 of the *Resuscitatio* appeared in 1657 and 1661, part 2 in 1670; both together in 1671. Citations are from the text of the 1671 edition, but as its pagination is chaotic, page references will usually be given to Spedding's edition.

¹¹ *The Medical Remains of Lord Bacon* and the *Medical Receipts* were printed in another posthumous collection of miscellanies, the *Baconiana* of Archbishop Tension (1679, 1684; see B, 3, 795ff). In the related *Physiological Remains* there is much about compounding metals and minerals, and Bacon also wrote a *History of Sulphur, Mercury and Salt*. Different candidates for the satire here are proposed by R. C. Olson, 'Swift's Use of the *Philosophical Transactions* in Section V of *A Tale of a Tub*', *Studies in Philology*, Vol. 49 (1952), pp. 459–467.

¹² See Marjorie Nicolson and Nora Mohler, 'The Scientific Background of Swift's "Voyage to Laputa"', *Annals of Science*, Vol. 2 (1937), pp. 299–334; G. R. Potter, "Swift and Natural Science", *Philological Quarterly*, Vol. 20 (1955), pp. 97–118; and W. P. Jones, *The Rhetoric of Science* (London, 1966), pp. 65–78. "Satire on Science, 1660–1760".'

¹³ XI, 197–8 and IV, 122–3; quoted by Herbert Davis, *Jonathan Swift. Essays on his Satire* (NY, 1964), p. 206–7.

¹⁴ Both works are translated by Benjamin Farrington, *The Philosophy of Francis Bacon* (Liverpool, 1964). My quotation is from Peter Shaw, *Bacon's Philosophical Works Methodized, and made English* (London, 1733), Vol. 2, pp. 52–3.

¹⁵ It was also used by Hobbes in the closing paragraphs of *Leviathan*: see the edition by Michael Oakeshott (Oxford, 1946), p. 467.

¹⁶ *Philosophical Transactions*, Vol. 5, Sig *3r*. The quotation made above (pp. 29–30) by Dr. Rogers from Boyle's *Christian Virtuoso* ('an Experimental Philosopher may be compar'd to a *skilful Diver* . . .') is completely Baconian, and strengthens my argument. Further examples of 'diving' images in the New Science have been collected by R. F. Jones, 'The Rhetoric of Science in England of the Mid-Seventeenth Century', in *Restoration and Eighteenth-Century Literature*, ed. C. Camden (Rice Univ., Texas, 1962), pp. 10–11.

¹⁷ Kathleen Williams, 'Gulliver's Voyage to the Houyhnhnms', *ELH* Vol. 18 (1951), p. 275; Nigel Dennis, *Jonathan Swift* (London, 1965), p. 28.

¹⁸ In the Essay 'Of Fortune' (B, 6, 472), following the phrase 'the mould of a man's fortune is in his own hands'; in the *Resuscitatio* often (pt. 1, pp. 11, 176, 216), etc.

¹⁹ Gibson, 51–6, 235.

²⁰ 'Bacon and the Architect of Fortune', *Studies in the Renaissance*, Vol. 5 (1958), pp. 186–195; and 'Bacon, Pepys, and the *Faber Fortunae*', *Notes and Queries*, Vol. 201 (1956), pp. 511–4.

²¹ See F. O. Matthiessen, *Translation, an Elizabethan Art* (Harvard, 1931), p. 198. In his *Discourse touching help for the intellectual powers* Bacon alludes to it metaphorically as a 'trade of carpenters' (B, 7, 98).

²² Oxford, 1920; references are to the second edition (Oxford, 1958) abbreviated as 'GS',

²³ The details of these and further allusions are given in Appendix A.

²⁴ In addition to its use in the *Novum Organum*, it also occurs in the *Apophthegms* (B, 7, 177; *Baconiana*, p. 58).
²⁵ See the classic article by R. F. Jones, 'Science and English Prose Style in the Third Quarter of the Seventeenth Century', reprinted in *The Seventeenth Century* (Stanford, 1951, 1965), pp. 75–110.
²⁶ *History of the Royal Society* (1677), p. 36; Samuel Sorbière, *A Voyage to England* with Thomas Sprat's *Observations on the Voyage* (London, 1709 edition), p. 163–4.
²⁷ I have briefly chronicled the vicissitudes of critical reaction to Bacon's style from Sprat to the present day in the final chapter of my book, *Francis Bacon and Renaissance Prose* (Cambridge University Press, 1968).
²⁸ IV, 46 (Essay, 'Of Superstition'); X, 120 ('Of Wisdom for a Man's Self'); V, 85; X, 55; X, 162; XII, 39; XII, 48.
²⁹ On Dr. Johnson's comment that the *Tale* has 'more colour' than Swift's other work Herbert Davis rightly observes that this 'is due to the fact that he has put into it so much material from the world of letters in order to make play with it and to shake himself free from it'. *Jonathan Swift, ed. cit.*, p. 116. R. Paulson, who is the most perceptive critic of the style of the *Tale*, writes that the work 'offered a whole spectrum of stylistic problems itself and seemed to stand off from the rest of Swift's writings' (*Theme and Structure in Swift's Tale of a Tub*, New Haven, 1960, p. ix). His interesting remarks on the Hack's use of doublets (p. 50 n. 6) may suggest another connection with Bacon, who is very fond of this effect in all his works. The paragraph quoted by Paulson (GS, p. 175) might be compared, e.g. with the beginning of the paragraph (I, 2, 1) in *The Advancement of Learning* (B, 3, 268), or almost anywhere in that work. It was another thing that the first of the Augustan critics, Budgell, objected to, saying that Bacon was 'ever in the tedious style of declaimers, using two words for one', and explaining that it was probably Bacon's 'application to the law that gave him a habit of being so wordy'. (*The Guardian*, no. 25; April 9, 1713).
³⁰*Advancement of Learning* (..'*AL*'), B, 3, 472; also found in works reprinted in the *Resuscitatio*, the *Apophthegms* (B, 7, 159) and the dedicatory letter to *Henry VII* (B, 6, 88).
³¹ This quality of Swift's imagery at this time is put down by I. Ehrenpreis (*Swift*, p. 176, 180) to the influence of Temple, but Bacon is perhaps the original influence, as the account of Temple's style given by Professor Ehrenpreis shows definite affinity with Bacon.
³² Swift may have had this passage in mind when elaborating his comparison of Libraries to Cemeteries: 'So, we may say, a restless Spirit haunts over every *Book*, till *Dust* or *Worms* have seized upon it' (p. 144), caught up again in the rumour that Bentley 'had a Humour to pick the *Worms* out of the *Schoolmen*, and swallow them fresh and fasting' (p. 146).
³³ This analogy is perhaps a parody of Dryden's observation, in the penultimate paragraph of the *Essay of Dramatic Poesy*, on the fact that rhyme was not used in the drama of the last age but has been triumphantly applied in that of the present: 'Thus, then, the second thoughts being usually the best, as receiving the maturest digestion from judgment . . .', ed. G. Watson (London, 1962), 1. 92.
³⁴ For example, Swift does use some of Bacon's favourite images in this early volume: sinews of body—mind (I, 140) fountains-streams-source (p.

107), back-door (p. 41) and porch (p. 32), seed-fruit (p. 92), foundation-building (p. 247), ends . . . thread (p. 48), plants and roots (p. 174), and lanthorns (p. 183). On the dominant images in Bacon see my *Francis Bacon and Renaissance Prose*, pp. 174–201, 250, and W. R. Davis, 'The Imagery of Bacon's late Work', *Modern Language Quarterly*, Vol. 27 (1966), pp. 162–73. Certainly Swift is aware of the sources of imagery characterising a writer, as we see in his marginal comments on Burnet's *History of his Own Times*, where besides making sour remarks about 'so ill a style', clumsy, ungrammatical, and with 'Pretty Jumping periods', he three times seizes on expressions like 'the tables were turned' or 'in the management of that run of success' and notes: 'A metaphor, but from gamesters'—'style of a gamester' (V, 275, 278, 283).

35 Swift singles out one of the most famous metaphors of the last age, Donne's compasses, for satirical comment in the *Tale* (p. 137).

36 R. Paulson attributes these 'homely images' to an attack on the Puritan sermon (op. cit., p. 160); and E. Rosenheim to the mock of L'Estrange (op. cit., pp. 77–82)—it can now be seen that the passage of L'Estrange on 'the Wisdom of the Ancients' quoted by Rosenheim on p. 80 is a direct borrowing from Bacon.

37 The New Science certainly objected to it, and Glanvill, in the *Vanity of Dogmatizing* (1661) attacked 'this vain Idolizing of Authors, which gave birth to the silly vanity of *impertinent citations*; and inducing Authority in things neither requiring, nor deserving it. That saying was much more observable, *That men have beards, and women none*; because quoted from *Beza*; and that other *Pax res bona est*; because brought in with a, *said St. Austin*'. In 1678 he says that 'the custom is worn out everywhere except in remote, dark corners'. Jones, 'Science and Prose Style', p. 84n. See also Swift's own comments in his *Letter to a Young Gentleman, Lately entered into Holy Orders* (IX, 75–6).

38 I list these for convenience in Appendix B ('Possible parodies'): other readers may feel the pressure of context suggests a stronger connection.

39 *Tale*, ed. A. C. Guthkelch and D. Nichol Smith, p. 241. Other Bacon sources noted here are: the image of light things floating on the surface of time (I, 19; GS 32 to B, 4, 72: also 6, 502 and *Baconiana*, 1679, p. 73; 3, 292); the maxim 'For all colours will agree in the dark', I, 84; GS 134 to B, 6, 383 —also 8, 165, a passage reprinted in *Resuscitatio*.)

40As, for example, a part of an analogy between human and natural union: '*Water* and *Oyl*, though by *Agitation*, it be brought into an *Ointment* yet after a little settling the *Oyl* will float on the Top' (*Resuscitatio*; B, 10, 94); also B, 4, 219 (in *Resuscitatio*) and B, 6, 88.

41 'For all colours will agree in the dark', *Studia Neophilologica*, Vol. 25, p. 158.

42 In fact Swift may not have invented this aphorism, for I have recently come across the phrase in Grimmelshausen's *Simplicissimus* (Book 5, ch. 24) and in two pieces of Elizabethan prose. It may have been a proverb, but I find it neither in Tilley nor in the *Oxford Dictionary of Proverbs*.

43 The similar passages quoted by Philip Harth, *Swift and Anglican Rationalism* (Chicago, 1961), pp. 90–1, seem to stem directly from Bacon here. Swift also mocks the phrase in his *Letter to a Young Gentleman*, attacking preachers who 'fill their sermons with philosophical Terms, and Notions of

the metaphysical or abstracted kind' or 'are fond of dilating on *Matter* and *Motion*, talk of the *fortuitous Concourse of Atoms* . . .' (IX, 77).

[44] The related device of omission is used beautifully in the (imaginary?) anecdote which follows Diogenes' answer to Alexander (p. 248; B, 7, 163): 'which was almost as extravagant as the Philosopher that flung his Money into the Sea, with this remarkable saying,—' The hiatus leaves all to the imagination.

[45] It also seems to be referred to in *A Letter to a Young Lady on her Marriage*: 'a wise Man, who soon grows weary of acting the Lover, and treating his Wife like a Mistress, but wants a reasonable companion, and a true Friend through every stage of his Life.' (IX, 86).

[46] *Essay* 'Of Goodness and Goodness of Nature' (B, 6, 403). The sentence is also excerpted as a memorable maxim in Tenison's *Baconiana* (pt. 2, p. 67).

[47] The language of these scientists is completely Baconian, and an account such as the professor's 'project for improving speculative knowledge by practical and mechanical operations' could be duplicated hundredfold from the Baconians: even a critic such as Sorbière has it, describing Bacon's purpose as being 'usefully to reduce the Knowledge we have in Natural Things into Practice, without being incommoded with the Disputes of the Schools, to the End we may apply them to Mechanism, and resolve the Difficulties that occur to us in our Lives.' (*Voyage*, ed. cit.; p. 32).

[48] See also essay 'Of Negociating' (B, 6, 493-4).

Appendix A: Possible non-ironic borrowings from Bacon

(i) *A Tale of a Tub*: first, two possible 'scientific' references:

Bacon: 'rotten wood which shines in the night and yet doth not feel hot' (*Resuscitatio*, from the *Novum Organum*: B, 4, 132). Also *Sylva Sylvarum* (B, 2, 456-7).

Swift: 'Because it is the Quality of rotten Wood to give *Light* in the Dark' (p. 37).

Swift's reference to the bird of Paradise, which has no feet and therefore cannot land until it dies (p. 99) may come from Bacon (*Resuscitatio*; B, 12, 43). The *Sylva Sylvarum* would have provided information about Macrocephali (§ 28), or the white powder which killed noiselessly (§ 120), or the chameleon (§ 360).

The most interesting possible source for the Aeolists section is Bacon's *History of the Winds*—it is certainly more suggestive than any details in other obviously scientific works that I have consulted, such as Boyle's experiments[1] on the *Spring and Weight of the Air*, *The Rarefaction of the Air*, and the *History of the Air*, or Royal Society papers such as Dr. Garden's on *The Cause of Winds, and of the Change of Weather*, and other ones on *Trade-winds* or *A Whirlwind in Northamptonshire*, or even than such Baconian works as Robert Dingley's *Vox Coeli* (1658) and R. Bohun's *Discourse concerning Wind* (1671).[1] Bacon's work was first published in Latin in the important *Historia*

---

[1] Full details of the Boyle works are given in J. Fulton, *A Bibliography of Robert Boyle* (Oxford, 1961, second edition), items 13, 16, 18, 94, 198; for the Royal Society see Paper no. 175, p. 1148; 1705 *Abridgement* Vol. 2, p. 129 ff; 1809 *Abridgement*, Vol. 3, p. 210 ff; for the Baconians, see Gibson 375 and 296.

Naturalis et Experimentalis (1622), the 'First-Fruits of his Lordship's Natural History' as Tenison called it (*Baconiana*, 1679, p. 36), and had 12 Latin editions by 1696; the English translation of 1653 was reprinted in part 2 of the *Resuscitatio* (1670, 1671; B, 2, 17–78; translation, B, 5, 139–200). This *History of the Winds* has many details which might have been suggestive to Swift—several references to Aeolus (*Resuscitatio*, Sig. b; p. 17; p. 42), and several to bellows, (p. 26, 42, 43, 59) both connected here: 'Bellows are with men as the bags of Aeolus, whence a man may draw wind according to the proportion of man' (B, 5, 195). It is important to see the possible *double-entendre* in each reference to 'wind', and how it is produced.

The analogy with man is carried even further in the section on 'Imitations of Winds', where we have just the same kind of 'scientific' comparison of phenomena in a totally abstract way, seemingly unaware of the ridiculous nature of what is *really* being said, that we find in the parallel between man and a plant cited for the *Meditation on a Broomstick* below. The fourth of Bacon's observations on this point is this:

> The breath in mans *Microcosmos*,[2] and in other Animals, do very well agree with the winds in the greater world; For they are engendred by humours, and alter with moisture as wind and rain doth, and are dispersed and blow freer by a greater heat. And from them that observation is to be trans-ferred to the winds, namely, that breaths are engendred of matter that yields a tenacious vapour, not easie to be dissolved; as Beans, Pulse, and Fruits; which is so likewise in greater wind (p. 43).

The scientific approach masks the grotesqueness as well as the potential crudity of this account of 'wind' in the human, physical context: Swift would expose and develop both tendencies. This section continues with the same analogy used for the handling of metals—

> In the distilling of Vitriol and other Minerals which are most windy, they must have great and large receptacles, otherwise they will break . . . there lies hidden a flatuous and expansive spirit in Quicksilver. . . .

There are further remarks about the bottling-up and release of winds from subterranean places (p. 44 and 46) and from a man's mouth (p. 59)—all of which has certain satiric possibilities given our hindsight knowledge of the Aeolists' belching and modes of communication.

The Windmill is the last major feature of Swift's satirical landscape on which Bacon's *History of the Winds* can shed some light. He deals with them in the section on 'The Motion of Winds in other Engines of Mans Invention', with a peculiarly detailed and imaginative explanation:

> The Motion of wind-mills hath no subtilty at all in it . . . and yet usually it is not well explained nor demonstrated. The sails are set right and

---

[2] The index records: 'Breath in Microcosmos parallel to the Winds which blow.' Swift refers to 'Man's little World' (a very common analogy in Bacon) here (p. 97) and earlier had gone out of his way to satirize this cliché, asking 'what is Man himself but a *Micro-Coat*', adding a footnote—'*Alluding to the Word* Microcosm, *or a little World, as Man hath been called by Philospohers*' (p. 47).

direct opposite against the wind which bloweth. One side of the sail lies to the wind, the other side by little and little bends itself, and gets itself away from the wind. But the turning and continuance of the Motion is always caused by the lower part, namely that which is farthest from the wind. But the wind over-casting itself against the Engine, is contracted and restrained by the four sails, and is constrained to take its way in four spaces. The wind doth not well endure that compression; wherefore of necessity it must as it were with its elbows hit the sides of the sails, and so turn them, even as little Whirligigs that Children play withal are turned with the fingers (p. 35).

Here we have as close a parallel as is possible to Swift's 'Monster', who 'with four strong Arms, waged eternal Battel with all their Divinities, dextrously turning to avoid their Blows, and repay them with Interest' (p. 100).

But why does he call it 'Moulinavent'? This may well be more than Swiftian mystification, for the French translation of the *History* by I. Baudoin, (1649 and 1650: Gibson, nos. 113 and 114) had a remarkable engraved title-page which shows bellows, windmill, the various destructive functions of the winds, together with a verse which, in its naive moral,

> L'Homme ce Maistre de la Terre,
> Où l'amuse un Bien decevant,
> Qu'est-il qu'un Ouvrage de verre,
> Puis qu'il se casse au moindre vent?

recalls Swift's 'What is a man but a micro-coat', and 'What is a man but a topsy-turvy creature?' of the *Broomstick*. Given Swift's fondness for French books, he may have seen this edition. Other parallels such as the points of the compass and the classical names (I, 97—just after the syllogism 'Words are but Wind'; Bacon p. 33), and the use of 'eructation' (I, 97; Bacon p. 57) may be coincidental, but a more stimulating detail is one which looks forward to Gulliver in Lilliput: W. A. Eddy[3] is satisfied that Philostratus was a source for the sleeping giant (Hercules: Gulliver) being attacked with bows and arrows by pygmies, but he offers no suggestion for the difference whereby in Swift the giant cannot get up and rout the pygmies because he has been pinioned by them. In the next section of the *History of the Winds*, a study of Motion, Bacon would supply this point: 'For if anyone through striving be kept down stretched out upon the earth, with his arms and legs bound, or otherwise held, and yet he with all his force strive to get up, his striving is nothing the less, though it doth not availe' (p. 89). The relation between the works is not as close as some of the other references to Bacon—but this is one of his most popular scientific works (Dr. Johnson refers to it familiarly in *Rambler* 14) and it certainly offers many more suggestive details for this section of *A Tale* than any contemporary scientific work I have read.

[3] *Gulliver's Travels, A Critical Study* (Princeton, 1923), pp. 53, 76–77.

(ii) *The Battle of the Books.*

Bacon: 'Wars, in ancient times, seemed more to move from east to west; But East and West have no certain points of heaven; and no more have the wars, either from the east or west, any certainty of observation. But North and South are fixed; and it hath seldom or never been seen that the far southern people have invaded the northern, but contrariwise; . . . when there be great shoals of people, which go on to populate, without foreseeing means of life and sustenation, it is of necessity that once in an age or two they discharge a portion of their people upon other nations; which the ancient northern people were wont to do by lot.' (*Essay*, 'Of Vicissitude'; B, 6, 515).

Swift: 'Invasions usually travelling from *North* to *South*, that is to say, from Poverty upon Plenty' (p. 141).

(iii) *Meditation upon a Broomstick.*

Bacon twice refers to the common classical and Renaissance comparison of man to an inverted tree. The first of these, in the *Sylva Sylvarum*, an extended parallel concluding—'Homo est planta inversa: Man is like a plant turned upwards: for the root in plants is as the head in living creatures' (B, 2, 530) is mentioned by A. B. Chambers in his well-documented study of this idea,[4] but he has not noted the second one, which is nearer home than many of the parallels he cites, from the *Novum Organum*:

> Item non absurda est Similitudo et Conformitas illa, ut homo sit tanquam planta inversa. Nam radix nervorum et facultatum animalium est caput; partes autem seminales sunt infimae, non computatis extremitatibus tibiarum et brachiorum. At in planta, radix (quae instar capitis est) regulariter infimo loco collocatur; semina autem supremo. (B, 1, 279).

This can be compared with Swift's 'application';

> BUT a *Broom-stick*, perhaps you will say, is an Emblem of a Tree standing on its Head; and pray what is a Man but a topsy-turvy Creature? His Animal Faculties perpetually mounted on his Rational; his Head where his Heels should be, grovelling on the Earth (I, 240).

None of the passages quoted by Chambers have Bacon's phrase 'facultatum animalium', and the closeness of Swift's 'Animal Faculties' may be convincing.

Appendix B: Possible parodies of Bacon

(i) *A Tale of a Tub*

Bacon: 'But (my lord) as it is a principle in nature, that the best things are in their corruption the worst, and the sweetest wine makes the sharpest vinegar. (*Baconiana* 1679, p. 2: B, 12, 131, and B, 6, 317, *Henry VII*).

---

[4] 'I was an inverted plant,' *Studies in the Renaissance*, Vol. 8 (1961), p. 291–299. But his references to Gascoigne and Rabelais seem to be indebted, though unacknowledged, to the work of other scholars, C. M. Webster (*MLN* 1936, p. 196) and G. P. Smith (*PQ* 1926, p. 218–9) respectively.

Swift: 'for we are taught by the tritest Maxim in the World, that Religion being the best of Things, its Corruptions are likely to be the worst' (p. 3).

Swift: 'For, upon the Cover of these Papers, I casually observed written in large Letters, the two following words, DETUR DIGNISSIMO' (p. 13–4)—GS (p. 23) cannot give an exact source, and suggests that the phrase 'may be a modification of the common *detur digniori*'. Although common, the phrase does occur in a letter in the *Resuscitatio*: B, 11, 254.

Bacon: 'For many times the things deduced to judgment may be *meum* and *tuum* (*Essay*, 'Of Judicature'; B, 6, 509 and 'what influence laws touching *meum* and *tuum* may have into the public state' (*AL*, B, 3, 475—and twice in the *Resuscitatio*; (B, 10, 309; B, 12, 143).

Swift: 'because it is a preferment attained by transferring of Propriety, and a confounding of *Meum* and *Tuum*' (p. 38). Although this is, according to OED: 'a popular phrase used to express the rights of property', it is striking how often Bacon uses it.

Bacon: 'This new opinion, whereof there is *altum silentium* in our Books of Law' . . . (*Resuscitatio*: B, 7, 651; and 10, 152). It is found at least twice elsewhere in Bacon: B, 12, 236; B, 7, 605.

Swift: 'Upon Recourse to the Will, nothing appeared there but *altum silentium*' (p. 51).

Swift: 'a compleat Body of Civil Knowledge, and the *Revelation*, or rather the *Apocalyps* of all State-*Arcana*' (p. 41). Book VIII of the *De Augmentis* is entirely concerned with 'Civil Knowledge' (Wats' translation) the phrase being often repeated, though the nearest Bacon comes to calling his work 'a complete body' is the final summing-up: 'Thus have we made as it were, a *small Globe of the Intellectual world*' (Wats, p. 476). The use of 'Arcanum' throughout the tale is doubtless at one level a satire on occultists and alchemists, but the phrase is also found frequently in Bacon, almost always in the form Swift chooses, the mysteries being those 'of State', as here from the *Resuscitatio*: 'And therefore that this matter, which is *arcanum imperii* one of the highest mysteries of estate, must be suffered to be kept within the veil.' (B, 10, 358); 'which were wont to be held *arcana imperii*' (B, 11, 313); 'not entering into particulars, which are *Arcana Imperii*, and not to be divulged'—(B, 12, 26); 'matters of state . . . are '*secreta & arcana*' (B, 13, 23; and B, 14, 172; B, 10, 195–6). It is also found in the *De Augmentis*, it being difficult for History to present '*imperii arcana*' (B, 2, 504).

Swift: 'For, if we take a Survey of the greatest Actions that have been performed in the World, under the Influence of Single Men, which are, *The Establishment of New Empires by Conquest*; *the Advance and Progress of New Schemes in Philosophy, and the contriving, as well as the propagating of New Religions*.' (p. 102). These are the three main categories of insanity in the 'Digression on Madness' and Bacon must surely have been an automatic response when a writer in 1704 offered to 'examine the great introducers of new schemes in philosophy'; and when we read that all the 'grand innovators' have been 'persons crazed, or out their wits' then we must conclude that Swift's most violent revenge on Bacon was to reveal him as a madman. But also Swift seems to be mocking several specific Bacon targets: first the maxim from the *Essay* 'Of Marriage and Single Life' that 'the best works, and of greatest merit for the public, have proceeded from the unmarried or childless men' (B, 6, 391); combined with this Swift parodies the frequent occasions when Bacon praises founders, as when in the *Essay* 'Of Honour and Reputation' he lists the 'degrees of sovereign honour' and puts in the first place 'conditores imperiorum, founders of states and commonwealths' (B, 6, 505), or such statements as 'A *Founder* of *Estates* or *Kingdoms*, excelleth all the rest' (*Resuscitatio*; B, 11, 116) or: 'For it appears that he had in Notion a triple Good. . . *Relief of Poor*; *Advancement of Learning*; *And Propagation of Religion*' (*Resuscitatio*; B, 11, 250).

Bacon: (The new Natural History must) 'be made after the measure of the Universe, for the World ought not to be tyed into the straightness of the understanding (which hitherto hath been done) but our Intellect should be stretched and widened, so as to be capable of the Image of the World, such as we find it.' (*Resuscitatio*; B, 4, 255–6: *Parasceve* § 4) and: 'For we desire that men should learn and perceive, how severe a thing the true inquisition of nature is; and should accustom themselves by the light of particulars to enlarge their minds to the amplitude of the world, and not reduce the world to the narrowness of their minds.' (*Sylva Sylvarum*; B, 2, 436).

Swift: 'For, what Man in the natural State, or Course of Thinking, did ever conceive it in his Power, to reduce the Notions of all Mankind, exactly to the same Length, and Breadth, and Heighth of his own?' (p. 105).

(ii) *The Mechanical Operation of the Spirit.*
Bacon: 'As may be well expressed in the tale so common of the philosopher, that while he gazed upwards to the stars fell into the water'. (*AL*, B, 3, 332; also *Resuscitatio*, *Apophthegms*, no. 44).

Swift: 'they seem a perfect Moral to the Story of that Philosopher, who, while his Thoughts and Eyes were fixed upon the *Constellations*, found himself seduced by his *lower Parts* into a *Ditch*' (p. 190). Whether or not Swift is mocking Bacon, this is a beautiful example of deflation by exaggeration.

Swift: 'The Practitioners of this famous Art, proceed in general upon the following Fundamental; That, *the Corruption of the Senses is the Generation of the Spirit*' (p. 176). As GS notes (p. 269) this is a common idea, stemming from Aristotle, but, in the form of the sententia, *Corruptio unius generatio alterius*, it is frequently found in Bacon. In the *Colours of Good and Evil*, appended to Swift's copy of the *Essays*, it is found twice (B, 7, 85, 90), twice also in the *Resuscitatio* (B, 7, 663; B, 4, 176–7), and in the *Sylva Sylvarum* (B, 2, 451), in a form which echoes the Sense/Spirit opposition: 'corruption is reciprocal to generation: and they two are as nature's two terms or boundaries.'

(iii) *A Tritical Essay upon the Faculties of the Mind.*

Bacon: 'Of this kind of learning the fable of Ixion was a figure, who designed to enjoy Juno, the goddess of power; instead of her had copulation with a cloud, of which mixture were begotten centaurs and chimeras.' (*AL*; B, 3, 362).

Swift: 'Thus Men are led from one Error to another, till with *Ixion*, they embrace a Cloud instead of *Juno*;'

Bacon: (a) 'Epimetheus when griefs and evils flew abroad, at last shut the lid, and kept hope in the bottom of the vessel' (*Essay* 'Of Seditions and Troubles'; B, 6, 411). (b) (The Gods give Pandora) 'an elegant vase, in which were enclosed all mischiefs and calamities; only at the bottom remained hope' (*De Sapientia Veterum* c. 26, B, 6, 746).

Swift: 'But the various Opinions of Philosophers, have scattered through the World as many Plagues of the Mind as *Pandora's* Box did those of the Body; only with this Difference, that they have not left Hope at the Bottom (p. 248).

Bacon: 'But I will conclude this part with that saying turned to the right hand: "*Si gratum dixeris, omnia dixeris*" ' (*Resuscitatio*: B, 14, 177).

Swift: 'Not that I would reflect on those wise Sages, which would be a Sort of Ingratitude; and he that calls a Man ungrateful, sums up all the Evil that a Man can be guilty of. *Ingratum si dixeris, omnia dicis.*' (p. 248).

Bacon: 'All men can see their own profit, *that part of the wallet hangs before*' (Stephens, *Letters of Bacon* p. 128, and *Cabala*, p. 87).

Swift: 'These Men could see the Faults of each other, but not their own; those they flung into the Bag behind; *Non videmus id manticae quod in tergo est*' (p. 248).

Bacon: 'or for not accepting *Polyphemus* Courtesie, to be the last that shall be eaten up.' *Resuscitatio*: B, 14, 477).

Swift: 'The utmost Favour a Man can expect from them is that which *Polyphemus* promised *Ulysses*, that he would devour him the last' (p. 349).

Bacon: '*Walled townes* . . . Ordinance, Artillery and the like; all this is but a sheep in a Lion's skins. . . . (*AL*, Wats (1640) p. 430 and *Essay* 'Of Greatness of Kingdoms'; B, 6, 445).

Swift: 'For, in spite of their terrible Roaring, you may with half an Eye, discover the *Ass* under the *Lyon's* skin' (p. 249).

Bacon: 'I know your Majesty is* '*Nunquam minus solus quam cum solus*' (Stephens, p. 105, with marginal note *'Never less alone than when alone':

B, 12, 231). 'I perceive his Majesty is never less alone than when he is alone.' (Stephens, p. 102–3, B, 12, 282).

Swift: 'And, therefore, a wise Man is never less alone, than when he is alone: *Nunquam minus solus, quam cum solus*' (p. 249).

Bacon: 'Because a man in fury is not himself, '*Ira furor brevis*' wrath is a short madness'—(*Resuscitatio*; B, 11, 272; also 11,404; 4, 335; 6, 742.)

Swift: 'Besides, these Orators inflame the People, whose Anger is really but a short Fit of Madness. *Ira furor brevis est*' (p. 250).

Bacon: 'like Penelope's web, doing and undoing' (*Resuscitatio*; B, 13, 191).

Swift: 'else we shall be forced to weave *Penelope's* web; unravel in the Night what we spun in the Day' (p. 250).

Bacon: 'Saying, that I did not marvel seeing Xerxes shed teares to think None of his great Army should be alive once within a 100 years'. (Stephens, p. 193: B, 13, 114).

Swift: '*Xerxes* wept when he beheld his Army; to consider that in less than an Hundred Years they would all be dead' (p. 250).

Bacon: 'And therefore, as Plato said elegantly, "That virtue if she could be seen, would move great love and affection."' (*AL*; B, 3, 310); repeated in *De Augmentis*; B, 4, 456, but with the note added: *licet jam in trivio decantetur* —'though it has now grown into a commonplace''.

Swift: 'Yet *Plato* thought that if Virtue would appear to the World in her own native Dress, all Men would be enamoured with her' (p. 251).

Bacon: 'For that more men adored the sun rising than the sun setting.' (*Essay* 'Of Friendship'; B, 6, 438; *AL* B, 3, 449).

Swift: 'For Men, now-a-days, worship the rising Sun, and not the setting.' (p. 251).

CONCLUSION. The reader (if any) who has reached this point will have mixed feelings about the relevance of these parallels: some may seem convincing, others (especially from *A Tritical Essay*) will seem merely commonplaces shared by Bacon with many other writers. I share these feelings; indeed my own reactions vary on the scale between acceptance and disbelief each time I read through the list. But as I argued earlier, this kind of evidence at its weakest shows that at least Bacon was among the users of maxims which to Swift seemed threadbare, and as there are surely signs of a definite satiric intent elsewhere then it seemed safer to include than omit. At least the reader can feel sure that he has all the evidence before him, however he may evaluate it.

Irony and the English Tongue

HUGH SYKES DAVIES

I

Though all writers are forced to attend closely to the qualities of the language in which they write, and at every turn to make choices determined by its special powers and limitations, there are few who organise these myriad *ad hoc* decisions and impressions into fully conscious and systematic reflexions upon it. Fewer still set down such reflexions with care and at length. In English, Swift is the most notable of this small company, both for the extent and for the quality of his writings on the language. Only Wordsworth and Johnson might be considered to rival him in this way. The former, in the *Preface* and the *Essays on Epitaphs*, is more perceptive than Swift, but also more limited in range, for his concern is with certain special problems of poetic English, and not with the language in general. And Johnson, when he writes on the language, is not so much a writer, an amateur, as a professional lexicographer. After all, the preface to an English dictionary could hardly be anything other than an extended discussion of the vocabulary, and its writer could not divest himself, even when writing in other contexts, of his vast and specialist experience.

Swift's concern with English stretches over a long period, from the *Tatler* paper No. 230 in 1710 and the *Proposal for Correcting, Improving and Ascertaining the English Tongue*, to the *Letter to a Young Gentleman* in 1719–20, and *A Complete Collection of Genteel and Ingenious Conversation* in 1738. There are, besides, many other passing comments, and many linguistic curiosities, jokes, puns, etc., which show both his range of interest and the peculiar character of his approach to language: and which make him almost the only English writer who might be regarded as a forerunner of Lewis Carroll. It is, therefore, very natural to ask how far these theorisings throw any light on his practice as a writer, and also whether his practice throws any further light on his theories.

The answer to these questions must be prefaced by another: to what extent are his linguistic theories 'right', or at least sensible? For only insofar as they are to some extent enlightened can they throw light on anything else. Insofar as they may be moonshine, their illumination will be both dim and distorting.

There is not much difficulty in pointing to the worst and the best in Swift's writings on English. He is at his worst in commenting on a handful of abbreviations in pronunciation and spelling which he supposed to be outstanding examples of recent corruption. Professor Wyld, in his *History of Modern Colloquial English*[1] showed that Swift's handling of these usages was quirky and pedantic. Most of the contemporary corruptions to which he objects were long established, and his selection of instances was both narrow and erratic; a host of similar usages went without comment, and indeed appeared regularly in his own English. In this field, he is inferior, both as an informant and as a commentator, to the humble manuals of his time on pronunciation and spelling, written by less distinguished but more diligent observers like Wallis, Cooper and Jones. He is at his best, on the other hand, in his sustained attacks on clichés and proverbs in the *Tritical Essay* and in *Polite Conversation*. The range of material collected is great, and brilliantly chosen—it is also recorded with a fidelity which proves Swift to have had, almost above all other writers in English, a 'good ear'. He holds, indeed, a pivotal position in the long decline of the proverb from the ancient and medieval worlds to the present time: a decline whose stages and implications still await coherent study. In this side of Swift's linguistic works he would expect, and we shall find, significant and intimate relations with his own writings.

Between the worst and the best, however, there is a sizeable streaky patch, in which interesting ideas are closely mixed with silly ones, so that discrimination is needed, and difference of opinion as to how it should be exercised is inevitable. Broadly speaking, it would seem, Swift is at his worst when he is repeating, with little real reflexion on his own part, hallowed prejudices, near-myths about language in general. He is at his most useful when he modifies and adapts these traditional views in the light of his own perceptions and of his feelings about England and English.

Among these hoary beliefs, two are central to his general approach to the language. The first, inherited from the classical critics and rhetoricians, and from the innumerable scholars and grammarians of the intervening ages, taught that Latin had passed through a typical series of changes, from crude origins to a period of perfection, and from this to decadence; and that these periods had coincided with the political fortunes of Rome itself. As an outline of the history of Latin, this time-honoured theory was lacking in precision and detail, and it seems to have depended less on stylistic and linguistic criteria than on the mythology of metals, of a Golden Age followed by a Silver one, down to the last dull thud on iron or clay. But it contained, in however germinal a form, the important truth that the development of a language is inextricably bound up with the changing conditions of the society which uses it, and when Swift came to apply this truth to the history of English and England, it led him to make some interesting observations. First, he naturally asked himself when had been the 'Golden Age' of English, at what period had the language 'received most Improvement'. His answer was a striking departure from that usually given in the generation before his own, for which Dryden's attitude was typical: that English had reached its period of perfection in their own day, after the Restoration, and that they had clearly surpassed the standards of the Elizabethans and Jacobeans. Swift, on the other hand, placed the best period between the accession of Elizabeth and the beginning of the Civil War, and was thus the first writer of some eminence to enunciate the principle which Johnson was to adopt in the choice of sources for his dictionary. Swift went on to make the further observation that since the Civil War, English had in some ways deteriorated:

> From that great Rebellion to this present Time, I am apt to doubt whether the Corruptions in our Language have not, at least, equalled the Refinements of it; and these Corruptions very few of the best Authors in our Age have wholly escaped. During the Usurpation, such an Infusion of Enthusiastick Jargon prevailed in every Writing, as was not shaken off in many Years after. To this succeeded that Licentiousness which entered with the *Restoration*; and from infecting our Religion and Morals, fell to corrupt our Language: Which last, was not like to be much improved by those who, at that Time, made up the Court of King *Charles* the Second; either such who had followed him in his Banishment, or who had been altogether conversant in the Dialect of those *Fanatick Times* . . . (IV, 9–10).

This passage is more often quoted than any other in the *Proposal*, and it deserves the attention it has received. It is the first clear statement of the feeling, the intuition, that the changes in English life associated with the Civil War had been crucial for the development of the language, which had also changed its course decisively. 'Dissociation of sensibility' is one of the more recent and famous descriptions of the same change.

What is missing, of course, from this very perceptive statement is illustration, a reference to concrete instances to clarify the very general descriptions of the two kinds of 'corruption'. For one of them, the 'Licentiousness' of the Restoration Court, we can fairly safely supply illustration from other passages in the *Proposal* and from other writings of Swift on the same general topic; what he had in mind was the sloven-

K

liness of abbreviations in speaking and in writing, and the characteristic 'cant' of the rakehells, words such as *mob*, *banter*, *sham*, *bamboozle*, against which he campaigned all through his life: as Shadwell had campaigned twenty years earlier in *The Squire of Alsatia*, a play of much linguistic interest, besides its other merits. For the other corruption, however, that of 'fanatic' or 'enthusiastic' jargon, we have no very ready indications, though they might perhaps be found by a careful lexical study of *The Mechanical Operation of the Spirit*. This absence of illustration is probably the natural result of the processes by which Swift had reached this view of English in his own day. He had not worked towards it by an analysis of actual usage in detail, but had felt that it must be so because of the changes in English society, of which as an acute political animal he was deeply aware. His description is, in fact, quite as much a political as a linguistic declaration, and the picture of the two opposing dangers in language exactly matches his political convictions about the two threats of a decadent court and aristocracy on the one hand, and disloyal dissent on the other. And of course it followed naturally that in language, as in politics, the remedy lay in some kind of middle course, in the predominance of the more sober, orderly, and educated classes, using—as they would wish to use —that kind of English which was well established, free from eccentricity, vulgarity, extreme colloquialism, 'cant' and slang.

The other central belief, of more recent origin and of still more questionable status, concerned the manner in which this policy of restriction, above all in vocabulary, might be put into practice. Here the example of the French Academy invited imitation, and Swift was only one of that long line of English writers who believed that a similar institution was needed here, and that it could have a beneficent influence on the language. Modern students of language tend to dismiss such a notion as doubly chimerical, in that there is no clear basis for choosing to prescribe one usage rather than another, and no means of enforcing such prescriptions even if they were made. Their task, they usually believe, is that of description only, and it turns out to be quite arduous and extensive enough to keep their minds off any kind of prescription for a very long time ahead. Thus preoccupied, they are inclined to dismiss earlier attempts at prescription as being of little significance in the study of language and the history of particular languages. In the main, they are no doubt right. But there are, perhaps, some special circumstances in which past prescriptions merit a little attention, because they have in fact coincided to some extent with what actually happened after they were made. This coincidence does not, of course, necessarily imply that the changes have been brought about by the prescriptions. There are parts of the world in which, when the sun goes into eclipse, the inhabitants make a great clatter with pots and pans, designed, so they say, to frighten away the evil spirits which are hovering in front of the sun. They are invariably successful in achieving their object: indeed few human beliefs are so regularly and firmly supported by experiment. But for all that, the rest of the world prefers to believe that they succeed for quite other reasons, and that the sun was going to reveal itself in any case, quite apart from the pot-banging. There might, however, be circumstances in which one might not wish to dismiss the noise as altogether of no account. Suppose that a sceptical visitor to these regions were to be sitting in a windowless hut, and were to hear outside a sudden din of beaten metal, he would at least be justified in concluding that an eclipse must be in progress, and that it might be worth his while to go out of doors if he happened to have a fancy for seeing such things. In much the same way, it is possible to look with interest upon those few linguistic prescriptions which have happened to coincide broadly with later developments. The illusion they provide of causing certain effects proceeds from the fact—the interesting fact—that those who formulated them had a fairly correct sense, a perceptive intuition, for the general tendencies of the languages which concerned them. And Swift was successful in this way. Not alone, for Dryden, Pope, Addison—to name only the major writers concerned—all held the same view, which was handed down, almost unaltered, to Johnson, who made the final heroic attempt to enforce the restriction of vocabulary in his *Dictionary*. The principles on which he acted, the particular words which he sought to discourage, the effects of his work on the standard of English usage—these are large subjects which concern us for the moment no further than to note that Johnson's restrictive policy was essentially that of Swift, in its main outlines, in its historical justification by the assumption of an Elizabethan-Jacobean standard of 'highest Improvement', and in many of its condemnations of particular words. Swift, in short, though it may well be doubted whether he 'caused' to any extent at all the attitude to words which ran through the next half-century, had at least sensed very accurately what this attitude was likely to be. And his sense of it was accurate because he had made the right kind of political guesses, and related them neatly with a few obvious linguistic prophecies.

His political and linguistic perceptions, however, presented him with a problem in the practice of writing. They tended to confine him to that part of the English vocabulary which he felt to be central, uneccentric, free from the taints of vulgarity, colloquialism and slang.

They imposed upon him, in fact, a restrictive policy which was none the less difficult to observe for being self-imposed: indeed the more difficult.

II

But there is, after all, something at first sight a little odd in the spectacle of so many writers—Swift, Pope, Addison, Johnson among them—agitating to have the vocabulary of English restricted, if need be by official action. One would have thought that any writer would, in the nature of things, wish to feel free to use any words that took his fancy, and that he would be the last person to accept, let alone to propose, the deliberate amputation of his native tongue. More natural, surely, is the attitude of those modern writers who doggedly include in their compilations words which are under various legal and social taboos in our own society, and their customary defence before the beaks that they need such words to express their innermost thoughts and feelings rings very true, whatever the verdict of the court may happen to be. This posture, however, only makes sense for a writer who conceives himself to be in the very van of human progress (or regress), a lonely and heroic pioneer, clearing a path for the common herd who blunder about behind him, impeding his exploration with abuse and persecution. This is of course not the only possible social and linguistic posture for writers. It is merely that dominant at the present time. From Dryden to Johnson, writers commonly regarded themselves rather as a rearguard than as a vanguard. They were in the last ditch, defending the ancient and traditional culture against its vulgarisation and destruction at the hands of venal politicians like Walpole, and the illiterate filth pouring from the sewers of Grub Street. They were, so to speak, passionately active reactionaries in their social and political beliefs, and it was therefore natural that they should also be linguistic reactionaries, devoted to a policy of restricting innovation in words as well as in things. And since their attitude to the language was based, not upon any serious linguistic study, but upon their political and social prejudices, it was as natural and logical for them as are the social and linguistic policies of extreme laissez-faire to the linguistic expansionists of the twentieth century.

But natural and logical though it may have been, their policy of linguistic restriction brought them up against some very prickly problems. They placed themselves in a position rather like that of the Director of an art gallery, large and astoundingly well stocked with Old Masters, with neither room nor desire for any additions, since all additions would be rather a come-down; but upon such a Director there might sometimes come a desire for a little change or a demand for it from the public. And all he could ever do would be to arrange the existing exhibits in a new order. Dryden, Swift, Pope and those of their contemporaries who shared their political and social beliefs were similarly placed. Outright innovation in thought, feeling or expression they gravely mistrusted, and their chosen role was to rearrange, perhaps to re-express, the best of what had already been thought and felt, not to go off on dangerous and fruitless explorations into the absolutely novel:

> True Wit is Nature to advantage dress'd,
> What oft was thought, but ne'er well so express'd.

Novelty, however, in its two distinct forms, absolute and confined to re-expression or re-arrangement, furnished the horns of a dilemma which, if it did not gore them outright, often enough left their arguments pretty ragged. Thus Johnson, in one of those staggering inconsistencies only made possible for him by the sustained imposture of his characteristic 'style', in one short critique[2] both praised and blamed Gray for precisely the same quality:

> In the character of his *Elegy* I rejoice to concur with the common reader. . . . The *Churchyard* abounds with images which find a mirror in every mind, and with sentiments to which every bosom returns an echo.
>
> The *Prospect of Eton College* suggests nothing to Gray which every beholder does not equally think and feel. His supplication to father Thames . . . is useless and puerile.

Such vagaries of navigation were perhaps inevitable for those who felt they had to pass between the Scylla of dangerous innovation, and the Charybdis of the trite, the threadbare and commonplace.

Of this Charybdis no one was more miserably conscious than Swift. The trite and threadbare horrified him the more intimately because he felt them to be so dangerous a travesty of his own deepest intuitions, ruining the past which he cherished by lifeless and automatic repetition. It was one of his chief butts in *Polite Conversation*, and his only butt in *A Tritical Essay*, which is a good deal funnier than most of *Polite Conversation*, partly because it is less laboured, and also because it rises, especially at the end, to a very high level of comic imagination. It was Swift too who, when all the poets and poetasters of the day were profiting from Dryden's hint about the 'music' of those notorious four lines in *Cooper's Hill*, warned them against any further treading down of the already trite through the mouth of Apollo himself:

> Nor let my Votaries show their Skill
> In apeing Lines from *Cooper's Hill*;
> For know I cannot bear to hear,
> The Mimickry of *deep yet clear*. (*Poems*, 271).

It was, indeed, this strain in Swift's sensibility which made so many of his close friends regard him as a reincarnation of Cervantes' 'serious air'. Lord Bathurst, for example, wrote to him that he was held in 'high estimation' in Spain, under the name Don Swifto, 'being thought to be lineally descended from *Miguel de Cervantes*, by a daughter of *Quevedo's*' (*Corr.*, IV, 390). No small part of Swift's admiration for *Don Quixote* rested on its massive comic attack on the follies of repeating outworn forms of thought and expression (as in Sancho's use of proverbs) when life had left them.[3]

As a writer on politics and society, Swift had to tread along the knife-edge between the dangerously novel and the trite; and his language had to follow the same narrow path between the degraded novelties of Grub Street and the threadbare. The feat would have been difficult enough had he never attempted anything other than straight exposition of his beliefs. But it became doubly difficult when he assumed the role of the satirist. For then it was not only a matter of disproving, of laying bare the folly and wickedness of his enemies; it was also needful to cover them with contempt. And the most direct and powerful way of doing this was, as it had always been, to employ the method of 'railing', to contaminate the policies of one's opponents by smearing them with the filth of the language in which they were described. But to do this was to trespass against taboos of all kinds, above all verbal, and to descend to the vulgarest of terms. Thus Gabriel Harvey had accused his raffish enemies of using the language of the stews, and prided himself on avoiding it:

> I WOTT not what these cutting Huffe-snuffes meane:
> Of Alehouse-daggers I haue little skill:
> I borrow not my phrase of knaue, or queane . . .[4]

And Hamlet, after a bout of railing against the King, 'Bloody, bawdy villain etc.', pulls himself up with this sobering reflection on the sociology of swearing:

> This is most brave
> That I, the son of a dear father murder'd,
> Prompted to my revenge by heaven and hell,
> Must, like a whore, unpack my heart with words,
> And fall a-cursing like a very drab,
> A scullion!

Railing of this type, with all the imaginative and linguistic developments of which it was capable, had been the usual medium of Elizabethan
satire, as in Marston and Donne. But it was almost wholly excluded
from among the possibilities open to Swift by his convictions about the
restriction of vocabulary in English. The one thing he could not do
was to attack Grub Street in the language of Grub Street. How, then,
was his satire to be waged?

The choice of weapons is often determined by the kind of war to
be fought or by the kind which the warrior desires to appear to be
fighting. For all these writers, from Dryden to Johnson, and most of
all for Swift, their political and social beliefs, with the convictions about
the decent standard of language which followed from them, involved
severe limitations. But as so often happens in art, limitations prove to
be the essential stimulus to the exploitation of new possibilities. It is,
for example, commonplace to note that the mock-heroic genre provided
the poets of this period with a mould singularly well fitted to shape their
contrasts between a heroic, dignified past and the degraded present, so
that it became, in their hands, much more than a clever literary device.
In something of the same way, the specialised patterns of the 'heroic'
couplet proved to be capable of development from a literary device to a
singularly rich and appropriate mode of thought and feeling. Dryden
had seen clearly that the spirit of what he had to utter accorded ill
with the 'wit' of the Elizabethans, and that metaphor, with its restless
exploratory quality, its tendency to catachresis, to violent changes in
the relations between words and meanings, could not be the dominant
device in an actively reactionary poetry. He saw almost as clearly
that the only alternative was 'turns' of word and phrase, which left
them with their usual, even with their commonplace meanings, but
sharpened and intensified by being made to reverberate with one another
in those balanced lines which appeal both to the apparently innate
human liking for bilateral symmetry and to those basic qualities of
vocabulary which provide the ordonnance of the Thesaurus, synonymy
and antinomy. As he and his ablest successors practised it, the couplet
combined exactly the right kind of vocabulary, restricted and 'central',
with the new precision and force derived from these formal collocations.
Thus, to take an elementary example, the statement 'It's light' conveys
very little. But if either of the two antithetical additions 'it's dark' or
'it's heavy' are made, there is a notable increase in lucidity. The same
basic device, used with varying skill and complexity, underlies the
heroic couplet in this period. And it was a providentially adequate
mode for the expression of an active reactionary posture, in which
such novelty as was permissible must be gained, not by absolute

innovations in thought, feeling or language, but by shifting what had already been thought and felt and said into its most impressive, its most lively order of exhibition.

But Swift's characteristic development of literary technique was neither in mock-heroic nor in the heroic couplet. It was in irony. And this too was a providentially suitable mode of expression for satire of precisely the kind which he had to write. It was pre-eminently the one device to replace that railing which was on all grounds impossible. The nature of its special aptness, however, can only be made clear if we look closely at its actual mechanism. Luckily, we shall have no occasion for a full and final description of irony: it will be quite enough to hold it up to the light, and turn it around until we have the right facet for our immediate purpose.

III

Irony is a special modification of the normal mode of communication, and its speciality is only to be understood by comparison with this norm. For this purpose we need some account of normal communication, but it need not be very sophisticated, and the following will serve for the moment: when A is speaking to B, or writing for X (any reader), he constructs a set of linguistic signals which correspond more or less with the concepts in his mind, and transmits them with voice or the written word. As B begins to receive these signals, he responds by constructing from them a set of concepts in his own mind—of course quite unconscious of the nature of his activity. In making this re-construction, he must respond both to individual signals, such as words, and also to the patterns which give them the order of a set (grammar, the sentence, etc.), and this response takes the form of a 'sentence' in his own mind, matching the unfolding pattern of A's signals, and also anticipating those still to come, modifying his expectations in accordance with the constantly changing probabilities suggested by those already received. When B ends by constructing, in his own mind, a sentence more or less like that transmitted by A, understanding may be said to have taken place. Where something else has been constructed, B may perhaps observe, 'I thought you were going to say . . .', and then A must try again. Or B may announce his failure to make any coherent internal sentence from the signals, and A must transmit them again, perhaps in an improved form. But throughout this process, whether it succeeds or fails, the essential characteristic is that the *message* (the set of concepts in A's mind) is embodied as directly as possible in the set of signals which he transmits, in order that B shall reconstruct it as nearly as possible and relate it with very similar concepts in his own mind. The message, in fact, coincides as closely as possible with the set of signals. A designs it in such a manner as to ensure this coincidence, and B receives it on the same, albeit unconscious, assumption.

In ironic utterance, on the other hand, there is no such simple coincidence between the message and the set of signals transmitted. Here, the signals are a deliberately altered version of the message. But the alteration is by no means at random. It is systematic, in the manner of a code, though a simple one, and they must be systematically de-coded by the receiver. If he were to deal with these coded signals according to the normal procedure for reception, they would communicate a message very different from, and quite possibly opposite to, the concepts which had originated them in A's mind. Thus if A and B were to meet amid the haze and hullaballoo of a cocktail party, A might remark to B 'What a lovely party, isn't it?' His actual message, however, might well be something more like 'What a ghastly episode —how on earth did we land up here?' If this is the case, B's task is much more complicated than in the normal case of communication. He must, if he is to 'understand' A, not merely receive the set of signals; he must also de-code them, and so reconstruct in his own mind the uncoded version, which has never been uttered. He cannot achieve this, however, unless the set of signals has included some warning that it is in code, not *en clair*, so that he perceives some de-coding to be necessary, and unless he already possesses, or is given in the same set of signals, an effective indication of the 'key' to the code, so that he is able to reverse its operation and construct the actual message from the ostensible one. In the very simple case just given, the set of signals might well have included special distortions of the normal patterns of emphasis and intonation which would serve both as a warning and as a key to the code.[5] In the whole of this process, we must distinguish clearly—it is our first basic distinction—between the general pattern or process of irony, which is probably much the same in all examples of this kind of expression, and the much more varied types of code which can be employed within this general pattern, the wide range of warnings that a code of some kind is in use, and of the corresponding keys to their de-coding.

Something of the nature of these warnings and keys may be learned by pushing the analogy with codes and de-coding a little further—but not, of course, too far. A message transmitted in code can be deciphered by the receiver only if he knows the system on which the coding was done, so that he can, by reversing its direction, reconstruct the original message from the coded one. And this knowledge must be given to him through the normal modes of communication. A key to a code which was itself in code would be of no use to him. When ciphered messages are used for diplomatic or military purposes, it is obviously unwise to include this key along with the coded message, and it is communicated to the receiver beforehand, or through a different channel. But the coded sets of signals which make up irony must include this key, *en clair*, along with that part of the message which is in code, since neither the listener nor the reader can be expected to go through some special course of instruction beforehand, or to have recourse to normal information through some quite different channel. He must, in fact, be put in a position to carry out the de-coding while the message is actually being transmitted, or at latest immediately after its transmission is finished. One of the major problems for the ironist is to enable the receiver to distinguish without ultimate obscurity between the 'keys' which are *en clair*, and the ironic signals which are in code.[6] And one of his most powerful resources is to produce temporary confusion between the two, so that the receiver thinks that he is dealing with signals in the normal, uncoded mode of communication, when in fact he is receiving coded signals. The shock of recognising his error, and of having to rectify his interpretation of the previously misunderstood signals, forces him to perceive even more clearly the magnitude of the difference between the signals and the real message, so that the message itself is powerfully reinforced in his mind. And thereafter, even while he is fully aware of the difference between the two, he gets much the same effect from making a running comparison between what is being said and what is being meant.

Another useful prolegomenon to the study of 'keys' and codes in irony depends on the fact that it is by no means the only mode of expression which makes use of them. It shares them with allegory and metaphor,[7] and some of the keys and codes used in irony can be studied more easily if they are compared with the processes met with in these other forms of expression. For example, in all three modes one of the most widely used keys to the existence and de-coding of a coded message is the presentation to the receiver of a statement which, if taken to be un-coded, *en clair*, is manifestly incompatible with its context in the rest of the utterance. Thus the reader of *The Faerie Queene* sets out with a gentle knight pricking across a plain in company with a fair lady for a distance of twelve Spenserian stanzas. In the thirteenth (so closely did the writer follow a Platonic notion of the magic in numbers) he learns that they have come to a cave called '*Errours den*'. Now all the proper nouns so far encountered have been in italic type; 'Errour' too is in italic, and though it is not at the beginning of a line it begins with a capital letter, so that it must be taken as some kind of proper noun. But the reader also knows, since he must be acquainted with English to be reading the poem at all, that 'Errour' is an abstract concept, and one which is not usually associated with so concrete a thing as a den, the haunt of a wild animal: 'Errour,' taken *en clair*, is incompatible with its immediate context. He is thus warned that the use of the word in this passage is different from that which he usually encounters, and he is thereby prepared to regard the abstract concept as being, for the nonce, also a creature or person of some kind. This enables him to de-code the message conveyed in the set of signals about a filthy hag of serpentine aspect, with a long knotted tail, and a large horrible progeny. They are all both creatures of a sort, and abstract concepts, the nature of which can readily be de-coded from various puns and other verbal signals. This is, with many variations, the rather tedious method of allegory. It is worth noting, by the way, that the Greek word from which irony comes was one of the words which in ancient Greek meant what we now mean by allegory; and also that allegory is one of the possible vehicles for satire, as in Orwell's *Animal Farm*, where the 'keys' are of the same type as Spenser's '*Errour's den*'. There is, for example, a horse called 'Napoleon', which is not, as both my usual bookmakers have assured me, a possible name for a real horse in English.

Metaphor uses keys and codes in a less tedious, and more varied manner. For example, the reader of Yeats' *A Prayer for my Daughter* hears in the first five stanzas of a father's natural forebodings and wishes for his infant daughter, and in the sixth he is told of his wish that she should become 'a flourishing hidden tree'. Now all the other things that he has wished for her have been good or in some way favourable. It is therefore most unlikely that this wish is meant literally, since for a girl to grow up into a tree would be neither usual nor wholly pleasant for her parents. The reader is thus warned that the expression is not to be taken literally, and that it is in some sort of code, the essence of which is that only those aspects of a tree's existence which might be pleasant for a girl are to be taken as being desired for her. The following lines confirm the rightness of this de-coding, and guide it more closely. The verse ends, for example, with the wish that the girl should 'live like a green laurel', and specifies the 'likeness' in the line 'Rooted in one dear perpetual place'.

As an example of the difference between key and coded signals in irony, we may take Swift's *Modest Proposal*. The first eight paragraphs of the pamphlet are concerned with the unhappy state of the Irish poor and their children, and they establish in the reader's mind, by the normal mode of communication, the writer's deep concern for their sufferings, and his indignation with those responsible for them. When, therefore, in the next paragraph he advances the suggestion that they should be fattened, sold, and eaten, the reader has been quite sufficiently alerted to the incompatibility of such a course with the writer's real feelings, and warned that the message must not be taken at its face value. He has been assured, moreover, that the writer himself is not a cannibal: his knowledge of the tastiness of children's flesh, he carefully explains, has come to him at second hand from 'a very knowing *American* of my Acquaintance in *London*' (XII, 111).[8] There is, moreover, the plain fact that in the society which uses the English language —and used it in Swift's time—cannibalism is generally frowned on, save under certain extreme conditions such as shipwreck, war in the jungle and Outward Bound endurance courses. Indeed English law discountenances it even under these extreme conditions, if the verdict in Stevenson's case may be taken as representing the last word of our lawyers on the subject. This incompatibility of the particular proposal with everything else that can be learnt about the writer and his background, both from the text itself and from its context, is the key which warns the reader of the need for de-coding, and suggests to him how it should be done: that what the writer really means is that the children of the Irish poor should *not* be eaten, as, in a manner of speaking, they actually are being eaten, by the English—including the reader.

The *Modest Proposal* also illustrates very clearly the compatibility between irony and metaphor—a compatibility to be expected from the similarity between their basic modes of communication. For the initial suggestion that the children should be eaten is immediately followed by this metaphor which itself provides a key to the correct de-coding of the ironic message:

> I grant this food will be somewhat dear, and therefore very *proper for Landlords*; who, as they have already devoured most of the Parents, seem to have the best Title to the Children. (XII, 112).

And towards the end of the pamphlet, this key is repeated, with a very slight variation in the choice of key-word:

> For, this kind of Commodity will not bear Exportation; the Flesh being of too tender a Consistence, to admit of long continuance in Salt; *although, perhaps, I could name a Country, which would be glad to Eat up our whole Nation without it.* (XII, 117).

In both of these passages, it is the metaphor which provides the key to de-coding the ironic signals. But it must be observed that if metaphors are to carry out this function, they must obey the general law for keys of codes: they must not themselves be in code. That is to say, they must be so commonplace that there will be no risk of their being taken literally, and in this respect Swift's metaphors are very different from the tree-metaphors in Yeats' poem, for they (despite some slight reference to the Daphne-laurel myth) are essentially novel and exploratory, as are most of the metaphors of modern poets. Both of the key-words used by Swift here have long histories of use in very much the same sense which makes them effective warnings of the existence of coded signals in the *Modest Proposal*. The first, 'devours', occurs in a famous description of the Devil in the Bible. He is said to go to and fro in the earth, like a roaring lion, seeking whom he may *devour*, and it is, of course, understood that the Devil, for all his faults, is no cannibal. It is men's souls, not their bodies, that he is roaring for. The phrase has acquired something of proverbial currency and force, and may well have exercised some influence over the whole lexical history of this word. Shakespeare uses it often in this metaphorical sense; 'time' and 'pestilence' devour, so do wars and the sea; good deeds past are 'scraps devoured', and so on. In Milton, the scythe of Time devours, and so do death and war. Swift himself used the same word in such contexts as these:

> The utmost Favour a Man can expect from them is, that which *Polyphemus* promised *Ulysses*, that he would devour him the last. (*A Tritical Essay*, I, 249).
>
> . . . there is hardly any remainder left of Dean and chapter lands in Ireland; that delicious morsel swallowed so greedily in England under the fanatick Usurpations. (XII, 185–6).
>
> (The synonymy of 'devour' and 'swallow' used in this special sense can be extensively paralleled in Shakespeare, Milton, etc.)

As for 'eat up', there are examples by the score in the same predecessors: in Shakespeare, for example, 'Appetite, a universal wolf,/So doubly seconded with will and power,/Must make perforce a universal prey,/And last eat up itself'. 'He that is proud eats up himself'; 'if the wars eat us not up, they will'. This group of nearly synonymous metaphors was, in fact, already so commonplace that none of these words could be misunderstood, or be taken literally, and the conventional mode of de-coding them was a clear pointer to the de-coding of the more elaborate coded signals which they accompany. Indeed there is a sense in which the *Modest Proposal* can be regarded as a deliberate expansion of these conventional metaphors, with all their associations; all it does is to take them literally, and so suggest that they are, in the particular case, much more nearly true in the literal sense than their habitual users might care to believe.

No doubt many other types of key to ironic codes could be identified, but for the moment we are concerned only with one more. And this is a direct extension of flatness, of commonplace, just noted in Swift's key-metaphors. Flatness of language, commonplaceness, can itself serve as a key of the de-coding of ironic messages, especially when it is brought into vivid contrast with the opposing qualities of violence and outrageousness of expression. Thus, to return for a moment to our cocktail-party victims, A and B: one of the possible, even probable intonations which A might use for his coded utterance 'Isn't this a lovely party?' would be abnormally monotonous, perhaps with a slight fall in pitch at the end instead of the rise more usual at the end of questions. And this abnormal flatness would serve to make B aware that the utterance was a statement rather than a question, and so suggest to him that it required to be looked at with special care, and perhaps de-coded into a quite different message.[9]

It is here, at last, that we rejoin the main thread of our argument. For it was this excessive flatness of style, this exaggerated commonplaceness of diction and structure, which at one and the same time conformed admirably with Swift's doctrine on the restriction of the vocabulary to a central core of simple words, and also enabled him to exploit precisely this lifeless quality as a key to ironic coding, thus conferring on it new force of meaning. It was also a linguistic medium well fitted for that powerful ironic effect noted above, whereby the ironist temporarily blurs the distinction between the coded and uncoded parts of his set of signals, so that the receiver has the shock of discovering that he has made (or been led into) a mistake, and that he must revise his interpretation of the signals so far received. But it is high time for us to leave these very abstract descriptions, and see how they apply to actual examples.

IV

One characteristic and effective way in which Swift uses the flat, trite restricted vocabulary is in passages which follow immediately on pieces of railing, which have made his real attitude quite clear by the normal mode of communication. The sharp, sudden contrast between the two vocabularies gives the needed warning that coding of the signals is in play, though even an alert reader may need a sentence or two to realise what has happened. The attitude communicated in the open railing, moreover, leaves no doubt as to the manner in which the de-coding should be done.

There are several early examples of this pattern in *A Tale of a Tub*, and one of the most interesting is in the *Preface*, where it is part of a discussion of the aims and methods of satire. Swift sets up a contrast between satire and panegyric, recommending the young author to practise the former rather than the latter for a variety of ironic reasons. One of these is that the panegyrist can praise but a few, and will thereby excite envy among many, while the satirist will cause universal satisfaction, since every individual will suppose the satire to apply to everyone but himself. The argument goes on:

. . . you may securely display your utmost *Rhetoric* against Mankind, in the Face of the World; tell them, '*That* we *all are gone astray*; *That there is none that doth good, no not one*; *That we live in the very Dregs of Time*; *That Knavery and Atheism are Epidemick as the Pox*; *That Honesty is fled with Astraea*; with any other Common places *equally* new and eloquent, which are furnished by the *Splendida bilis*. And when you have done, the whole Audience, far from being offended, shall return you thanks as a Deliverer of precious and useful Truths. Nay farther: It is but to venture your Lungs, and you may preach in *Covent-Garden* against Foppery and Fornication, and *something else*: Against Pride and Dissimulation, and Bribery, at *White Hall*: You may expose Rapins and Injustice in the *Inns of Court* Chappel: And in the *City* Pulpit be as fierce as you please, against Avarice, Hypocrisie and Extortion. 'Tis but a *Ball* bandied to and fro, and every Man carries a *Racket* about him to strike it from himself among the rest of the Company. But on the other side, whoever should mistake the Nature of things so far, as to drop but a single Hint in publick. How *such a one* starved half the Fleet, and half-poison'd the rest; How *such a one*, from a true Principle of *Love* and *Honour*, pays no Debts but for *Wenches and Play*: How *such a one* has got a Clap and runs out of his Estate: How *Paris* bribed by *Juno* and *Venus*, loath to offend either Party, slept out the whole Cause on the Beach: Or, how *such an Orator* makes long Speeches in the Senate with much Thought, little Sense, and to no Purpose; whoever, I say, should venture to be thus particular, must expect to be imprisoned for *Scandalum Magnatum*; to have *Challenges* sent him; to be sued for *Defamation*; and to be *brought before the Bar of the House*. (I, 30–2).

Now the vocabulary in play here is very near to that of railing—as near as Swift may have felt inclined to go, and there is an open, or very lightly encoded attack on various vices, together with a guide to their distribution round London. In the last section, it would seem that scandalous attacks on individuals are being freely made—and the 'such a ones' are clearly very scandalous people. The great taboos are invoked—pox, clap and wenching. Swift's attitude to all these things is quite open, and the reader is left in no doubt whatever about his moral standards, and the extent to which the world falls below them. But all

this is merely by way of preparation for the real blow, which is introduced with a sudden change of diction, from railing and satire to the
inexpressible blandness of panegyric, where not a word lies outside the
central core of simple and gentlemanly English:

> But I forget that I am expatiating on a Subject, wherein I have no
> concern, having neither a Talent nor an Inclination for Satyr. On
> the other side, I am so entirely satisfied with the whole present
> Procedure of human Things, that I have been for some Years
> preparing Materials towards *A Panegyrick upon the World*, to which I
> intended to add a Second Part, entituled *A Modest Defence of the
> Proceedings of the Rabble in all Ages*.

This reads as smoothly as a prospectus for the South Sea Company, and
contrasts so clearly with the tone of what has preceded it, that the
reader is warned of the existence of coded signals. What the contrast
signals, in fact, is not the expression of a different and changed attitude
to the vices of the world, but a continued condemnation of them by
that kind of panegyric which, in Swift's hands, is so much more deadly
than open satire.

The same contrast in choice of words is found in one of the most
notable passages described by Swift himself as 'irony'. It is in *A Short
View of Ireland*, and here the 'panegyric' comes first, in a description of
the state of the country as it is represented by English official observers:

> Let the worthy *Commissioners* who come from *England*, ride round the
> Kingdom, and observe the face of Nature, or the faces of the
> Natives, the Improvements of the Land; the thriving numerous
> Plantations; the noble Woods; the Abundance and Vicinity of
> Country-Seats; the commodious Farmers-Houses and Barns; the
> Towns and Villages, where every Body is busy, and thriving with
> all Kind of Manufactures; the Shops full of Goods, wrought to
> Perfection, and filled with Customers; the comfortable Diet and
> Dress, and Dwellings of the People; the vast Numbers of Ships in
> our Harbours and Docks, and Ship-wrights in our Seaport-Towns.
> The Roads crouded with Carriers, laden with rich Manufactures;
> the perpetual Concourse to and from of pompous Equipages.
> With what Envy, and Admiration, would those Gentlemen
> return from so delightful a Progress? What glorious Reports would
> they make, when they went back to *England*? (XII, 10).

The 'glory' of the reports is, of course, as misleading as the exaggeration
of the panegyric implies, but here Swift himself, overcome by the
bitterness of the truth, himself undertakes the de-coding of the whole
passage:

> But my Heart is too heavy to continue this Irony longer; for it is
> manifest, that whatever Stranger took such a Journey, would be apt

to think himself travelling in *Lapland* or *Ysland*, rather than in a Country so favoured by Nature as Ours, both in Fruitfulness of Soil, and Temperature of Climate. The miserable Dress, and Dyet, and Dwelling of the People. The general Desolation in most Parts of the Kingdom. The old Seats of the Nobility and Gentry all in Ruins, and no new Ones in their Stead. The Families of Farmers, who pay great Rents, living in Filth and Nastiness upon Butter-milk and Potatoes, without a Shoe or Stocking to their Feet; or a House so convenient as an *English* Hog-sty, to receive them. (*Ibid.*)

It will be apparent from this passage that Swift himself was, at any rate by 1728, very clearly aware of the nature of his own irony, and of the special use to which he had put the vocabulary and tone of 'panegyric' since *A Tale of a Tub*. It was, indeed, the device which he had used again and again in *Gulliver's Travels*, not least in the long account given by Gulliver of the state of England. This is carefully introduced as an official panegyric, and by an invocation so exaggeratedly and pompously patriotic that it serves to warn the reader of the coded signals to come:

Imagine with thy self, courteous Reader, how often I then wished for the Tongue of *Demosthenes* or *Cicero*, that might have enabled me to celebrate the Praises of my own dear native Country in a Style equal to its Merits and Felicity. (XI, 111).

The flattest and drabbest of styles would not, of course, match Swift's actual estimate of these merits and this felicity, but the announcement warns the reader that in the ensuing account he is to expect the same strain of apparent panegyric, which is to be constantly de-coded into its opposite, aided by frequent reminders of the need for this de-coding, and the direction it should take. For example, the King puts questions such as these, by way of clarification of what Gulliver has told him: 'What Qualifications were necessary in those who are to be created new Lords: Whether the Humour of the Prince, a Sum of Money to a Court-Lady, or a Prime Minister; or a Design of strengthening a Party opposite to the publick Interest, ever happened to be Motives in those Advancements.' And when the King has been possessed of all the information he needs, he takes Gulliver into his hands, strokes him (just as Swift has been stroking the reader with his panegyric on England), and gives, both for himself and for the reader, the final de-coding of all that has been said: 'My little friend *Grildrig*; you have made a most admirable Panegyrick upon your Country . . . by what I have gathered from your own Relation, and the Answers I have with much Pains wringed and extorted from you; I cannot but conclude the Bulk of your Natives, to be the most pernicious Race of little odious

L

Vermin that Nature ever suffered to crawl upon the Surface of the
Earth.' (XI, 116).

As a final example of the same deployment of contrasting modes
of communication and diction, the 'panegyrick' and the 'satyrick', we
may take a passage from the conclusion to the *Travels*. Here Swift
affects to be giving his reasons for not reporting to the government his
discoveries of new lands, so that they could be duly conquered and
added to the British Empire. This is his last reason against performing
this patriotic duty:

> But, I had another Reason which made me less forward to enlarge
> his Majesty's Dominions by my Discoveries: To say the Truth, I
> had conceived a few Scruples with relation to the distributive
> Justice of Princes upon those Occasions. For instance, A Crew of
> Pyrates are driven by a Storm they know not whither; at length a
> Boy discovers Land from the Top-mast; they go on Shore to rob
> and plunder; they see an harmless People, are entertained with
> Kindness, they give the Country a new Name, they take formal
> Possession of it for the King, they set up a rotten Plank or a Stone for
> a Memorial, they murder two or three Dozen of the Natives, bring
> away a Couple more by Force for a Sample, return home, and get
> their Pardon. Here commences a new Dominion acquired with a Title
> by *Divine Right*. Ships are sent with the first Opportunity; the Natives
> driven out or destroyed, their Princes tortured to discover their
> Gold; a free Licence given to all Acts of Inhumanity and Lust; the
> Earth reeking with the Blood of its Inhabitants: And this execrable
> Crew of Butchers employed in so pious an Expedition, is a *modern
> Colony* sent to convert and civilize an idolatrous and barbarous People.
> (XI, 278).

This is not in code. It is open railing. After the quiet warning 'a few
Scruples', it rises steadily to an openly outraged climax, in the contrast
between the 'execrable crew of Butchers' and the conversion and
civilization of 'idolatrous and barbarous people'; this is not an ironic
statement, since no de-coding is needed to realise that neither religion
nor civilisation can be propagated by those who so conspicuously
lack both qualities. The structure of the sentences very aptly keeps
pace with the mounting force of the condemnation. The auxiliary verb
is carried on from the sentence beginning 'Ships are sent . . .' to the
next two sentences, but it can hardly be made to operate at all in the
final phrase, 'the Earth reeking with the Blood of its Inhabitants',
which strikes the reader with the open violence of an exclamation.
It is, in itself, a very good piece of railing, but its purpose is something
quite beyond itself. It is to give the reader the key to what is coming,
the encoded version of the same opinions. And the last sentence, by

opposing so powerfully the customary official version of the aims of British colonialism, at once introduces the ironically coded passage, and warns the reader of its true nature and interpretation. This very clear warning is reinforced by an abrupt change in the whole character of the diction. The violent and open indignation of words like 'rob, plunder, murder, rotten, tortured, lust, reeking, butchers' is left behind, and the ensuing description has all the deadly smoothness of all those official versions which all governments and their defenders have used throughout history to justify their acts of ignobility and inhumanity:

> But this Description, I confess, doth by no means affect the *British* Nation, who may be an Example to the whole World for their Wisdom, Care, and Justice in planting Colonies; the liberal Endowments for the Advancement of Religion and Learning; their Choice of devout and able Pastors to propagate *Christianity*; their Caution in stocking their Provinces with People of sober Lives and Conversations from this the Mother Kingdom; their strict Regard to the Distribution of Justice, in supplying the Civil Administration through all their Colonies with Officers of the greatest Abilities, utter Strangers to Corruption: And to crown all, by sending the most vigilant and virtuous Governors, who have no other Views than the Happiness of the People over whom they preside, and the Honour of the King their Master. (XI, 278–9).

It is enough for the modern reader to take note of this bland tone, this gentlemanly choice of words, to know that there is not a word of truth in the whole grim panegyric. If he tries, *ex tempore*, to summon up some knowledge of the actual facts, he may succeed in recalling that the colonies at that time were indeed not stocked with 'People of sober Lives and Conversations', but with convicted felons. And he will not be astray in concluding that every other statement made here to the honour of the British People is to be turned upside down in precisely the same fashion: that colonies were conducted with no care for learning, or religion, justice, common honesty, or the happiness of the colonists, but solely for the advantage of that execrable crew of pirates who described themselves, according to their eminence and success in their profession, as Pastors, Magistrates or Governors, to the measureless dishonour of the King who was insufficiently their Master (or perhaps himself insufficiently Honourable) to make them behave any better. This is the 'message' which the reader discovers for himself, and in a sense in himself, when the set of signals has been de-coded in the light of the key previously given. But in its coded form, it has none but the mildest, the most respectable of words. There is no trace of violence in the vocabulary, or even of individuality. On the surface, we have nothing but the official language of the various orders of pirate, in a series of clichés as sterling as the sovereigns of old.

It would be easy to multiply examples of that heavily clichéd use of metaphor, and the ironic expansion of stock metaphors, which has been mentioned above. A notable instance would be the well-known passage from the *Digression on Madness* in *A Tale of a Tub* on the advantages of 'Credulity' over 'Wisdom', of being 'a Fool among Knaves'. The whole argument is developed by expanding the commonplace metaphors involved in the contrast between the 'surface' of things and their 'inside', and by joining this with that metaphorical extension of 'anatomy' which had been current at least since Burton wrote on melancholy, and had received a new impetus from the investigations of members of the Royal Society. The same passage would illustrate the extreme delicacy of which Swift was master in handling the ambiguities of the normal, the central and mild English vocabulary. When he tells us that he had lately seen a woman flayed, and that we would hardly believe how 'much it altered her Person for the worse', the word 'Person' is doing double duty, and performing both of its duties superbly well. It means, indeed, in the 'coded' set of signals, nothing more than her body; but in the de-coded 'message', it summons up the whole series of resonances going back at least as far as Cleopatra's 'person', which beggared all description, and the use of the same word by Swift's contemporaries to describe, with mock-gallantry and real salaciousness, a woman's body considered as an object of lust: thus Shamela was to say, a generation later, 'I thought once of making a little fortune by my person. I now intend to make a great one by my vartue.'[10]

Further illustrations, however, are not needed for the main point of my argument: that the kind of language to which Swift was restricted by his linguistic and social doctrines was precisely the kind of language capable of carrying the coded messages of irony; and that there was, in this sense, a kind of providential coincidence between his sense of the language and his special need for a satirical instrument. By this means, he was able to defend the traditional values, and to rail against those who were subverting them, while yet keeping the full decorum of a polished and civilised diction, and so escaping from the dilemma (which has sadly gored many a satirist since) of letting down his own side by his mode of defending it.

V

Some apology may well be needed for the laborious analysis of
irony given here, beyond the need to demonstrate its relation with a
particular phase in the history of the language. The excuse must be
that the device really is rather delicate, and that it has already suffered a
little from rough handling. There are critics who, because they have
failed to examine patiently the mechanism of irony, have insufficiently
distinguished between the coded signals in Swift and his real messages,
and have concluded that his outlook on mankind was 'negative' or
despairing. They have, indeed, been clumsy enough to fall into the
error thus described by Peacock's character, Mr. Sarcastic, who in the
twenty-first chapter of *Melincourt* explains his habit of 'reducing practice
to theory' and thereby gaining 'inexhaustible amusement':

> This then is my system. I ascertain the practice of those I talk to,
> and present it to them as from myself, in the shape of a theory: the
> consequence of which is, that I am universally stigmatized as a pro-
> mulgator of rascally doctrines.

In just the same way, all too many readers and critics of Swift have
supposed him to be 'a promulgator of rascally doctrine'—and for much
the same reason. He was, in fact, about as much of an optimist as any
man can possibly be, provided he is not a fool and is fully capable of
understanding the knavery of those around him. And the essential
optimism, the positiveness of outlook, implied in the ironic method is
very clearly explained again by Mr. Sarcastic in the same discourse—
which should be regarded as one of the great commonplaces on irony:

> *Mr. Forester.* Your system is sufficiently amusing, but I much
> question its utility. The object of moral censure is reformation, and
> its proper vehicle is plain and fearless sincerity. . . .
> *Mr. Sarcastic.* I tried that in my youth, when I was troubled with the
> *passion for reforming the world*; of which I have been long cured, by the
> conviction of the inefficacy of moral theory with respect to producing
> a practical change in the mass of mankind. Custom is the pillar round
> which opinion twines, and interest is the tie that binds it. It is not
> by reason that practical change can be effected, but by making a
> puncture to the quick in the feelings of personal hope and personal
> fear.[11]

It was precisely this 'puncture to the quick' that Swift too hoped to
make by the delicate instrument of irony. And it was the more likely
to be successful because the ironic signals must be de-coded by their
recipient, giving him something of the impression that they have
indeed originated partly in himself. He has been an active partner in

working out the message from the signals, and the whole system of keys and codes forces him into a kind of complicity with the satirist, who thus penetrates beneath his carapace of custom and interest, and has some prospect of stimulating 'to the quick the feelings' within. This special intimacy of relation between the ironist and his victim is possible only because the signals emitted are not messages in the normal mode of communication, but, as it were, complex stimuli designed to provoke the reconstruction of the real messages by an unusual activity on the part of the recipient. And this activity involves him in, perhaps commits him to, the content of the message he has in a sense made for and from himself.

There is a certain similarity between this process and that studied in what Communication Theorists a few years ago were calling 'the cocktail party problem'. They had discovered, that in the din of a social gathering under the influence of alcohol, a tape-recorder was unable to pick up enough signals to make an intelligible record of what A might be saying. How, then, did B manage to receive it? The answer was that in communicating under these conditions, A and B entered into a kind of unspoken compact, by which they undertook to do much more than merely use their mouths and ears. Eyes came into it too, for watching the lips—and for not watching other people, even pretty ones; gestures too were to be observed; and over and above these describable phenomena there was to be, for the time being, a special rapport between the two communicators the nature of which was a large part of 'the cocktail party problem'—and so far as I know it is still incompletely solved. Just the same kind of rapport is necessary between the ironist and his recipient, or at least a very similar kind of temporary intimacy. Sterne used it to tease his reader for having a dirty mind—sometimes even played with it almost as an end in itself, as an aesthetic game. Swift used it because he saw in it a way to puncture the hard carapace of habitual stupidity and greed, and to arouse within it the common feelings of humanity, pity and that sense of fair play which is, on occasions, among the virtues of the English. To believe in the existence of this central core of decency, and in the possibility, given stimuli sharp and subtle enough, of rousing it from its customary dormancy, was not negative, but intensely and practically positive.

NOTES

[1] Oxford, 1920; 3rd ed., reprinted, 1953; pp. 158–161 on Swift's views on language; pp. 392–4 on *Polite Conversation*.
[2] *Lives of the Poets* (Everyman edition), II, 392, 389.

³ It is probably for this reason that Swift paid tribute to two translators of *Don Quixote*, Ozell and Stevens, in the *Introduction* to *Polite Conversation* (IV, 118).

⁴ Sonnet VI, 'His Pallace of Pleasure', in *Foure Letters and Certeine Sonnets*, ed. G. B. Harrison (London, 1922), p. 89.

⁵ The term used by the great Sanskrit grammarians to mean irony, or something very like it, is in fact a word for a particular pattern of intonation.

⁶ That Swift was aware of his problem, in a manner not very different from my description of it, appears from the lines quoted by the Editor from *Cadenus and Vanessa* on p. 17.

⁷ As the classical rhetoricians clearly saw. There is a useful discussion of all three 'figures' in Quintilian, *Inst. Orat.* VIII. vi.

⁸ The real helpfulness of this 'key' is blunted for some unwary readers by a change in the language. In Swift's time, 'American' was never used of the white colonists; it always meant an Indian. The whole phrase is made up of ambiguous words: 'knowing' can be fairly good or pretty bad, 'of my acquaintance'—not a friend, certainly, nor a frequent companion. Taken one way, the whole phrase is quiet and bland; but only just beneath its surface lurks something very like 'a very fly Redskin I happened to come across in London', and a much more emphatic warning as to the proper decoding of what is to follow in the next words.

⁹ It seems to me very probable that Swift wished to indicate special intonations and stresses to the 'inner voice' of his readers by means of italic. This probability is suggested by many of the passages quoted here, not least by those from the *Modest Proposal* above, where two key-phrases (in my special technical sense) are in italic. I refrain from pursuing this point further because it would involve a long excursion into typography, and an even longer into phonetics, but would note in passing that, as so often, Swift was fully conscious of his own practices and their implications. In *On Poetry: A Rapsody*, he wrote:

> To Statesmen wou'd you give a Wipe,
> You print it in *Italick Type*.
> When Letters are in Vulgar Shapes,
> 'Tis ten to one the Wit escapes;
> But when in Capitals exprest
> The dullest Reader smoaks the Jest. (*Poems*, 643).

¹⁰ *Shamela*, end of Letter X; in Fielding, *Joseph Andrews and Shamela*, ed. M. C. Battestin (London, 1965), p. 325.

¹¹ T. L. Peacock, *Novels*, ed. D. Garnett (London, 1948), pp. 222–5.

Swift's Use of Irony

HERBERT DAVIS

I propose to examine some examples of Swift's different uses o-
irony, keeping in mind particularly the risk he took of being misf
understood; and not forgetting that some problems in the interpretation of irony may become more difficult with the passage of the
centuries, as changing ways of life and standards of behaviour sometimes throw into obscurity the original intentions of the writer.

Swift himself was aware of the danger of being misunderstood
even by his first readers. In the Apology which he wrote for the fifth
edition of *A Tale of a Tub*, in 1710, he admits that he had played some
tricks, which might well have provoked some of his unsophisticated
readers, but appealed to '*the Men of Tast*, [who] *will observe and distinguish
. . . that there generally runs an Irony through the Thread of the whole Book
. . . which will render some Objections that have been made, very weak and
insignificant*'. (I, 4). I propose now that as readers 'of Taste' we should
'observe and distinguish' the irony that runs through the thread
of all his work, for it is a way of writing which he seems almost to
claim as his own special gift. In this art he was the great master and
could brook no rival:

> ARBUTHNOT is no more my friend,
> Who dares to Irony pretend;
> Which I was born to introduce,
> Refin'd it first, and shew'd its Use. (*Poems*, 555)

But that is itself not to be taken too seriously. Swift might have
forgotten the irony of Shakespeare which is often refined enough, but
he would not have forgotten the claims of Socrates. And if pressed,
he would probably have admitted that in the generation just before
him, Andrew Marvell, whose work we know he admired, had shown
some gift that way. He even anticipated that particular mixture of
parody and irony which marks *A Tale of a Tub*; and Swift would have
found it difficult to improve upon Marvell's parody of Charles II in
his 'Most Gracious Speech to Both Houses of Parliament':

> If you give me the revenue I desire, I shall be able to do those things
> for your religion and liberty, that I have had long in my thoughts,
> but cannot effect them without a little more money to carry me
> through.

After explaining the kind of things he will do for them, he ends with this splendid irony:

> I desire you to believe me as you have found me; and I do solemnly promise you, that whatsoever you give me shall be especially managed with the same conduct, trust, sincerity and prudence, that I have ever practised since my happy restoration.

But this is still the simplest form of irony—to talk of the sincerity and prudence of Charles II, or to talk as Swift did of 'the singular Humanity' of Dr. Bentley; it is what Puttenham had called 'the drye mocke'. And we must look for something more sustained as well as more refined, which runs through the thread of the whole *Tale*. Perhaps the chief cause of difficulty for modern readers is Swift's refinement of Marvell's mixture of parody and irony. In his parody of Dryden and L'Estrange, which he particularly draws to our attention so that we shall not miss the point, he adds a touch of contempt by assuming the role and the style of a Grub Street hack, who lives in a garret, and writes under the stimulus of hunger and want of money, and complains of the unfair competition of these two '*Junior* start-up Societies . . . of *Gresham* and of Will's', who have made 'continual Efforts . . . to edify a Name and Reputation upon the Ruin of OURS'. (I, 38). Here with one stroke he is able to reduce the Royal Society and the literary establishment who pay their court to Dryden at Will's Coffee-House to the Grub Street level. In his satire on the corruptions of the world of letters, Swift does not hesitate to use the extravagances and absurdities of tone and manner of the hack; and he makes the most of his role, to indulge in all kinds of follies and enjoys the freedoms and the privileges which are allowed to those who wear a mask. But recent critics like William Ewald and Ronald Paulson, in their attempts to analyse Swift's methods, seem to me in their emphasis on the use Swift makes of his disguise—of the language and tricks of Grub Street—to be in danger of confusing us so that the much more important element—the play of irony—is obscured. What I would contend is that here, just as with all his other later disguises, Swift simply makes use of a mask as it suits him; it is never permanently moulded over his face, and it always allows him to use his own voice. It is a mask which he holds in his hand, like a comedian, which may be withdrawn at any moment to show a sardonic grin or a humorous smile. Thus, when in his role of Grub Street hack he goes on to tell us of his literary plans, explaining that he has 'neither a Talent nor an Inclination for Satyr' and is 'so entirely satisfied with the whole present Procedure of human Things' that he has been 'for some Years preparing Materials towards *A Panegyrick upon the World*' (I, 32), we can observe the very moment when parody turns into irony; and that satirical rogue—the real author —very conscious of the completeness of his own dissatisfaction with the whole world of religion and learning, removes the mask for a moment and indulges in the simplest form of irony. In fact, he never surrenders his pen into the hands of a Grub Street hack, whose manner and point of view are substituted for his own. He always remains himself in complete charge; he never becomes the sport of his own characters. Indeed, I cannot think of any writer who is at every moment in more complete and more conscious control. The puppets he is using are always being manipulated by his fingers, and their voices, however disguised, are always his voice.

I do not wish to be thought to suggest for a moment that there is not to be found in Ronald Paulson's study of *A Tale of a Tub* some excellent comments on Swift's irony. He has shown how often we ought to be reminded of such favourite books of Swift's as Erasmus' *Praise of Folly* and Cervantes' *Don Quixote*, how like his irony is to theirs, and his use of the fool and madman, to expose the world of reality underneath the world of illusion. The whole of the clothes imagery, whether applied to the universe—'a large *Suit of Cloaths*, which *invests* every thing' (I 46)—or to the globe—'What is that which some call *Land*, but a fine Coat faced with Green? or the Sea, but a Wastcoat of Water-Tabby?' (47) or 'the *vegetable* Beaux,' or man himself, 'a complete suit of Cloaths with all its Trimmings'—is so inexhaustible in its possibilities that he can't let it alone. It may be used to frighten us with a vision of all these mirrors of illusion surrounding us; or it may finally be turned to account to be used at his own expense to remind us of the tricks he is playing upon us, all the finery he has put on for our amusement:

> *Embroidery*, was *sheer Wit*; *Gold Fringe* was *agreeable Conversation*, *Gold Lace* was *Repartee*, a huge long *Periwig* was *Humor*, and a *Coat full of Powder* was very good *Raillery*: All which required abundance of *Finesse* and *Delicatesse* to manage with Advantage, as well as a strict Observance after Times and Fashions. (I, 48).

In the digressions that interrupt the tale of the three brothers and their coats, he is concerned to expose the fakes and absurdities of the learned world—its criticism and its scholarship—and finally to strip off all the show and trappings of the professions and the world of rank and society and reveal the Bedlam which surrounds us.

Two of these digressions will provide us with opportunity to observe the 'Thread of Irony'—the first, concerning critics, Section III, which begins with a grave apology for having got so far without having performed the usual politenesses expected by 'my *good Lords* the

Criticks'. He proposes to make up for this unpardonable omission by looking into the 'Original and Pedigree of the word, and considering the ancient and present State thereof'. He defends the critics against their detractors who say

> that a *True Critick* is a sort of Mechanick, set up . . . at as little Expence as a *Taylor* . . . on the contrary, nothing is more certain, than that it requires greater Layings out, to be free of the *Critick's* Company, than of any other you can name. For, as to be a *true Beggar*, it will cost the richest Candidate every Groat he is worth; so, before one can commence a *True Critick*, it will cost a Man all the good Qualities of his Mind. . . . (I, 62–3).

and he concludes with three maxims, which can be used to distinguish a true modern critic from a pretender. I will quote the first, which shows alike the thread and the embroidery:

> The first is, That *Criticism*, contrary to all other Faculties of the Intellect, is ever held the truest and best, when it is the very *first* Result of the *Critick's* Mind: As Fowlers reckon the first aim for the surest, and seldom fail of missing the Mark, if they stay for a Second. (63).

Then, having brought his chapter to a successful conclusion, he returns to the main story with the hope that he has 'deserved so well of their whole *Body*, [the critics] as to meet with generous and tender Usage at their *Hands*.' (64).

I do not find it very helpful to be told that the particular tone of the raillery here is due to the fact that a Grub Street hack is speaking; nor do I share Mr. Paulson's impression 'that the guiding hand of the satirist is not so evident as in the work of Marvell or Eachard, because the gesturing Hack is all that is in sight'. I always hear the voice of Swift—the words are in fact his own—and the tone seems to me to come directly from the ironic intention of the author, when he refers, for instance, to 'our Noble *Moderns*; whose most edifying Volumes I turn indefatigably over Night and Day, for the Improvement of my Mind and the good of my Country.'

But it is in the superb rhetoric of Section IX, the Digression on Madness, that we recognize for the first time the peculiar intensity of Swiftian irony and realize that he had good reason to claim this as the particular kingdom where he ruled alone. Dr. Johnson must, I think, have had this particularly in mind when he said that Swift exhibits in the *Tale* 'a vehemence and rapidity of mind, a copiousness of images, and vivacity of diction such as he afterwards never possessed or never exerted'. Yet I would maintain that, in spite of all the exuberance and wit, the tricks and gaieties of the book, we can find there also Swift's characteristic directness and concreteness, the liveliness of racy, living speech: 'when a Man's Fancy gets *astride* on his Reason, when Imagination is at Cuffs with the Senses, and common Understanding, as well as Common Sense, is Kickt out of Doors; the first Proselyte he makes, is Himself.' (I, 108).

Even when he moves to subtler and more abstract propositions, the language remains almost conversational in tone; it never becomes academic or professional. The result is that the calm surface of the prose allows us to perceive very clearly the depth beneath; we are led on quietly and unsuspecting, and then suddenly faced with the horror of the real situation:

> For, if we take an Examination of what is generally understood by *Happiness*, as it has Respect, either to the Understanding or the Senses, we shall find all its Properties and Adjuncts will herd under this short Definition: That, *it is a perpetual Possession of being well Deceived*. And first, with relation to the Mind or Understanding; 'tis manifest, what mighty Advantages Fiction has over Truth; and the Reason is just at our Elbow; because Imagination can build nobler Scenes, and produce more wonderful Revolutions than Fortune or Nature will be at Expence to furnish. (108).

Then, after a couple of paragraphs, sparkling with wit full of exuberance and the delight of the young man in the realization of the splendid performance he was putting on, we are brought back to this theme again, and the whole is resolved in those final closing notes:

> He that can with *Epicurus* content his Ideas with the *Films* and *Images* that fly off upon his Senses from the *Superficies* of Things; Such a Man, truly wise, creams off Nature, leaving the Sower and the Dregs, for Philosophy and Reason to lap up. This is the sublime and refined Point of Felicity, called, *the Possession of being well deceived*; The Serene Peaceful State of being a Fool among Knaves. (110).

Swift's meaning here should be clear enough, as he points so triumphantly to the only way which could lead in this sorry world to any kind of felicity or serenity or peace.

I want to make quite clear what I think is the position of the writer here, for this passage, with its striking repetitions and underlinings, has always seemed to me to reveal very clearly something that we need to bear in mind in our interpretation of all Swift's work. The irony appears, I think we should agree, in such statements as refer to the 'mighty advantages Fiction has over Truth' or to the wisdom of the man who 'creams off Nature', content with the '*Images* that fly off . . . from the *Superficies* of Things'. But the whole argument is arranged to leave us with nothing but utter scepticism. There can be no happiness or felicity in this world except in the 'perpetual Possession' of full and complete deception, no serenity or peace except for the fool who does not allow himself to be disturbed by the knaves. Lest we should be under any doubt about his position, Swift devotes the rest of the chapter to a very thorough examination of the world's knavery, and triumphantly proves its madness by taking us on a visit to Bedlam, and showing us there the talents and qualities essential for the highest success in all the professions, which 'are here mislaid'. He vividly describes the behaviour of the inmates—even adding a memorable illustration of the cells that were then open for the entertainment of the public—and explains his 'high Esteem' for 'that honourable Society, whereof I had some Time the Happiness to be an unworthy Member.' (111). He shows us some splendid examples of just those very qualities needed to command a regiment of dragoons, or required for success in Westminster Hall, the Court, or the City; and then he presses the irony a little further, by assuring us that it is not merely a matter of rescuing these talents now buried, 'but all these would very much excel, and arrive at great Perfection in their several Kinds; which I think, is manifest from what I have already shewn . . .' (113–4).

*   *   *

I am not myself aware that the conditions and circumstances under which we now live have made Swift's *Tale of a Tub* out of date or his irony difficult to interpret; but this may not be true when we come to deal with that splendid piece of sustained irony, in which he attempted to meet the attacks of the Deists and the Whigs on the Established Church. He made sure that they would read it by providing this alluring title: *An ARGUMENT To Prove, That the Abolishing of CHRISTIANITY in ENGLAND, May, as Things now Stand, be attended with some Inconveniences, and perhaps, not produce those many good Effects proposed thereby.* (II, 26).

The attitude of the writer is exactly shown by the tone of this statement. There will be parody as well as irony; for here is a case to be argued, to be drawn up with all the care, the necessary qualifications and detailed consideration of all objections, which could possibly come into the minds of judge or jury, anticipating every possibility that learned counsel on the other side might bring forward—*in England, may, as things now stand—and perhaps*. He never forgets for a moment how difficult a case he has taken on; he knows that he is reasoning against the general humour and disposition of mankind. Yet, however absurd it may be and whatever the consequences, he cannot but insist that:

in the present Posture of our Affairs at home or abroad, . . . I do not yet see the absolute Necessity . . . of extirpating the Christian Religion from among us.

This perhaps may appear too great a Paradox, even for our wise and paradoxical Age to endure: Therefore I shall handle it with all Tenderness, and with the utmost Deference to that great and profound Majority, which is of another Sentiment. (27).

Here I feel, in addressing a modern audience, under the very different circumstances from those of 250 years ago in England, it may be necessary to state that Swift is being ironical when he speaks of 'that great and profound Majority, which is of another Sentiment.' Then even the Tolands and the Tindals, the Deists and the Free-thinkers would have understood the irony; for they would only have claimed to be an advanced and enlightened minority, in their desire to overthrow the Established Church. Now, again, it may indeed be that there is no irony left at all in Swift's reminder that he had even heard it affirmed by some very old people that they could remember the time that 'a Project for the Abolishing of Christianity 'would' have appeared as singular . . . as it would be at this Time to write or discourse in its Defence.' But I hope there is still a little sting left in that paragraph where he is careful to protect himself against any suspicion that he might be fool enough

. . . to stand up in the Defence of *real* Christianity; such as used in primitive Times (if we may believe the Authors of those Ages) to have an Influence upon Mens Belief and Actions: To offer at the Restoring of that, would indeed be a wild Project; it would be to dig up Foundations; to destroy at one Blow *all* the wit, and *half* the Learning of the Kingdom; to break the entire Frame and Constitution of Things; to ruin Trade, extinguish Arts and Sciences with the Professors of them; in short, to turn our Courts, Exchanges and Shops into Desarts. (27).

And I am afraid there is still rather a grim irony in the objection he makes to doing away with the clergy: 'here are ten Thousand Persons reduced by the wise Regulations of *Henry* the Eighth, to the Necessity of a low Diet, and moderate Exercise, who are the only great Restorers of our Breed.' (30–31).

A good many of his other points are rather outdated, depending as they do on such forgotten practices as assembling in churches and other forms of Sunday observance. But Swift was right in his forecast that abolishing Christianity would do nothing to extinguish parties among us; and his final warning has quite a familiar ring about it in introducing considerations which still seem to influence public policy:

Whatever some may think of the great Advantages to Trade, by this favourite Scheme; I do very much apprehend, that in six months Time, after the Act is past for the Extirpation of the Gospel, the Bank and the *East-India* Stock may fall, at least One *per Cent*. And, since that is Fifty Times more than ever the Wisdom of our Age thought fit to venture for the *Preservation* of Christianity, there is no reason we should be at so great a Loss, meerly for the Sake of *destroying* it. (38–9).

We can perhaps be pretty sure of the objects of his attack in 1708, and therefore we are not likely to mistake the general intention beneath the irony. But if we probe further, hoping to discover exactly what sort of man the writer of the *Argument* was and, in particular, what was his own religious faith—what meaning did Christianity have for him— we may even here find ourselves baffled. To put it quite bluntly, when he talks about the *real* Christianity of primitive ages and shows that he is aware of its complete incompatibility with the whole structure of English society in his time—which side is he on? He is saying clearly enough that primitive Christianity would dig up the foundations, i.e., it would cause a revolution. When he goes on to say, 'I hope, no Reader imagines me so weak as to stand up in the Defence of *real* Christianity', is that an ironical statement, which we have to turn upside down, so that it would mean that he is weak enough, fool enough nevertheless, to stand up for real Christianity?

But I must come to the more controversial questions, concerned with the interpretation of Swift's meaning and intentions in *Gulliver's Travels*. In the first book, the irony is sufficiently obvious. There can be no doubt of Swift's intentions when Gulliver gives his account of the intrigues of his great enemies at court and the barbarous proposals that they made for his destruction, and the final kindly suggestion merely to put out both his eyes, which he owed to his friend Reldresal: 'he humbly conceived, that by this Expedient, Justice might in some measure be satisfied, and all the World would applaud the *Lenity* of the Emperor, as well as the fair and generous Proceedings of those who have the Honour to be his Counsellors.' (XI, 70). Gulliver's considerations on what he ought to do provide further opportunities for irony:

. . . as to myself, I must confess having never been designed for a Courtier, either by my Birth or Education, I was so ill a Judge of Things, that I could not discover the *Lenity* and Favour of this Sentence; but conceived it (perhaps erroneously) rather to be rigorous than gentle . . . if I had then known the Nature of Princes and Ministers, which I have since observed in many other Courts, and their Methods of treating Criminals less obnoxious than myself; I should with great Alacrity and Readiness have submitted to so *easy* a Punishment. (XI, 72–3).

If we need an image which it would be useful always to have in mind to symbolize the relationship between Gulliver and his creator, we can find it in that dramatic moment so vividly described in the Second Book, when his gigantic Majesty the King of Brobdingnag, after listening to all of Gulliver's account of his own country, delivers his judgment. Here we get the full force of the dramatic irony, as Gulliver so honestly and so naively tells us what happened to him: 'His Majesty . . . taking me into his Hands, and stroaking me gently, delivered himself in these Words, which I shall never forget, nor the Manner he spoke them in. . . .' There is Gulliver, the little manikin, the very symbol of poor silly, stupid, wretched man, and Swift—his Creator— enlarged into this majestic figure who suddenly speaks with the authority of a mythical prophet-king. Not from a distant throne or like Zeus, thundering from the heavens; but he takes him into his hands and strokes him gently, and then, without irony, but with plain merciless invective with the whole authority of the prophetic tradition behind him, he denounces the corruptions of that society Gulliver had described, and concludes the bulk of them 'to be the most pernicious Race of little odious Vermin that Nature ever suffered to crawl upon the Surface of the Earth.' (132).

Swift continues to make use of Gulliver—the irony is at his expense in the next chapter, when he tries to explain that this king lives remotely from the rest of the world, and it would be hard 'if so remote a Prince's Notions of Virtue and Vice were to be offered as a Standard for all Mankind.' (133). Then he gives an extraordinary example of the king's blindness, when the king refuses Gulliver's offer to provide him with artillery of a size proportionable to all other things in that kingdom:

He was amazed how so impotent and grovelling an Insect as I (these were his Expressions) could entertain such inhuman Ideas and in so familiar a Manner as to appear wholly unmoved at all the Scenes of Blood and Desolation, which I had painted as the common Effects of those destructive Machines. (134–5).

But Gulliver continues to give himself away, chattering about the defectiveness of the Brobdingnagians' learning and their legal system and their ignorance of the whole art of government.

There is no difficulty here in the interpretation of Swift's meaning. No one could mistake his intention that we are to accept the values of the Brobdingnagians; Gulliver's views are quite clearly not those of Swift. Swift has picked him up and is looking at him with pity and amusement.

In the Third Book, where it has often been noticed that Gulliver is not given such a prominent role, he is again made use of, on one occasion where he adds to the effect of horrible surprise at the revelation of the Struldbruggs by describing his 'inexpressible delight' when he first heard of this race of Immortals:

> Happy Nation, where every Child hath at least a Chance for being Immortal! Happy People who enjoy so many living examples of antient Virtue. . . . But, happiest beyond all Comparison . . . those excellent *Struldbruggs* . . . (208).

He notices that his companions are amused by his enthusiasm, and they lure thim on to tell them what schemes of living he would have formed, if he had chanced to have been born a Struldbrugg. They then tell him the truth and afterwards he saw five or six of different ages— 'the most mortifying Sight I ever beheld'. But Gulliver learns from his experience and confesses: 'my keen Appetite for Perpetuity of Life was much abated. I grew heartily ashamed of the pleasing Visions I had formed. . . .' (214).

Here there is no doubt that Gulliver's education has been successful, and he is allowed to express the moral which Swift intends us to draw from this particular adventure. But in the last book, we are faced with real difficulties, since in the last twenty or thirty years we have been offered entirely new interpretations of Swift's meaning. We have been told that the dramatic irony has been entirely overlooked, and that Swift's intentions have been entirely mistaken. We should have realized that Gulliver was a dramatic character in the story, and that the last voyage to the country of the Houyhnhnms and the Yahoos is really an account of his final folly in his admiration for this rationalist society and his worship of 'his Master and Lady', as he calls those gifted horses who were his hosts, whom he finally had to leave— 'mine Eyes flowing with Tears, and my Heart quite sank with Grief.' How else are we to understand Gulliver's ridiculous behaviour when he takes his final leave before getting into his boat:

> . . . as I was going to prostrate myself to kiss his Hoof, he did me the Honour to raise it gently to my Mouth. I am not ignorant how much I have been censured for mentioning this last Particular. Detractors are pleased to think it improbable, that so illustrious a Person should descend to give so great a Mark of Distinction to a Creature so inferior as I. (282).

M

How else are we to explain his absurd behaviour, when found by the Portuguese seamen who were astonished that this strangely dressed creature answered them in their own language, but at the same time fell alaughing at his strange tone in speaking like the neighing of a horse? In spite of all the kindness of Don Pedro, the Portuguese captain, Gulliver continues to behave like a madman, and when he finally gets back to his wife and family, his behaviour is so atrocious that it is obviously Swift's intention to alienate our sympathy for Gulliver entirely, and use him as a symbol of the fate of those who cannot accept the human compromise, but give themselves up to strange ideals of purely rationalist existence untouched by folly and evil passions. For he tells us that the sight of his family filled him with disgust and contempt:

> . . . my Memory and Imaginations were perpetually filled with the Virtues and Ideas of those exalted *Houyhnhnms*. And when I began to consider, that by copulating with one of the *Yahoo*-species, I had become a Parent of more; it struck me with the utmost Shame, Confusion and Horror. (289).

It is certainly true that—whatever his purpose—Swift was careful to leave us in no doubt about Gulliver's feelings after his unfortunate exile from the Houyhnhnm country:

> As soon as I entered the House, my Wife took me in her Arms, and kissed me; at which, having not been used to the Touch of that odious Animal for so many years, I fell in a Swoon for almost an Hour. At the Time I am writing, it is five Years since my last Return to *England*: During the first Year I could not endure my Wife or Children in my Presence, the very Smell of them was intolerable; much less could I suffer them to eat in the same Room. To this Hour they dare not presume to touch my Bread, or drink out of the same Cup. . . . (289–290).

I do not think it would have been possible for any Anglican priest to use such words unconsciously, and such a one as Swift must have been willing to allow these overtones to remain—the bread and the cup; and even the word *presume*, from the opening phrase of the prayer before the act of communion; even the phrase *suffer them*, of the children's eating in the same room; even the tone ringing so clearly in the phrase *to this hour*. There is here, it seems to me, evidence enough of Swift's intention to emphasize Gulliver's complete estrangement from the human race, his inability to live any longer in communion with his own kind.

But the question at issue is what conclusion did he wish his readers to draw from Gulliver's behaviour. It has been in recent years the subject of lively debate—particularly in the United States, where if you go into any paperback-book shop you will almost certainly find two volumes entirely devoted to a discussion of the subject. It is largely concerned with the use of irony. One view is that Gulliver in this last voyage and final adventure in the land of the Houyhnhnms must be seen as the victim himself of Swift's irony. Swift has allowed him to become more and more fascinated by this rationalist society only to expose his folly and madness in accepting their values, which we ought to recognize as those of the Deists and Freethinkers—the modern rationalist faith of the enlightment. We are reminded that Swift was an orthodox clergyman, who had spent his life in attacking the views of Deists and Freethinkers, and that his purpose in the Fourth Book could only have been to use it as a dramatic parable to uphold the doctrines of Augustinian Christianity. In short, to quote from one of the most recent pronouncements on the subject; 'When placed in their proper historical and ideological context, the horses are in every important respect like the Deists', or, to quote from another, 'as symbols of Swift's religious irony, the horses could only represent Deists.'

It is perhaps fair to point out that this is to challenge the interpretation of Swift's meaning which was accepted unchallenged for two hundred years. It also seems to me to ignore Swift's manifest intention in revising *Gulliver's Travels* for the Dublin edition of his *Works* in 1735, to restore certain long passages which the printer of the London edition had been afraid to include because they so ruthlessly exposed the vices of human nature and the horrible corruptions of human society, as Gulliver tries so helplessly to explain them to the innocent mind of his Houyhnhnm master. Can there be any doubt what is the intention of Swift as Gulliver speaks of war, and politics, and the scandals of the law? Can we possibly forget the likeness of his position to that he had held in the land of Brobdingnag, when in one of these conversations (where Gulliver prides himself on 'being no stranger to the Art of War') he tells us:

> I was going on to more Particulars, when my Master commanded me Silence. He said, whoever understood the Nature of *Yahoos* might easily believe it possible for so vile an Animal, to be capable of every Action I had named, if their Strength and Cunning equalled their Malice. But, as my Discourse had increased his Abhorrence of the whole Species, so he found it gave him a Disturbance in his Mind, to which he was wholly a Stranger before ... when a Creature pretending to Reason, could be capable of such Enormities, he dreaded lest the Corruption of that Faculty might be worse than Brutality itself. He seemed therefore confident, that instead of

Reason, we were only possessed of some Quality fitted to increase our natural Vices; as the Reflection from a troubled Stream returns the Image of an ill-shapen Body, not only *larger*, but more *distorted*. (247–8).

Can anyone who reads that—without preconceived notions—doubt on which side Swift himself stood at this moment, and that what he wanted to do was to make his readers feel the horror that had caused this 'disturbance in the mind' of this innocent, truthful horse. The spell that he casts over us, the power of the narrative, the parody of the traveller's tale, make us almost forget that it was his imagination that had created this scene, forcing Gulliver to give us away so badly, and his mind that found the dread words which fall from the lips of Gulliver's master. But if we do forget him, we are likely to be made maddeningly aware of the power of his presence, as he embroiders the thread of his irony with that last striking image of the reflection of an ill-shapen body, as it appears not only *larger*, but more *distorted* in a troubled stream.

When Gulliver goes on to describe the virtues of the Houyhnhnms, we are given a picture of calm beauty, of classical virtue—of friendship and benevolence, of decency and civility—something which is as remote as possible from everything that Swift ever said or wrote about the Deists, whom he does, in fact, in one of his doggerel verses, describe as Yahoos. And in the tenth chapter, just before Gulliver is told that he must depart, he gives an account of his little economy, which is indeed a Swiftian parody of Utopia. The only irony here is that the poor fellow does not yet know that he is about to have to give it all up—and return into this sorry world. Finally, Swift brings Gulliver to the point where he can no longer bear to have any communion with humanity. I am not sure that it is a mistake to think that he never allowed Gulliver to represent his own view.

In the last chapter of the book, Gulliver concludes the story by giving some account of his design in publishing the work for the public good; and finally, I think, Swift allows himself to emerge and make a little ironical speech of his own. For Swift's real intentions were not, I think, without malice; indeed he confessed privately that he had written with one intention—'to vex the world.' And perhaps that is just what he means, if we understand the irony, when he says:

I am not a little pleased that this Work of mine can possibly meet with no Censurers. . . . I meddle not the least with any *Party*, but write without Passion, Prejudice, or Ill-will against any Man or Number of Men whatsoever. I write for the noblest End, to inform and instruct Mankind, over whom I may, without Breach of Modesty, pretend to some Superiority, from the Advantages I received by conversing so long among the most accomplished *Houyhnhnms*. I write without any View towards Profit or Praise. I never suffer a Word to pass that may look like Reflection, or possibly give the least Offence even to those who are most ready to take it. So that, I hope, I may with Justice pronounce myself an Author perfectly blameless. . . . (292–3).

*   *   *

There is no difficulty in interpreting another work which he planned for the public good; for it is, I suppose, the most completely sustained and unbroken irony that he or anyone else ever wrote. He did not live to finish it, but what he had done was printed shortly after his death under the title *Directions to Servants*. I am afraid the topic is one that has no longer much relevance today, and this remains one of his works which only has a sort of historical appeal. It was planned to give proper directions for the performance of every single detail in the duties of a very large staff, such as was required to run a great house in Swift's time; and though he had a wide experience of English society, I rather think it is particularly coloured by his intimate knowledge of the ways of the servants' hall in the houses of his Irish friends. It is what he called a 'perfection of folly', and the irony that runs through the whole is quite simple and direct. Like *Polite Conversation*, an amusement of his leisure, which he kept long by him, it shows the very habit of his mind—his constant tendency to play with parody and irony. But thus kept in exercise, it could be turned to dangerous purpose when required, and could reveal how deeply Swift continued to be engaged in public affairs in the years which followed his final return to Ireland after the success of *Gulliver's Travels*.

From time to time, there appeared a number of small pamphlets printed at the same press and looking very much like the Drapier's Letters, but with no other indication of authorship on the title page. The first was called *A Short View of the State of Ireland*, where he allows himself to describe the delightful progress the Commissioners from England might make through the country, wondering at the improvement of the land, the thriving towns and villages, the vast numbers of ships in the harbours, and carriers crowding the roads, laden with rich manufactures. Suddenly he breaks off and gives up—'my Heart is too heavy to continue this Irony longer.' (XII, 10). Two years later, however, in 1729, when he has come to find all his proposals utterly useless in the face of both English exploitation and the discouragement and misery of the people of Ireland, the only satisfaction that was left for him was to indulge in the savage irony of *A Modest Proposal*, which I am inclined to regard as the most perfect piece of writing that ever came from his pen. He made no mistake here. There could hardly be any doubt of his meaning, or of the completeness of his scepticism, as he contemplates the face of Ireland with utter despair. Yet, he must still lift up his voice in a last protest, parodying the proposals of the economists in this imaginative discovery of his, the only possibility left, this plan which he presents with irony and wit and humour.

Here his attack is mainly against the people of Ireland—'I desire the Reader will observe, that I calculate my Remedy *for this one individual Kingdom* of IRELAND, *and for no other that ever was, is, or I think ever can be upon Earth*' (XII, 116)—and then he goes on to list all the things that might have been done and that have often been suggested, and charges them with being unwilling ever to try and put them in practice. But he does not forget the crimes of the absentee landlords—'I GRANT this Food will be somewhat dear, and therefore very *proper for Landlords*; who, as they have already devoured most of the Parents, seem to have the best Title to the Children' (112)—nor fail to include among the advantages of his proposal the fact that it is one 'whereby we can incur no Danger of *disobliging* ENGLAND':

> For, this Kind of Commodity will not bear Exportation; the Flesh being of too tender a Consistence, to admit a long Continuance in Salt; *although, perhaps, I could name a Country, which would be glad to eat up our whole Nation without it.* (XII, 117).

There is a strange intensity throughout, an imaginative fire which leaps from one point to another devouring everything it can reach. There would be so many advantages in this scheme to fatten healthy infants to be sold as meat at twelve months old:

> It would increase the Care and Tenderness of Mothers towards their Children. . . .
>
> Men would become as *fond* of their Wives, during the Time of their Pregnancy, as they are now of their *Mares* in Foal. . . .
>
> [It would make a fitting dish for] *merry meetings*, particularly *Weddings* and *Christenings*. (115–6).

He admits that it would not deal with the problem of that vast number of people, who are aged, diseased, or maimed, 'But I am not in the least Pain upon that Matter; because it is well known, that they are every Day *dying*, and *rotting*, by *Cold* and *Famine*, and *Filth* and *Vermin*, as fast as can be reasonably expected' (114). Here the force of the irony depends upon the violence of the impact of the words—the horrible excess of the added phrase *and rotting* and the repetition of it again in the words *filth* and *vermin*.

Swift continued for several years in various ways to concern himself with the miseries of Ireland, the corruptions and enormities of the city of Dublin, and even produced another 'Proposal to pay off the National Debt without raising any taxes', which was included in his *Works* with this warning note at the head of the page: *'The Reader will perceive the following Treatise to be altogether Ironical'* (XII, 207). But in none of his other papers do we find the perfection, the completeness, which must, one feels, have been enough even to satisfy Swift himself. He could hardly have done better in his attempt to go on 'vexing the world', forcing his readers at least to recognize his revulsion, and to understand the cause of his despair. Here is his last challenge. Having made his proposal, he bursts out, 'Therefore, let no man talk to me of other Expedients', (116) and adds, 'THEREFORE I repeat, let no Man talk to me of these and the like Expedients; till he hath, at least, a Glimpse of Hope, that there will ever be some hearty and sincere Attempt to put *them in Practice*' (117). It is the same despair, the same pessimism, as he had expressed in the Letter of Captain Gulliver to his cousin Sympson, complaining that there had been no sign of any reformation anywhere since the publication of his travels:

> And, it must be owned, that seven Months were a sufficient Time to correct every Vice and Folly to which *Yahoos* are subject; if their Natures had been capable of the least Disposition to Virtue or Wisdom . . . I must freely confess, that since my last Return, some Corruptions of my *Yahoo* Nature have revived in me . . .; else I should never have attempted so absurd a Project as that of reforming the *Yahoo* race in this Kingdom; but, I have now done with all such visionary Schemes for ever. (XI, 7–8).

I must confess that I find a remarkable similarity between the attitude of Captain Gulliver and the author of *A Modest Proposal*. The quality of the irony, the very ring of the words they use—their tendency to despair because of the Yahoo nature of man. Did then, you may ask me, this orthodox Anglican dean give up all Christian hope, and have to content himself with the foolishness of doing little charitable deeds, such as making small loans to poor craftsmen who were willing to work? Or was he perhaps driven by the very depth of his despair back to the Christian faith?

I recently found a comment of his on the creed of the Christian church which I should like to know the meaning of. It is written clearly in his own hand on the margin of a page towards the end of the seventh volume of Baronius' *Ecclesiastical History* (which he notes that he finished reading in 1729, the same year as *A Modest Proposal*). In the appendix to that volume, Baronius prints the document accepted by the Russian Church as the statement of the Christian Faith when they were received into communion with the Church of Rome. This included the *Credo* text of the Nicene Creed in Latin, exactly as it is translated in the English prayer book, then in use at the cathedral of St. Patrick's. Over against the opening words Swift has written:

> *Confessio fidei*
> *barbaris digna*

(XIV, 35).

which I suppose must be translated, 'A creed worthy of the barbarians', or, perhaps, 'fit for the Russians'.

Does this mean that, after all, Swift had become a creature of the Enlightenment, a real contemporary of Voltaire, or at least so much an Augustan as to find the source of his morality in Republican Rome rather than among the Christian barbarians? This, I suppose, would be easily acceptable to many of Swift's modern readers, probably to all of his admirers in Russia and in Asia. But might there be another remote possibility, that he was here indulging himself for a moment in a sort of Pauline irony, where he admits that having had to give up all hope of the world—that Augustan civilized world his friends still believed in (he separates himself from them in that phrase in a letter to Pope—*vous autres*)—nothing now was left for him but the faith of the barbarians, that primitive Christianity which he had once said it would indeed be a wild project to offer to restore?

Swift's Fallen City:

A Description of the Morning

ROGER SAVAGE

As to your Blank-verse, it hath too often fallen into the same vile
Hands of late. One *Thomson*, a *Scots*-Man, has succeeded the best in
that Way, in four Poems he has writ on the four Seasons. Yet I am
not over-fond of them, because they are all Description, and nothing
is doing, whereas *Milton* engages me in Actions of the highest
Importance, *modo me Romae, modo ponit Athenis.*
(Swift to Charles Wogan, July 1732; *Corr.*, IV, 53.

In 1709, Swift contributed a lean, unflorid poem to the ninth of
Richard Steele's *Tatlers*. He called it *A Description of the Morning*. The
title may strike us as prosaic, appropriately prosaic considering the
bald way Swift treats his unromantic sunrise. But we shall miss the
point of the piece if we assume that Swift gave it a plain name because
plain names are aptest for lean poems. If title underlines treatment
here, it does so ironically, for the associations of 'description' in
Augustan poetics were far from prosaic. In fact, *descriptio* was a
respected ingredient of the Grand Manner. Le Bossu has a chapter
on it (VI.ii) in his *Traité du poëme épique*—a book admired and mined
extensively by Dryden, Addison and Pope—while Rymer chooses to
spend half the preface to his version of Rapin's *Reflexions sur la poetique*
analysing specimens of description from the *Argonautica*, the *Aeneid*,
The Conquest of Mexico and so on. But the work best preserving the
glamour of Augustan *descriptio* is a verse-essay with which Swift
himself was closely connected only a few years after the *Morning*
appeared. This was the ambitious *Essay on the Different Stiles of Poetry*
which his Irish protégé Thomas Parnell published in 1713. The year
before, Swift had generously appointed himself stage-manager of
Parnell's reputation at Court, and decided that the half-finished *Essay*
could play a vital part in his plan to give the unknown Irishman 'a
little friendly forwarding'. He chivied Parnell into finishing it, helped
him correct it, got him to add a eulogy of Lord Secretary Bolingbroke
at its climax. And though Swift was chiefly interested in the poem as
a device for putting his gifted friend in the way of some enviable
Court patronage, it would be hard to believe under the circumstances
that he strongly disapproved of its themes and arguments. Yet

Parnell demonstrates in his *Essay* that proper *descriptio* is the reverse of lean and unflorid.[1]

The *Essay*, as its preface explains, is an allegory: 'Wit *is made to be* Pegasus, *and the* Poet *his* Rider, *who flies by several* Countries *where he must not touch, by which are meant so many vicious* Stiles, *and arrives at last at the* Sublime'. *En route* Parnell is much concerned with varieties of poetic Description and Narration, and when it comes to discussing them, as we might expect of someone soon to be an intimate of Pope's, he drops into the dialect of classicist idealism. For instance, one of the countries his Pegasus makes a point of avoiding is the land of lean literalism, where Description and Narration are skimped:

> Here flat *Narrations* fair Exploits debase,
> In Measures void of ev'ry shining Grace;
> Which never arm their *Hero* for the Field,
> Nor with *Prophetick Story* paint the Shield,
> Nor fix the Crest, or make the Feathers wave,
> Or with their Characters reward the Brave;
> Undeck'd they stand, and unadorn'd with Praise,
> And fail to profit while they fail to please. (vv. 75-82)

The landscapes of 'forc'd *Description*' here are equally bare and un-memorable:

> The liveless Trees may stand for ever bare,
> And Rivers stop, for ought the Readers care. (vv. 85-86).

But when at last we reach the Sublime, *narratio* comes into its own 'by boldly vent'ring to dilate in Praise', and so does *descriptio*—as an Italianate fresco-painter:

> Above the Beauties, far above the Show
> In which weak Nature dresses here below,
> Stands the great *Palace* of the *Bright* and *Fine*,
> Where fair Ideas in full Glory shine . . .
> Here bold *Description* paints the Walls within,
> Her Pencil touches, and the World is seen:
> The Fields look beauteous in their flow'ry Pride,
> The Mountains rear aloft, the Vales subside . . .
> The Skies extended in an open View,
> Appear a lofty distant Arch of *Blue*,
> In which *Description* stains the painted Bow,
> Or thickens Clouds, and feathers out the Snow,
> Or mingles Blushes in the Morning ray,
> Or gilds the Noon, or turns an Evening gray.
> (vv. 189–192, 237–240, 247–252).

Parnell gives no details of the landscape produced when his *descriptio* 'mingles Blushes with the Morning ray', so we cannot compare her work directly with Swift's *Description of the Morning*. But we can be sure that her paintings are more like Claude's or Poussin's than Breughel's, for we know generally that her art heightens 'weak Nature', transcends mere appearances and idealises every beauty it touches. And beyond this we can assume that her techniques of making images of 'the *Bright* and *Fine*' are essentially those of just *narratio*. Just Narration's methods can be established by reversing the faults (already shown us) of *flat* Narration; and this makes her an out-and-out classicist. The arming of the hero, the roll-call of his companions, the recital of the legends carved on his shield: each of these shining graces has a sound pedigree in ancient poetry. It seems, then, that sublime presentation of superior nature (superior to that dull, weak, untidy reality which commonly passes for nature) will best be achieved through adaptation of the classics. What Goldsmith says sixty years later of Parnell's own poetic achievement can well be applied to the narrative-descriptive techniques recommended under the eye of Swift in the *Essay*:

> Parnell . . . appears to me to be the last of that great school that had modelled itself upon the ancients, and taught English poetry to resemble what the generality of mankind have allowed to excel. A studious and correct observer of antiquity, he set himself to consider nature in the lights it lent him; and he found that the more aid he borrowed from the one, the more delightfully he resembled the other. To copy nature is a task the most bungling workman is able to execute; to select such parts as contribute to delight, is reserved only for those whom accident has blest with uncommon talents, or such as have read the ancients with indefatigable industry.[2]

As Goldsmith suggests, Parnell's circle shared a belief—a belief they saw increasingly threatened—that imitation of the ancients was the modern artist's surest guide to *la belle nature*. In the spring of 1713, when his *Essay* appeared, Parnell was seeing more and more of Pope (it may well have been Parnell who introduced Pope to Swift about that time); and it was Pope who two years before had embodied the belief most memorably in his fable of the poetic education of Virgil:

> When first young *Maro* in his boundless Mind
> A Work t'outlast Immortal *Rome* design'd,
> Perhaps he seem'd *above* the Critick's Law,
> And but from *Nature's Fountains* scorn'd to draw:
> But when t'examine ev'ry Part he came,
> *Nature* and *Homer* were, he found, the *same*.
> (*An Essay on Criticism*, vv. 130–135).

Nature at her worthiest=Homer. Parnell implies the same in his

Essay on the Different Stiles. His *narratio* is an emulator of ancient epic ritual. His *descriptio* can be seen as an active connoisseur of classic landscape poetry.

But if Parnell only implies this about *descriptio*, John Hughes the following year makes it explicit. In the thirty-ninth *Lay Monk* (February 12th, 1714) he has an unsigned essay, reprinted in his collected works of 1735, on how the great poets have classicised their dawn-scenes. The essay is in the line started by Rymer with his discussion of night-scenes in the Rapin preface; but where Rymer is careful to save his highest praise for his most modern exhibit, Hughes puts the emphasis on the workings of tradition. 'There is no particular Description', he says, 'which the Writers of Heroick Poetry seem to have labour'd to vary so much as that of the *Morning*. This is a Topick on which they have drawn out all the Copiousness, and even the Luxury of their Fancies.' Description is copious and luxuriant, not lean and unflorid, and description of the morning especially so:

> The Morning is most frequently figur'd as a Goddess, or divine Person, flying in the Air, unbarring the Gates of Light, and opening the Day. She is drawn by *Homer* in a Saffron Garment, and with Rosy Hands (which is the Epithet he almost constantly bestows on her) sprinkling Light thro' the Earth. She arises out of the Waves of the Sea, leaves the Bed of *Tithon* her Lover, ascends the Heavens, appears to the Gods and to Men, and gives Notice of the Sun-Rising. . . . She is usher'd in by the Star which is her Harbinger, and which gives the Signal of the Morning's Approach.

Now though Hughes says at the outset that descriptions of the morning have been more varied than any others, we soon see that what has been treated in so many ways is an event in classic art, not an event in nature. Homer's Aurora is the common *datum*. 'On this, as a Ground, the Poets following *Homer*, have run their Divisions of Fancy'. Their variations, such as the dawn-formula Virgil uses twice in the *Aeneid*—

> Now rose the ruddy morn from Tithon's bed,
> And with the dawns of day the skies o'erspread[3]

—are on a Homeric rather than a natural theme, *if* the two can be distinguished. But it seems they cannot, for Hughes, going on to quote some lines of Tasso to show 'how the same Images have been copy'd or diversify'd by the Moderns', adds significantly that 'our own *Spenser*, who excells in all Kinds of Imagery, following the same Originals, represents the Morning after the like manner'. Spenser excels in all kinds of imagery and is working in a descriptive mode friendly to copious fancy; yet still he sees imitation of the classics as the best imitation of ideal nature, representing morning as the Renaissance in general represented it by following the same originals. Nature's dawn and Homer's are, Spenser finds, the same.

The trouble with a demonstration like Hughes's, however high-minded its intentions, is that it gives the untalented modern poet rich scope for disguising his lack of talent. To copy nature delightfully, says Goldsmith apropos of Parnell's classicism, is 'reserved only for those whom accident has blest with uncommon talents, or such as have read the ancients with indefatigable industry'. The more the lineaments of ideal *descriptio* or *narratio* are vulgarised by analysis in *Lay Monks* or exhibition in commonplace-books, the less intense this industry will need to be, the more the Grub Street hack will be able to apply classical formulae mechanically in and out of season, and the more any 'uncommon talent' will be provoked into looking for an entirely different way of describing nature. It is significant that it should be an anonymous, faceless entry in one such commonplace-book —Edward Bysshe's *British Parnassus*, also published in 1714—which offers us the fullest Augustan embodiment of Hughes's dawn-topos. Day's harbinger, her aged lover's bed, the gates of day, the blushing sky and lingering stars: all the images are there in the lines quoted below, supplemented with fitting generalities from an Arcadian landscape. By the early eighteenth century, such cataloguing of landscape was as traditional as the Aurora-motifs themselves. In his chapter on *descriptio*, Le Bossu had recommended the 'fine *Description* of a Calm and quiet Night' in the *Aeneid* (IV, 522–528), where Virgil describes the repose of nature—woods, waves, stars, cattle, birds—and so 'renders the cruel Disturbances of *Dido* a great deal more moving, since they rob her of that Rest which all Nature enjoy'd, to the very vilest and most despicable Creatures'.[4] Le Bossu's recommendation was not lost on the Restoration dramatists. Not only sleepy night-catalogues but Arcadian dawn-catalogues too are reeled off by the soliloquists of Otway and Nathaniel Lee before they announce in Dido's vein that they alone of all creation know no rest or happiness. So the couplets which follow from Bysshe's *Parnassus* present the classical ideal—and the classical cliché—both in the invocation of a revered myth and in the segmentation of a picturesque landscape:

> —And now Aurora, Harbinger of Day,
> Rose from the Bed, where aged Tithon lay;
> Unbarr'd the Doors of Heav'n, and overspread
> The Path of Phoebus with a blushing Red.
> The starry Lights above are scarce expir'd;
> And scarce the Shade from open Plains retir'd;

The tuneful Lark has hardly stretch'd her Wing;
And warbling Linnets just begin to sing;
Nor yet industrious Bees their Hives forsake;
Nor skim the Fish the Surface of the Lake;
Nor yet the Flow'rs disclose their various Hue;
But fold their Leaves, oppress'd with hoary Dew;
Blue Mists around conceal the neighb'ring Hills:
And dusky Fogs hang o'er the murmuring Rills;
While Zephyr faintly sighs among the Trees;
And moves the Branches with a lazy Breeze.
No jovial Pipe resounds along the Plains,
Safe in their Hamlets sleep the drowzy Swains.[5]

When Parnell, Swift's protégé, presents Description 'mingling blushes in the morning ray', he has surely something like these eighteen lines in mind. We are to look over the poet's shoulder for a distant, harmonious, elevated landscape. But when Swift himself presents *A Description of the Morning* in eighteen lines, it is of quite another scene:

Now hardly here and there an Hackney-Coach
Appearing, show'd the Ruddy Morns Approach.
Now *Betty* from her Masters Bed had flown,
And softly stole to discompose her own.
The Slipshod Prentice from his Masters Door,
Had par'd the Dirt, and Sprinkled round the Floor.
Now *Moll* had whirl'd her Mop with dext'rous Airs,
Prepar'd to Scrub the Entry and the Stairs.
The Youth with Broomy stumps began to trace
The Kennel-Edge, where Wheels had worn the Place.
The Smallcoal-Man was heard with Cadence deep,
'Till drown'd in Shriller Notes of Chimney-Sweep,
Duns at his Lordships Gate began to meet,
And Brickdust *Moll* had Scream'd through half the Street.
The Turnkey now his Flock returning sees,
Duly let out a Nights to steal for Fees.
The watchful Bailiffs take their silent Stands,
And School-Boys lag with Satchels in their Hands.

(Poems, 124–5).

Unless we are aware of such Augustan stock-responses to Swift's title as those suggested above, we are not likely to achieve more than a partial reading of his poem. The *Description of the Morning* has often been seen as a piece of uncomplicated realism, vivid and assured or barren and pointless, according to the taste of the critic; but its realism is not simply the result of a walk through London at dawn with a camera. It is determined and moulded by what Swift has learned from the masters of the descriptive tradition and by the attitude to them he has come to adopt. The poem is basically mock-*descriptio*, a comic imitation of the classical ideal; and on this level it reads like a parody of the dawn-scene in Bysshe's *Parnassus*. Each begins with two mythological couplets which lead to seven of appropriate amplification from nature. Swift's nature, though, has no distancing or elevation: it is a world of scavengers and bailiffs, dirt and dust, scrubbing and screaming.[6] Warbling larks and tuneful linnets become coalmen and chimney-sweeps; the shepherd-swain about to wake and sound his jovial pipe becomes the turnkey counting his flock of thieves as they come in from night-pasture: and this because Swift's is a nature amplified from a mythology of hackney coaches and fallen Pamelas. The mythology is adapted daringly and wittily from the classical tradition, and the result is rich burlesque.

Apart from two couplets of morning-description in the 'tragical elegy' *Cassinus and Peter* (vv. 31–34), so perfunctory in themselves, so cruelly ironic in their context, Swift the poet only once allows himself to make significant use of the conventional dawn-myth. This is in the enthusiastic epistle *To Lord Harley on his Marriage* (1713), a tribute to the son of one of Swift's few modern heroes, Queen Anne's Lord Treasurer. Harley's bride, Lady Holles (whose unfashionable red hair may have provoked the comparison) is 'as Aurora bright':

> Thus the bright Empress of the Morn
> Chose, for her spouse, a mortal born . . .
> Tho' like a virgin of fifteen,
> She blushes when by mortals seen. (vv. 65–66 and 69–70).

The myth—which Spenser had kept alive in his *Faerie Queene* and Milton in his Latin Elegy *In Adventum Veris*, which Guercino and Agostino Carracci had both illustrated in Roman frescos[7]—celebrates an amorous, blushing dawn-goddess escaping from Tithonus, her domestic Struldbrugg, to drive her eager horses Lampos and Phaethon ahead of the sunrise. In Dryden's Virgil the 'ruddy morn' rises from 'Tithon's bed'; and in Hughes she is 'usher'd in by the Star which is her Harbinger, and which gives the Signal of the Morning's Approach'. In Swift's *Description* the myth is revised. Here the ruddy morn's approach is signalled by quite other harbingers and the dawn-spirit leaves the bed of a very different lover. Hackneys deputise for the stars (and perhaps for the Lampos and Phaethon too) of a conventional fresco, while Betty takes over the role of the Aurora. The pat symmetry of 'from her Masters Bed had flown—stole to discompose her own' persuades us to take it as a matter of course that when a *modern* Aurora is 'figur'd as a Goddess, or divine Person, flying in the Air' she will have something more pressing to do before the other folk are up than 'unbarring the Gates of Light, and opening the Day'. The low nature Swift presents makes a mockery of high art.

And a nature of sorts it certainly is, though an untidy and corrupt one, which makes the mockery. Swift here is not simply putting a moustache on the *Mona Lisa*, reducing outworn tradition to mere grotesque. Throughout the *Description* he is working from the jottings of an on-the-spot reporter in an average street, not very far from one described by his journalist contemporary, Tom Brown:

> Some carry, others are carried. 'Make way there,' says a gouty-legged chairman, that is carrying a punk of quality to a morning's exercise; or a Bartholomew baby-beau, newly launched out of a chocolate-house, with his pockets as empty as his brains. 'Make room there,' says another fellow, driving a wheelbarrow of nuts, that spoil the lungs of the city 'prentices. . . . 'Stand up there, you blind dog,' says a carman, 'will you have the cart squeeze your guts out?' One tinker knocks, another bawls, 'Have you brass-pot, iron-pot, kettle, skillet or a frying-pan to mend?' . . . Here a poet scampers for't as fast as his legs will carry him, and at his heels a brace of bandog bailiffs, with open mouths ready to devour him and all the nine muses; and there an informer ready to spew up his false oaths at the sight of the common executioner.[8]

The tone is very different. Brown has a journalist's camera: Swift is working on a canvas prepared for formal *descriptio*. But their Londons are recognisably the same. Again, comparison with other mock-descriptions of the age will also show how positive the element of realism is in Swift's burlesque. We may take what another of his contemporaries, Francis Hutcheson, calls the 'fantastical imitation of the poetical imagery and similitudes of the morning' in Butler's *Hudibras*, a poem Swift himself admired immensely:

> The Sun, had long since in the Lap
> Of *Thetis*, taken out his *Nap*,
> And like a *Lobster* boyl'd, the *Morn*
> From *black* to *red* began to turn.[9]

The calculated vulgarity of 'taken out his *Nap*' is not unlike Swift's more potent shock-tactics with Aurora the chamber-maid (more potent because, with the names of his *dramatis personae* changed, Swift is able to preserve ideal epic dignity and mock it at the same time, while Butler's travesty can only coarsen). But the simile of the lobster has no counterpart in Swift. It is a metaphysical-farcical conceit, and its witty surrealism only intensifies by contrast the low-life naturalism of *A Description of the Morning*. Swift's imitation is not fantastical. And neither is it merely literary. Here a burlesque Description of the Night from the *Orpheus and Euridice* in William King's *Miscellanies* of 1707 is relevant:

> 'Twas Night, and Nature's self lay dead,
> Nodding upon a Feather-bed;
> The Mountains seem'd to bend their Tops,
> And Shutters clos'd the Mill'ners Shops,
> Excluding both the Punks and Fops.
> No ruffl'd Streams to Mill do come,
> The silent Fish were still more dumb;
> Look in the Chimney, not a Spark there,
> And Darkness did it self grow darker.

King's butt here is the Dryden purple passage from *The Conquest of Mexico* (III. ii):

> All things are hush'd, as Nature's self lay dead,
> The Mountains seem to nod their drowsie head

as Rymer quotes and praises it in his discussion of night-scenes. Dryden's solemnity and Rymer's connoisseur tone presumably make King uneasy. His reaction is good-natured, whimsical parody, with no holds barred. Deflation (mountain tops and milliners' shops), fantasy (night's feather-bed), low realism (the fops and punks), homely button-holing (look in the chimney!), nonsense-hyperbole (darker darkness, dumber dumbness)—anything which can help ridicule the traditional descriptive mode is brought into play. And the indiscriminateness with which the weapons are chosen suggests that King's criticism of that mode is not a constructive one: that is to say, he has no directing awareness of a sordid actuality which demands to be presented. His *descriptio* is simply a pleasant literary joke. Swift's, on the other hand, is anchored to the Here and Now; and it is the tension between a positive and demanding poetic convention and a positive and demand-ing low reality which makes it more than a *jeu d'esprit*. Where King sees realism as one device among many useful to the parodist, Swift seems to be using burlesque of the formal *descriptio* just so that he can draw attention to the real, to common city nature. There is no place in his strategy for conceits *or* whimsies.

In this yoking of the poetic and the day-to-day, Swift stands closer to Samuel Garth in parts of *The Dispensary*. *The Dispensary*, which was published ten years before *A Description of the Morning*, is a baroque allegory satirising abuses among doctors. Its events are narrated in epic style, to give them enough significance to interest the layman and also to make a fitting framework for the personifications of Envy, Fortune, Health and so on which dominate the poem. But the abuses

N

themselves and the stock-in-trade of the doctors who practise them are not at all sublime, and so the poem, for lack of any cohesive power on Garth's part, breaks up into an aimless alternation of epic and satiric paragraphs, with eulogies of the House of Nassau rubbing shoulders uneasily with indignant accounts of quacks' consulting-rooms. This uneasiness sometimes infects Garth's epic descriptions of evening, night and dawn. Most of these are perfectly lofty and well-behaved, like the evening scene in Canto IV, with its reeds and aspens, drowsy cattle and amorous birds. But some are tempted to visit the satiric-realist camp for the occasional detail, and the bathos which results must have appealed to Swift. For example, the Description of the Morning in Canto III, which begins

> With that, a Glance from mild *Aurora's* Eyes
> Shoots thro' the Chrystal Kingdoms of the Skies

could perfectly well go on like this without being untypical of *The Dispensary*:

> Now Trav'llers from their Eyes soft Slumbers shake,
> And for new Labour, Swains their Beds forsake.
> The roaming Lion, surfeited with Spoil,
> Comes to his Den fatigu'd with bloody Toil.

But in fact these two couplets come from a patriotic epic of Sir Richard Blackmore's; and what Garth actually writes here is

> The Savage Kind in Forests cease to roam,
> And Sots o'ercharg'd with nauseous Loads reel home.
> Light's chearful Smiles o'er th' Azure Waste are spread,
> And Miss from Inns o' Court bolts out unpaid.[10]

The relating of distant sky and jungle with furtive whoring and vomit on the pavement is certainly Swiftian, and yet Garth only makes a physical compound of these opposites where Swift's compound is chemical. In Garth, two pictures are put side by side. One belongs to the same world as the *Aurora* painted by Sir James Thornhill in 1715 for the Queen's Bedroom at Hampton Court: the goddess leaving Tithon and his starry mantle and rising on a cloud of Cupids to mount her golden coach. The other is closer to the urban morning scene of London in mid-winter from Hogarth's *Four Times of Day*, with its very different heroine, the frosty *à-la-mode* spinster pointedly ignoring the Covent Garden whores at their work as she sails into Inigo Jones's church. In Swift, instead of alternating, the two pictures are super-imposed.[11]

But it is symbolic that Thornhill was Hogarth's father-in-law, that Hogarth engraved high baroque illustrations for *Paradise Lost* as well as low realistic ones for *Hudibras*, and that when he was making studies for his portrait of the murderess Sarah Malcolm (a visual analogue to Fielding's Jonathan Wild, Gay's Macheath and Swift's own Clever Tom Clinch) his father-in-law was sketching beside him in the condemned cell.[12] Clearly the two men and the two manners, idealistic and naturalistic, found a *modus vivendi*. Is there a similar *modus* in *A Description of the Morning*? It is not enough just to say that in it Swift is using ironic imitation of the classical *belle nature* as an enabling device, as his means of rendering the immediate nature of contemporary London. Burlesque of this sort can hardly be neutral, cannot juxtapose two jarring natures without implying some sort of judgement. If low reality makes a mockery of high art in the *Morning*, with which does the blame lie?

According to the paragraph which introduces it in *Tatler* 9, we are to see the poem as a judgement against high art, a triumph of revolutionary realism over dead tradition. Swift, says the *Tatler*, 'has run into a Way perfectly New, and described Things exactly as they happen: He never forms Fields, or Nymphs, or Groves, where they are not, but makes the Incidents just as they really appear'. In other words, the Phoebus and Zephyr, open plains and drowsy swains of Bysshe's commonplace have been dismissed. Swift, we are to infer, has gone back to nature; her fountains are his true source. This praise of Swift in the *Tatler* strangely anticipates Joseph Warton's praise of James Thomson in his *Essay on the Genius and Writings of Pope*. Thomson, Warton says, has

enriched poetry with a variety of new and original images which he painted from nature itself and from his own actual observations. His descriptions have, therefore, a distinctness and truth which are utterly wanting to those of poets who have only copied from each other and have never looked abroad on the objects themselves. Thomson was accustomed to wander away into the country for days . . . while many a poet who has dwelt for years in the Strand has attempted to describe fields and rivers and generally succeeded accordingly. . . . Hence that disgusting impropriety of introducing what may be called a set of hereditary images without proper regard to the age or climate or occasion in which they were formerly used.[13]

Swift has not wandered for days in the country, but his method —according to this reading—is the same as Thomson's. A poet of the Strand, he has drawn from nature's fountains by *describing* the Strand: his poem, the *Tatler* points out, is 'a Description of the Morning, but of the Morning in Town, nay, of the Morning at this End of the Town, where my Kinsman at present lodges'. Swift and Thomson both 'describe things exactly as they happen'; both scorn to draw on the 'set of hereditary images' offered them by art; both have 'a proper regard to age and climate'. In all this they recall one of the favourite Augustan images of Shakespeare, as the poet of direct realism, untutored and uninhibited. This is the Shakespeare who triumphed, according to Pope, by doing what Pope's own 'young *Maro*' was not allowed to do, that is by taking his characters 'immediately from the fountains of nature', while those of all other dramatists 'have a constant resemblance which shows that they received them from one another and were multipliers of the same image; each picture, like a mock-rainbow, is but the reflection of a reflection'.[14] Swift, interpreted in this way, is an unambiguous Shakespearian realist, and we should ignore any slight hint of dusty traditions or hereditary images we may find in his poem as so much irrelevant husk.

But this would be to assume too hastily that the analogy with Shakespeare could tell us the whole truth about *A Description of the Morning*. Actually it is a dangerous analogy for an Augustan poet to draw, since a just unclassical imitation of nature could only be a contradiction in terms after the revelation that Nature and Homer were the same. In Shakespeare's time such a *mimesis* had been possible because, as Pope put it, Elizabethan poets 'had no thoughts of writing on the model for the ancients'.[15] But things were different by 1709. Unclassical imitation by then could only mean anticlassical imitation: which is to say that, in spite of Swift's Shakespearian schoolboys with their satchels out of *As You Like It*, the apparent naturalism of the *Description* is really closer to the painter Caravaggio's than to Shakespeare's in its relation to ideal antique tradition. Granted Caravaggio was Shakespeare's contemporary, but their situations were different in so far as the Italy of the 1600s had been fully exposed to the learned enlightenment of the Renaissance, while England at the time was still in outer darkness. Caravaggio's concern for 'mere' appearances was held up as a terrible example by classicising theorists. He was 'esteemed too natural', as Dryden puts it, translating from G. P. Bellori's *Vite de' Pittori* in his own *Parallel of Poetry and Painting*, because 'he drew persons as they were'. The sordid and anticlassical implications of this are brought out in Bellori's life of the revolutionary Italian published in 1672. Caravaggio, he says,

> not only ignored the most excellent marbles of the ancients and the famous paintings of Raphael, but he despised them, and nature alone became the object of his brush. Thus when the most famous statues of Phidias and Glycon were pointed out to him as models for his painting, he gave no other reply than to extend his hand

toward a crowd of men, indicating that nature had supplied him
sufficiently with teachers. . . . With the majesty of art thus suppressed
in Caravaggio, everyone did as he pleased, and soon the value of the
beautiful was discounted. The antique lost all authority, as did
Raphael. . . . Now began the representation of vile things; some
artists began to look enthusiastically for filth and deformity. If they
have to paint armour they choose the rustiest; if a vase, they do not
make it complete but broken and without a spout. The costumes
they paint are stockings, breeches and big caps and when they paint
figures they give all of their attention to the wrinkles, the defects
of the skin and the contours, depicting knotted fingers and limbs
disfigured with disease.[16]

In the *Description* Swift too looks for the sordid. The crowd he points
to is slipshod, raucous and none too clean; and there are obviously as
many moral wrinkles and deformities as physical. Along with the
brick-dust and coal, gutters and dirty doorsteps, there is Betty's
whoring, his Lordship's profligacy, the prison system abused and the
need for a secret police of watchful bailiffs. It is as though Swift, in his
determination to avoid the sterilized purity of Phidias, Virgil and the
rest, feels forced to insist that the fountains of true nature are dirty
fountains; and it is apt that Goldsmith, when he characterises Swift's
poetry later in the century, places the poet firmly in Caravaggio's camp:

> Dean Swift . . . perceived that there was a spirit of romance mixed
> with all the works of the poets who preceded him; or, in other
> words, that they had drawn nature on the most pleasing side. There
> still therefore was a place for him, who, careless of censure, should
> describe it just as it was, with all its deformities.[17]

'Persons as they were,' 'nature just as it was': Swift, like Caravaggio,
makes a conscious rejection of antiquity and a conscious return to the
fountains of nature, but with this difference in emphasis—that the
consciousness of rejection is central to Swift's poem. As a result, he
does not dismiss Phidias absolutely in favour of the crowd. The
antique has not lost *all* authority for Swift. For all his low realism—
and however ironically—he *is* 'writing on the model of the ancients'.
When the *Tatler* announces 'a Description of the Morning, but of the
Morning in Town', the implication is that the poem does owe some
sort of allegiance to a *genre* with rules and hereditary images; while the
assertion that Swift 'never forms Fields, or Nymphs, or Groves, where
they are not' is only a half-truth. The gaoler's 'flock' return from
burlesque fields; the chimney-sweeps and coalmen sing in makeshift
groves; Betty takes on the role of a classical nymph, however degrad-
edly she plays it. Swift is pointing to a crowd of men and setting them

beside the sculptures of Phidias and Glycon. In *News from Parnassus*, a tribute to Swift written in 1721, his friend Dr. Delany recalls the *Tatler's* phrase about Swift running into 'a Way perfectly New'; but he makes a better balance than the *Tatler* does between new and old. Swift for Delany is 'like *Virgil* correct, with his own Native Ease'. Speaking in the *persona* of the verse-god Apollo, he goes on to describe him as a poet

> Who admires the Ancients, and knows 'tis their due,
> Yet writes in a Manner entirely new;
> Tho' none with more Ease their Depths can explore,
> Yet whatever he wants he takes from my Store. (*Poems*, 269).

But even this is a little glib. Swift's exploration of ancient depths cannot be sealed off entirely from his novel manner. He must surely have been aware of the dilemma of being a modern among ancients and an ancient among moderns. A similar dilemma faced James Thornhill when commissioned to paint the momentous landing of George I at Greenwich in 1714. Thornhill, as a baroque idealist and as a servant of the Government, has to make a sublime epiphany of the event. But as an honest observer, he knows that the event was not at all sublime visually. For instance (as he notes in the margin of one of his preliminary sketches), 'the king's own dress' was 'then not graceful, nor enough worthy of him to be transmitted to posterity'. And who were the other figures in the picture to be? 'If the real nobles that were there, then some of them are in disgrace now and so will be so much party in picture.' And worst of all, 'there was a vast crowd which to represent would be ugly, and not to represent would be false': ugly by the standards of classical beauty appropriate to a painting of the Golden Age Restored, false by the standards of naturalism appropriate to the literal transcription of a notable event.[18] The event in Swift, an ordinary morning, is less notable; but it is one haunted by potent poetic ghosts. However, Swift refuses to be 'false': he knows what morning at his end of the town is like, and will not compromise himself with mechanical goddesses or swains like a Grub-Street description-monger. One of the self-denying ordinances he puts into *Apollo's Edict*, the poem he sent Dr. Delany in reply to Delany's verses quoted above, covers this very point:

> No Simile shall be begun,
> With *rising* or with *setting* Sun . . .
> No Son of mine shall dare to say,
> *Aurora usher'd in the Day*.　　　(vv. 12–13 and 20–21)

And yet Swift knows too that what he sees in the urban dawn is 'ugly'; and so he contrives to give his poem meaning and permanence

by counterpointing this ugliness with elevated *descriptio*. Tradition
is weighed in the balance with 'the representation of vile things', and
it is the balance which animates the poem. Both sides have things to
be said in their favour, but both are found wanting. The *Description*
is at once a vigorous, no-nonsense parody of the sort of dawn-scene
Bysshe would put into a commonplace book, and a classicist's mocking
exposé of the corruption, triviality and untidiness of what passes for
day-to-day reality in 1709. Swift both chafes at the classical ideal
because it seems so little relevant to the reality he sees in the Strand,
and is drily ironic about the reality he sees in the Strand because it will
not live up to the standards set by the classical ideal.

A *Description of the Morning* was published in April, 1709. Two
months later, Swift left London for Ireland. He came back to the
capital in September, 1710, and found it a political chaos. 'We shall
have a strange Winter here,' he reports to Stella, 'between the struggles
of a cunning provoked discarded party, and the triumphs of one in
power; of both which I shall be an indifferent spectator.' To be
indifferent at such a time, or at least unpartisan, was certainly prudent.
For instance, when Swift was on his way across London to visit Sir
Godfrey Kneller's studio at the beginning of October, 'the rabble
came about our coach, crying A Colt, a Stanhope, etc., we were afraid
of a dead cat, or our glasses broken, and so were always of their side'.
But Swift's private life was peaceful enough in those weeks, and this
entry in the *Journal to Stella* is typical: 'we dined at the Chop-house with
Will Pate, the learned woollen-draper: then we sauntered at china-
shops and book-sellers.' And, for most of September at least, the sun
shone: 'we have had a fortnight of the most glorious weather on earth,
and still continues.' But the weather broke on September 27th; and
between then and October 13th Swift wrote his companion-piece to the
Morning, *A Description of a City Shower*. Coach-hire, saunterers in shops
dining out, dead cats and the political crisis all feature in the poem, and
in November, when it is already in print, Swift writes to Stella apropos
of his London lodgings that 'I am almost st—k out of this with the
sink, and it helps me to verses in my *Shower*.[19] 'The whole poem,'
writes Sir Harold Williams, 'is built on scenes and incidents observed'
—the scenes being presented so circumstantially that at one point a
textual problem can be cleared up by 'reference to any good map of
London in the eighteenth century'. (*Poems*, 137, 139). As with the
Morning, Swift's subject is common city nature: coffee houses, whirling
mops, dirty overcoats, stinking cesspools. Art could not mirror
empirical life more closely. But at the same time, the mode in which
Swift chooses to present London 'just as it is with all its deformities'

announces that the crude actual is being weighed against a high style
deeply involved with 'nature drawn on the most pleasing side'. The
poem was in fact later subtitled '*In Imitation of* VIRGIL'S Georg.'
More exactly it is the final section of the first *Georgic* which provides
the counterpoise for Swift's low *mimesis* here; and reference to a good
Augustan translation of Virgil—Dryden's is the obvious choice—is as
important for a full reading of the *City Shower* as reference to a good
map of London.

The 'Essay on Virgil's *Georgics*' which Addison wrote to preface
Dryden's translation can help too. Addison brings out clearly what
it was an Augustan critic expected from ideal description of weathers.
'A georgic', he explains,

> is some part of the science of husbandry put into a pleasing dress,
> and set off with all the beauties and embellishments of poetry. Now
> since the science of husbandry is of a very large extent, the poet
> shows his skill in singling out such precepts to proceed on as are
> useful and at the same time most capable of ornament. Virgil was
> so well acquainted with this secret that to set off his First Georgic
> he has run into a set of precepts which are almost foreign to his
> subject, in that beautiful account he gives us of the signs of nature
> which precede the changes of the weather. . . . He delivers the
> meanest of his precepts with a kind of grandeur; he breaks the clods
> and tosses the dung with an air of gracefulness. His prognostications
> of the weather are taken out of Aratus, where we may see how
> judiciously he has picked out those that are the most proper for his
> husbandman's observation, how he has enforced the expression and
> heightened the images which he found in the original.[20]

Georgic *mimesis* demands a high antique decorum to turn raw nature
into *la belle nature*, a nature fit for sublime art. Mean scientic fact must
be embellished with beauty and grandeur; image and expression must
be heightened with ornament and grace; all this being made very clear
to the modern poet (the poet planning the georgic description of a
storm for instance) by the inescapable presence of Virgil, supreme
example and judge of how it is to be done. The danger of course is that
Virgil's demands may be more than the modern poet's material is able
to bear. Thus Swift begins his account of the prognostics of a storm
grandly enough; but he soon finds that the Virgilian decorum of his
style is at odds with the indecorousness of his subject, that the attempt
to heighten and embellish a sublunary London accurately observed has
ironic consequences both for London and for *la belle nature*:

> Careful Observers may fortel the Hour
> (By sure Prognosticks) when to dread a Show'r:

While Rain depends, the pensive Cat gives o'er
Her Frolicks, and pursues her Tail no more.
Returning Home at Night, you'll find the Sink
Strike your offended Sense with double Stink . . .
A coming Show'r your shooting Corns presage,
Old Aches throb, your hollow Tooth will rage. . . .

Compare Dryden's Virgil:

And that by certain signs we may presage
Of heats and rains, and wind's impetuous rage,
The sov'reign of the heav'ns has set on high
The moon, to mark the changes of the sky . . .
The crow with clam'rous cries the show'r demands,
And single stalks along the desart sands.
The nightly virgin, while her wheel she plies,
Forsees the storm impending in the skies,
When sparkling lamps their sputt'ring light advance,
And in the sockets oily bubbles dance.
                    (*Georgics* I, 483–486 and 533–538)[21]

An alley-cat for the austere crow, corns and toothache for the distant
moon, a poor citizen with drain trouble for the virgin at her spinning-
wheel; this is the poor best the city can offer, however orotund the
language in which it is presented. And this is the theme of the *City
Shower* throughout—the ludicrous attempt of an imperfect, trivial
London to live up to classical dialects and situations.

As the storm gathers, the sky over the city makes a fine show of
elemental grandeur:

Mean while the South rising with dabbled Wings,
A Sable Cloud a-thwart the Welkin flings . . .

And it is a grandeur closely linked with high art, witness its sinister
echo of the biblical Flood in *Paradise Lost*:

Meanwhile the Southwind rose, and with black wings
Wide hovering, all the Clouds together drove
From under Heav'n; the Hills to their supplie
Vapour, and Exhalation dusk and moist,
Sent up amain.   (XI, 738–742).

But when Swift's storm breaks, the grandeur of the elements is reduced
to the level of the citizenry they drench, as London's moist exhalations
fill a sordid cloud

That swill'd more Liquor than it could contain,
And like a Drunkard gives it up again.

Again, the downpour itself is a fine Latinate one:

> Now in contiguous Drops the Flood comes down,
> Threat'ning with Deluge this *Devoted* Town . . .

but since the crowds in doomed London are too petty-minded even to merit equation with Noah's wicked generation, the Latinity has to be dropped:

> To shops in Crouds the dagged Females fly,
> Pretend to cheapen Goods, but nothing buy.

It is as though Swift's Miltonic Jehovah were too contemptuous of the citizens to bother with any sublime retribution, verbal or physical, just as Swift's Jove in *The Day of Judgement* twenty years later will summon the sinful world to his judgement-seat only to dismiss it again with the ultimate bathos:

> "I to such Blockheads set my Wit!
> I damn such Fools!—Go, go, you're bit." (*Poems*, 579).

We have bathos of another sort at the climax of the *Description*, which presents the overflowing drains rushing the city's garbage down to Fleet Ditch and the Thames:

> Now from all Parts the swelling Kennels flow,
> And bear their Trophies with them as they go.

'Trophies' of course cries out to be undercut; but Swift's closing triplet offers more than simple deflation:

> Sweepings from Butchers Stalls, Dung, Guts and Blood;
> Drown'd Puppies, stinking Sprats, all drench'd in Mud,
> Dead Cats and Turnip-Tops come tumbling down the Flood.

No one could say that Swift tosses the dung about with an air of gracefulness here; but it is less easy to say just what he *is* doing. Clearly he cannot allow himself room for the hygenic storm-scenes of the georgic tradition,

> When the fleecy skies new clothe the wood,
> And cakes of rustling ice come rolling down the flood.
> (Dryden's *Georgics* I, 417–418).

But why not exactly? Because they are fatuous in themselves, or because modern London is not worthy of them, or because they have been degraded by bad poets? What sort of weight should we give Swift's own commentary on these lines? This is to be found in a letter of 1735, as part of a general attack on the triplet-form. Triplets, he writes, are 'a vicious way of rhyming, wherewith Dryden abounded. . . . He was poor, and in great haste to finish his plays, because by them he chiefly supported his family, and this made him so very uncorrect;

he likewise brought in the Alexandrine verse at the end of the triplets. I was so angry at these corruptions, that above twenty-four years ago I banished them all by one triplet, with the Alexandrine, upon a very ridiculous subject' (*Corr.*, IV, 321). Triplets with the Alexandrine certainly abound in Dryden's Virgil; and on this level of ridicule, the dung, puppies, cats and turnips are to be seen simply as aids to a destructive parody of Drydenisms like

> The dykes are fill'd, and with a roaring sound
> The rising rivers float the nether ground;
> And rocks the bellowing voice of boiling seas rebound.
>   (*Georgics* I, 441–443).

It is as though Swift were getting the 'needy Poet' he introduces earlier in the *Description* to write the end of the poem for him. And yet this is less than half the truth about Swift's triplet, for to see no more in it than an angry stylistic joke is to ignore its positive vitality, a vitality which is its own justification and which has an effect transcending mere parody. Almost in spite of itself, mockery of inept classicism here leads to a vivid rendering of modern nature.

Swift confronts modern with classical more openly in his treatment of the stranded beau earlier in the *Description*. The beau is puny enough in himself:

> Box'd in a Chair the Beau impatient sits,
> While Spouts run clatt'ring o'er the Roof by Fits;
> And ever and anon with frightful Din
> The Leather sounds, he trembles from within.

But his puniness is intensified when we see in him the city counterpart of Virgil's Earth Mother as she trembles at the din of Jupiter scattering his thunderbolts:

> The Father of the Gods his glory shrouds,
> Involv'd in tempests, and a night of clouds;
> And, from the middle darkness flashing out,
> By fits he deals his fiery bolts about.
> Earth feels the motions of her angry god;
> Her entrails tremble, and her mountains nod.
>   (I, 444–449).

And as if it were not enough to place the impatient beau against Virgil's ideal natural world, Swift carries the shrinking process still further by dropping him into the ideal heroic world of the *Aeneid*:

> So when *Troy* Chair-men bore the Wooden Steed,
> Pregnant with *Greeks*, impatient to be freed,
> (Those Bully *Greeks*, who, as the Moderns do,
> Instead of paying Chair-men, run them thro'.)

Laoco'n struck the Outside with his Spear,
And each imprison'd Hero quak'd for Fear.

Swift's beau is to the Greeks in the Trojan horse as his Betty is to Aurora—here-and-now pettiness beside classic magnificence. The epic significance of the myth stresses the insignificance of the beau's world. The sedan chair imprisons one petulant fop where the horse is 'Pregnant with *Greeks*': Virgil's equivalent phrase in the *Aeneid* is *feta armis* (II, 238), which Dryden renders 'Big with destruction', the destruction of Troy which is in its turn the creation of Rome and western civilisation. Yet the beau's world, however insignificant, is inescapably our world; so the modern poet must allow it to cut the ancient myth down to size. In our world the heroic Trojans would be mere chairmen and the Greeks mere bullies, and so that is how they must be presented in an up-to-date Description. The Restoration poet John Oldham provides a similar case. He can write a *Praise of Homer* which makes the poet's work as sublime a fountain as nature's:

Thou art the unexhausted Ocean, whence
Sprung first, and still do flow th'eternal Rills of sense.
To none but Thee our Art Divine we owe,
From whom it had its Rise, and full Perfection too.

Yet when he has to put Homeric themes into a Restoration context, Oldham can describe Homer as

He, who sung on *Phrygia's* Shore,
The *Grecian* Bullies fighting for a Whore.[22]

Traditional ideal art, then, in the *Shower* as in the *Morning*, is at once a yard-stick and a dead letter, while the crude actual is both a source of vitality and a target for neoclassical irony. Swift's is certainly 'a Manner entirely new', but he is not suggesting that, because his immediate concerns must be with petulant fops and good-for-nothing chamber-maids, the classical heroes and weather-gods are poetically irrelevant. Rather, there seems to be this sort of pattern in his assumptions: the classics embody a just and beautiful nature; the contemporary realities of a sordid Queen Anne London are no more than a travesty of true nature; so to copy these apparent realities (as I must if I am not to be quite out of touch with life as it is lived) is to travesty the classics. For an open-eyed city-dweller who knows that modern life does not live up to ancient art, the sublime second nature of young Maro's vision has a double function. It enables him to channel his explosive Hogarth-ian energies into burlesque; and at the same time it validates his hints that somewhere, however far away, order, decorum and nobility do really exist.

Swift had written as a committed Ancient in *The Battle of the Books*, some fifteen years before the *Descriptions*. He was to do so again in the third part of *Gulliver's Travels*, about fifteen years after them. Though it is never safe to assume that Gulliver's judgements in the *Travels* are identical with Swift's, the confrontation of ancient and modern seems to be one episode in which the hero does speak unequivocally for the author. Asking the wizards of Glubbdubdrib 'that the Senate of *Rome* might appear before me in one large Chamber, and a modern Representative, in Counterview, in another', Gulliver reports that 'the first seemed to be an Assembly of Heroes and Demy-Gods; the other a Knot of Pedlars, Pick-pockets, Highwaymen and Bullies'. (XI, 196). The *Descriptions* too set ancient demigods and modern bullies in counterview. But where the counterviewing in the Glubbdubdrib episode can be seen as sane and constructive—after all, it is in the power of a modern parliament to reform itself in emulation of a classical senate—there is a sound Swiftian reason for declaring the counterviews of the *Morning* and the *Shower* dangerously insane.

A favourite device of Swift's for satirising wrong-headed idealisms is to dramatise the madness which seizes the idealist when he is forced to face the facts of the real world. For example, Cassinus in *Cassinus and Peter* loses his wits on discovering that his adored Celia is not a disembodied goddess, and Strephon in *Strephon and Chloe* reacts to the same discovery by falling into a crazy bestiality. Both have let themselves be gulled into believing that the human creatures they worship are pure spirit, angels without bowels, etherial nymphs; and both pay the penalty. Similarly, Lemuel Gulliver comes to adore those ethical equivalents to etherial nymphs, the perfectly rational Houyhnhnms, and his disgust on returning to the world of men drives him mad. But is our description-writer any less sick than the Gulliver who brands all his fellow countrymen as Yahoos and hides in the sanctum of the stable-yard from the odious affections of his wife and children? Our *descriptor*, his mind clouded by the antique perfection of hero and demigod, can see nothing in contemporary London but pocket-picking, bullying and pedling. Granted that he exploits the counterviewing of ancient and modern brilliantly; but one wonders what he would have his fallen city do to redeem itself. Try to become another ancient Rome? The *Descriptions* nowhere imply this, and the *Satires* of Juvenal would have argued against it. Or try to transform itself into the English countryside of the early eighteenth century? Swift doubtless had as few illusions about *that* as a potential ideal as his friend Gay in *The Birth of the Squire* or *The Shepherd's Week*. Rather, the charade he forces his London to play is to disguise itself inadequately, grotesquely

as Virgilian landscape and classical fresco. His basic grievance seems
to be that Modern Town is not Ancient Country, which is as pointless
as torturing oneself with the sad truth that the men one knows are not
as virtuous as one's fantasy Houyhnhnm and the women not as anti-
septic as one's fantasy Diana. We may accept that Augustan London is
dirty, trivial and immoral; but can we honestly allow that our *descriptor*
is any less deranged in his way than Strephon or Gulliver in theirs
when he measures the facts of London life by the standards of Arcadian
art and finds London odious as a result?

Perhaps Swift would agree with us. Perhaps the poker-faced,
tight-lipped observer who speaks the *Descriptions* is an ironic *persona*, a
dramatic creation not to be taken at his face-value. Perhaps the reader
of this essay should substitute '*descriptor ridiculus*' for 'Swift' every time
the name has been used in connection with the attitudes of the *Morning*
and the *Shower*. But this would be to ignore not only Swift's declared
allegiance to the Ancients but also the fact that, though arguments
ultimately proving the madness of the *descriptor* may hold good by
Swiftian logic, Swift himself never allows us time to apply such a logic.
Both *Descriptions* are short considering the issues they bring up, and
both are so busy with surface action that there is no room for *reductio ad
absurdum*. Though it may be illuminating in one way to see the *Description of the Morning* as a fragment from a lost *Macheathiad*, in another it
is as important to remember that Swift gave his poem no such context.
Though here and in the *Shower* he pushes his ideas far enough to let
them resonate with rich irony, in both poems he stops them far short
of any *reductio*.

And even if it is a mad delusion to believe that Homer equals
Nature, that decorum, nobility and order are vested uniquely in remote
classic forms, and that our modern cities should aspire to the condition
of Virgilian commonplaces, we may still find that the delusion has a
positive use, just as the crazy fantasies of the rational horse and the
sweatless goddess, though dangerous if taken in the wrong way, may
do good if taken in the right one. The heroes of *The Lady's Dressing
Room* and *Strephon and Chloe* are partly figures of satiric fun because they
should have known better than to idealise their mistresses in the first
place; but they are also figures to sympathise with because their
awakenings are unnecessarily traumatic: even as physical human
creatures, their Celias and Chloes need not have been so filthy in their
habits or so concerned to cover that filth with a gaudy veneer. Then
Gulliver among the horses is stupidly wrong to make the glib equation
of Yahoo with *homo sapiens*, but there are extenuating circumstances, for
English *homo sapiens* in the eighteenth century has given Gulliver every

provocation to make the equation: had his contemporaries been less single-mindedly vicious and less preoccupied with perverting their gift of reason to compound their vices, perhaps Gulliver would not have been gulled. A loved woman should try, as far as her limiting human condition allows, to deserve the praise of a Wholesome Nymph. And a civilised man should to the same degree try to emulate everything emulable which deserves emulation in the Good Horses. Similarly, the raillery of the *Descriptions*, however unsure its basis in logic or common sense, can serve usefully to deflate the complacency of the routine classicising poet or the routine citizen. These Houyhnhnm *Descriptions of the City of the Yahoos* may not be comprehensive photo-surveys of life in London, but their ludicrous gravity may provoke a few Londoners to look more intently at their neighbours, their drains, themselves. And to the irrelevant hack-classicist they may serve as eye-openers, as London's equivalent to the Laputian 'flapper', who is

> employed diligently to attend his Master in his Walks, and upon Occasion to give him a soft Flap on his Eyes; because he is always so wrapped up in Cogitation, that he is in manifest Danger...in the Streets, of jostling others, or being jostled himself into the Kennel. (XI, 159-60).

NOTES

[1] Quotations from the *Essay* are from the 1713 ed., with line-numberings from the modernised text in *Minor Poets of the Eighteenth Century*, ed. Fausset (London, 1930), pp. 185–197. For Swift's 'forwarding', see *Journal to Stella*, ed. H. Williams (Oxford, 1948), II, 586, 597, 611–612, 623, etc.

[2] 'Life of Thomas Parnell', *Works*, ed. J. W. Gibbs (London, 1884–6), IV, 172.

[3] IV, 584–585 and IX, 459–460 (Dryden's version of the latter).

[4] *Monsieur Bossu's Treatise of the Epick Poem*, tr. 'W.J.' (1695), p. 240.

[5] *The British Parnassus* (1714), II, 578–579. It seems, though the lay-out of his text is not clear at this point, that Bysshe ascribes these lines to Creech's translation of Lucretius; but I have not been able to find them there or elsewhere. For dawn-soliloquies, see Otway's *Orphan* IV.i.81–97 (*Works*, ed. J. C. Ghosh [Oxford, 1932], II, 54–55), and Lee's *Massacre of Paris* V.i.1–11 (*Works*, ed. Stroup and Cook [New Brunswick, 1954–5], II, 48).

[6] Two other poems by Swift dating from the late 1700s show similar attitudes to *descriptio* and to the tension between town and country: *Baucis and Philemon*, vv. 163–164, and *In pity to the empty'ng Town*, vv. 5–16.

[7] Spenser, *Faerie Queene* I. xi.51; Milton, *Elegia Quinta*, vv. 49–54; for the Carracci and Guercino paintings of Aurora, *inter alia*, see Irving Lavin, 'Cephalus and Procris', *Journal of the Warburg and Courtauld Institutes*, XVII (1954), plates 39 and 40.

[8] *Amusements Serious and Comical*, ed. A. L. Hayward (London, 1927), pp. 11–12.

[9] *Hudibras* II.ii.29–32; Hutcheson, *Dublin Journal* 10 (*Eighteenth Century Critical Essays*, ed. Scott Elledge [Ithaca, 1961], I, 378).

[10] *The Dispensary*, 6th ed. (1706), p. 34; Blackmore, *Eliza* (1705), p. 22.

[11] For the Thornhill, see F. Saxl and R. Wittkower, *British Art and the Mediterranean* (London, 1948), Section 50; for the Hogarth, see F. Antal, *Hogarth and his Place in European Art* (London, 1962), plate 58a.

[12] Antal, *op. cit.*, p. 56.

[13] *Essay*, I (1756), ii (Elledge, *op. cit.* [note 9], II, 730).

[14] *Preface to Shakespeare* (1725); Elledge, *op. cit.* I, 279.

[15] *Ibid.*, I, 281.

[16] *Vite de' Pittori* (1672), p. 5, tr. Dryden, *Essays*, ed. W. P. Ker (Oxford, 1900), II, 119; *Vite*, pp. 202–203 and 212–213, tr. Walter Friedlaender, *Caravaggio Studies* (Princeton, 1955), pp. 246 and 253.

[17] 'History of England', *Works*, ed. J. W. Gibbs (London, 1884–6), V, 345.

[18] Thornhill's notes are printed by Edgar Wind, 'The Revolution of History Painting', *Journal of the Warburg Institute*, II (1938), 123.

[19] *Journal to Stella*, ed. H. Williams (Oxford, 1948, I, 24, 42, 43, 28 and 87.

[20] Elledge, *op. cit.*, I, 2 and 6.

[21] Dryden, *Poetical Works*, ed. G. R. Noyes, 2nd ed. (Cambridge [Mass.], 1950), pp. 450–451. (All quotations from Dryden's Virgil are taken from this edition, the line-numbers being those of the translation.)

[22] *The Works of Mr. John Oldham* (1686), pt. ii, p. 63, and pt. iii, p. 167.

Jonathan Swift: The Poetry of 'Reaction'

GEOFFREY HILL

In general, when we use the word 'reaction', we may be referring to a supposedly 'retrograde tendency' in politics or to a 'revulsion' of feeling. Since the political and pathological aspects of Swift's work have been amply debated, the purpose of the present exercise may appear open to question. It should be emphasised that, in proposing the term 'reaction' for this discussion, my chief endeavour is to define and describe an essential quality of Swift's creative intelligence: the capacity to be at once resistant and reciprocal.

I am aware that, in the consideration of Augustan poetry in general and Swift's poetry in particular, arbitrary assumptions as to the irreconcilability of wit and feeling still carry weight; and Swift is especially vulnerable to those distortions of interpretation which occur when ideas are extracted from the texture of language. To state my own case in its most basic terms is to say that if, as a moralist, Swift's concern is with the ordering of acceptance and rejection, as a moral artist he can transfigure his patterns. We may readily perceive that this demands from the poet a most sensitive awareness of the things which are beii ; reacted against and that in his finest work this sensitivity works a a catalyst to transform, say, autocratic disdain into a cherishing par cularity. We recognize just as readily that this awareness can be fully realized only in the medium of language itself, the true marriage, in words, of wit and feeling.

I

It is no longer possible to explain Swift's genius in terms of convenient myth. That he was not 'mad' is attested by eminent medical and scholarly authority[1]; that he suffered, in 1742, a brain-lesion followed by senile decay seems probable and, in view of his advanced age, unremarkable. Nevertheless, for a considerable part of his life he was certainly ill and demonstrably eccentric, concerned to the point of obsession with manifestations of the absurd and irrational in himself, in particular enemies and friends and in society at large. Certain episodes in his career would have justified such concern, among them his fruitless efforts to reconcile the quarrel between Bolingbroke and Oxford, the oppressive infatuation of Esther Vanhomrigh, the threat of arrest by the Walpole Administration and of physical assault by Richard Bettesworth. These were matters of more than clinical observa-

O

tion, but such observations, in the form of philosophical and political theory, were not overlooked. Swift read and annotated his volumes of Machiavelli, Bacon, Harrington and Hobbes.[2] Sir William Temple had been attracted by the truism that events in history could be largely explained by noting the 'passions and personal dispositions' which rule the private lives of public men; and the master's fondness for the commonplace seems to have been shared by his pupil.[3] One may feel, therefore, that to view the intimate eccentricities of Swift in their larger context is in accord with his own creative disposition. Such poems as *An Apology to the Lady Carteret, Lady Acheson Weary of the Dean,* and *Verses on the Death of Dr. Swift* suggest that, as a poet, he could represent personal predicaments emblematically and turn private crisis into public example. W. B. Yeats, whose view was understandably influenced by the prevailing myth of Swift as *poète maudit,* to some extent justified his acceptance of the legendary figure by making it representative of the destruction of an epoch. The final silencing of Swift was the silencing of the voice of moral authority in his place and time: 'more than the "great Ministers" had gone.'[4]

In Swift a sense of tradition and community is challenged by a strong feeling for the anarchic and the predatory. A necessary qualification is that the appeal of Community exists not as a fine Platonic idea but as something soberly lived, taken up into the daily pattern of conduct and work. A reader of his correspondence, as of the *Journal* and birthday poems to Stella, comes to accept the real presence, as well as the ritual, of his friendships. This affects the poetry, in particular its power to move with fluent rapidity from private to public utterance and from the formal to the intimate in the space of a few lines. At times, in the letters to Bolingbroke and Oxford, what is private is simultaneously public in its implications. It is of course true that when one has a few good friends and those friends happen to be the most important men in England, E. M. Forster's injunction 'only connect' has a particularly happy significance. It might be objected that such ideal conditions hardly existed for Swift after the debacle of 1714; it might also be remarked that the familiar verse which, we are told (*Poems,* 965), 'occupied so much of Dean Swift's leisure' in Ireland became a half-defensive exaggeration of the sudden failure to connect, a play on the vicissitudes of being 'in' or 'out':

> When I saw you to-day, as I went with Lord Anglesey,
> Lord! said I, who's that parson? how awkwardly dangles he!
> When whip you trot up, without minding your betters,
> To the very coach side, and threaten your letters.
>   (*The Dean to Tho: Sheridan,* 1718; *Poems,* 978).

This is the conversion to familiar nuance of the public admonitory tone of seventeenth-century satire, but for the intimate joke to have bite it still needs the public contact, an edge of hard fact. In a letter to Pope, years afterwards, Swift wrote that:

> I was t'other day reckoning twenty Seven great Ministers or men of Wit and Learning, who are all dead, and all of my Acquaintance within twenty years past... (*Corr.*, V, 271).

And continued, as though trying to balance his account, with the names of nineteen 'men of distinction and my friends who are yet alive'. Primarily an ageing man's game of Patience, it is still a suggestive catalogue both for the timbre of the voice and for the data it provides. Several of those named, including Lord Berkeley, Lord Carteret, the Duke of Ormonde and the Earl of Pembroke had held high office as Lord Justice or Lord Lieutenant in Ireland. The younger Swift, 'taking his ease at the Castle,'[5] had enjoyed friendly acquaintance with Berkeley and Pembroke. Carteret's term of office (1724–30) enabled the old and celebrated writer to exercise a nice intricacy of formal yet familiar association with a man whose intellect was at once engaged and frustrated in the practicalities of government. However daunting the periods of Irish reclusion may have seemed, they were far from bringing total eclipse.

Swift has been called 'a practical politician in everything he wrote';[6] he was, in a variety of senses, a born administrator. Dr. Johnson, who was not over-indulgent towards Swift's memory, admitted his capability as Dean of St. Patrick's.[7] Professor Ehrenpreis has remarked that, in Ireland, the administrative class to which Swift's family belonged could be 'numbered in the hundreds' yet formed 'a kind of social capital on which he drew interest for the rest of his life'.[8] It was necessarily a self-contained society. Ireland's ruling caste, as the historian William Lecky pointed out, was 'planted in the midst of a hostile and subjugated population'.[9]

Among the coterie of Swift's Dublin years were a number of people, active in their public lives, who wrote occasional verses and sometimes took part in humorous rhyming contests with the Dean and other friends. His literary acquaintance included Dr. Patrick Delany, Dr. Richard Helsham, George Rochfort, William Dunkin and the Earl of Orrery. Stella also wrote, and a character in Yeats's *The Words Upon the Window Pane* claims that she was a better poet than Swift; though on the evidence of the three pieces which are attributed to her the argument is untenable. These verses are less impressive than some by Swift's other close friend, Dr. Thomas Sheridan. *Tom Punsibi's Letter to*

Dean Swift (c. 1727) is an immaculate example of that style of familiar naturalism in which Swift himself excelled:

> When to my House you come dear Dean,
> Your humble Friend to entertain,
> Thro' Dirt and Mire, along the Street,
> You find no Scraper for your Feet:
> At this, you storm, and stamp, and swell,
> Which serves to clean your Feet as well:
> By steps ascending to the Hall,
> All torn to rags with Boys and Ball.
> Fragments of Lime about the Floor,
> A sad uneasy Parlor Door . . .   (*Poems*, 1045).

Sheridan's description of the miry street may be an admiring echo of Swift's earlier *A Description of a City Shower* (1710) but it is clear from the accuracy of his writing that Swift had found a reciprocating talent.[10] Apparently:

> so successful was Sheridan in imitating Swift's style that even Delany found it difficult to distinguish the work of one from that of the other.[11]

But if *Tom Punsibi's Letter* is imitation, it is so in the good neo-classical sense and is distinct from simple mimicry or mere plagiarism. Familiarity with Sheridan's work may have given Swift a much-needed incentive for his own familiar verse, a more racy and immediate contact than the admired Pope and a disciple and confederate in the 'Hudibrastic' line.

Swift, in his old age, is reputed to have had the whole of Butler's *Hudibras* by heart[12] and it is somewhat surprising to find no mention of this work in the catalogue of his library. Swift's library was admittedly not widely representative of the achievements of modern English poetry. He had Spenser, Milton,[13] Pope, Prior, Gay and Parnell but not, apparently, those two predecessors with whom, as a satirist, he is now most often associated. Of these, Butler is one, and for the absence of Rochester there may have been sufficient reason since even the libertine Earl's return to Christianity had been made under the aegis of the detested latitudinarian Bishop Burnet. Although Swift 'never was one of his Admirers' (IV, 274) it is difficult not to be in sympathy with those critics who cite the 'agony and indignation'[14] of Rochester's major satires as a precedent for Swift's own work in the genre and hard not to suppose that the Dean had read them, perhaps with mixed feelings about their 'Hobbesian' views but with a professional attention to detail:

> With Mouth screw'd up, and awkward winking Eyes,
> And breast thrust forward; Lord, Sir, she replies:

It is my goodness, and not my deserts,
Which makes you shew your Learning, Wit and Parts.
He puzzled, bites his Nails, both to display
The Sparkling Ring, and think what's next to say.
And thus breaks out a fresh: Madam, I gad,
Your Luck, last Night, at Cards was mighty bad
At Cribbidge; Fiftynine, and the next shew,
To make your Game, and yet to want those Two.
                    (Rochester: *Tunbridge-Wells*)[15]

'Stand further Girl, or get you gone,
'I always lose when you look on.
Lord, Madam, you have lost Codill;
I never saw you play so ill.
'Nay, Madam, give me leave to say
''Twas you that threw the Game away;
'When Lady *Tricksy* play'd a Four,
'You took it with a Matadore.
        (Swift: *The Journal of a Modern Lady*, 1729; *Poems*, 452).

That the advantage of this comparison appears to be with Rochester is
not wholly due to the exigencies of arbitrary selection. He is a lyric
dramatist: the 'mouth screw'd up,' the gesture with the ring, seem to
occur in a sequence of human cause and effect. Rochester peoples a
situation with actors who themselves grasp that they are 'situated' and
must therefore act to live. Swift, it might seem, though often praised
for his sense of situation, shows less concern for human predicament
than for the more obvious tones of social behaviour. He converts
manners into mannerism; or he presents a formal setting which serves
as a *pied-à-terre* for punitive excursions:

My female Friends, whose tender Hearts
Have better learn'd to act their Parts
Receive the News in *doleful Dumps*,
'The Dean is dead (*and what is Trumps?*)'
        (*Verses on the Death of Dr. Swift*, 1731; *Poems*, 562).

Here, though, the rhyming wit itself works like a 'trump' or triumph to
snatch brilliant personal success from a position of elected disadvantage.
A constant pre-occupation with verbal routines is a characteristic of
Swift, as may be seen in *A Proposal for Correcting, Improving and Ascer-
taining the English Tongue* (1712) or *A Compleat Collection of Genteel and
Ingenious Conversation* (1738), and his satiric art in *Verses on the Death of
Dr. Swift* depends on a seemingly-perfect rapport between clichés.
The effect does not merely require the bathos of the move from 'dead'
to 'Trumps'; it also needs a constant frisson or sympathetic vibration
between truisms, 'Friends', 'tender', 'doleful'. There is even a reverse

thread of ironic suggestion linking 'News' and 'Friends'. The very solidity of Rochester's characterisation is itself releasing. Swift's nuance-haunted repartee puts the burden of correct or incorrect response on the reader and is capable of employing pathos as a trap for obtuse decency:

> 'The Dean, if we believe Report,
> 'Was never ill receiv'd at Court:
> 'As for his Works in Verse and Prose,
> 'I own myself no Judge of those:
> 'Nor, can I tell what Criticks thought 'em;
> 'But, this I know, all People bought 'em;
> 'As with a moral View design'd
> 'To cure the Vices of Mankind:
> 'His Vein, ironically grave,
> 'Expos'd the Fool, and lash'd the knave:' (*Poems*, 565).

II

In order to isolate and describe Swift's own idiom it is necessary to recognise contacts, both those which excite and those which inhibit the growth of idiosyncratic art. If Swift's friendship with Thomas Sheridan stands at one pole of the creative field, Addison's influence possibly represents the opposite extreme. It is known that Addison drastically edited two of Swift's poems, *Vanbrug's House* and *Baucis and Philemon* by 'cutting out many strokes that gave vigour and force to the description'.[16] Although Swift always referred to Addison in terms of personal respect it is clear that Swift's creative tact was a very different thing from Addison's literary taste. Nor was there always a perfect understanding with such close acquaintances as Delany and Orrery who were sometimes disturbed by Swift's breaches of etiquette. It is not altogether astonishing to find in Swift's poetic satire a certain amount of irritation at the spurious proscriptions of false delicacy and a clear distinction between squeamishness and decorum. The question of 'reaction' implies more than a manipulation of antitheses. With many aspects of the consensus of taste Swift was undoubtedly able to agree and it would be patronising to suppose that he necessarily regarded himself as sacrificing original liberty on the altar of caste. Despite the possibly inhibiting surveillance of Addison or Temple and the sympathetic reservations of Delany and Orrery, Swift's poetry gained more than it lost by his overall adherence to the major canons of his class. *The Journal of a Modern Lady* contains a scathing account of the trivial malice of social gossip:

> Nor do they trust their Tongue alone,
> To speak a Language of their own;
> But read a Nod, a Shrug, a Look,
> Far better than a printed Book;
> Convey a Libel in a Frown,
> And wink a Reputation down;
> Or by the tossing of the Fan,
> Describe the Lady and the Man.   (*Poems*, 450).

But, setting ethics aside, this 'language' is no mean achievement in quick, economical mimicry. Swift never did leave ethics aside but it is still true that his poems have a good deal of the gadding energy and, at times, something of the spleen and complacency of the society which they inhabit.

It may be that close-knit communities need to evolve sophisticated weapons of control. Eighteenth Century verse sometimes aims to 'disarm'. *The Rape of the Lock* is such a poem; Swift's *Cadenus and Vanessa* (1713) is another. This work originated in the Esther Vanhomrigh affair; Swift was 'embarrassed but unwilling to end the situation'. (*Poems*, 684). Ostensibly a tale in verse, *Cadenus and Vanessa* is a working blue-print for the kind of poem which it then discovers itself to be; its task is to test various techniques against varying situations and successfully reduce a dangerous immediacy to a more remote hypothesis:

> She railly'd well, he always knew,
> Her Manner now was something new;
> And what she spoke was in an Air,
> As serious as a Tragick Play'r.
> But those who aim at Ridicule
> Shou'd fix upon some certain Rule,
> Which fairly hints they are in jest,
> Else he must enter his Protest:
> For, let a Man be ne'er so wise,
> He may be caught with sober Lies;
> A Science which he never taught,
> And, to be free, was dearly bought:
> For, take it in its proper Light,
> 'Tis just what Coxcombs call, *a Bite*.   (*Poems*, 707–8).

Given the situation between Swift and Vanessa, such terms as 'in an Air', 'As serious as', 'may be caught', 'a Tragick Play'r' are a breathtaking defiance of gravity. The passage turns on the words 'railly'd' and 'Bite', two technical terms out of the social rhetoric of the time. The requirements for a successful 'bite' were specified by Swift himself:

You must ask a bantering question, or tell some damned lie in a
serious manner, and then she will answer or speak as if you were in
earnest; and then cry you, 'Madam, there's a *bite*. (*Corr.*, I, 40).

Receiving an answer 'as if you were in earnest' suggests, in the Swift-
Vanessa relationship, a dénouement more far-reaching than the crisis of
a rhetorical game; yet the whole point of the rhetoric is to defuse the
emotional charge.

The somewhat complex question of Raillery as an eighteenth-
century social and literary phenomenon has been the subject of much
able and detailed discussion.[17] In terms of pure theory it is possible to
distinguish two major types: 'ironical praise that is really satire or
reproof' and its opposite, 'something that at first appeared a Reproach
or Reflection; but, by some Turn of Wit unexpected and surprising,
ended always in a Compliment, and to the Advantage of the Person it
was addressed to.'[18] Swift favoured, in principle, the second type and
was particularly careful to make the distinction between constructive
raillery and mere abuse:

> So, the pert Dunces of Mankind
> Whene're they would be thought refin'd,
> Because the Diff'rence lyes abstruse
> 'Twixt Raillery and gross Abuse,
> To show their Parts, will scold and rail,
> Like Porters o'er a Pot of Ale.
>   (*To Mr. Delany*, 1718; *Poems*, 216).

In the light of these meticulous distinctions and the insistence on the
social and ethical advantages of the art, one recognises all the more
sharply those occasions when it is bungled or simply set aside. When
Swift was at Market Hill, 'the neighbouring Ladies', according to
Faulkner, 'were no great Understanders of Raillery'. (*Poems*, 890 n.)
Market Hill was a rural estate and the implication here may be that
country cousins are no match for urban wit. But it seems that these
same urbanities frequently wore thin. Sheridan angered Delany and,
in the end, lost Swift's friendship with raw remarks that were ill-taken.
Participants in the humorous verse 'battles', which were a feature of the
intellectual circle, not infrequently lost their tempers; Swift was at
various times culprit, victim and peace-maker. His own poem *The
Journal*, describing in terms of affectionate raillery the household
activities of the Rochforts and their guests, led to his being criticised
for abusing the hospitality of friends. (*Poems*, 277). The casualty-rate
could, admittedly, have been higher; but the point would seem to be
that notwithstanding the precise distinctions between fine raillery and
coarse insult, mistakes were frequently made, even by such skilled

practitioners. It may seem that infringements occurred through the necessity to turn in small tight circles of mutual exacerbation and the obligation to demonstrate superior skill.[19] Despite accidents this high-strung technique had its value in a close community, permitting the reiteration of such real or imagined values as accuracy, tact and feeling. It offered a way of beating the bounds between the permissible and the unspeakable, of driving out the drones and instructing the rest. In a letter to William Pulteney of March 7th, 1736–7 Swift acclaimed his recipient's 'more than an old Roman spirit' which had been 'the constant Subject of Discourse and of Praise among the whole few of what unprostituted people have remain[ed] among us'. (*Corr.*, V, 7). Swift had a tendency to count heads.[20] 'Few' and 'unprostituted' is what the drama of unity required, in the teeth of human limitation, for the sake of the *manes*. He wrote to the Earl of Oxford, July 3rd, 1714:

> For in your publick Capacity you have often angred me to the Heart, but, as a private man, never once. So that if I only looktd towards my self I could wish you a private Man to morrow. (*Corr.*, II, 44–5).

In one sense this is telling praise; in another, it is a courteous and restrained lament for the failure to achieve unity of Being. In one important respect, the mutual regard of two 'unprostituted' people is everything; but at the same time, given the ideal integrity of public life, it is not enough. Perhaps this is the value for Swift, emotionally and philosophically, of the defeated man and it may be the truly creative thing that he received from the ideas and example of Sir William Temple. Defeat restores Unity of Being, if only hermetically and in isolation.[21] Although critics quite properly stress the manifest differences between the early Pindarics and the mature verse,[22] it is possible to detect a thread of continuity, a line of development starting with the Pindaric celebration of the defeated man (Temple; Sancroft), continuing through the 1716 poem to Oxford, 'How blest is he, who for his Country dies', and culminating in the comic exorcisms of Swift's own defeat. His political and ecclesiastical embarrassment, his 'exile', were factors to which he personally refused to succumb, but, which, as a poet, he provoked into a series of difficult encounters. The situation of *An Apology to the Lady Carteret* (1725) and *Verses on the Death of Dr. Swift* (1731) is defeat, either by bodily humiliation or the trivia of daily encounters or the triumph of philistine life, but wit converts the necessitous failure into moral and rhetorical victory. The prime significance of Swift's 'sin of wit' is that it challenges and reverses in terms of metaphor the world's routine of power and, within safe parentheses, considers all alternatives including anarchy.

Swift's attitude towards the anarchic was significantly ambiguous. In principle he abhorred all its aspects, from lexical and grammatical to social and political; pragmatically he played along with it to some extent;[23] poetically he reacted to it with a kindling of creative delight. While, in the main, anarchy was a mob-attribute, it is open to suggestion that Swift also recognised a Jonsonian sense of disorder, an imbalance of humours in those who governed policy or money. Viewed in this light, great bad men like Marlborough or Walpole were a threat to the Body Politic. Although Swift, in common with other contemporaries, offered analyses of raillery and although a subsequent process of scholarly abstraction has tended to give such discussions an apparent universality in Augustan literary and social debate, his work is noteworthy for its 'so-called', 'ungenerous' and 'inexcusable'[24] attacks on Marlborough and somewhat lesser figures like Baron Cutts and Archbishop Hort, poems in which he abandons the salon of raillery for the pillory of invective. There seems little to distinguish the tone of *The Character of Sir Robert Walpole* or the anti-Marlborough piece *On the Death of a Late Famous General* from the kind of procedure that Swift, in *To Dr. Delany*, purported to despise. It should be stressed that in considering the poems themselves, when one notes the distinction between raillery and invective one is describing the difference between two equal forces rather than between superior and inferior kinds. If *Verses on the Death of Dr. Swift* is the apotheosis of raillery it is equally apparent that *The Legion Club* (1736) is Swift's masterpiece of invective:

> Keeper, shew me where to fix
> On the Puppy Pair of *Dicks*;
> By their lanthorn Jaws and Leathern,
> You might swear they both are Brethren:
> *Dick Fitz-Baker, Dick* the Player,
> Old Acquaintance, are you there?
> Dear Companions hug and kiss,
> Toast *old Glorious* in your Piss.
> Tye them Keeper in a Tether,
> Let them stare and stink together;
> Both are apt to be unruly,
> Lash them daily, lash them duly . . . (*Poems*, 835).

Invective is a touchy subject. Sir Harold Williams, to whose researches all students of Swift are indebted, writes of *The Legion Club* as an 'uncontrolled outburst', (*Poems*, xvi) but it is difficult to see quite what he means. In these lines Swift describes the vicious as being also, in a sense, helpless. 'Stare' perfectly expresses fixated energy. 'Old Acquaintance' seems equally well judged: the two 'Companions',

Richard Tighe and Richard Bettesworth, were well-known opponents
of Swift, participants in lengthy feuds. In the poem he makes them
'old' in the sense that the devil is 'old' Nick; that is, their sinful madness is inveterate. This is the fusion of familiar and formal in a word.
Or consider:

> Bless us, *Morgan*! Art thou there Man?
> Bless mine Eyes! Art thou the Chairman?
> Chairman to yon damn'd Committee!
> Yet I look on thee with Pity. (*Poems*, 837).

Here an 'impossible' rhyme (there Man/Chairman) toys with the
'impossibility' of finding a decent man like Morgan in such a place,
while its thumping obviousness simultaneously confirms his presence.
The magisterial tone quite transcends the real source of Swift's outrage,
a pot-and-kettle dispute between the Irish clergy and the landowner-
dominated Irish Parliament over the question of pasturage-tithes.[25] It
is poetically convincing and technically invulnerable: not an 'uncontrolled outburst' but in places a deft simulation of one. Because it is
so convincing it could even be said to react upon its source. While
admitting the parochial nature of the original feud, one is prepared to
accept that universal principles of human conduct—justice, dignity and
right dealing—are here involved and that Swift's protest is uttered on
behalf of common honesty and freedom.

III

Supposedly 'uncontrolled' outbursts also affect that most sensitive
area of Swiftian research, the so-called 'unprintable' poems. There is
a line of defence on these which laudably aims to explode the pathological fallacy but requires careful qualification. It has been said that
Swift 'is hardly more scatological than others of his contemporaries'[26]
and Professor Ehrenpreis has drawn attention to possible parallels in
Dryden's version of Juvenal's 'Tenth Satire', in a burlesque (dated
1702) of L'Estrange's *Quevedo's Visions* and in *Le Diable Boiteux* of Le
Sage.[27] Parts of Smollett's *Humphry Clinker* and *Adventures of an Atom*
also constitute admissible evidence. But when all has been allowed
Swift still remains more comprehensively and concentratedly scatological than his English contemporaries. One cannot seriously compare
such squibs as the anonymous *On a Fart Let in the House of Commons*[28]
with *Cassinus and Peter*, or *Strephon* and *Chloe* with the mild and modish
pornography of Prior:

> At last, I wish, said She, my Dear—
> (And whisper'd something in his Ear)[29]

'Whisper'd something' is truly symptomatic of the mode and perhaps helps to explain by contrast the nature of Swift's verse, which cuts through that barrier of shame and coquetry where it is only too easy to excite a snigger with gestures of mock reticence. The best of Swift's scatological poems can therefore be called 'harrowing' in the true sense of that word. It is open to argument that the best are those which are most susceptible to accusations, on the part of hostile critics, of violent morbid obsession. The range of these poems is extremely varied and Swift at his worst is quite capable of polite innuendo, superior to Prior in verbal *brio* but hardly superior in ethos.

It may be proper, as a preliminary step, to establish the robustness of Swift's scatological humour:

> My Lord, on Fire amidst the Dames,
> F[art]s like a Laurel in the Flames.
> (*The Problem*, 1699; *Poems*, 66).

Here it subsists in the comedy of 'on Fire' and 'like a Laurel', in the suggestion of genial heat and sparkling Olympian success. It occurs in later work such as *Strephon and Chloe* (1731):

> He found her, while the Scent increas'd,
> As *mortal* as himself at least.
> But, soon with like Occasions prest,
> He boldly sent his Hand in quest,
> (Inspir'd with Courage from his Bride,)
> To reach the Pot on t'other Side.
> And as he fill'd the reeking Vase,
> Let fly a Rouzer in her Face. (*Poems*, 589).

'He boldly sent his Hand in quest' is the language of lyrical pornography applied to an unlyrical situation. The catharsis of the episode has been well described by Maurice Johnson who speaks of 'the surprise of the line in which that word ['Rouzer] appears, startling the reader to laughter or at least to exclamation' (*op. cit.*, p. 112). It would be difficult to find a word that blends the outrageous and the festive more effectively than this. Swift is capable of outrage at the world of spontaneous reflexes but he is equally offended by the false notions of 'divinity' previously entertained by Strephon about women and by Chloe about men; hence the real importance of the perception in '*mortal*'.[30] In a basic sense these anarchic explosions are more real than the sublimities of attenuated fancy but they are still grotesque, Swift suggests, when contrasted with the proper decencies and restraints of life:

> On Sense and Wit your Passion found,
> By Decency cemented round; (*Poems*, 593).

But the very fact that these basic functions do have this element of truth in the situation, and come with a mixture of unexpectedness and inevitability, produces something of the festive energy of farce. However deliberately the retrenching moralist may stand at guard (e.g. the routine phraseology of the concluding lines) the poetic imagination still cherishes the creatures of its invention.

It would be a mistake to enter a plea for Swift's defence merely on the evidence of 'healthy laughter', which is something of an escapist term and fails to cover the dominant characteristics of Swift's major scatological work. It could be said that the embarrassments of Strephon and Chloe are trivial and susceptible to robust treatment but that *The Lady's Dressing Room* (1730) and *A Beautiful Young Nymph Going to Bed* (1731) reveal an appalled, and appalling, obsession with filth and disease; that we are far from the delighted surprise of 'Rouzer' in lines like these:

> The Bason takes whatever comes
> The Scrapings of her Teeth and Gums,
> A nasty Compound of all Hues,
> For here she spits, and here she spues.
> (*The Lady's Dressing Room. Poems*, 527).

Although this may be basically comparable to passages in Dryden and Le Sage, its emotional and verbal concentration is undeniably unique. So far as accusations of simple 'bad taste' are concerned, there is no great difficulty in showing that, in terms of the eighteenth-century conditions of life, it would be virtually impossible to exceed plain reality. Objections on this ground alone are like the tasteful reservations of Swift's aristocratic friends, such as the Earl of Orrery, who saw, but didn't enjoy what they saw. On the other hand it is true that the language of such poems may seem excessive when compared with Swift's equally-unflinching work in *A Modest Proposal*. There he can cover the small circle of a mean intelligence (the 'persona') with the ample radius of the Intellect itself and make his tacit reservations tense with humane implication. In *A Beautiful Young Nymph* it may seem that the superior intelligence can assert itself only by extravagant gestures of revulsion. Notwithstanding these objections, a modern critic who appeals to the supposed imperative of Compassion is gesturing towards little more than a modern version of pastoral. To fret at its absence from Swift is really to miss the point:

> The Nymph, tho' in this mangled Plight,
> Must ev'ry Morn her Limbs unite.
> But how shall I describe her Arts
> To recollect the scatter'd Parts?
> Or shew the Anguish, Toil and Pain,

Of gath'ring up herself again?
The bashful Muse will never bear
In such a Scene to interfere.
Corinna in the Morning dizen'd,
Who sees, will spew; who smells, be poison'd.
                    (*A Beautiful Young Nymph* . . ., *Poems*, 583).

The perfect dryness of 'recollect', the charged portentousness of
'dizen'd', inviting and awaiting the sharp crack of the final rhyme-word,
have complete control over the plangencies of 'Anguish, Toil and Pain'.
If one argues for compassion here it has to be admitted that it exists
principally for the eye of the beholder; and this is not a currently-
acceptable form today, when pity is all for the object. One would also
observe that if Swift's view of Corinna is scarcely charitable neither is
it unfeeling.

   Professor Ehrenpreis has convincingly answered a certain kind of
objection to the emotional intensity of some of Swift's scatological
verse by remarking:

> the complainants' case would be best proved if Swift were *not* intense
> on such subjects.[31]

The accuracy of this as a general ethical observation can be sustained,
even though the immediate defence-plea for Swift is damaged, by citing
A Panegyrick on the Dean, in the Person of a Lady in the North (1730).
This poem does not seem to be among those generally selected for
attack, though it ought to be. Composed as a contribution to the mirth
of the Achesons at Market Hill, it is cast in the form of an address of
commendation to the Dean by Lady Acheson herself. One of its main
themes is the erection of two latrines on the estate and the consequent
partial reformation of manners:

> Yet, some Devotion still remains
> Among our harmless Northern Swains;
> Whose Off'rings plac't in golden Ranks,
> Adorn our chrystal River's Banks:
> Nor seldom grace the flow'ry downs,
> With spiral Tops and Copple-Crowns:
> Or gilding in a sunny Morn
> The humble branches of a Thorn. (*Poems*, 896).

One could, in theory, defend *A Panegyrick* as being an elaborate but
proper complaint about the recalcitrance of human behaviour: the
'swains', having been offered hygiene, still prefer their old casual filth.
The poem, however, eludes this kind of defence. If it is set against
The Lady's Dressing Room or *A Beautiful Young Nymph*, the intensity of

the sensuous attack in those poems appears as a valid human reaction; one is convinced that the virtuosity of description is necessary to contain and express the range of Swift's feelings. *A Panegyrick*, on the other hand, is Swift's only scatological poem that seems in any sense coprophilous. It is, significantly enough, the one which most nearly approaches the conditions of *salon* verse. The poem's tonality suggests that Swift is writing, not out of fascinated disgust or angry contempt, but under the obligation to amuse: it is the very coolness of the verbal draughtsmanship, the detailing of the faecal coils, that is so chilling. The fact that Swift parodies the namby-pamby of fashionable pastoral is, I think, beside the point so far as the larger issues are concerned. *A Description of a City Shower* also parodies pastoral but this fact neither explains nor limits that poem's total effect. In *A Panegyrick* any plea of parody is really an alibi for the indulgence of a taste that is itself more dubious than 'straight' pastoral. It is a pity that terms like 'perfectly calculated'[32] have become, out of context, mere laudatory commonplaces in criticisms of Swift. As a generalisation this could apply to a great deal that he wrote; but between the perfect calculation of *A Description of a City Shower*, *Verses on the Death of Dr. Swift* or *The Legion Club* and the perfect calculation of *A Panegyrick* there stretches a wide terrain of ethical and aesthetic distinction.

It is possible that 'perfectly calculated' could, in some instances, be better expressed as 'predetermined' or even 'academic'. The academic Swift is a significant figure, notable in *A Proposal for Correcting, Improving and Ascertaining the English Tongue*, an attempt to predetermine the future shape of the language in accordance with his over-riding political convictions and apprehensions. Swift's linguistic attitude is a kind of Tory stoicism, a rather simpler form of resistance than that of the poems. Its limitations are perhaps best described by Dr. Johnson, in the Preface to his *Dictionary*. Johnson remarks on the futility of trying to secure language from corruption and decay and of imagining that one has the 'power to change sublunary nature, and clear the world at once from folly, vanity and affectation'.[33] One recalls Yeats's saying that Swift 'foresaw' Democracy as 'the ruin to come'.[34] If this is so, it only intensifies the creative paradox of his poetry whose energy seems at times to emerge from the destructive element itself. In his own copy of Dr. Gibbs's paraphrase of the Psalms Swift scribbled unflattering comments alongside examples of slovenly rhyming. Of 'more–pow'r' he commented 'Pronounce this like my Lady's woman'.[35] Yet in Swift's own poetry this lexical and grammatical arrogance is transfigured, as in such a work as *The Humble Petition of Frances Harris* (1701). Mrs. Harris was one of Lady Berkeley's gentlewomen:

> Yes, says the *Steward*, I remember when I was at my Lady
>   *Shrewbury*'s,
> Such a thing as this happen'd, just about the time of *Goosberries*.
>   ....
> The *Devil* take me, said she (blessing her self), if I ever saw't!
> So she roar'd like a *Bedlam*, as tho' I had call'd her all to naught;
>   (*Poems*, 71).

Some years later, in 1718, Swift wrote a further poem, *Mary the Cook-
Maid's Letter to Dr. Sheridan*, along similar lines of character and idiom.
A number of his polemical pieces adopt, or affect, the form and phrasing
of the popular street-ballads of the day: *Peace and Dunkirk: Being an
Excellent New Song upon the Surrender of Dunkirk* (1712); *An Elegy upon
the Much-Lamented Death of Mr. Demar, the Famous Rich Man* (1720);
*An Excellent New Song Upon His Grace Our Good Lord Archbishop of
Dublin* (1724); *Clever Tom Clinch Going to be Hang'd* (1726); *The Yahoo's
Overthrow; or the Kevan Bayl's New Ballad . . . to the tune of 'Derry down'*
(1734). The Bagford, Pepys and Roxburghe Collections contain
possible precedents and analogues, such as the anonymous *South Sea
Ballad* of 1720,[36] which could be compared and contrasted with Swift's
poem, *The Bubble*, of the same year. If we refer to the confrontation of
two distinct kinds of poetic tradition and method, a popular and an
aristocratic, and if we relate Swift's Pindaric 'aberration'[37] to the kind
of portentous sublimity advocated by Sir William Temple in his *Essay
on Heroick Virtue* (1690) there will be a temptation to claim that a timely
encounter with popular colloquial verse 'redeemed' Swift as a poet.
But there is no simple and obvious way in which this could be affirmed.
Some of Swift's poems may have achieved immediate popular success,
but one still has reservations about calling him a 'popular' poet; he
did not so much use as demonstrate the colloquial; the very kind of
accuracy he achieved was the result of a certain aloofness. He was able
to fix his perspectives:

> And so say I told you so, and you may go tell my Master; what
>   care I?
> And I don't care who knows it, 'tis all one to *Mary*.
> Everybody knows, that I love to tell Truth and shame the Devil,
> I am but a poor Servant, but I think Gentle folks should be civil . . .
>   (*Mary the Cook-Maid's Letter*, 1718; *Poems*, 986).

If one is conscious, throughout, of the dualistic nature of Swift's
genius and achievement, it is not inappropriate that so much of his
energy should have been expended upon, and re-charged from, the
dualistic nature of Irish life and politics, or that one should be able to
find both the cold disdain and the fervent identification of the poems

co-existing in the style of *The Drapier's Letters*, whose effect on the Irish people is well described by Lecky:

> He braced their energies; he breathed into them something of his own lofty and defiant spirit; he made them sensible at once of the wrongs they endured, of the rights they might claim, and of the forces they possessed.[38]

Given the current English political attitude, to be in Ireland, the 'depending kingdom', as a member of the so-called governing class was to be in a 'situation' of considerable difficulty. Swift polemically rejected the situation as a principle in the fourth *Drapier's Letter* but encountered it daily as a fact. His sensitive reaction to this situation, both personal and national, resulted in a release of creative energy which could not have been produced by the application of principle alone. Swift had little sympathy with Shaftesbury; but the crowning paradox is that his own poetry is one of the most powerful expressions in eighteenth-century English Literature, prior to Blake, of that kind of resistance which the Whig philosopher so eloquently described:

> And thus the natural free Spirits of ingenious Men, if imprisoned and controul'd, will find out other ways of Motion to relieve themselves in their *Constraint*. . . 'Tis the persecuting Spirit has rais'd the *bantering* one. . . The greater the Weight is, the bitterer will be the Satir[e]. The higher the Slavery, the more exquisite the Buffoonery.[39]

NOTES

[1] See Irvin Ehrenpreis, *The Personality of Jonathan Swift* (London, 1958), pp. 117–126.

[2] H. Williams, *Dean Swift's Library* (Cambridge, 1932), p. 54 and appendix p. 15.

[3] I. Ehrenpreis, *Swift* (London, 1962), I, 98.

[4] W. B. Yeats, *Explorations* (London, 1962), p. 358.

[5] R. Quintana, *Swift: An Introduction* (London, 1955, ed.), p. 11.

[6] Yeats, *op. cit.*, p. 354.

[7] Johnson, *Lives of the English Poets* (World's Classics edition), II, 211–2.

[8] *Swift*, I, 71, 77.

[9] *History of England in the 18th Century* (1883 ed.), II, 221.

[10] In making this assertion one is obliged to acknowledge, though not to over-estimate, Swift's reference to Sheridan's 'bad Verses' (*Corr.*, II, 307). He had recently been annoyed by the tone of Sheridan's 'The Funeral'.

[11] F. Elrington Ball, *Swift's Verse* (London, 1929), p. 244.

[12] Though this may be mythical. For a discussion of Swift in relation to Butler see C. L. Kulisheck, 'Swift's Octosyllabics and the Hudibrastic Tradition', *J.E.G.P.* Vol. 53 (1954), pp. 361–68.

[13] *Dean Swift's Library*, p. 76: 'Paradise Lost' noted 1715; missing 1745.

[14] *Poems by John Wilmot, Earl of Rochester*, ed. V. de Sola Pinto (London, 1953), p. xxix.

Ibid., p. 90.

16 Craik, *Life of Jonathan Swift* (1894 ed.), 175; cf. *Poems*, 88–90.

17 See e.g., A. O. Aldridge, 'Shaftesbury and the Test of Truth', *PMLA* LX (1945), pp. 129–56; P. Dixon, 'Talking Upon Paper', *English Studies*, XLVI, No. 1 (February, 1965), pp. 36–44.

18 Dixon, *op. cit.*, p. 38: his sources are Steele and Swift: cf IV, 91.

19 See *Corr.*, V, 269, Appendix XXIX for a fine 'free fall' demonstration of Raillery of the second type: Swift to Lord Charlemont.

20 *Ibid.*, p. 270, Appendix XXX, 'Swift's Friends Classed by their Characters'.

21 For a fuller discussion of this theme see R. Paulson, 'Swift, Stella, and Permanence', *E.L.H.* Vol. 27 (1960), pp. 298–314.

22 E.g., H. Davis, *Jonathan Swift* (1964), pp. 171–2: Davis's argument, originally published in 1931, that Temple's influence distorted Swift's 'natural bent' and that the Pindarics are a temporary diversion rather than a false start, is a suggestive one. It is necessarily qualified by later debate and research into the authorship of doubtful poems in the Christie Book and *The Whimsical Medley*.

23 As a 'practical politician' Swift took a shrewd view of the usefulness of anarchy: e.g. *Corr.*, II, 113: 'I have been long afraid that we were losing the Rabble' (to Charles Ford, August 7th, 1714); *Corr.*, II, 131: 'If any thing witholds the Whigs from the utmost Violence, it will be onely the fear of provoking the Rabble . . .' (to Charles Ford, 27 September, 1714).

24 *Poems*, 296; 82. C. Peake, 'Swift's *Satirical Elegy on a Late Famous General*', *R.E.L.*, Vol. 3 (1962), pp. 80–89, indicates Swift's method.

25 L. A. Landa, *Swift and the Church of Ireland* (Oxford, 1954), p. 135 ff.

26 M. Johnson, *The Sin of Wit* (New York, 1950), p. 117.

27 *The Personality of Jonathan Swift*, pp. 43–48.

28 Formerly attributed to Prior, but rejected by Wright and Spears, *The Literary Works of Matthew Prior* (Oxford, 1959), II, 791. Apparently of mid-seventeenth century origin.

29 Prior, *ed. cit.*, I, 264: 'Paulo Purganti and His Wife. . . .'

30 Cf. K. Williams, *Jonathan Swift and the Age of Compromise* (1965), pp. 148–53.

31 *The Personality of Jonathan Swift*, p. 43.

32 The phrase happens to be taken from Professor Quintana's humane and stimulating *Swift: An Introduction*. I quote it quite out of context because this is what frequently happens. It should be read here simply as a 'representative phrase': I am in no sense trying to short-circuit Professor Quintana's discussion.

33 M. Wilson (ed.), *Johnson: Prose and Poetry* (1957), p. 319.

34 *Op. cit.*, p. 350.

35 M. Johnson, *op. cit.*, pp. 26–7.

36 *Roxburghe Ballads*: VIII, part i (1897), 256.

37 Ball, *op. cit.*, p. 16.

38 Lecky, *ed. cit.*, II, 427.

39 *Sensus Communis: an Essay on the Freedom of Wit and Humour* (1709) I, iv; also cited in W. K. Wimsatt (ed.), *English Stage Comedy* (1955), p. 5.

Swift and the Comedy of Evil

IRVIN EHRENPREIS

Comedy and evil used to seem hard to mix. Only a few authors have in the past represented a successful villain, at the height of his evil career, as the main figure in a purely comic episode. Often enough, evil in defeat has suffered ridiculous humiliations. Equally often, an audience could watch petty vice and harmless obsessions become the occasion for elaborate farce. But unmitigated badness remained in general a figure for tragedy, melodrama, invective. If one thinks of Shakespeare's Iago, Racine's Nero, or George Eliot's Grandcourt, one can hardly imagine them in a comic setting without softening their monsterhood or enlarging their humanity.

Among the exceptions to this rule are parts of works by a few celebrated satirists. In these rare, brilliant scenes a successful villain appears at the centre of a detached piece of comedy with no loss of his frightening power to embody evil. For one example, I recall Juvenal's picture of the self-deified Domitian, holding a high council in order to determine the best means of cooking a fish. The action grows monumentally absurd as the supreme advisors of the despot of the world quickly enter, cringing, to meet as a cabinet and offer their judgment whether or not the chef should cut the turbot up because the available vessels are too small to hold it entire. As one would expect, the furious poet stays outside the scene, making the emperor and his cronies into figures quite separate from himself; and he speaks almost like a reporter or moral commentator who, with all his anger, never feels responsible for the frightfulness he may have to describe. At the same time, Domitian is no way reduced by Juvenal's episode. The *pallor amicitiae*, the servility, haste, and loquacity of his corrupt ministers, while they devote their full intelligence to the contemptible question, only darken the abominations of their master.

Of course, Satan himself took the first of all comic rôles. Excluded from the range of our sympathy, he may have terrified us by his power; yet we laughed at the tricks he played on his stupid, irrational victims. I suggest that their foolishness has been essential to his comic operations. Since the absurd is a necessary element in humour, those ages which called irrationality evil could not regard rationality as an object of ridicule; and the satirists of imperial Rome agreed with those of King Charles and King George when they treated reason as coterminous with virtue. To show how the same lesson could be applied in another country, let me refer to the peripety of *Tartuffe*. Act IV, Scene V, of Molière's masterpiece is the famous courtship of Elmire by Tartuffe, with Orgon listening under a table. The comedy of the episode invariably succeeds. Even clumsy actors can hardly prevent an audience from feeling delight when Elmire signals to her stupefied husband and he fails to halt the process of seduction. Yet the satanic Tartuffe suffers no diminution. 'J'ai de quoi confondre et punir l'imposture,' he announces, after retreating from Orgon's arms; and he walks off with his sinister dignity intact. Like Domitian and Satan, he will not laugh at himself, because for him the drama is tragic. This self-absorbed lack of moral intelligence seems at last determined by the *ir*rationality of a complete villain, for the great satirists gave reason dominion over moral as well as narrowly intellectual issues. Both Tartuffe and Domitian must fail to recognize the absurdity of their entanglements if they are not to see the malignity of their actions. At the same time, a character like Orgon must be more than an innocent victim or butt. Our laughter remains only partly sympathetic: we feel some degree of contempt for his cooperation in his own ruin, and we hesitate to identify ourselves with him.

In Brecht's play, *The Resistible Rise of Arturo Ui*, there is another instance of the same sort. Ui, a gangster whose life becomes an allegory of Hitler's progress, reaches the peak of his criminal achievements and then decides to have lessons in the arts of oratory and public deportment. The scene that follows is like a vaudeville turn, with the straight man taken by Ui and the end man by a broken-down actor who teaches him elocution. Every piece of instruction is farcical, and Ui accepts each one as sagacious. When the tutor declares that the properest way for Ui to manage his hands, during a speech, is to hold them over his private parts, the audience giggles, but the gangster obeys. Yet the scene does not make Ui less ominous. On the contrary, the more unreasonable he grows, the more terrifying he seems. Brecht also follows the example of Molière and Juvenal in excluding himself from any responsibility for the triumph of vice. Like most playwrights he seems no more than the historian of the events he shows us. Similarly, the gangsters and grocers who become Ui's victims seem willing tools or foolish weaklings. Like Domitian's counsellors, they discourage sympathy.

The effect I have been describing seems to me among the deepest ends of satire. In a reader's memory the crimes of a Domitian or a Tartuffe are too vivid for them to be put aside. These men can only seem objects of detestation. At the same time, the comedy of the scenes I have reviewed is detached, almost a free fantasy, never involving the villain's enormities. How, then, can a reader avoid a continuous, guilt-ridden sense of ignoring horrors which ought to obliterate any humourous aspect of a literary work? So long as the humour is compelling, I think he cannot.

If these principles appear elementary, let me complicate them now with some examples from the prose of Jonathan Swift. In 1712 appeared his *Letter of Thanks from My Lord Wharton to the Lord Bishop of St. Asaph.* A year and a half earlier, Swift's art had conferred immortality on Thomas, Earl of Wharton when the satirist wrote, 'He is a Presbyterian in Politics, and an Atheist in Religion; but he chuseth at present to whore with a Papist' (III, 179). Elsewhere, Swift describes his lordship in language drawn from Milton's representation of Satan (III, 8); and he worked hard to have the Earl impeached for treason. Constantly in Swift's political essays, Wharton manifests himself as the supreme Whig and supreme villain, a compound of the filthiest vices, devoid of patriotism, charity, or religion. Since Wharton's father had been a Parliamentary Presbyterian, Swift, as a devoted churchman and constitutional monarchist, could trace the son's political corruption to his ancestry: 'He hath imbibed his father's principles in government, but dropt his religion, and took up no other in its stead: Excepting that circumstance, he is a firm Presbyterian' (VII, 10). When Swift blamed the Earl for defecating on the high altar of Gloucester Cathedral, there were protests; so the journalist apologized in print: 'it was neither in the Cathedral, nor City, nor County of *Gloucester*, but some other Church of that Diocess' (III, 57, 69).

Now I take up my chosen passage from Swift's *Letter of Thanks to the Bishop of St. Asaph.* The whole pamphlet is a satire on a Whig bishop for his wretched prose and worse venality as exhibited in the half-dozen paragraphs of a composition praising the old, ousted Whig administration. In the pamphlet the author pretends to be the Earl of Wharton writing to Bishop Fleetwood and congratulating his grace on these remarks. According to this mock-Wharton, the Bishop had never believed that the English people should live under a true monarchy or obey their rightful king unless his majesty gave in to every caprice of the mob. Addressing Fleetwood himself, the mock-Wharton continues: 'This [i.e., republicanism] you say is the opinion of CHRIST, St. *Peter*, and St. *Paul*: And, faith I am glad to hear it; for I never thought the Prigs had been Whigs before' (VI, 152). In a tribute to Fleetwood's style the mock-Wharton fixes on some episcopal regrets for the fall of the Whigs, regrets which the satirist inevitably links to a sympathy with the Presbyterians in their Nonconformist meeting houses. I quote:

Oh Exquisite! How pathetically does your Lordship complain of the Downfal of Whiggism, and *Daniel Burges's* meeting-house! The generous Compassion your Lordship has shewn upon this tragical Occasion, makes me believe your Lordship will not be unaffected with an Accident that had like to have befallen a poor Whore of my Acquaintance about that Time, who being big with Whig, was so alarmed at the Rising of the Mob, that she had like to have miscarried upon it; for the Logical Jade presently concluded (and the Inference was natural enough) that if they began with pulling down Meeting-houses, it might end in demolishing those Houses of Pleasure, where she constantly paid her Devotion. (VI, 154).

Without determining the ultimate literary value of Swift's performance in this pamphlet, I will say the humour is not easily withstood. Whether or not we know who Wharton was and what Swift thought of him, the burlesque of a rake praising an ambitious clergyman has its comic power. Adding to that general effect the identification of Wharton as a diabolical villain, can anyone who laughs escape the guilt of seeming indifferent to crimes that ought to excite indignation?

If my question sounds like an effort merely to place Swift in a class with Juvenal, Molière, and Brecht, let me now try to distinguish him. Those authors, like most creators of satire or comedy, avoided bringing themselves directly into their work; so far from accepting a part of the responsibility for the triumph of evil, they covertly absolved themselves of blame. No historian or paid journalist could be further from involvement (except as a judge) in the events he retails.

But it is a well-known mark of the workings of Swift's imagination that he loves to speak in a parody of people he detests; and so he assigns himself in fantasy the very rôle of the character he means to attack. It is also typical of Swift that when he does attack a man's character, he blackens it to a depth where the villainy seems to have no mitigation. Whether he ever even attempts the subtle, controlled characterization of an evildoer that Dryden produces in the character of Achitophel, seems doubtful. If we may trust Swift, each one of his enemies aspires to the condition of Satan. In denigrating Wharton, therefore, just as in assuming his identity, Swift merely follows what to him are normal procedures.

If we now digress and search for the emotional or psychological origin of such procedures, we may speculate along familiar lines: are we to deny that in producing his flavorsome fantasies of atheistic whoremongering, the rigidly moral and devout Dr. Swift enjoyed some *frissons* of ambiguous self-indulgence? I suspect that the comical parody of Lord Wharton gave Swift a delicious chance to leap in fantasy over the steep walls of his own ethical judgment. The contemplation of pure evil in a human shape released Swift's imagination till he could slip inside the diabolical nature and taste its sensations. Yet it was as the private, weak victim of such public monsters that he deliberately issued his ferocious political satires. In childhood he had been the half-orphaned son of an impoverished widow, and had suffered continually the bitter sensation of powerlessness to resist the will of those who took charge of him. As the adult moralist and patriot he made his pen an instrument for punishing traitors like Wharton, too great to be attacked openly.

Whatever may have been the hidden spring of Swift's impulse, its visible effect becomes a brilliant feature of his rhetoric. Instead of standing aloof, like most satirists, he plunges into the prospect of evil, establishing himself in the immediate foreground of the scene. For the reader, the consequence seems an exact, required direction for the flow of guilt which the comedy of evil produces. There is no comfortable outlet to relieve the reader's uneasiness, because every element of the absorbing comical situation forces him to share in the devil's work. In Swift's hoaxes and satires the victims are under attack as well as the criminals—the Ireland that helps England make men into beasts, the superstitious customers of quack astrologers, the tasteless readers of hack authors. Juvenal, Molière and Brecht excite our indignation and may even drive us toward action; but we are free, in their work, to join the high, mountain view of the cities of the plain. With them as with Swift we cannot hide in the abominable villains or contemptible victims. Yet we do retire by an instinct of revulsion to the consciousness of the poet, sheltering ourselves in his detachment or his outrage.

But when we recoil from Swift's comedy, we face a disquieting mirror. The author himself looks like the villain, and we find our reflection in both. If the scene he presents makes us uneasy, any meditation sharpens our guilt. Swift was always ready to imitate directly the irrationality on which rests his conception of evil. As early as *A Tale of a Tub* he admits his own complicity, writing, 'even, I my self, the Author of these momentous Truths, am a Person, whose imaginations are hard-mouth'd, and exceedingly disposed to run away with his *Reason*, which I have observed from long Experience, to be a very light Rider, and easily shook off' (I, 114). On the contrary, Pope, in his magnificent denunciations of social corruption, regularly excepts himself:

> Yes, I am proud; I must be proud to see
> Men not afraid of God, afraid of me.
> *(Epilogue to the Satires*, ll. 208–9).

I suppose Pope's many disabilities kept him from risking the sacrifice of dignity which could result from admitting that he had a hand in the sins he condemns. But by excluding his own case, he can only invite us to exclude ours. Swift, by risking more, wins more.

The greatness of Swift's whole achievement as a satirist can be expressed in terms of this comedy of impersonated evil, which forces us not simply to grow indignant but also to admit we helped perpetrate the crime we deplore. Thanks to the dramatic qualities of Swift's ironical style, such an analysis is far from limited to those works in which he adopts the name or reputation of a known villain. To suggest what may be happening, his tone by itself is enough. For Swift, it was natural to employ the cynical voice of a debauchee when describing the vileness that every honest priest wishes to eradicate. Although the reader feels disgust, he will hardly look to the author for comfort, because Swift sounds comically acquiescent in the scandal. Cannot the much-quoted, oddly detachable sentence in the *Digression on Madness*— 'Last Week I saw a woman *flay'd*, and you will hardly believe, how much it altered her Person for the worse' (I, 109)—be understood this way? Must not this amusing speaker be both irrational and evil to ignore the agony he has witnessed? If this is so, does not the wit of the sentence delight the reader to the point of making him feel guilty for appearing indifferent to the fate of the wretched woman?

It is hardly worthwhile to glance at works like the *Digression on Madness* or *A Modest Proposal*, because this pattern so obviously fits them. But I shall notice the most disquieting mixture of humour and guilt in Swift's works. How successful the last part of *Gulliver's Travels* really is, we may doubt. But that the author means to identify the Yahoos with evil, irrationality, *and* essential human nature as well, seems plain enough. What has offended most of those whom Swift nauseates in his masterpiece is this identity; and the method employed by several of his defenders has been to dwell on the comic implications of the Fourth Voyage. When Gulliver bathes in a river, and narrowly escapes being ravished by a female Yahoo—who relaxes her passionate embrace only because the sorrel nag drives her away—it may seem pedantic to look for anything but farce in the episode. Yet Gulliver insists that the lust of the young animal proves his own membership in the same species. Since Swift has been at pains to express Gulliver's revulsion from the Yahoos, the laughing reader is, in a sense, trapped between sympathetic humour and punitive ridicule; for to accept the black-haired Yahoo is to accept the most sickening bestiality; but to reject her is to reject oneself. Perhaps in no other work has Swift made the foundation of his moral distinctions so visible. Villain, victim, author, and reader are all united in the great, hideous teetering between laughter and outrage. Gulliver reiterates and bellows his conviction that the reader is a Yahoo like himself, that we all share in creating the satanic evil we abominate. In his reformer's zeal and comic humiliation he exemplifies that partnership of preacher and clown which is Swift's special mark. Surely Swift's pessimism concerning human nature deepened the amused consciousness of his own weakness; for the irrationality of the devil who desires to ruin man is at least equalled by the irrationality of the priest who hopes to save him.

The Social Circumstances of Several Remote Nations of the World

ANGUS ROSS

I

Not every commentator on *Gulliver's Travels* is as modest as Professor Ricardo Quintana, who in a celebrated essay offers the reader '*a* key that will unlock the first door' into Swift's satires.[1] The implication follows, that other keys are needed for other doors. Some of these barriers have been placed there by time; some of them by Swift himself. Several skeleton keys are on the market, however, warranted to open all the doors that Swift locked behind him. In addition, the possibility is sometimes persuasively canvassed, that the Dean's 'meaning' is accessible through one grand entrance. The ensuing activity, trying different keys, unlocking (and locking) doors, opening them bravely or triumphantly, is a topic worthy of the satirist himself. None of his works has been more severely handled in this way than *Gulliver's Travels*. All reductive criticism of Swift must 'explain' Book IV of this satire. It is true, that the best modern critics of Swift's art, some writing very recently, have used the vast extent of Swift scholarship to correct quite wrong readings of his works which had become commonplaces. Insights of great value have been opened up. The variety of these insights, and the differences between the points of view, to say nothing of the incompatibility of many of them however ably developed, only confirm the reader's wary skepticism. This is no frame of mind for reading the most dangerous, wily and profound eighteenth-century critic of human behaviour. The only reasonable conclusion is that there is no single 'meaning' to be found in Swift's works; that a book such as *Gulliver's Travels* is not to be 'explained' by any single notion, biographical, psychological, philosophical, or by any single critical method or rhetorical analysis.

A possible, limited but useful tactic in these circumstances is to consider something that permeates the work and so offers the prospect of establishing some pattern or framework, and of relating plausible 'meanings' together. Swift's use of the *persona* or mask has been brilliantly examined by W. B. Ewald and others. The awareness that Gulliver is not the satirist (nor yet a complete patsy either), that argument, rather than narration, description or story is the centre of the book, all add great and disturbing power as well as rich surprise to the satire. As for the content of the satire, however, and the strands which connect it, another possible perspective could be opened up through examining the social circumstances of the several groups which come before Gulliver's observation in the course of his voyage. The book, of course, had direct political relevance for contemporary readers, and as long ago as 1919, the historian Sir Charles Firth began elucidating a specific structure of this sort.[2] His aim, though, was to realise the hidden references in local areas of the text which would be appropriate to a political satire. These include the Flimnap-Walpole connections in Book I, or in Book III, the pseudo-Jacobite anagram, which is more than merely political:

> in a Letter to a Friend, *Our Brother* Tom *hath just got the Piles* . . . analysed into the following Words; R*esist,—a Plot is brought home—The Tour.* (XI, 191–2).

This provides an entertaining example of Swift's linguistic fooling, which touches on a more searching exploration of the treacherous nature of communication itself. Firth certainly succeeds in illuminating something of the work's contemporary political significance, as well as Swift's own political views. Even Swift obviously means his satire to be wider than a 'Tory' attack on 'Whig' measures and broadens the political considerations to include an attack on party strife in general as a social danger.[3] A modern reader is more likely, however, to regard this as simply one of the levels of meaning in the work, which must be related to a more general approach. If instead of solely *party political* considerations, we take the notion to include more broadly social circumstances, a different picture appears. In social circumstances we must include politics. Swift obviously believed, in common with his age, that great events are often, perhaps nearly always, brought about by individual actions and reactions. In Glubbdubdrib, Gulliver learns 'the true Causes of many great Events that have surprized the World: How a Whore can govern the Back-stairs, the Back-stairs a Council, and the Council a Senate.' (XI, 199).

We may also associate with political action, though, social and civic institutions, economics, class-structure and so on. This is to understand *politics* as Hume does, dealing 'with Men, as united in Society and dependent on each other.' Swift himself obviously related these things together. The Irish reference of Book III, for instance, fuses the wrong intellectual attitudes of the virtuoso, the inhuman political and economic thinking of the English ministers, the ill-judged programmes of the 'projectors' and the ill-digested opinions of the 'moderns' as comparable functions of human pride and mis-directed ingenuity. It is obvious also, that some of Swift's writings are direct comments on the Party politics of his day set within wider economic and social perspectives. *The Drapier's Letters* is perhaps the best instance of this. Even here, though, Swift's social and economic theory appears somewhat opportunistic: it has been systematised within a framework of religious thought or political philosophy, but little consistent attention has been given to informing ideas of economic or social structure.[4]

The title of *Gulliver's Travels* is itself rather strange. The travels are 'into several Remote Nations . . .', not drawing attention, that is, to strange places as might have been expected in a satirical title for a collection of spoof voyages, but at the risk of being untypical emphasising that Gulliver is to be surrounded with strange groups of people. In fact, setting up the classic Swiftian satirical situation. In the very first sentences of Gulliver's own account, the narrator himself is placed precisely in a plausible set of English social circumstances:

> My Father had a small Estate in *Nottinghamshire*; I was the Third of five Sons. He sent me to *Emanuel-College* in *Cambridge*, at Fourteen Years old, where I resided three Years, and applied myself close to my Studies: But the Charge of maintaining me (although I had a very scanty Allowance) being too great for a narrow Fortune; I was bound Apprentice to Mr. *James Bates*, an eminent Surgeon in *London*. (XI, 19).

Thereafter, with his social position established, he is made to describe and comment on various social groups and respond to their behaviour. Just as Gulliver is provided with a father in the person of a Nottinghamshire land-owner of small means, in the English fashion not forced by social or caste laws to ruin himself for a third son, so a considerable range of social arrangements, economic patterns and 'Manners and Dispositions' is provided for the English and Dutch seamen, the pirates, Lilliputians, Blefuscudians, Brobdingnagians, Luggnaggians, Laputans, Balnibarbians, Glubbdubdribians, savage islanders, Yahoos and Houyhnhnms. On one level, this is part of the primitive imaginative attraction of the book, the witty ingenuity and engaging air with which the fantastic is made possible and plausible. The social details, the kings, courts, ministers, servants, militiamen, agriculture, academies, cities, houses, laws, customs, contribute to the concrete side of the fable, to that part of the *Travels* which appeals to children and which has perhaps been undervalued in the close attention paid to more speculative matters. Of course, Gulliver's attempts to preen himself on an 'unvarnished' account are ironically deflated and attacked from time to time. No description in Swift is free from moral or argumentative complexity. Gulliver may 'intend to leave the Description of this Empire to a particular Treatise', 'a greater Work, which is now almost ready for the Press', with accounts of 'Matters very curious and useful': the reader is not allowed to forget that such travellers' tales, told without judgement or close thinking are worthless and negligible. The information pure and simple is nothing, but the judgement, the uncertainty of tone on which much of the satire depends, the painful probing into weakness and folly is partly based on the provision of carefully selected social details about those strange, remote nations.

II

The social structures of the nations visited by Gulliver are, as might be expected, markedly and rigidly hierarchical; this is to be expected, because it presumably reflects Swift's own traditional view of society. The 'Impertinence and probably Malice of the Rabble' is as much in Gulliver's consciousness in Lilliput as it no doubt was in Swift's mind in London or Dublin. The 'rude vulgar Folks' are never present except to be scorned, though the 'Women, Tradesmen, *Flappers*, and Court-Pages' were Gulliver's sole companions at the court in Laputa, and 'the only People from whom I received a reasonable Answer'. He is usually placed, however, in the situation of talking to and arguing with courtiers, kings, ministers, projectors or domestic sages. First as a monster, then as a pet, a kind of humanoid *splacknuck*, later as a voyager and traveller, he is able to make his way out and in, up and down, amongst different ranks and castes, 'The *Luggnuggians*,' for example,

> are a polite and generous People, and although they are not without some share of that Pride which is peculiar to all *Eastern* Countries, yet they shew themselves courteous to Strangers, especially such who who are countenanced by the Court. (XI, 207).

Gulliver had of course been introduced to the king in the approved manner and had

> many Acquaintance among Persons of the best Fashion, and being always attended by my Interpreter, the Conversation was not disagreeable. (*Ibid.*)

Finally in Book IV, he finds himself in a strange society, whereas a curiosity from the animal world again, a Yahoo prodigy, he discovers that he cannot use his accustomed, unthinking assumptions about social rank. This is one of the facts of the case that throws him off balance. Swift is no reformer, or leveller, but the final impression of the book, even allowing for his usual opportunism in seizing promising parallels with English affairs for political or personal satire, is surely that if social rank is necessary as one of the divine controls on human nature, it does not of itself confer value on the people it may dignify. Social rank too, under the manipulation of that very same proud and ingenious human nature, lets in certain possibilities of many evils, excesses and corruptions that face men with difficult choices in every-day life. The position is further complicated, or enriched, by the ambiguities of Gulliver's narrative. He is the only source of all the information about these social arrangements in the different nations, and both as a man and as a teller of travellers' tales is not always a reliable commentator on what he thinks he has observed.

Paradoxically, the simplest and most rudimentary social structures are found in Book IV, which is the most complex part of the whole satire. There are two reasons for this. Book IV is the most profound exploration of human nature, of the self, though not the most compli-cated, which Swift ever attempted. It is an examination, in part, of the conflict—to put it no more strongly—between reason on the one hand, the controller of behaviour, and on the other, the unregenerate animal part of man. This not a case of a fight between right and wrong, between superior and inferior powers. The 'lower' faculty is the source of life, of copiousness, of poetry. For instance, Gulliver, who is a poor literary critic, is allowed to claim that the poetry of the Houyhnhnms excels that of all other mortals in the rather thin qualities of

> the Justness of their Similes, and the Minuteness, as well as Exactness of their Descriptions . . . [and] some exalted Notions of Friendship and Benevolence, or the Praises of those who were Victors in Races, and other bodily Exercises. (XI, 273–4).

The 'superior' force is dry and lacking in sparkle, though to be prized, and essential for the good life. Placed in this book too is the very difficult attempt to relate social structures and beliefs, even economic doctrines, to the true nature of private existence. This is the point of chapters five and six, where Gulliver gives yet another of his defensive accounts of English society to a benevolently interested but puzzled interlocutor. Secondly, the dichotomy between reason and the uncon-scious (or sub-conscious) drives is set up in a fabular and simplified opposition between the Houyhnhnms and the Yahoos, in such a way that each is given a suitable social arrangement. The simplest structure in the book is one appropriate to

> these noble *Houyhnhnms* [who] are endowed by Nature with a general Disposition to all Virtues, and have no Conceptions or Ideas of what is evil in a rational Creature. (XI, 267).

To the Yahoos, 'those Animals, like other Brutes', as they are described by Gulliver's 'Master', is assigned a contrasting, primitive, rudimentary social structure.

The Houyhnhnms form the only republic in the book, not excepting the pirates. They are a kind of squirearchy without a king. Gulliver quickly comes in contact with a 'Master Horse', who orders around a 'Sorrel Nag, one of his Servants'. A visitor who comes and looks at Gulliver, is 'an old Steed, who seemed to be of Quality', and stays on for a kind of well-run, country-house dinner party. There are several 'Horses and Mares of Quality in the Neighbourhood' and Gulliver's master brings him 'into all Company', rather as in a kind of ideal rural society in a Jane Austen novel. The Houyhnhnms' own organisation, however, unlike that of *Mansfield Park*, is based on simple and incontrovertible principles. These are not without ironical implications. Gulliver is made to observe

> that among the *Houyhnhnms*, the *White*, the *Sorrel*, and the *Iron-grey*, were not so exactly shaped as the *Bay*, the *Dapple-grey*, and the *Black*; nor born with equal Talents of Mind, or a Capacity to improve them; and therefore continued always in the Condition of Servants without ever aspiring to match out of their own Race, which in that Country would be considered monstrous and unnatural. (XI, 256).

This is finely juxtaposed with an observation by the horse that on account of his shape and complexion, as well as attainments, Gulliver must be 'born of some Noble Family' in England. Since among the Houyhnhnms 'Controversies, Wranglings, Disputes, and Positiveness in false or dubious Propositions, are Evils unknown', their institutions can be simple and unequivocal too:

> EVERY fourth Year, at the *Vernal Equinox*, there is a Representative Council of the whole Nation, which meets in a Plain about twenty Miles from our House, and continueth about five or six Days. Here they inquire into the State and Condition of their several Districts; whether they abound or be deficient in Hay or Oats, or Cows or *Yahoos*? And where-ever there is any Want (which is but seldom) it is immediately supplied by unanimous Consent and Contribution. Here likewise the Regulation of Children is settled: As for instance, if a *Houyhnhnm* hath two Males, he changeth one of them with another who hath two Females: And when a Child hath been lost by any Casualty, where the Mother is past Breeding, it is determined what Family in the District shall breed another to supply the Loss. (XI, 270).

There is only ever one real discussion of moment in this Assembly, the 'old Debate', 'whether the *Yahoos* should be exterminated from the face of the Earth'. This is not an ideal society. The sentence about the Regulation of Children is embodied in a gross simplication of human affairs, and an ironical simplication. It would be interesting to know, though, whether 'Children' and 'Child' are slips by Gulliver or Swift.

The Yahoos' society, contrasting with the horses' republic, is a primitive kind of monarchy. Gulliver's master

> had heard indeed some curious *Houyhnhnms* observe, that in most Herds there was a Sort of ruling *Yahoo* (as among us there is generally some leading or principal Stag in a Park) who was always more *deformed* in Body, [not like the ruling Houyhnhnms] and *mischievous in Disposition*, than any of the rest. (XI, 262).

The ruler has a favourite who performs menial and degrading offices for him. The institution, however, is not regulated or regularised by the hereditary principle, that prized feature of a landowning society, and a bone of particular contention in the battles between the Hanoverians and the Jacobites. When a new monarch appears, the deposed ruler becomes the centre of one of those excremental visions so troublesome to some of Swift's readers, but so useful to others. In this case perhaps it is emblematic of some terrible kind of life and spirit among the Yahoos, a powerful madness or unreason that Swift wants to draw attention to. The Yahoos are also given to apparently causeless civil wars and other mass neuroses.

These two social patterns must be contrasted with the more complex details found in the other three books. No ideal society is anywhere presented, but the contrast between different groups is used to discuss or suggest a way of looking at society itself as a controlling force on human nature, *and* a corrupter of that nature. The impossible simplicity of the horses' society points to the difficulties of human government. In the three monarchies of Lilliput, Brobdingnag and Laputa, the hierarchical arrangements govern the way Gulliver enters 'into' these nations. A narrative as well as a symbolic structure is provided by the deployment of social details. The first three books do not really present three different societies, but three views of the same society. In Book IV, the joke at the outset is to see Gulliver walking into a completely different situation armed with assumptions and expectations as inappropriate as the 'Bracelets, Glass Rings, and other Toys' he has about him to 'purchase his Life'.

In Lilliput, Gulliver as a man-mountain, a monster, enters the society from the top down. After seeing the bow-man, a soldier who in this warlike and efficient country is a member of an important government service, he notices a detachment of forty soldiers, then other government workmen who erect a stage to allow the first communication with a Lilliputian. This turns out to be 'one of them who seemed to be a Person of Quality', 'a *Hurgo* (for so they call a great Lord)' sent 'by the King's Orders upon the first Intelligence he received of me'. The king is the efficient operator of a centralised government machine, which would have been the envy of an English monarch. He receives early notice of anything untoward by a well-organised system of expresses. Gulliver must, by reason of his size, view the social life of the country as a government, as a machine: this is of course only one way to look at it. Because of his size, *and therefore importance*, he deals directly with the administration in the person of the emperor. He is looked after by the royal 'Cooks and Butlers'; given 'an Establishment'. He is in a good position to notice somewhat patronisingly 'the prudent and exact Oeconomy of so great a Prince'. The image of the country itself is that of a beautiful model:

> The Country round appeared like a continued Garden; and the inclosed Fields, which were generally Forty Foot square, resembled so many Beds of Flowers. These Fields were intermingled with Woods of half a Stang, and the tallest Trees, as I could judge, appeared to be seven Foot high. I viewed the Town on my left Hand, which looked like the painted Scene of a City in a Theatre. (XI, 29).

Lilliput is apparently a rigorous autocracy. The king's ministers, Flimnap-Walpole and the rest are discussed cheek-by-jowl with the 'Emperor's Huntsmen' and 'the Master of his Woods'. The emperor issues a proclamation to forbid on pain of death deserting the capital to go and see Gulliver. Production was being lost. The autocrat, however, would please any old English conservative by living 'of his own' or as Gulliver says 'chiefly upon his own Demesnes'. This is a somewhat nostalgic view for an experienced politician such as Swift to take seriously as provision for the administration of a thriving nation. A kind of mediaeval purvey is exacted to feed Gulliver: 'An Imperial Commission was issued out, obliging all the Villages nine hundred Yards around the City to deliver in every Morning' the vast quantities of provender the man-mountain consumed. (XI, 32). Sumptuary laws are in existence to restrict, for instance, parents' expenses on their children. The rewards a man may earn by seventy-three moons' good conduct is 'according to his Quality and Condition of Life', though it does include a kind of B.E.M., the non-hereditary title of *Snilpall*. The government, or the emperor, does the 'chusing of Persons for all Employments'.

Swift in this first voyage enjoys himself, using all the technicalities of court and official procedure with which he had become familiar as a

Q

court hanger-on in the reign of the late queen. The 'Articles of Impeachment' for example are drawn up in form, as Swift no doubt himself assisted in drafting official documents for Bolingbroke or Oxford. Gulliver is allowed to find out at first hand about the 'Dispositions of great Princes and Ministers'. Viewed from above down, and rather unsympathetically, human society is seen to be a rather terrible engine. Gulliver is allowed to come to some fairly easy conclusions about the nature of government, not of his own society yet, but of society generalised and diminished 'in so remote a Country, governed, as I thought, by very different Maxims from those in Europe'.

The hierarchical nature of the Lilliputian society is also used to define further the point of view of the *persona*. Gulliver is carried away by talking to those 'persons of quality'. How unctuous that phrase is, and how typical somehow of the eighteenth century! He plumes himself on having

the Honour to be a *Nardac*, which the Treasurer himself is not; for all the World knows he is only a *Clumglum*, a title inferior by one Degree, as that of a Marquess is to a Duke in *England*. (XI, 66).

In Brobdingnag, as befits the change in his point of view, Gulliver enters the society from the bottom upwards. Again he finds a monarchy, but ruled this time by a philosopher-king, 'as learned a Person as any in his Dominions'. This king is more than a match for Gulliver as a disputant, and both from his own experience as a ruler, and from keenly analysing Gulliver's not very astute account of European affairs, puts forward a series of political and economic doctrines, which have direct importance as a comment by Swift on contemporary English politics. Gulliver cannot take a bird's-eye-view of the state this time. Instead he has his attention forced on to his own social and political ideas by what he is made to experience, and by the king's shrewd questioning. Brobdingnag, 'wholly secluded from the World', has a prosperous, isolated, agricultural economy. It is a sizeable country with cities and towns, but 'a large number of Villages'. This contrasts with Lilliput, which has 'great Intercourse of Trade and Commerce' with Blefuscu, and is altogether a more urban, mercantile and mechanic organisation. It may be noted that the four books of voyages pair off into I and III, where there is trade and commerce between different nations, and the more introspective II and IV, where the nations are each isolated. This must be so because the giants and the horses are both unique, but it also allows a special kind of argument to engulf Gulliver.

Brobdingnag's well organised rural life is stressed at the beginning of the voyage, with the appearance of market-days, neighbouring gentlemen, a country inn, and a market-town crowd. Imagery is also an important part of the voyage's structure. The parody of a voyage-writer's frenzied employment of a barrage of technical terms precedes a closely organised normal-image network, and a powerful and suggestive use of homely, rustic comparison which has both picturesque and moral importance. When Gulliver lands, it is harvest time, and after struggling for an hour to walk the length of a field, he sees a man 'as tall as an ordinary Spire-steeple', followed by seven monsters, 'with Reaping-hooks in their Hands' as big as scythes. Far from talking to persons of quality, Gulliver first tries to converse with one of the 'Reapers', who is employed by 'a substantial Farmer' awarded a 'low Bow' by the terrified narrator. Even at court the analogies are from agriculture: 'the Queen took up at one mouthful, as much as a dozen English Farmers'; her knives were 'twice as long as a Scythe set strait upon the Handle'. The king's 'Razor was almost twice as long as an ordinary Scythe'. This imagery and its related economic structure is used in the rhetorical logomachy between Gulliver and the king. Gulliver's dishonesty and unwittingly bad argument is opposed by the king's almost rustic, solid (if limited) honesty. It is the king in Book II, who speaks one of Swift's most celebrated sentences:

> he gave it for his Opinion; that whoever could make two Ears of Corn, or two Blades of Grass to grow upon a Spot of Ground where only one grew before; would deserve better of Mankind, and do more essential Service to his Country, than the whole Race of Politicians put together. (XI, 135–6).

This springs naturally out of the social circumstances of this nation, where socio-economic doctrines are really important, not the *roman-à-clef* aspect which Firth tends to identify with the political importance of the book. Swift of course held very strong views on these matters and a study of the economic basis of his satire could be as valuable as similar studies of economic doctrines in the fiction of Defoe, and as useful in judging properly his imaginative power. Brobdingnag is an admirable, if not ideal community. The rustic labourers, the substantial farmers and their families are brutal, coarse and avaricious, but citizen Gulliver sees much to commend in the nation, such as:

> their military Affairs; they boast that the King's Army consists of an hundred and seventy-six thousand Foot; and thirty-two thousand in the several Cities, and Farmers in the Country, whose Commanders are only the Nobility and Gentry, without Pay or Reward . . . every Farmer is under the Command of his own Landlord, and every Citizen under that of the principal Men of his own City, chosen after the Manner of *Venice* by *Ballot*. (XI, 138).

Gulliver's first glimpse of the Flying Island affords not persons of quality, nor reapers, but 'numbers of People', and 'some People fishing'. When he is spotted, 'four or five Men' run up the stairs to the top of the island for orders, and only on a closer view, 'Those who stood nearest over-against me, seemed to be Persons of Distinction, as I supposed by their habit'. Once on the island, in a crowd, 'those who stood nearest seemed of better Quality', and then he notices their peculiar 'Shapes, Habits and Countenances'. So he enters Laputa in a process of detached observation and judgement. The obviously public, social feature of this part of the story is the wrong-headed, colonising rule by the mis-directedly ingenious Laputians of the 'Continent' below, Balnibarbi. The Island is the 'King's Demesn', and the Irish application is obvious.[5] Book III, otherwise full of social, economic and political absurdities, does contain one of the few truly admirable figures in the whole satire in Lord Munodi. Not surprisingly his admirable character functions in a realised social setting. He is a Swiftian paragon:

> not of an enterprizing Spirit, [but] content to go on in the old Forms; to live in the Houses his Ancestors had built, and act as they did in every Part of Life without Innovation. (XI, 177).

For this, he and some others are considered 'ill Commonwealth's-men'. Gulliver, being neither a monster, nor a pet, is able to continue developing his detached view as a traveller. He is shown Lord Munodi's estate in Balnibarbi, a well-run and beautiful enterprise. It is the ideal country retreat, perhaps for Swift, following classical, Horatian values, the ideal of human existence. It is contrasted with the faction-ridden fooleries and oppression of the Flying Island, and the 'Soil so unhappily cultivated, Houses so ill-contrived and so ruinous, [and] People whose Countenances and Habit expressed so much Misery and Want' in the rest of the country. This is the social setting of the Grand Academy of Lagado. The political and socio-economic details are an important aspect of the point being made, which is not mere satire on mis-directed learning, but a unified attack, in the best Augustan manner, on the moral, political, practical and personal results of intellectual pride, as well as its disastrous mental effects. The thread of social argument in the satire is now more, now less important, but always there acting as an important unifier.

There are three considerable passages on education in *Gulliver's Travels*: the first in chapter 4 of the voyage to Lilliput, the second in chapters 5 and 6 of the voyage to Laputa (this is one way to consider the account of the Academy), and the third in chapter 8 of the voyage to Houyhnhnmland. In Lilliput and in Houyhnhnmland the emphasis, in contrast with the corrupt attitudes of the Laputians, is on the socialising aspect of the educational process. As far as Lilliput is concerned, this process is not presented in a straightforward fashion. It is difficult to distinguish between the Lilliputians' 'Notions relating to the Duties of Parents and Children' and Gulliver's account of these Notions, that:

> the *Lilliputians* will needs have it, that Men and Women are joined together like other Animals, by Motives of Concupiscence; and that their Tenderness to their Young, proceedeth from natural Principle: For which Reason they will never allow, that a Child is under any Obligation to his Father for begetting him, or his Mother for bringing him into the World. (XI, 60).

As might be expected, Gulliver reports that the Lilliputians draw a statist conclusion from this tendentious argument. The government must take over the process of education. But why shouldn't children owe obligations to their parents for other reasons? The question is never fully examined in the text, by the Lilliputians, or by Gulliver. Mingled with this, though, are some sharp comments on the unfortunate social effects of education in Swift's own day, especially of upper-class children by servants. In the nineteenth century (and even now) it was, and is, not very fashionable to stress the important and obviously explicit socialising intent of educational systems. Thus humanist writers like Sir Thomas More in *Utopia* and Milton in the *Tractate on Education* seem to be no less quaint theorists than the arguers in *Gulliver's Travels*. But an awareness of the importance of the social matrix of the arguments enables the reader to place and deal with the thorny arguments about education that appear in this satire. The horses' 'Method is admirable, and highly deserveth our Imitation' begins Gulliver, and then plunges into a ludicrous sentence about oats, milk and grazing, that ought to put us on our guard. The point of the argument, though, is societisation, *not* the acquisition of knowledge, information or expertise, and it is not a ludicrous question, however peculiar the answer.

In some such way as has been suggested, a network of political, social and economic connections can be formed, which is one way of considering Swift's many-sided book, a satire that continually astounds by its unpredictable energy, and its refusal to be pinned down to any monistic interpretation. For instance, in Book IV, Gulliver (not the didactic Houyhnhnm) is allowed the biting insight:

> *Poor* Nations are *hungry*, and *rich* Nations are *proud*; and Pride and Hunger will ever be at Variance. (XI, 246).

Political and National action is here presented in personal terms. There is a grim humour in this, but the social frameworks of the different preceding voyages allow the reader to put it in perspective, to consider this bleak generalisation in a wider context. There is no point in arguing whether Swift meant this to be so: it is what happens. Gulliver is not becoming wiser altogether—though he does a bit—but simply sees different sides to the old arguments about the nature of society, and its role in the world over against individual, personal, human life. It does not seem to me that Swift has any simplistic answer to this conflict, but he did have a various vision of the complexities of the problem.

The social, political, economic network, the structure of social circumstances, is only one of the number of possible networks in the book, but obviously an important one. Much attention has been focussed on Gulliver's personal sensibility, thought-processes and rhetorical ability (or defects). Swift seems to be saying, however, that the social matrix of personal life and judgement must also be considered in forming a just picture of the good life, of man's potential for good, or ill.

> Man, like the gen'rous vine, supported lives;
> The strength he gains is from th'embrace he gives.
> On their own Axis as the Planets run,
> Yet make at once their circle round the Sun:
> So two consistent motions act the Soul;
> And one regards Itself, and one the Whole.[6]

NOTES

[1] R. Quintana, 'Situational Satire: A Commentary on the Method of Swift', *Univ. of Toronto Quarterly*, xvii (1948).

[2] Sir C. Firth, 'The Political Significance of *Gulliver's Travels*', *Proc. British Academy*, ix (1919).

[3] See Z. S. Fink, 'Political Theory in *Gulliver's Travels*', *ELH*, xiv (1947), 151–61. Swift owned Petty's *Essays in Political Arithmetick* (1699): see the 1745 Sale Catalogue, item no. 412.

[4] P. Harth, *Swift and Anglican Rationalism: The Religious Background of 'A Tale of a Tub'* (Univ. of Chicago Press, 1961) deals closely with religio-political ideas; A. Bloom, 'An Outline of *Gulliver's Travels*' in J. Cropsey ed., *Ancients and Moderns: Essays in the Tradition of Political Philosophy* (N.Y., 1964) is an account of Swift's traditional, classical political philosophy. Both essays are about ideas, making little connection with Swift's own social behaviour or his views of economic problems. On the other hand discussions of mercantilism such as E. F. Hecksher, *Mercantilism* (revised English edition, London, 1953) and P. W. Buck, *The Politics of Mercantilism* (New York, 1942; reprinted 1964) provide little comment useful for dealing with a publicist and polemicist like Swift. The field is open for investigation.

[5] O. W. Ferguson, *Jonathan Swift and Ireland* (Univ. of Illinois Press, Urbana, 1962), pp. 135–6.

[6] Pope, *An Essay on Man*, III, ll. 311–316.

The Satiric Structure of Gulliver's Travels and More's Utopia

BRIAN VICKERS

The possibility that More's *Utopia* provided a model for parts of *Gulliver's Travels* does not seem to have been taken very seriously. Despite the fact that Swift owned a copy of 'Eutopia' and often referred to More with admiration, the connection between these two great satiric works remains shadowy. In the most thorough study of the sources of Swift's book W. A. Eddy mentions *Utopia* only to dismiss some extravagant claims made for it by a German scholar;[1] similarly Irvin Ehrenpreis mentions one connection proposed by R. W. Chambers and at once diminishes it.[2] Émile Pons has made a thorough study of the imaginary languages in the two works,[3] and it is a pity that the scholarship and judgment shown there are quite lacking in what seems to be the only study to attempt a fuller examination of the connection, a confusing article by John Traugott which misinterprets *Utopia* even more fundamentally than it does *Gulliver*.[4] One cause of this reluctance to consider Swift's debt to the most famous of imaginary voyages is perhaps that it is only recently that *Utopia* has been fully recognised as a work of satire,[5] and even so I shall argue that some of its crucial satiric methods have not yet been rightly understood. Much could be made of the relative doctrinal contents in the two works (that is, the positive attitudes to man and society) but in this essay I want to focus on the satiric targets and techniques common to them.

I

More's *Utopia* was written between 1514 and 1516, and was published in 1516 at Louvain, under the care of Erasmus. It consists of two books: the second contains the account of *Utopia* (Nowhere) as reported by the imaginary traveller Raphael Hythlodaeus; the first is made up largely of an imaginary dialogue between Raphael and two real people, More himself and Peter Giles, concerning the problems of giving counsel to rulers and the chaotic state of Europe in the sixteenth century. The interplay between these two books is important, and although it has long been known that Erasmus reported that More had written the second book 'because he was at leisure, and the first part he afterwards dashed off as opportunity offered', it was left to J. H.

Hexter[6] to make the right deductions from this remark. By a shrewd analysis of the joins between the sections and various inconsistencies in the factual account of Raphael, Hexter has shown that the work originally consisted of Book II with the introductory conversation setting the scene for Raphael's account which still opens Book I (in '*Y*', the Yale edition, pp. 46–58, in '*P*', the Penguin, pp. 37–41), and that this part was probably written while More was on a time-consuming diplomatic mission in the Netherlands in 1515. Between his return to London in October 1515 and his despatch of the completed book to Erasmus in September 1516, More added two parts, first a large section in Book I consisting of the only piece of dialogue in the work (the rest is narrated discourse)—a section which Hexter calls the 'Dialogue of Counsel', complete with an exordium which leads directly into the 'Discourse on Utopia' (*Y*. 58–108, *P*. 41–68), and secondly he added to Book II a peroration and conclusion (*Y*. 236–246, *P*. 128–132).

This reconstruction of the process of composition may seem to be solely of interest to students of More, but it gives valuable support to what can be deduced from the text without this special information, the existence in *Utopia* of various planes of irony and satire. A large part of the additions in Book I is concerned with purely contemporary problems, whether or not Raphael (=More?) should give in to the recurrent Renaissance duty of becoming a counsellor to his ruler, and how the abuses in the law, in the economic structure, and in imperial ambition are ruining England and indeed all Europe. Some passages are added as a definite prologue to Book II, and Hexter has shown (1952, p. 36 ff.) how More the writer achieves a tactical success by making More the persona in the dialogue object to Raphael's enthusiastic advocacy of communism as practised in Utopia with some serious arguments against this system:

> I disagree. I don't believe you'd ever have a reasonable standard of living under a communist system. There'd always tend to be shortages, because nobody would work hard enough. In the absence of a profit motive, everyone would become lazy, and rely on everyone else to do the work for him. (*P*. 67; *Y*. 107).

To these and further objections Raphael answers that if they knew what Utopia was like they would realize that such difficulties could be overcome, and indeed in Book II we see that this is so: the wit lies in the fact that More has already solved the problems, and has in fact tailored the objections to fit the answers which follow. This keen sense of the particular social consequences resulting from any system is one of More's strengths as an inventor of an ideal society, but while Hexter's later surmise (*Y*. xxxviii–xl) that one purpose in adding the dialogue in

Book I and the peroration to Book II was to tie the satiric planes implied in the discourse (which is often rather rambling and loosely-constructed) more firmly to the actuality of sixteenth-century society, I believe that a more important literary, ethical and social purpose was to promote the process of comparison, a process which Swift carries further than More could ever have visualized.

In the 'Discourse on Utopia' in Book II Raphael offers a straight-forward description of this society, in which *their* virtues are implicitly the antitheses of *our* vices; the qualities absent in Utopia can be extrapolated from their virtues and make a rather frightening list: greed, ostentation, pride, ambition—in war as in peace, inequality, corruption, sloth, envy. It is a kind of definition by negatives, for all these qualities are conspicuously present in our society today as they were in sixteenth-century England, as indeed they always will be in any secular society given the values and appetites of men. But as Book II stands on its own, in order to be perceived these deductions have to be made positively by the reader himself (and preferably by a reader familiar with the ethical basis of More's non-satirical work), and thus the danger exists that some readers would not be able to see the connection, for Swift's general law that satire is 'a sort of Glass, wherein Beholders do generally discover every body's Face but their Own' (I, 140) would apply particularly here. Although in the original design of Book I, just before his insertion of the dialogue, More had expressly recorded that Raphael (like Gulliver) had balanced criticism of imaginary and actual societies: 'just as he called attention to many ill-advised customs among these new nations, so he rehearsed not a few points from which our own cities, nations, races, and kingdoms may take example for the correction of their errors', More's characteristic vein of irony led him to disclaim any such reforming intent: 'These instances, as I said, I must mention on another occasion. Now I intend to relate merely what he told us of the manners and customs of the Utopians' (*Y.* 55; *P.* 40–41). Knowing More's fondness for irony the educated reader may be prepared to start extrapolating points from which our own society could 'take example for the correction of their errors', but nevertheless the instinct of comparison of this hypothetical society with his own is not really produced in Book II, and as if to combat this More adds several details in Book I which make comparison unavoidable. In Mr. Sykes Davies' phrase, he begins to set up his 'code'.

The major literary device in Book I is the dialogue, but Hexter's description of it as a 'Dialogue of Counsel' is misleading, for although it does involve a discussion on the duty to advise the ruler this takes up only a small part of the dialogue (*Y.* 55–9, 87, 99–103; *P.* 41–3, 57,

63–5)—indeed the dialogue between More, Giles, and Raphael is itself only a part of the whole. The major events in this section are a number of imaginary conversations narrated by the imaginary character Raphael, one of them with a real figure, Cardinal Morton, the wise and good Chancellor, and with a corrupt lawyer (*Y.* 59–85, *P.* 43–56) and two other hypothetical conversations with the French King (*Y.* 87–91, *P.* 57–9) and an undesignated King (*Y.* 91–97, *P.* 60–3). As will be seen from this analysis the discussions about counselling are brief, and are interspersed with the imaginary conversations between Raphael and the three rulers, conversations which may be incidentally designed to provide concrete examples for the theoretical problems but which in their final state exceed in size and interest the discussion of counsel. There is thus a cyclic structure in the way that the discussions between More and Raphael alternate with those between Raphael and a foreign ruler, and a further symmetrical element which becomes very important in terms of the process of comparison is that in each of his conversations Raphael is made to compare the organization of real European societies on a particular point with those of imaginary countries which he is supposed to have visited: those of the Polylerites (*Y.* 75–9; *P.* 51–3), the Achorians (*Y.* 89–91; *P.* 58–9), and the Acarians (*Y.* 97; *P.* 62–3). Thus within the framework of an imaginary conversation More has constructed a play within a play within a play, but by presenting reality twice removed he lulls his reader into a state of security in order to create a considerable surprise when it materializes that the topics discussed within this double framework are in fact the burning issues of 1516. Within these hypothetical conversations Raphael exposes the condition of England: robbers are being hanged all over the place but petty theft continues; the noblemen 'live like drones' off their tenants (*P.* 44) and exploit them so much that they are reduced to poverty and so to theft; the economic chaos of the enclosure system is destroying the agricultural life, demolishing towns: a sheep's wool seems to be the *summum bonum*; everywhere there is extravagance. Within a receding plane this is a remarkably direct piece of satire, and could be compared to Swift's direct attacks in *Gulliver* on the condition of England in the 1720s—with the proviso that because Swift's attack is less open, more disguised, it will hardly be possible to fix the details of his political satire with any comparable exactness.

But rather than develop this point about direct satire I prefer to look at the more general issue of the use of indirect satire for purposes of comparison: as More the *persona* says to Raphael, there is no point in attempting to convince opponents of the strength of your argument by mere force, the 'indirect approach' (*obliquo ductu*) must be used (*Y.* 98–9;

P. 64). To step out of this framework and consider the issue as it must have presented itself to him in the process of composition: by inventing these hypothetical societies More is starting from a definite moral or political conviction and trying to embody it in an oblique (but realistically conceived) form which will provoke corrective comparison—here, in a very simple state, is what Swift does with his imaginary societies. In his first conversation with Cardinal Morton Raphael attacks the use of capital punishment for theft, and is asked by the Cardinal to explain why he thinks 'that theft ought not to be punished with the extreme penalty, or what other penalty you yourself would fix, which would be more beneficial to the public' (*Y.* 73; *P.* 49). In reply Raphael devotes five paragraphs to a sensible ethical and pragmatic condemnation of capital punishment before explaining what happens in the commonwealth of the Polylerites, a country 'far from the sea, almost ringed round by mountains, and altogether satisfied with the products of their own land' (an economic isolation like the Brobdingnagians, *pace* Dr. Ross). If caught, a thief must restore the goods or their value to the owner, and once convicted he is not imprisoned but put to public works. The convicts are treated humanely, but if they attempt to escape or form a faction they are severely punished. Thus from his moral conviction that capital punishment for theft is wrong More has developed a realistic, practical scheme to replace it, and it is here that he most differs from Swift: whereas both writers invent imaginary societies in order to attack some political or moral weakness in our society, More is a reformer who is sufficiently sanguine about the chances of success to invent definite proposals (Raphael is given a quite practical six-point plan to cure the crisis in agriculture—*Y.* 69–71; *P.* 48–9), Swift devotes his energies to exposing our weaknesses. Swift's is not the inferior process, it is merely the first stage of More's, carried to its ultimate in destructiveness.

In his hypothetical conversation in the French Privy Council Raphael is given a slightly different tack: in the midst of a discussion on how France can best play off her enemies against each other and win absolute command in Europe he considers what the reaction would be if he advised the French to be content with what they have and if he cited 'the decisions made by the people called the Achorians who live on the mainland to the south-south-east of the island of Utopia' (*Y.* 89; *P.* 58). They conquered a neighbouring kingdom but discovered that the expenses of maintaining it were reducing them to a chaos in which morals were being corrupted, robbery, murder, and all kinds of illegal practice were flourishing, and so they made their King give up the conquest. Here the satire seems to be directed against sixteenth-century England (Henry VIII's difficulties in maintaining France), but the invention certainly exposes the corrupting effect of imperial ambitions. The parallel suggested with Lilliput and Blefuscu is strengthened in the following sequence, where Raphael imagines being present at another European council which discusses all sorts of vicious schemes for raising money, and to which he thinks of explaining the law of his third imaginary nation, the Macarians, who insist that their King should never have at one time in his coffer more than a thousand pounds of gold. The satiric target here is more universal, and completes a trio of imaginary nations used mainly for lessons of political administration: these are More's Lilliput and Brobdingnag, and it is significant that the nation whose structure is based on a sensible ethical rather than political basis, Utopia itself (Raphael's fourth 'voyage'), should have most resemblance to Swift's Houyhnhnms-Land.

Still within the section in Book I which he added later, More now begins to prepare us for the structure of Utopia by making Raphael introduce its most novel feature, the abolition of private property. From this basis all other virtues flow, especially the destruction of the abuses of the legal system, and Raphael is made to develop at some length the various exploitations of the law in a way which brings him quite close to Gulliver:

> when in my heart I ponder on the extremely wise and holy institutions of the Utopians, among whom, with very few laws, affairs are ordered so aptly that virtue has its reward, and yet, with equality of distribution, all men have abundance of all things, and then when I contrast with their policies the many nations elsewhere ever making ordinances and yet never one of them achieving good order—nations where whatever a man has acquired he calls his own private property, but where all these laws daily framed are not enough for a man to secure or to defend or even to distinguish from someone else's the goods which each in turn calls his own, a predicament readily attested by the numberless and ever new and interminable lawsuits,
>
> (*Y*. 103–5; *P*. 65–6)

when he considers these facts he agrees with Plato that communism is the only perfect remedy. But more important than any specific details at this stage is the process (More's 'code') by which we are gradually drawn into wishing to compare these remote nations to our own, the positive movement towards comparison which was lacking in the original form of Book II. Thus having finished his account of the Polylerites' humane punishment for theft Raphael explicitly connects their method with England's:

I then added that I didn't see why this system shouldn't be adopted in England. It would produce far better results than the so-called 'justice' that the lawyer had praised so highly.

At this our learned friend—I mean the lawyer—shook his head. 'Such a system,' he announced, with a smile of contempt, 'could never be adopted in England, without serious danger to the country.' That was all he said—and practically everyone else agreed with him.

(*P.* 53–4; *Y.* 79–81).

The further tactical ploy of having the lawyer reject the system out of hand arouses our sympathy and makes us want to interpose that their method *could* be tried. Thus we are in the position of wanting to compare the social structures of these remote nations with our own, and this wish for comparison is given further impetus at the end of Book I by the subtle device of making Raphael eulogize the totally un-Yahoo teachableness of the Utopians. But first the least talkative partner in the dialogue, Peter Giles, objects in advance: 'I must say, I find it hard to believe that things are so much better organized in the New World than in the Old. I should think we're just as intelligent as they are, and our civilization is older.' Again More has set up a sitting duck, and Raphael at once pots it by telling how, twelve hundred years ago, when some Romans were wrecked off Utopia,

the citizens learned from them every useful technique practised anywhere in the Roman Empire. . . . But if, by any similar accident, a Utopian has ever found his way over here, we've completely forgotten about it, as I dare say people will soon forget that I was ever there. On the strength of our first meeting, they immediately adopted all the best ideas that Europe has produced—but I doubt if we'd be quite so quick to take over any of their arrangements which are better than ours.   (*P.* 68; *Y.* 109).

Again the psychological effect of this is to make us *want* to compare the two systems, to see if we could take over any of their arrangements. Thus More, in addition to the other direct satirical attacks made in Book I, has achieved a more lasting reinforcement by giving us the motive force to read Book II and its fully-worked-out account of Utopia and to compare their ethical, rational, equitable system with our own. And it is at this point that the ethical satire begins to work, for each such confrontation grates: the European societies come off worst. The triumph of the alteration of Book I in order to include additional imaginary kingdoms is that the readers now take part in the criticism of extant societies: we do the work ourselves, and so our discoveries strike us harder, all the more so because we have been given a blank cheque. Each of us, seeing this ideal state and with the will to compare it to our own, will estimate the corruptions of our society at a different rate, and thus the range of its working its infinite. It is also private, for unless we each published our commentary on *Utopia* no one else would know just how to rate the gap: *Utopia* lives on in the individual mind.

II

More's *Utopia*, then, offers an ethical criticism of our society which is given additional impetus by various satiric devices and by the instinct of comparison. That summary description brings it near to *Gulliver's Travels*, and I think that these elements are truly common to both, but at the same time there are great divergences. More's satire works partly by indirection, but his ethical purpose extends to providing fully-formed replacement systems. It would be possible to read *Gulliver's Travels* in this way, extracting those elements in the various social systems which Swift seems to be approving—the Lilliputians' choice of public servants with 'more Regard to good Morals than to great Abilities' (XI, 59), and their simple principles for the education of children, which 'differ extremely from ours' (60–63), the Brobdingnagian King's concept of government being limited 'to common sense and Reason, to Justice and Lenity' (135) the admirable example of Lord *Munodi* (175), the Houyhnhnms' dedication to Reason[7] and to a number of admirable human virtues: 'FRIENDSHIP and *Benevolence*', 'TEMPERANCE, *Industry*, *Exercise* and *Cleanliness*' (267–9), their sensible reaction to death (274–5), the absence in their society of the abuses and corruptions which pester ours (276–7—a devastating list, ending cryptically: 'No Lords, Fidlers, Judges or Dancing-masters'), and their enlightened way of conducting conversations (277–8). But the scarcity of these unambiguous positives shows that Swift is not really concerned to provide an alternative social system but to castigate the vices inherent in our own, and throughout the most positive examples, those of Houyhnhnms-Land, the effect is complicated—although not totally undercut—by the fact that this ideal human behaviour is being practised by horses. Whereas More is a social reformer who uses satire, Swift is a satirist who hopes to vex society into reforming itself. In this distinction lies a further difference, in their attitude to their audience: with his subtle stress on comparison More lures the reader into an active co-operative process of analysing the defects of our society by reference to an ideal model. In reading *Gulliver's Travels* the reader is (by comparison) passive, for although he sometimes has to infer the weaknesses of his own society by comparison with that of a remote nation, during much of the time the parallel is inescapably drawn for him by Swift through Gulliver. And whereas More is essentially working with the reader towards a better system, at the most biting parts of his satire Swift is attacking us, for we watch embarrassed and powerless as Gulliver (omitting our good points) exposes to the Brobdingnag King and his Houyhnhnm master the full corruption of our society, and we can only assent to their condemnation of us. And if their criticism is just, on the basis of the evidence presented, then it becomes still more so in retrospect when we learn that Gulliver has in fact falsified even that, not mentioning many of our worst faults.

Swift's satiric method of comparison is almost an inversion of More's, for while in *Utopia* we see a traveller recounting details of imaginary societies and from them we deduce the weaknesses of our own, in Swift's satire we see a traveller telling the representatives of imaginary societies the weaknesses of our own society, and the direct nature of such satire being put in an indirect frame is reinforced by the destructive comments of the listener—discourse becomes dialogue, for Swift adds a second actor and revolutionises the form as much as Aeschylus did his. Again while in *Utopia* our deductions as to our society's corruption have an infinite range because they are implicit and personal, in *Gulliver's Travels* the criticism of society is finite and particular, sharply focussed and transfixing both Gulliver and the reader. It seems to me, indeed, that Swift's satire-by-social-comparison is the most effective mode within his work, for although he uses a great variety of satiric methods—exaggeration and diminution, relativism carried to the ultimate, dichotomies between physical size and moral worth or between reason and the passions, mock computations which increase grotesqueness, descriptions of peculiar practices in imaginary societies which turn out to be extremely similar to our own (the political scheming in Lilliput, marital infidelity and scientific incompetence in Laputa), the humiliation and ultimate over-inflation of his narrative *persona*—nevertheless I find that the most telling blows, those which most destroy man's pride in his political or legal systems, his moral standards and intellectual achievements, even his unalterable possession of human nature, this whole satiric annihilation of man is most forcibly achieved in the dual process of Gulliver explaining to a foreign interlocutor how we live, and faithfully recording that foreigner's comments on us. Of course Swift far exceeds More in the complexity and force of his satire, but I think that none of the accepted sources for *Gulliver's Travels* presents a closer parallel for the basic situation of a political and ethical attack on our society by juxtaposition with that of an imaginary one. There seem to be further connections between the two works both in satiric targets and satiric techniques.

The similarity in some of the satiric targets may just be due to the fact that European society had not changed much between 1516 and 1726, but it seems to go deeper than this and be the extension of similar ethical convictions. Thus there is an ironic parallel between the characters of soldiers and sailors: in *Utopia* the corrupt lawyer argues that the idle attendants of noblemen who fall into poverty and theft, once cast off are valuable in the army, and Raphael counters that 'you might as well say that for the sake of war we must foster thieves', and that soldiers and robbers have much in common (*Y*. 63; *P*. 45). Two hundred years later Gulliver explains that sailors can only be recruited from 'Fellows of desperate Fortunes, forced to fly from the Places of their Birth, on Account of their Poverty or their Crimes' (XI, 243–4), but Swift's imagination at once enlarges their crimes to a great catalogue of evil. Both writers mock the absurdities of the system of mercenary soldiers: Raphael describes the Zapoletans (and Erasmus adds in a marginal note 'A People Not at all Unlike the Swiss', *Y*. 207), who fight bravely for the country which pays them yet could change sides to the enemy if more pay is offered them', and then the day after, if a trifle more is offered to tempt them back, return to the side they took at first.' Swift makes capital out of the miserliness of those Princes 'who hire out their Troops to richer Nations for so much a Day to each Man; of which they keep three Fourths to themselves' (XI, 247).[8] In both works we are reminded of the horror and futility of war; throughout *Utopia* but especially in the second book, where although the Utopians fight to defend themselves we are reminded that they loathe war 'as an activity fit only for beasts and yet practiced by no kind of beast so constantly as by man' (*Y*. 199). Swift's exposition of this theme hardly needs comment.

Still more unanimous is their agreement as to the corruption of lawyers, an antipathy so strong in More that in a prefatory letter to in words which Swift must have read with pleasure:

one must necessarily confess the object of legal and civil arts and sciences to be this: with spiteful and watchful cunning a man should behave toward his neighbor, with whom he is joined by rights of citizenship and sometimes of family, so as always to be taking something or other away, drawing it away, shaving it away, swearing it it away, squeezing it out, beating it out, scooping it out, twisting it out, shaking it out, hammering it out, taking it quietly, stealing it away, plucking it away, pouncing upon it, and partly with the connivance and partly with the sanction of the laws—purloining it and embezzling it. (*Y*. 7).

Budé goes on much longer in the same violent way, and Swift's account of how a neighbour could with the help of a lawyer fiddle Gulliver's cow away from him may by comparison not seem over-cynical (XI, 248–9). More himself directs bitter satire at lawyers, from the corrupt representative who figures in Book I to the Privy Council which advises a King to bribe the judges to 'find some loophole whereby the law can be perverted' (*Y.* 93; *P.* 60), and to Raphael's preliminary comparison of Utopian happiness with our corrupt system, already cited. (*Y.* 103–5; *P.* 65–6). Of course attacks on the abuses of the law have long been traditional in satire, and it would not do to suggest *Utopia* as a source for Swift here. Nevertheless he must have derived amused agreement from the sequence in Book II where Raphael explains that in reaction against the situation in the rest of the world where people are 'bound by laws which are either too numerous to be read through or too obscure to be understood by anyone', the Utopians have few laws and furthermore 'absolutely banish from their country all lawyers, who cleverly manipulate cases and cunningly argue legal points'. (*Y.* 195, *P.* 106). Again a marginal note draws our attention, to 'The Useless Horde of Lawyers' ('*Aduocatorum inutilis turba*') and More continues with satire directed against the way in which treaties are broken, sometimes as lawyers find some 'loophole in the wording', loopholes which 'are often incorporated deliberately in the original text' (*P.* 108, *Y.* 199). Of all the faults in the law which Swift attacks, perhaps the most compelling is this ambidextrous quality:

> I SAID there was a Society of Men among us, bred up from their Youth in the Art of proving by Words multiplied for the Purpose, that *White* is *Black*, and *Black* is *White*, according as they are paid.
> (XI, 248).

Like Utopia, Brobdingnag has few and short laws, and 'to write a Comment upon any Law, is a capital Crime' (XI, 136). But Swift's invention on this *topos* far exceeds More's in ingenuity and bite.

The Houyhnhnm Master's reaction to the concept of Law both echoes a point made in *Utopia* and parallels a satiric technique used frequently there:

> he was at a Loss how it should come to pass, that the *Law* which was intended for *every* Man's Preservation, should be any Man's Ruin. (248).

This is a simple observation, although a fundamental one, and its satiric power derives much from the particular context in which it appears: More engineers similar situations in which equally simple comments achieve great force. As in Swift, it is all a question of point-of-view, and although More does not involve Raphael in a dialogue

R

with a foreign observer he creates an analogous effect in a smaller way through the people of Utopia. By inventing a fully-formed society whose ethical values are almost diametrically opposed to our own (a point which he is at some pains to stress), More often inverts our values so that we begin to see that much of what we prize has no intrinsic value but is merely relative. This technique is best seen in the question of gold and precious jewellery. Raphael explains that the Utopians only use money to pay their mercenaries, and

> silver and gold, the raw materials of money, get no more respect from anyone than their intrinsic value deserves—which is obviously far less than that of iron. Without iron human life is simply impossible, just as it is without fire or water—but we could easily do without silver and gold, if it weren't for the idiotic concept of scarcity-value. (*P*. 86; *Y*. 151).

Placed in this light we agree that the value of gold and money is entirely relative and arbitrary. But instead of satirising our values, as Swift might have done, More goes on with his favourite tools of paradox and inset anecdote. He admits that it would be of little use simply to confiscate gold, and that to get around such difficulties the Utopians have

> devised a system which, while perfectly consistent with their other conventions, is diametrically opposed to ours.

They use gold and silver 'for the humblest items of domestic equipment, such as chamber-pots'; chains of gold are used to fetter slaves,

> and anyone who commits a really shameful crime is forced to go about with gold rings on his ears and fingers, a gold necklace round his neck, and a crown of gold on his head. In fact they do everything they can to bring these metals into contempt. (*P*. 86–7; *Y*. 151–3).

If that invention is ingenious, More improves on it with regard to jewels: children are taught to associate precious stones with the nursery, and as they grow up their self-respect prompts them to give up all childish things.

The imaginative power which has constructed these paradoxical inversions now exploits them with a beautifully-placed anecdote, as Raphael records how the Anemolian ambassadors visited Utopia in ignorance of their customs and in all the splendour of silken clothes, gold chains and rings, in fact—as More reminds us—'they were fully equipped with all the things used in Utopia for punishing slaves, humiliating criminals, or amusing small children'. The reactions of the Utopians are well dramatized, from the citizens who welcome the retainers thinking that they must be the ambassadors, to the children who create a literal inversion by imagining that the ambassadors must be clowns. Again More reminds us of the point:

> You see, from the Utopians' point of view—apart from a few who'd had occasion to go abroad—all that splendour was merely degrading.

Thus the point-of-view has been set up on a sound and sympathetic ethical basis and then well exploited using satire and dramatisation to reinforce the underlying idea. More develops the attack on relative values further, marvelling 'how anyone can be silly enough to think himself better than other people, because his clothes are made of finer woollen thread than theirs'. The Utopians are fundamentalists, but they are right:

> Nor can they understand why a totally useless substance like gold should now, all over the world, be considered far more important than human beings, who gave it such value as it has, purely for their own convenience.

This is another point that More can exploit with a keen eye for the absurd in human behaviour, and it is not impossible that his attack on relativism should have influenced Swift in his much more thorough-going development of this idea to discredit even the validity of human perception.

More's literary method of handling the satiric contrast in viewpoint differs from Swift's in being more extended with paradoxical inversion and anecdote. But the root position of a fundamental truth about life being uttered by a person from an imaginary nation when confronted with our society is clearly the same. In both writers, once it is accepted that this foreigner comes from a society quite different to our own, then a truism—a truth about life which on its own would be too obvious or banal for it to have any force (that the laws are meant to help not to confuse, that money is of arbitrary value)—such a simple but funda-mental truth becomes energised by its satiric context. Thus the point-of-view of the Brobdingnagian King is set up in optical as well as moral terms, and is then exploited in such a way that we have to agree with the result, and Gulliver is even made to reflect that the King is right to say 'how contemptible a Thing was human Grandeur, which could be mimicked by such diminutive Insects as I' (XI, 107), for the present vision of 'a Company of *English* Lords and Ladies in their Finery and Birth-day Cloaths' would produce the same conclusion. This technique is used intermittently in Book II but reaches its apotheosis in Book IV, where the reactions of the Houyhnhnm interlocutor are very similar to those of the Utopians. Their lack of understanding of Western (or human) behaviour and the way that exposure to it forces them back on their fundamental ethical principles are both seen in the Houyhnhnm response to the concept of lying:

> it was with much Difficulty that he comprehended what I meant; although he had otherwise a most acute Judgment. For he argued thus; That the Use of Speech was to make us understand one another, and to receive Information of Facts; now if any one *said the Thing which was not*, these Ends were defeated. (XI, 240).

There is another irrefutable truth (that speech is the medium for communication) one which is so obvious that we may be in danger of forgetting it—thus modern, post-Freudian man responds with amusement (for a Houyhnhnm it would be with 'some Expressions of great Indignation') to such a cynical aphorism as 'Most people use language not to reveal what they think but to conceal it.'

The Houyhnhnms and the Utopians view us with amazement and puzzlement, and by use of this *tabula rasa* we are forced to take fresh stock of cynical or corrupt assumptions about the actual nature of life and society which have hardened to the point of our not noticing them. The Houyhnhnms exist in a state of innocence which exposes our corruptions, their language lacks even the words for crimes, and Gulliver's inquisitor responds to their explanation with that recurrent 'Amazement and Indignation' which makes us uncomfortably aware of our perversions:

> He was wholly at a Loss to know what could be the Use or Necessity of practising those Vices. To clear up which I endeavoured to give him some Ideas of the Desire of Power and Riches; of the terrible Effects of Lust, Intemperance, Malice, and Envy. All this I was forced to define and describe by putting of Cases, and making Suppositions. After which, like one whose Imagination was struck with something never seen or heard of before, he would lift up his eyes with Amazement and Indignation. Power, Government, War, Law, Punishment, and a Thousand other Things had no Terms, wherein that Language could express them. (244).

But they are all words which we humans become accustomed to from early childhood, and the blunting of our moral sense to such concepts is exposed by the effect that they have on the pristine mind of the Houyhnhnm:

> as my Discourse had increased his Abhorrence of the whole Species, so he found it gave him a Disturbance in his Mind, to which he was wholly a Stranger before. He thought his Ears being used to such abominable Words, might by Degrees admit them with less Detestation. (248).

Swift's use of the *tabula rasa* as recording agent here is rather similar to Shakespeare's use of innocence to record corruption in *Hamlet*, both for the Prince ('My tables! Meet it is I set it down') and for the mad Ophelia '(she does hear there's tricks i' th' world.').

If that reaction by the Houyhnhnm is the absolute in this direction, Swift has not yet finished with the device, and his Master is allowed to make further fundamentalist objections: he could not understand why lawyers should

> perplex, disquiet, and weary themselves by engaging in a Confederacy of Injustice, merely for the Sake of injuring their Fellow-Animals; neither could he comprehend what I meant in saying they did it for *Hire*. Whereupon I was at much Pains to describe to him the Use of *Money*, the Materials it was made of, and the Value of the Metals. (251).

Here subject-matter as well as technique come close to *Utopia*, and Gulliver's explanation that 'when a *Yahoo* had got a great store of this precious Substance, he was able to purchase whatever he had a mind to'—clothing, houses, land, 'the most costly Meats and Drinks; and have his Choice of the most beautiful females' can be directly compared to Raphael's attack on the random power of money in the hands of an equally worthless being:

> a man with about as much mental agility as a lump of lead or a block of wood, a man whose utter stupidity is paralleled only by his immorality, can have lots of good, intelligent people at his beck and call, just because he happens to possess a large pile of gold coins.
> (*P.* 89; *Y.* 157).

Gulliver enlarges on his point in the satiric vein, and his Master again stops him with a fundamental truth: 'For he went upon a Supposition that all Animals had a Title to their Share in the Productions of the Earth; and especially those who presided over the rest.' That is an entirely unexceptionable comment, but the Houyhnhnm's truisms may be deliberately subject to the law of diminishing returns, for a later comment in this vein seems double-edged: 'our Institutions of *Government* and *Law* were plainly owing to our gross Defects in *Reason*, and by consequence in *Virtue*; because *Reason* alone is sufficient to govern a *Rational* Creature.' (259). After the demoralizing effect of these juxtapositions that truism does not somehow seem certain.

In addition to this shared satiric technique of a fundamental truth being energised by its narrative context so that we see the particular abuse with new eyes, a number of targets within their respective sequences of comparison seem common to More and Swift. Connected with the worship of gold is that of luxury goods. In the Utopian economy money has been abolished, so freeing many more workers for essential occupations:

> for where money is the only standard of value, there are bound to be dozens of unnecessary trades carried on, which merely supply luxury goods or entertainment. (*P*. 77; *Y*. 131).

In his peroration to Book II Raphael returns to this point to denounce the injustice in all countries except Utopia, where

> People like aristocrats, goldsmiths, or money-lenders, who either do no work at all, or do work that's really not essential, are rewarded for their laziness or their unnecessary activities by a splendid life of luxury.

whereas the real workers are exploited and live in poverty. In fact all other social systems seem to him conspiracies 'of the rich to advance their own interests under the pretext of organizing society'(*P*. 129–130; *Y*. 239–241). Gulliver makes a very similar report on the organization of his society:

> That, the rich Man enjoyed the Fruit of the poor Man's Labour, and the latter were a Thousand to One in Proportion to the former. That the Bulk of our People was forced to live miserably, by labouring every Day for small Wages to make a few live plentifully. (251).

Significantly enough it is in the same context that Swift satirizes human dependance on delicacies, though with more humour than Raphael:

> I assured him, that this whole Globe of Earth must be at least three Times gone round, before one of our better Female *Yahoos* could get her Breakfast, or a Cup to put it in. (252).

In England all the surplus trades abolished in Utopia are necessary to preserve the appurtenances of quality:

> BUT beside all this, the Bulk of our People supported themselves by furnishing the Necessities or Conveniencies of Life to the Rich, and to each other. For Instance, when I am at home and dressed as I ought to be, I carry on my Body the Workmanship of an Hundred Tradesmen; the Building and Furniture of my House employ as many more; and five Times the Number to adorn my Wife. (252–3).

These are not the most spectacular or most frequently-quoted pieces of satire in *Gulliver's Travels*, but they are essential and effective. The climax to this exposure of the vanity of money and precious stones is the report that the Yahoos are inordinately fond of 'certain *shining Stones*' which they dig up in fields and treasure with vicious and illogical love, and the Houyhnhnm's acid comment uses the same device that More sometimes applies, that of pointing out the mere uselessness of the commodity. (260–1).

More's fundamentalism is extended to a greater number of targets than Swift's, most of them traditional objects of complaint: the Utopians fail to understand the importance of etiquette and foolish honours:

> isn't it equally idiotic to attach such importance to a lot of empty gestures which do nobody any good? For what real pleasure can you get out of the sight of a bared head or a bent knee? (*P.* 94, *Y.* 169).

Again a fundamental truth is given impetus by its satiric perspective, and again we are reminded of the spurious and purely relative value of gems: 'the value of such things varies according to where and when you live', and a marginal note points out that 'Human Imagination Gives Value to Gems or Takes It Away' (*Ibid.*). The same simple logical reasoning reduces to absurdity human love of gambling and with more rancour, hunting, and here too the *tabula rasa* exposes the irrationalities and vain assumptions on which much of our society is built (*P.* 95; *Y.* 171). Another common target within these sequences of comparison is the assumptions of traditional logic—a target which, although it is not near the surface in Swift's work, is clearly there, for R. S. Crane has shown how Swift uses the stock logical definitions of man as *animal rationale* in such treatises as that of Burgersdicius or Narcissus Marsh and exposes the contradictions on which they are built.[9] Similarly More ironically records that although skilled in all other branches of knowledge known to the Ancients, the Utopians 'are no match for the Moderns when it comes to logic'. They are ignorant of the rules learned by heart in our schools, and

> so far from being equal to investigating Second Intentions, they're even blind to the existence of that notorious Universal, MAN. Now he, as you know, is a pretty conspicuous figure, bigger than any giant you ever heard of—but, though we pointed him out quite clearly, none of them could see him. (*P.* 90, and Notes 141; *Y.* 158–9).

This passage seems to mock the arrogance of our systems, the assumption of human dominance which is found even in the school-book examples in logic, and in case we are too slow to see the jest Erasmus added a marginal note: 'Evidently This Passage Is Satiric.' Finally in this series of parallel satiric targets energised by the process of comparison there is the perfectly serious mockery of the human fear and fuss about death. The Utopians even practise voluntary euthanasia in cases of painful and incurable illness (*Y.* 187, *P.* 102), and as for normal death they treat it with sorrow and solemnity but without mourning (they are confident of an after-life), and if someone dies in a cheerful and optimistic mood they rejoice—at all events the burial and funeral are handled with a minimum of fuss (*P.* 121; *Y.* 223). In this they again resemble the Houyhnhnms (I do not suggest that Swift's horses are always admirable, but it is undeniable that they are given some good qualities): thus the death of a Houyhnhnm is not a time for extremes of joy or grief or even regret, although one in which to 'take a solemn Leave', and their burials are so inobtrusive that they are hardly noticed (XI, 274–5).—'How different from our practice', we think, and indeed this is one of the few places where Swift has not made the comparison for us.

III

If Swift and More resemble each other in their use of satiric techniques and targets, then they do so in one other essential feature, the use of a *persona*. Gulliver and Raphael are the mediators whose experience brings the idea of our society into corrosive contact with that of an imaginary society. As personalities (or rather, as instruments of satire) they are quite different in tone, Raphael giving a consistently positive account of social reforms, Gulliver moving from embarrassed agreement with the King of Brobdingnag (his reservations about that ruler's intelligence only reinforce the criticism) to an absolute acceptance of the Houyhnhnm point of view (again complicated by his acceptance of their viewpoint on the purely physical inferiority of man —which is patently ridiculous; as well as man's moral inferiority— which is undeniable.) But although the satiric *personae* differ in application there are some interesting similarities, two minor, one major. First their surnames: 'Hythlodaeus' means 'dispenser of nonsense', and more than one critic has suggested that 'Gulliver' has overtones of 'gullible' and 'gull', a suggestion of a hoax. Secondly their reliability: Swift is at great pains to establish Gulliver's accuracy as a recording agent, from the Publisher's letter to the Reader announcing that a great many of his factual and 'minute Descriptions' have had to be deleted (XI, 8–9), through the whole process by which Gulliver measures, computes, and estimates size, quantity, and value—a process wonderfully adapted to satire, as several recent studies have shown. More has nothing as complex as this, but in his prefatory letter to Peter Giles he goes out of his way to establish his own accuracy and that of his *persona* by writing that Raphael

> has caused me to feel very doubtful on one point. According to my own recollection, Hythlodaeus declared that the bridge which spans the river Anydrus at Amaurotum is five hundred paces in length. But my John says that two hundred must be taken off, for the river there is not more than three hundred paces in breadth.

Giles is urged to consider the problem because, as More writes, 'I'm extremely anxious to get my facts right' (*Y*. 41; *P*. 30). Again More and his friends surround his work with testimonies to its veracity and to the actual existence of Raphael and Utopia, including its geographical position (e.g. *Y.* 13, 25, 43, 45, 113, 251) and in the same vein, in addition to providing us with maps, Gulliver complains that some critics 'have gone so far as to drop Hints, that the *Houyhnhnms* and *Yahoos* have no more Existence than the Inhabitants of *Utopia*' (XI, 8).

The final resemblance is the most important. Both *Gulliver's Travels* and *Utopia* use an invented *persona* who is the main medium for a critical examination of how our civilization functions. In both works, with the help of this *persona* the satire moves backwards and forwards, from direct attack to more subtle insinuation, from accounts of imaginary practices which turn out to resemble our own to carefully chosen damaging accounts of our society which are exposed for comment by a representative of a remote nation who can pierce our irrationalities and remind us of fundamental truths often forgotten. But more significant even than this important connection is the fact that while the satire moves on various direct and indirect planes, at the end of both works the author's *persona* moves unambiguously out of the satiric framework to deliver an uncompromising attack on human vices, especially that of pride. After the description of Utopia Raphael is given a peroration which sums up the virtues of that society and relates them caustically to our own weaknesses. It is one of the sections which Hexter argues, and I think rightly, was added later, for in addition to completing the satiric perspectives formed by the earlier revisions it is set aside from the rest of the work by its force—as Hexter has said, 'if we read *only* the somewhat diffuse and rambling, occasionally gay and sportive Discourse we are not wholly prepared for the sharp focus, the consistently intense tone, the steady drive of the peroration.' (*Y.* xxi). In the first part of his indictment *in propria persona* Raphael attacks the unjust distribution of wealth in society, a passage from which I quoted earlier and which resembles Gulliver's account of how the rich exploit the poor. But More's attack is of a much greater intensity and has a rising force, moving through the variety of evils produced by money and greed (*P.* 128–131; *Y.* 237–243), and acquiring ever more power.

At the climactic point of this indictment—three paragraphs from the end of his book—More returns to that motive of comparison which he established at the outset to say that 'either self-interest, or the authority of our Saviour Christ . . . would have led the whole world to adopt the Utopian system long ago, if it weren't for that beastly root of all evils, pride.' Now he can deliver the final blow at the 'root-cause of ambition, political conflict', dissension at home and abroad, and indeed many other human vices, the insatiable vice of pride:

For pride's criterion of prosperity is not what you've got yourself, but what other people haven't got. Pride would refuse to set foot in paradise, if she thought there'd be no underprivileged classes there to gloat over and order about—nobody whose misery could serve as a foil to her own happiness, or whose poverty she could make harder to bear, by flaunting her own riches. Pride, like a hellish serpent gliding through human hearts—or shall we say, like a sucking-fish that clings to the ship of state?—is always dragging us back, and obstructing our progress towards a better life. (*P.* 131).

The impact of this denunciation on a sympathetic reader is considerable, for in place of the willing active comparison which we have been so far involved in we are now passive, shot at, caught uncomfortably as when reading *Gulliver*. Raphael now seems to have the power and authority of a prophet—as Edward Surtz has put it, here 'he emerges as a blend of social reformer and religious prophet, dramatically and passionately denouncing the one thing which holds the whole world from adoption of the Utopian system, namely, pride. Apocalyptically he calls pride a serpent from hell . . .' (*Y.* cxli). However, I cannot agree with Surtz that More 'subtly . . . renders the reader less favorable by having the uncompromising Hythlodaeus overstate his case' (*Ibid.*). On ethical and human grounds Raphael is surely right—this *is* the vice which produces human contentiousness and ambition, and on literary grounds the placing of the attack could hardly be bettered. Certainly Erasmus had no doubt as to its value, for he added a marginal note here: '*Mire dictum*' (*Y.* 242), and for More it was clearly a topic of the greatest importance as we know from his attacks on pride in other works.[10]

Gulliver reaches the identical conclusion as Raphael, also at the climactic stage of the book (two paragraphs from the end), and with a similar moral force (in the headnote to this chapter Swift laconically summarizes: 'The Author . . . gives good Advice, and concludeth'): Gulliver writes 'I am not in the least provoked at the Sight of a Lawyer, a Pick-pocket, a Colonel' and so on through another of those Swiftian catalogues of the professions, apparently random but suggesting some secret unifying evil, until the 'root-cause' is reached:

But, when I behold a Lump of Deformity, and Diseases both in Body and Mind, smitten with *Pride*, it immediately breaks all the Measures of my Patience; neither shall I be ever able to comprehend how such an Animal and such a Vice could tally together.

The moral *tabula rasa* of the Houyhnhnms is again invoked, who even lack a word for this concept, one which is as universal for Yahoos outside this country as it is outside Utopia: his masters were not able to distinguish this of Pride, for want of thoroughly understanding Human Nature, as it sheweth it self in other Countries, where that Animal presides.

Gulliver is as correct in his diagnosis as Raphael is, and Swift is at pains to stress the moral intent in the final sentence:

> I dwell the longer upon this Subject from the Desire I have to make the Society of an *English Yahoo* by any Means not insupportable; and therefore I here intreat those who have any Tincture of this absurd Vice, that they will not presume to appear in my Sight. (XI, 296).

This conclusion is absolute and violently uncompromising but it is not to be dismissed. It is too easily described as 'misanthropy', and since critics have made the sensible step of not identifying Gulliver with Swift they have unfortunately reached the tidy-minded conclusion that therefore Gulliver is the misanthropist. Of course, Swift's satire lacks the sharply-defined ethical simplicity of More's, because he has deliberately complicated the issue by showing Gulliver's admiration for his Utopian horses to be partial, blind to man's virtues as it is to the Horses' weaknesses, and resulting in much ludicrous behaviour. But while accepting that this equophilic strand in Gulliver is unbalanced and absurd we cannot simply dismiss everything that he says: the dichotomy between physical shape or size and moral worth which was exercised in Books One and Two and again in the distinction between Houyhnhnm and Yahoo is applied most sharply here and in the 'Letter to Sympson'. Swift uses overlapping dichotomies to force us into relying on our reason and good sense (such as it is): we have to make crucial distinctions between a speaker, his subject, and his attitude to it; within what he says we have to make further separations of good sense from the limiting or distorting effects of his peculiar perspective, or even his physical shape and the assumptions which that fosters. These discriminations a person of balanced judgment is always making in the experience of literature as in life providing that he does not fall into the trap of deciding in advance that everything one person says is 'insane' or 'misanthropic': we can distinguish personal tinctures of malice in Shakespeare's Apemantus or Thersites from their unexceptionable attacks on human folly and vice—why can't we do the same for Swift? Of course Swift makes the trap of 'prior judgment' harder to avoid than in almost any other literary work (Shakespeare's most complex essay in this mode is *Coriolanus*), but if we hold on to this principle of judgment and if we remain aware of Swift's methods then we will avoid a hasty or one-sided decision. Here his dichotomy divides Gulliver's acceptance of the horses' physical perceptions (foolish), from their moral judgments on man (sensible): although their way of life is not, as he thinks, wholly admirable, as commentators on our faults they must be reckoned with.[11]

Certain modern critics[12] have proposed variants on Gulliver as misanthropist: he has gone mad here, temporarily lapsed into insanity; he is to be laughed at; he is himself suffering from the sin of pride, taking super-human power of moral criticism upon himself (this explanation may express a certain modern discomfort about the motives of any person attacking human vices, but it is a right which has to be granted the satirist). All these explanations have in common the result that what Gulliver says here can be safely ignored, and in formulating them the critics seem to me to have behaved in the face of uncomfortable satire in the way that Swift predicted, taking a racket and bandying the ball out of their own court. I suggest that Gulliver's attacks on human pride are to be taken seriously, both here and in the Letter to Captain Sympson, and that as well as in the content and placing of the attack on pride More provides a suggestive model in the subsequent reactions of the *persona*.

To be sure, *Utopia* ends in a much quieter way than *Gulliver's Travels*. More restores the narrative framework which he set up at the beginning, reminding us that he himself was said to have been listening to Raphael's discourse, and then adding a neat ironic touch in a double-inversion as he pretends to dismiss the whole account, thinking of 'various objections':

> The laws and customs of that country seemed to me in many cases perfectly ridiculous. Quite apart from such things as their military tactics, religions, and forms of worship, there was the grand absurdity on which their whole society was based, communism minus money.

But under this stalking-horse he looses his sharpest arrow:

> Now this in itself would mean the end of the aristocracy, and consequently of all dignity, splendour, and majesty, *which are generally supposed* to be the real glories of any nation.
>
> (P. 132; Y. 245; my italics).

—*ut publica est opinio*—so much for the public's values. This conclusion, although extremely witty in itself, is not much use to Swift, except perhaps for the irony-by-inversion which he developed so wonderfully. But in two details concerning Raphael's attitude to man there are near and illuminating parallels. After his crushing attack on pride More's *persona* dismisses any hope of reform and is content that one nation at least (like the Houyhnhnms) has cured it:

> But as this fault is too deeply ingrained in human nature to be easily eradicated, I'm glad that at least one country has managed to develop a system which I'd like to see universally adopted. (P. 131; Y. 245).

The consequences for any person who has experienced such a system when faced with the imperfections of Western civilization (or 'human': Swift complicates the issue profitably by making the difference between them and us not simply national or ethnic but animal) are also drawn by More: in Giles's letter to Busleyden reports are given concerning the whereabouts of Raphael:

> Others declare that, after his return to his native land, partly because he could not endure his countrymen's ways [*suorum mores non ferentem*] and partly because he was moved by his longing for Utopia, he made his way back again to that country. (*Y.* 25; *P.* 34).

Whether or not *Utopia* can be thought of as a source for *Gulliver's Travels* Swift makes the same two points about his *persona*, though of course with the violence appropriate to his growing disgust. Like Raphael, Gulliver would have gone back to his Utopia if the citizens would have had him, and he, too, is unable to 'endure his countrymen's ways' although this reaction is obviously given a more complex perspective. And like Raphael he discovers that pride is 'too deeply ingrained in human nature to be easily eradicated', only he makes the discovery not in that sad resigned way but in a torrent of bitterness, becoming himself for the first time the *tabula rasa* which sees our imperfections clearly. To take up a point made earlier, by making his comparison of societies a dialogue, not a discourse, Swift can give the added dimension of the second actor's reactions, and just as the King of Brobdingnag and the Houyhnhnm master responded to our corruptions with surprise and disgust so Gulliver now suffers the same disillusionment with man. R. S. Crane has indirectly summed up this strategy of what we might call 'the dialogue with a *tabula rasa*':

> though we must surely agree that there is a significant difference between Gulliver and Swift, why must we suppose that the difference has to be one of basic doctrine? Why could it not be simply the difference between a person who has just discovered a deeply disturbing truth about man and is consequently, like Socrates' prisoner in the myth of the cave, more than a little upset and one who, like Socrates himself, has known this truth all along and can therefore write of his hero's discovery of it calmly and with humour?[13]

Swift, like Raphael, is at the same stage as Socrates: but Gulliver has only just made the horrible discovery, and thus we must give all possible sympathy and force to his complaint to Sympson that

> instead of seeing a full Stop put to all Abuses and Corruptions, at least in this little Island, as I had Reason to expect: Behold, after above six Months Warning, I cannot learn that my Book hath produced one single Effect according to mine Intentions: . . . And,

it must be owned, that seven Months were a sufficient Time to correct every vice and Folly to which *Yahoos* are subject; if their Natures had been capable of the least Disposition to Virtue or Wisdom.

Again the fundamentalist truth—seven months would indeed be ample time—and although Swift reminds us of some of the absurdities inherent in his worship of horses, it is not surprising that Gulliver should end in despair that he ever

> attempted so absurd a Project as that of reforming the *Yahoo* Race in this Kingdom; but, I have now done with all such visionary Schemes for ever. (XI, 6–8).

If Raphael and Gulliver are mad, then they should bite the others.

NOTES

[1] *'Gulliver's Travels': A Critical Study* (Princeton, 1923), p. 67 on Borkowsky: 'his effort to prove indebtedness to More's *Utopia* is all but a parody of scholarship.' But on p. 112 Eddy accepts one parallel cited by Borkowsky: 'As in More's *Utopia*, "the disbelief of a Divine Providence renders a man uncapable of holding any public station".'

[2] 'In providing the Houyhnhnms with good qualities, [Swift] was therefore duplicating the method of More's *Utopia*; and, to only this extent, R. W. Chambers is correct in writing, "Just as More scored a point against the wickedness of Christian Europe, by making his philosophers heathen, so Jonathan Swift scored a point against the wickedness of mankind by representing *his* philosophers, the Houyhnhnms, as having the bodies of horses".' (*Sir Thomas More*, (London, 1935), p. 128). I. Ehrenpreis, 'The Origins of *Gulliver's Travels*' *PMLA* 1957, reprinted in *The Personality of Jonathan Swift* (London, 1958), p. 101.

[3] 'Les Langues Imaginaires dans le Voyage Utopique. Un Precurseur: Thomas Morus.' *Revue de Littérature Comparée*, Vol. 10 (1930), pp. 589–607.

[4] 'A Voyage to Nowhere with Thomas More and Jonathan Swift: Utopia and The Voyage to the Houyhnhnms', *Sewanee Review* Vol. 69 (1961), pp. 534–565.

[5] See A. R. Heiserman, 'Satire in the *Utopia*', *PMLA* Vol. 78 (1963), pp. 163–174; R. C. Elliott, 'The Shape of *Utopia*', *ELH*, Vol. 30 (1963), pp. 317–34, and the Introduction by Edward Surtz, S. J., pp. cxlvii–cliii in *Utopia*, Vol. 4 of the Yale *Complete Works*, ed. E. Surtz and J. H. Hexter (New Haven and London, 1965). This edition uses the translation by G. C. Richards (1923) and is hereafter referred to as '*Y*'. Reference will also be made to the lively contemporary version by Paul Turner (Penguin Books, 1965), abbreviated as '*P*'.

[6] See J. H. Hexter, *More's 'Utopia': The Biography of an Idea* (Princeton, 1952), pp. 99–102, and those sections of his Introduction on 'The Composition of Utopia' to the Yale edition (*Y*. xv–xxiii), and 'The Immediate Circumstances' (xxvii–xli).

[7] The fact that the Utopians place reason high on their scale of values is important but it is not a determinant factor in their society as it is with the Houyhnhnms (*Y.* 16, 163, 179 and notes 443–8, 452, 458, 460, 463–4). For reasons of historical and fictional credibility Utopia has not yet been converted to Christianity, although it has welcomed missionaries with great keenness and many of its philosophical and theological principles are specifically Christian.

[8] I. Ehrenpreis (*op. cit.* in note 2 above, p. 98, note) records a communication from Professor H. W. Donner to the effect that the presence of this satire on mercenaries 'is one more sign of *Gulliver's* connection (often slighted) with More's *Utopia*'.

[9] See R. S. Crane, 'The Houyhnhnms, the Yahoos, and the History of Ideas', in *Reason and the Imagination*, ed. J. A. Mazzeo (London, 1962), pp. 231–253.

[10] See e.g., the passages from More cited in the notes by Surtz (*Y.* 565), and the famous letter to Gunnell, quoted and discussed by Hexter (1952), pp. 119–120.

[11] Having evolved this argument I was pleased to discover that Martin Price has reached a similar conclusion: 'Clearly [Swift] is demanding of his readers what he never grants to Gulliver, the power to make necessary distinctions. . . . Gulliver fails to make the most important distinction of all —between *animal rationale* and *animal rationis capax*. Only after long exposure to human folly and perversity does he give up the dream of man as a rational animal, but instead of coming to terms with what in fact he is, Gulliver immediately turns to truly rational animals, the Houyhnhnms, and hopes to become one of them. His pathetic whinny and canter betray the fantasy of a literal-minded convert.' *To the Palace of Wisdom* (Doubleday paperback ed.), pp. 200–1.

[12] For a representative sample of critical judgments of Gulliver as a misanthropic, lunatic, overproud or simply comic figure see M. P. Foster's collection, *A Casebook on Gulliver among the Houyhnhnms* (New York, 1961), pp. 136–7 (J. F. Ross), pp. 187–9 (E. Stone), p. 200 (Kathleen Williams), pp. 233–4, 243–5 (S. H. Monk), and pp. 279–80 (C. Winton). For some critics who stress the consistency of Swift's satiric attack on pride in moral and Christian traditions, and do not regard the Houyhnhnms as wholly ironic (at any rate not in their intellectual world—no-one, so far as I know, maintains that they are correct in their physical judgment of man), see *Ibid.*, pp. 173–5 (Louis Landa), 176 (Herbert Davis), 208 ff. (R. M. Frye), 260–6 (George Sherburn), and 293–8 (C. Peake).

[13] *Op. cit.*, pp. 233–4.

Dean of St. Patrick's : A view from the Letters

JOHN HOLLOWAY

The sorry tale of Swift's last years is well known, and I shall not dwell on it. 'I am what I am,' it is said he muttered in his dotage in 1744, a year before his death. One wonders what trace there was in his mind of St. Paul in the First Corinthians: 'I am the least of the Apostles . . . but by the grace of God I am what I am'—with, he meant, an assurance of immortality. Swift's widowed cousin Mrs. Martha Whiteway, on whom he came to be quite dependent just before his collapse, writes a pitiful account of the crucial illness in November 1742. 'He walked [in the house] ten hours a day. . . . His meat was served up ready cut, and sometimes it would lie an hour on the table before he would touch it, and then eat it walking. . . . The torture he was in, is not to be described.' (*Corr.*, V. 207).

But I think one must see these years in proportion. Swift was then 75, his strong body survived into helpless old age, and unless we are very foolish we know that in greater or lesser degree, such things as these are part of the common lot. Old age had been coming to him for many years: old age, and also the isolation and ageing of friends that it brings. In April 1740 he complained to his cousin of excruciating pain all night—but noted that she would put it down only to gout; which his acquaintance John Boyle, fifth Earl of Orrery, had had 'settled, confirmed', though only 35. The winter of 1739–40 had been bitterly cold in Dublin. 'Our kingdom is turned out to be a *Muscovy*, or worse. . . . I walk only in my bed-chamber and closet, which hath also a fire'. (*Ibid.*, V. 173, 174). 'Still my garden is all in white', he wrote a month later (179). He is 72. Two years before this, he lamented that he was so much out of touch, he could no longer catch the references in Pope's latest satire. The year before again, he had several times felt near enough to death, to send his most private papers to the safe keeping of friends (42). 'I have not been out of Doors further than my Garden, for severall Months' (85). Also in 1737: 'I find such a weekly decay, that hath made it impossible for me to ride above five or six miles at farthest' (37); 'I have not one Rag of Memory left; and my Friends have all forsaken me' (28).

But after all, he was 70. No wonder if his friends were going. That same year, he had lamented the last days of Rebecca Dingley, erstwhile companion to his lifelong friend—or more than friend—Stella Johnson:

Mrs. Dingley 'quite sunk with years and unwieldiness . . . I do not find her nearest relations consider her in the least' (*Corr.*, V. 5). By now she was probably 70 too. Stella herself, of course, had died long before. Age was also taking some of Swift's best correspondents. Gay of *Beggars' Opera* fame died in 1732 aged 67; Arbuthnot, another of the circle in Swift's London days, and physician to the old queen, early in 1735, at 68. Young Orrery's father, one of Swift's good friends (unlike the son, if truth be told) died in 1731. In that year, Swift had become estranged from his old friend the lively, dogmatic, philandering landowner Knightley Chetwode. In 1735 died his housekeeper, the grave Presbyterian Mrs. Brent, whom he called Sir Robert (*Corr.*, V. 64), in honour of Walpole his most powerful opponent, ever-present to his mind. In his later years he had dined alone with her almost every evening of the week.

That was partly because his deafness made it hard for him to go much into company. It is now familiar knowledge that for many years Swift suffered from Ménière's disease, or *labyrinthine vertigo* in the middle ear; which was at that time beyond treatment or even diagnosis by medical science. He more or less knew this himself: 'I believe my disorder is particular, and out of the Experience of our Physicians here' (*Corr.*, IV. 197). That fact mingled in his mind, however, with his doubts in general about Irish doctors, and his recurrent sardonic gloom. Somewhere, he says, he has the *London Dispensary*, with remedies for deafness and giddiness: 'but my books are so confused that I can not find it, nor would value it if I did' (*Corr.*, IV. 210).

This illness of Swift's one must also put into perspective: painful and humiliating, but intermittent. Even as early as 1722 he was writing to Chetwode like this:

I have been these five weeks . . . so disordered with a noise in my ears and deafness, that I am utterly unqualified for all conversation or thinking . . . now the disease I fear is deeper rooted, and I never stir out (*Corr.*, II, 417).

But no less than twelve years later:

My head is every day more or less disordered by a Giddyness: Yet I ride the Strand here constantly when fair weather invites me.
(*Corr.*, IV. 536).

And this was the year in which the younger Lord Orrery said that the Dean 'enjoys more Health and Vivacity this winter than he has felt for some Years past' (*Corr.*, V. 3); and early in 1737; 'the Dean feasted his Clergy last week with Ladies, Music, Meat and Wine . . . as a Musician I gain'd admittance to join Chorus with *Away with Cuzzoni, away with*

S

Faustina' (*ibid*). One wishes one knew the tune of that chorus: John Boyle, on the other hand, is not the most reliable of witnesses about Swift. But even three years later, he and Mrs. Whiteway both described Swift as in 'excellent Health and Spirits' (*Corr.*, V. 168), and speak favourably of his hearing, though Mrs. Whiteway notes that he is very 'indolent in writing' (*Corr.*, V. 142). He was still well enough, at least from time to time; though by now an old man, and far from a satisfied one.

In some ways, the eighteenth-century spirit nearest to Swift was Samuel Johnson. 'A world where much is to be endured, and little is to be enjoyed', Johnson wrote in *Rasselas*. This is rather how Swift saw the 'cursed factious oppressed miserable country' he lived in after 1713. Yet at the same time he knew how to enjoy that little. He more than once told his friends that he could not settle in England again; not on any terms likely to come his way. With his indifferent health, he valued the comfort, and the circumstance, of his Deanery. In 1732 Oxford made him the offer of the living of Burghfield. He was not in two minds in declining, he preferred his plentiful wine, the dry Dublin strands to ride on, his horses and servants and quiet, and the respect he was shown in the Dublin streets. 'The dignity of my present Station damps the pertness of the inferior puppyes & Squires, which without plenty & ease on your side of the channel, would break my heart in a month' (*Corr.*, IV. 73); 'like Cesar I will be one of the first here rather than the last among you' (*Corr.*, IV. 269).

Swift cannot be said to write with enthusiasm of his domestic life as Dean: but from his *Letters* there emerges a taking picture of it. This is from a letter to Pope early on, in 1715:

> I live in the corner of a vast unfurnished house; my family consists of a steward, a groom, a helper in the stable, a footman and an old maid, who are all on board wages, and when I do not dine abroad, or make an entertainment (which last is very rare) I eat mutton-pye and drink half a pint of wine' (*Corr.*, II. 177).

From time to time he had a little trouble because the beef-steak is spoiled, the ale sour, Tom the groom too drunk to keep up when out riding (*Corr.*, II, 153), or none of his servants able to read or write properly (*Corr.*, IV. 476). This is how he wrote, in 1717, from Trim (he was probably staying with Stella there) to his friend and colleague in Dublin, Thomas Walls the Archdeacon of Achonry:

> I shall not have a Stocking to my Foot, unless Mrs. Brent sends them to you tomorrow and you put them in the Bishop's Bag (*Corr.*, II. 264).

Walls was one of his oldest friends—a 'grave and good man', Archbishop King had called him. Swift had known him in Ireland early on (Walls was then a schoolmaster), and again in the London years, when he figures not infrequently in the *Journal to Stella* of 1710–13.

Besides the Deanery itself, Swift had his garden, which he called 'Naboth's Vineyard'. 'I am as busy in my little spot of a town garden, as ever I was in the *grand monde*' he wrote in 1723 (*Corr.*, II. 449). And above all, he took his exercise, walking and riding. The sight of the elderly Dean, celebrated for harshness towards the great ('I hope your Lordship will please to remember . . . you are to speak to a clergyman, and not to a footman': *Corr.*, II. 326) and gentleness to the poor, became a famous Dublin sight:

> I walk the streets in peace, without being justled, nor ever without a thousand blessings from my friends the Vulgar. (*Corr.*, IV. 171).

That was in 1733. At the same time, one sees the great physical vigour that preserved him, perhaps unhappily, into extreme old age:

> I ride and walk whenever good Weather permits, and am reputed the best Walker in this Town and 5 Miles round. (*Corr.*, III. 381).

Swift wrote those words in early 1730. But eight years later there is still the same extraordinary vigour:

> I seldom walk less than four miles, sometimes six, eight, ten, or more, never beyond my own limits; or, if it rains, I walk as much through the house, up and down stairs (*Corr.*, V. 118).

Riding, his other exercise, still took him out into the Dublin countryside:

> I often ride out in fair weather, with one of my servants laden with a Joynt of meat and a bottle of wine, and Town bread, who attends me to some rural parson 5 or 6 miles round this Town. (*Corr.*, IV. 379).

*   *   *   *

It is from details like this that, fragment by fragment, one can build up from Swift's *Letters* a picture of his life day by day. In fact they make it possible to do this with a detail and immediacy that has no rival in earlier English letters—of any period—nor in our literature as a whole, until one gets back as far as Ben Jonson, or Shakespeare himself. Why this plain but rich immediacy and detail reappears with Swift, I hardly know. Perhaps because of his familiar acquaintance with Rabelais. Perhaps because he was the contemporary of Defoe, and lived when the English novel was becoming its true self. The same quality had shown already in some of Swift's poems, like those describing the morning, or a city shower, during his London years.

There went with the Deanship, about 25 miles out in the country from Dublin, the parish of Laracor just south of Trim. Almost the first thing Swift did when he arrived as Dean was to go there. But at that time the parsonage-house was of mud and straw (*Corr.*, II. 130), and had gone to ruin into the bargain. His stay there involved him, he records, in 'a field bed and an Earthern floor' (*Corr.*, I. 373); a curious situation, one cannot but reflect, for perhaps the finest mind in the British Isles, and one who only a few months before had been more or less at the heart of public affairs. But Swift liked Laracor: 'My River walk is extremely pretty, and my Canal in great Beauty, and I see Trout playing in it' (*Corr.*, I. 373). This was a fortnight after his arrival.

More than this, some of his best friends were close to him in the country. Surviving letters written not by, but to Swift, are testimony to the extraordinarily warm feelings, touched always with respect, that many of the most distinguished men of the day had towards him: and he had many good friends during his Irish years, though some he had to keep close to mainly by letter. There was, for example, John Barber, the printer who was imprisoned in 1714 for bringing out Swift's *Public Spirit of the Whigs*. Barber's wife Mary the poetess, author of *The Widow Gordon's Petition*, reflecting the distress of the poor, was one of the very few women poets whom Swift liked, and may even have slightly admired. Barber went back to London in 1730, when Swift supplied his wife with letters of introduction, and in 1732 became Lord Mayor. One of Swift's many small actions in advancing those he knew was to persuade the new Lord Mayor to take Matthew Pikington as chaplain. Charles Boyle, fourth Earl of Orrery, was a good friend of Swift's until his death in 1731, and at about that time Swift got to know his son the fifth Earl. Well enough too, it seems; for in 1736 he was sending the young nobleman an invitation 'commanding' him to dinner at the Deanery; and added, characteristically, 'Pray Give my Groom a *Guinea* for attending You, and for the Charges of his Horse' (*Corr.*, IV. 511). John Boyle's *Remarks on Swift* of 1751, however, though the first account of him, was an unsympathetic one.

Other friends included John Brandreth, who from 1731 was Dean of Armagh; and Carteret himself, who was Lord Lieutenant from 1724 to 1730—'What in God's name do you here? Get back to your own country, and send us our boobies again!' Swift burst out at him once, over some piece of astuteness on Carteret's part that he objected to. Carteret's boast was that when asked what he had done in Ireland, he could answer 'I pleas'd Dr. Swift' (*Corr.*, V. 18). Until they fell out, there was also Knightley Chetwode, who besides his main property near Portarlington, had another house near Navan. It was only a few miles from Laracor, and Swift visited him there in 1714. At Celbridge, just over the border into Co. Kildare, Vanessa herself had a house, and Swift visited here there too, for example shortly before 1720. Not altogether off the way to it, if one was coming from Dublin, lay Woodpark, the home of Charles Ford, for whom Swift had got the official post of Gazeteer in London in 1712—he soon lost it, though—and whom he visited at Woodpark in 1723. Then, at Gaulstown, south of Mullingar in Co. Westmeath, was the Rochfort family, whom Swift also visited in the country in 1723. Stella, Chetwode, Vanessa, Ford, the Rochforts—or if you like Trim, Celbridge, Woodpark, Gaulstown, Laracor itself—Swift's friends made something of an integrated little world out in the country as well as in Dublin; and one can begin to see a pattern of life for him there also. One of his later friends, William Richardson, had his house far away in the north, at Summerseat near Coleraine. Swift was invited, but it seems that he never managed to go so far. In 1736, Richardson sent him a 27 lb salmon, and mentioned in his letter that Swift had promised to come to Summerseat; but that is as far as it went. I shall come back, though, to the Richardsons.

Of course, Swift saw these country friends in Dublin also. So he did others, men like Henry Singleton, the Prime Sergeant from 1726 on, and one of the Dean's executors; or Archdeacon Walls, or one of his closest friends, Patrick Delany, a Junior Fellow at Trinity until 1727. The circle seems to have met sometimes at Delany's house in Stafford St.; but Delany also had a house outside the city, at Glasnevin. Swift's warmest relations, though (in spite of the fact that in the end there was a breach) must have been with Thomas Sheridan. Early on, Sheridan was celebrated as an outstanding Dublin schoolmaster, both classic and mathematician; 'the best Grecian among us', Swift said. He was gay, convivial, improvident, forgetful, scintillating, witty and richly warm-hearted. Swift loved him well enough to be unusually indulgent towards his faults. 'His greatest Fault is a Wife and seven Children' (*Corr.*, III. 58); 'he hath not overmuch Advertency' (*Corr.*, III, 97); 'if I do not *Sheridan* it, I mean forget it' (*Corr.*, III. 101); 'Sheridan is still the same, I mean in the Sense that Weathercocks are the same' (*Corr.*, III. 4); 'pray do not employ yr Time in lolling a bed till noon to read Homer' (*Corr.*, III. 69).

Sheridan, however, by marriage to a rich woman, had recovered the family house, which had been forfeited through the family Jacobitism. It was at Quilca, in the poor land of Co. Cavan, and outside the old limit of the Pale, while all the other properties I have mentioned (save of course Summerseat) were within it. In Swift's time—I sometimes wonder if not still a little today—that made a difference. 'I live in a cabin and in a very wild country', Swift wrote of a stay he made at Quilca in 1725 (*Corr.*, III. 60). The year before, as a tease, he had started a chronicle called *The Blunders, Deficiencies, Distresses and Misfortunes of Quilca . . . Proposed to contain One and Twenty Volumes in Quarto.* So there were enough Blunders and Deficiencies for a substantial work. 'But one Lock and a half in the whole House', we read . . . 'The Kitchen perpetually crowded with Savages . . . Not a bit of Turf this cold Weather, and Mrs. Johnson [Stella was there too, then] and the Dean forc'd to assist at the Bog . . . the Dean's great Coat was employ'd to stop the wind from coming down the Chimney . . . the Spit blunted with poking into Bogs for Timber, and tears the Meat into pieces . . . the Dean deaf and fretting . . . the Crew of Quilca . . . insisting on their right of not milking till eleven in the Forenoon'. Ten years later, in spite of praise for the beef and mutton and inexhaustible supplies of game, life at Quilca—as one might expect—seems not to have much changed:

> . . . but one pair of tongs in the whole house; the turf so wet, that a tolerable fire is a miracle; the kitchen is a cabin a hundred yards off, and a half; the back and fore door always left open, which, in a storm (our constant companion) threatens the fall of the whole edifice. . . . But we have a good room to eat in . . .[and] an honest neighbour, Mr. *Price*, who sits the evening, and wins our money at backgammon (*Corr.*, IV. 441).

—a racy, detailed first-hand picture emerges of Irish rural life at that time: or, I myself would add, apart from the turf, of rural life in a great many places, today as in Swift's time.

Quilca, however, and Sheridan, had something to offer Swift besides human (if not always material) warmth and hospitality. With Sheridan, Swift's powers of intellect and wit could come at least in large part into play. Indeed, Sheridan, grandfather of the great comic dramatist, sometimes gave Swift as good as he got. One thing he did was to write a Treatise on punning: the letters between them were in fact, often enough, puns a whole letter long. Sheridan writes a string of meaningless gibberish words:

> Eye wood heave yew take sum ray maid Eyes first, and then go in ash hays two week low, where Eye no yew will bee as well come as a knee 1 in ire land. Yew no eye promiss said too right yew a Nun inn tell liege eye bell Let her. He writ is. Eye main ass crop off it. (*Corr.*, IV. 281).

Fun to look at on the page, but quite hard to read aloud so that it *doesn't* sound what it is: 'I would have you take some remedies first, and then go in a chaise to Wicklow, where I know you will be as welcome as anyone in Ireland. You know I promised to write you an unintelligible letter. Here it is. I mean a scrap of it'. Those last words, I think, show how Sheridan was catching an Irish not an English voice. It makes me think of *Finnegan's Wake*, where again, a strong Irish accent very often brings the meaning straight out. They also played the same game in Latin: 'Mire se ver cannas vel res ad e villas a peni'—'my receiver can as well raise a devil as a penny' (*Corr.*, IV. 237–8). Doubtless Sheridan wrote the truth when he wrote that.

Trifling jests in a way, no doubt: yet important. One may treasure Swift's *Letters* for their racy, intimate domesticity; but after all, Swift is not Parson Woodeford. It was *Gulliver* that he is said to have put the finishing touches to at Quilca. Crucially, one is confronting, in all this, the greatest literary mind of the age as he says (to quote from a letter of 1735), 'thus I patch up life' (*Corr.*, IV. 379). In the end, the great quality of the *Letters* is a marvellous gift of language.

Not that, in this, Swift was alone. Those who wrote to him, many of them, also had it—not only the literary men who wrote from London, not only Pope and Arbuthnot and Gay, but also Oxford, Bolingbroke, Bathurst, Peterborough—for the noblemen too, the English of that time could indeed be radiant with vigour, elegance and nicety. None, though could match Swift in his own two chosen fields. These I see as raillery, and simplicity:

> . . . to put a stop to these Corruptions; and recover the simplicity which in every thing of value ought chiefly to be followed (*Corr.*, IV. 274).

Perhaps one thinks that while raillery may need explanation, what simplicity means is simple enough. But in Swift's day, English was like another tongue: richer, crisper, and for the daily affairs of life far stronger that anything at least we English can now make of it. 'It seems there is a trade of carrying stories to the government and many honest folk turn the penny by it' (*Corr.*, II. 175); 'you may count upon it, it lies very much at my Heart to make you easy.' (*Corr.*, II, 204). Everywhere, finds like these help to make the *Letters* rewarding; and these two, at any rate, one should see as issuing less from the genius of Swift, than from the genius of the language. But they shade into what was his own. 'I never could learn' he writes drily to Arbuthnot in 1734 —Arbuthnot's brother on the continent has sent him some wine— 'what kind of present from here would be acceptable in France' (*Corr.*, IV, 269). Behind these seeming-casual words lie not only his periodic outbursts over the 'dirty obscure nook of the world' (*Corr.*, II. 417), worse than Hottentot-land, he has to live in (but 'all these evils are effects of English tyranny': *Corr.*, IV. 34); also his indomitable pillorying of the commercial subjugation whereby Ireland could not export even the few fine things she could produce. One recalls how he sent the first two *Drapier's Letters* to the Lord Lieutenant: 'I have made bold to send you enclosed two small tracts . . . one written (as it is supposed) by the Earl of Abercorn; the other is entitled to a Weaver, and suited to the vulgar, but thought to be the work of a better Hand' (*Corr.*, III. 12).

In these passages, and as I myself believe, always and everywhere, triumph of style is not a knack with words. Behind the sharp edge lies the weight of a great mind and an iron firmness. 'I hope your Lordship,' he writes elsewhere, 'who were always so kind to me while you were a servant, will not forget me now in your greatness' (*Corr.*, II. 128). It means the converse of what it seems to mean: the service was the service of the old Queen, the greatness is the exile that comes to patriots in evil times. That was to Bolingbroke. To Oxford, just after his release from the Tower, he wrote: 'this glorious scene of your Life (I do not mean your Discharge but your . . . Imprisonment)' (*Corr.*, II. 276). In Ireland, I suppose, those words might have overtones that it hardly falls to an Englishman to underline.

Grand as it is, it is not quite on this note that I should wish to close. There is another side: the domestic Dean whom I have tried also to depict. And it is in these more relaxed and intimate contexts that Swift's raillery appears. Raillery, to praise by seeming blame, or more generally, to make oneself amiable through the seeming converse of amiability, was one of Swift's special loves. It could express at once the kindliness, and the rebarbativeness of his nature; and beyond that it is a great and subtle compliment to the hearer, a major act of trust both in his intelligence, and in his nearness of feeling to you. 'I begged some mutton of you, and you put me off with a Barrell of ale, these disappointments we must endure': that's what Swift writes to his colleague at St. Patrick's, the Reverend John Blatchford, in 1731 (*Corr.*, III. 452). Here is how, irresistibly to my mind, he shows his special warmth for Archdeacon Walls:

> This letter is to go to the Bp. of Clogher on Saturday and should have gone last Night, if I had not thought you might be such a Fool as to copy it today and send it to the Bp of Dromore on Saturday likewise. If you will come this morning and do it here we will dine together. . . . If there be a greater fool, than I who took Pains to write it, it must be he who Copyes it out. Adieu. (*Corr.*, II. 244).

And as late as 1738, this immortal letter is how he can repay Richardson's daughter Katharine, who had made him a half-dozen of shirts:

Madam,

I must begin my correspondence by letting you know that your uncle is the most unreasonable person I was ever acquainted with; and next to him, you are the second, although I think impartially that you are worse than he . . . I find you follow your uncle's steps, by maliciously bribing a useless man, who can never have it in his power to serve or divert you. . . . Your uncle came to me several times; and, I believe after several invitations, dined with me once or twice. This was all the provocation I ever gave him; but he had revenge in his breast, and you shall hear how he gratified it. First, he was told, that my ill stomach . . . forced me . . . to take a spoonful of usquebaugh: he discovered where I bought it, and sent me a dozen bottles . . . . He next . . . found out the merchant with whom I deal, by the treachery of my butler, and sent me twelve dozen bottles of [sweet Spanish wine]. . . . But what can I say of a man, who, some years before I ever saw him, was loading me every season with salmons, that surfeited myself and all my visitors? Whereby it is plain that his malice reached to my friends as well as myself. At last, to complete his ill designs, he must needs force his niece into the plot; because it can be proved . . . that you are his prime minister . . . and second in mischief, by sending me half a dozen of shirts, although I never once gave you the least cause of displeasure. And, what is yet worse, the few ladies that come to the Deanry assure me, that they never saw so fine linen, or better worked up, or more exactly fitted. It is a happiness they were not stockings, for then you would have known the length of my foot. . . . I have seen some persons who live in your neighbourhood . . . but I found you had bribed them all, by never sending them any such dangerous presents: For they swore to me, that you were a lady adorned with all perfections, such as virtue, prudence, wit, humour, excellent conversation, and even good housewifery; which last is seldom the talent of ladies of this kingdom. But I take so ill your manner of treating me, that I shall not believe one syllable of what they said, until I have it by letter under your own hand. (*Corr.*, V. 87–8).

It is not Swift's best letter of raillery. He was 71, and ill. But when one finds he could write a private letter like that, one's mind goes back to the great loss and waste in all these years of, 'patching up life':

I write Pamphlets and follys meerly for amusement, and when they are finished, [or] as I grow weary in the middle, I cast them into the fire, partly out of dislike, and chiefly because I know they will signify nothing. (*Corr.*, III. 434).

So in 1730. That, again, is the other side. And there, all in all, is the complex balance of his Irish years; one that goes back right to the beginning, to that evening of the 10th of June 1713, when the newly-appointed Dean of St. Patrick's stepped off the packet from England at what, ironically enough from Swift's point of view, came later on to be called *Kingstown*.

INDEX